09 03

D0164217

EVALUATIVE RESEARCH IN RECREATION, PARK, AND SPORT SETTINGS:

SEARCHING FOR
USEFUL INFORMATION

Carol Cutler Riddick
Gallaudet University

and

Ruth V. Russell
Indiana University

Interior book design and production coordinator: Deborah M. Bellaire .
Editor: Anne E. Hall
Cover design: Matthew Edwards

ISBN: 1-57167-245-1
Library of Congress Number: 98-89973

Printed in the United States.

www.sagamorepub.com

Dearest Mom, Aunt Ann, and Uncle Syd

Though your faces and laughter have begun to fade with the passing days, the fond memories of our times together have not! A belated thanks for all the love you gave me. I miss you.

— *Carol Cutler Riddick*

Fran, Katharine, Chris, Bill, and Baggins

— *Ruth V. Russell*

CONTENTS

Preface vi

PART I: FOUNDATIONS

Chapter 1: Introduction and Underpinnings 1

Chapter 2: Developing an Organization Evaluation System 17

Chapter 3: Ethics of Evaluation 43

PART II: EVALUATION PLANNING MODEL

Chapter 4: Literature Review 63

Chapter 5: Quantitative and Qualitative Frameworks 85

Chapter 6: Defining the Scope of Evaluative Research 97

Chapter 7: Designs Used in Evaluative Research 119

Chapter 8: Sampling and Sample Size 149

Chapter 9: Procedures 167

Chapter 10: Data Collection 185

Chapter 11: Making Sense of Quantitative Information 207

Chapter 12: Making Sense of Qualitative Information 231

Chapter 13: Writing and Presenting Reports 249

Chapter 14: From Results to Policy and Practice 271

PART III: EVALUATIVE RESEARCH IN ACTION

Chapter 15: Program Evaluation 286

Chapter 16: Assessment 305

Chapter 17: Personnel Performance Appraisal 319

Chapter 18: Evaluation of the Physical Plant 345

Chapter 19: Evaluation of Marketing 367

PART IV: The MISE-EN-SCÈNE

PREFACE

More and more frequently recreation, park, and sport-related organizations are calling upon professional staff to be more accountable by applying research skills to their work. The questions of accountability vary widely. They include measuring how effective a National Park Service policy has been in reducing the environmental impact of park users, determining the success of a new member recruitment campaign for a Girl Scout council, assessing how well an employee lunchtime exercise program affected the number of reported illness days, and understanding the best time for open-facility scheduling of the YMCA fitness center.

Managers of leisure service organizations need better and more definitive information for making intelligent decisions. Increased demand for services, coupled with shrinking public and more competitive private dollars, require intelligent decision making by professionals in all types of leisure service settings. Evaluative research is a stimulating and socially valuable genre of applied social research. In today's information-based society it is an important tool for making enlightened decisions.

The purpose of this book is to introduce evaluative research to those whose career interests (e.g., students majoring in recreation, leisure services, or sports management) or current professional positions will or do require them to monitor and manage programs and services. Within academic settings, this book is intended to be as useful for undergraduate, upper level evaluation and management courses. Within leisure service organization settings, this book is aimed at assisting the practitioner two ways: in the development of an evaluative research study, and review of an evaluative research proposal.

This book, however, was not written with the idea that the reader will be "made over," engage in a metamorphic experience, or otherwise transcend him/herself into a research expert. Nor is it meant to be an exhaustive coverage of social research—indeed, there are many fine texts that teach about research methods. Instead, this book advances a framework for evaluative research and discusses specific steps and guidelines for planning, executing, and reporting evaluative studies dealing with some aspect of leisure service or program operation. Understanding this foundation should empower you with the basic abilities to design and conduct, as well as read and critically interpret evaluative studies performed in leisure service settings.

We hope you will learn enough from this book to help you minimize or avoid the major pitfalls frequently experienced in conducting or understanding evaluative research. Indeed, evaluative research can be a powerful tool in our quest to acquire useful information that helps us better serve our clientele, organization, and profession. Our aim was to produce a reference that is pragmatic in content and writing style, building in the reader a "can do" readiness for actually conducting an evaluation project.

ORGANIZATION OF BOOK

The book is divided into three major parts. In the first part, or foundations section, we present an introduction (reviewing definitions and rationale) along with underpinnings of evaluative research; guidelines in developing an organization's evaluation system; and the ethics of evaluation. In the second part, a four-stage evaluative research planning model is discussed, along with a detailed presentation of the requisite steps necessary to execute the model. The third and final part, "Evaluative Research in Action," reviews ideas for how to proceed in conducting evaluative research related to specific programs (including a chapter on assessment), resources (such as personnel, physical plant), and marketing.

FEATURES

To assist you, a number of learning aids have been incorporated into the book. Each chapter is introduced by a statement of learning goals. New and important words are set off in chapters by being italicized. A summary of main points and study questions concludes each chapter. To reinforce what has been presented, schematics and case illustrations are sprinkled liberally throughout the chapters.

INSTRUCTOR MATERIALS

An instructor's manual has been prepared by the authors. This manual contains for each chapter: teaching goals, in-class activities, out-of-class activities, exam questions (multiple choice and essay), audiovisual resources, and overhead/transparency masters.

ACKNOWLEDGMENTS

A pivotal point in both our lives was entering Pennsylvania State University and having Dr. Betty van der Smissen as our mentor. It was our first semester research methods course taught by Betty that instilled within us an appreciation of the importance of evaluation. Through the years Dr. van der Smissen has always taken personal interest in our career developments. She has been a source of inspiration to us. Betty, from both of us, muchisimas gracias.

Another person who has become significant in our careers is Dr. Joe Bannon. Joe's encouragement and support throughout the conception of this book was unwavering. It simply has been a pleasure to work with a first-rate colleague and publisher, someone who has provided us with provocative insights along the way.

In pulling together this text, we relied on a number of "front-line" service colleagues to provide us with some real-life examples, figures, etc., to incorporate in this book. The following individuals' kindness is hereby acknowledged:

Dee Highnote, National Park Service
Doug Hawthorne, City of Boulder Park & Recreation Department
Linda Kotowski, City of Boulder Park & Recreation Department
Noe Villarreal, New Mexico State Park & Recreation Division

We also are indebted to: Dr. Tim DeSchriver, University of Massachusetts, for sharing resources and guidance related to evaluation of sport and fitness services; and Mr. Steve Wolter, Indiana University, for sharing resources on area and facility evaluation. Furthermore, Dr. Ernie Olson, California State University-Sacramento, and Dr. Kim Shinew, University of Illinois at Urbana-Champaign, invested significant time to provide us with quality feedback on a draft of the manuscript. Indeed, their constructive criticism and insights were extremely helpful in the revision stage.

Additionally, Carol acknowledges the support extended to her in writing this book by Drs. Ron Dreher, Anne Simonsen and Bill McCrone. Brother Ron, you are a fine person and great boss. Anne, your continuous support and unwavering empathy explain why you are such an outstanding colleague and therapeutic recreation professional. And Dean McCrone, I have appreciated your kind words and actions. I would also be remiss in not proclaiming to the world how much I enjoyed writing the book with Ruth. RVR you have been a great co-author. You repeatedly helped in crystallizing thoughts. Indeed, I feel both fortunate and grateful to have been able to work with you, my gentle friend. To Gallaudet University I am forever indebted—you were thoughtful enough to award me a sabbatical in order that I could begin writing the book I have dreamt about for the last 15 years. And finally, to my family, Howard, Blake, and Ryan, your acts of encouragement were exquisitely timed. Your understanding helped keep me on an even keel, propelling me forward so I could complete this book. Thank you all!

Ruth also extends appreciation to those who have both specifically and generally supported her enterprise on this book. I owe thanks to my faculty colleagues and students in the Department of Recreation and Park Administration at Indiana University Bloomington (IUB) for their trust and challenge. I also thank my colleagues in the University Division at IUB who gave me so many "real world" opportunities to test my thinking and skills on evaluation. My family, as always, have been supportive beyond what is reasonable and fair for them, but I appreciate it so very much anyway. Finally, I wish to ditto Carol's declaration about working together. We have been friends and colleagues since those early Penn State days in 1973, and this book project seems a fitting symbol of our mutual respect and enthusiasm.

FEEDBACK

In closing, we endeavored to write a book practitioners and "soon-to-be" practitioners alike would find useful. Comments and reactions to our work truly will be appreciated. We'd also love to learn about the evaluation success stories of your organization. Please let us hear from you!

Carol Cutler Riddick	Ruth V. Russell
Gallaudet University	Indiana University
800 Florida Ave N.E.	109 Bryan Hall
Washington, D.C. 20002	Bloomington, IN 47405

PART I: FOUNDATIONS

Chapter 1: Introduction and Underpinnings

Chapter 2: Developing an Organization Evaluation System

Chapter 3: Ethics of Evaluation

Evaluative research requires time and effort, not only for collecting and analyzing the data, but for conceptualization. An inexperienced evaluator sometimes moves too quickly into implementing the procedures of a study in order to meet deadlines for decision making. But this haste, in the long run, is foolhardy. Good evaluation takes substantial "up-front" work. Time and thought devoted to the preliminaries are justified because more accurate and useful results are yielded.

Part I concentrates on the preliminary considerations of the definitions, systems and ethics. In Chapter 1, basic definitions and rationale for evaluative research are presented. As leisure service organizations are monitored and managed, there are different reasons for conducting evaluation research. The first chapter in this unit discusses these distinctions. Additionally, the fit of the evaluation in its social and political contexts is discussed.

Chapter 2 presents ideas for developing a comprehensive evaluation system for an organization. Whether your organization is related to park, tourism, commercial recreation, natural environment, sport and fitness, or therapeutic recreation services, the point is the same. Organizations need to formalize evaluation activities as part of their operations; a systematic plan for evaluating is required.

Finally, Chapter 3 covers an increasingly important anchoring foundation for evaluation—ethics. The discussion in this chapter focuses on how to identify and deal with moral dilemmas that often accompany evaluation. Essentially the theme of the lesson is the importance of conducting the study with integrity.

CHAPTER 1

Introduction and Underpinnings

What Will I Learn in This Chapter?
I'll be able to:

1. Explain the various ways of knowing.

2. Distinguish between evaluation and evaluative research.

3. List some reasons leisure service organizations undertake evaluative research.

4. Recall the differences between evaluative research and basic research.

5. Recollect questions of a social ecological nature that should be asked at the initiation of an evaluation project.

Whether you realize it or not, you engage in evaluation on a daily basis—how to dress, where to eat breakfast, what to talk about to a friend or colleague, which television program to watch, what to do on the weekend, etc. All these activities require evaluation based decisions. *Evaluation* is using subjective judgement to arrive at or set the worth or value of something (Dressel, 1968, p. 11; Suchman, 1967).

Public and private human service programs (including park and recreation services as well as sport and fitness programs) require similar evaluation based decisions. For this, the casually formed subjective opinions of everyday evaluation should be replaced with a more formal evaluation process. Figure 1.1 provides an example of a formal evaluation study undertaken by Cleveland Metroparks. This organization provides conservation, outdoor education, and recreation services for over two million people in Northeast Ohio. The study was undertaken in order to plan for "quality" future services.

Ways of Knowing

What are the different ways we can "know" something? Walizer and Wienir (1978, pp. 8-13) point out there are essentially five ways we know. That is, knowledge can come from:

Figure 1.1: An example of evaluative research at work in a recreation organization.[1]

Cleveland Metroparks developed a master plan in order to guide decision making in the decades ahead. To make the best possible decisions, the park district asked the University of Akron's Research Center to assist in designing a telephone survey to determine: (1) how often people visit parks in Northeast Ohio; (2) what barriers or factors prevent some people from using parks; (3) what kinds of things public park agencies can do to help people use parks more often; and, (4) what variables are related to frequency of park visitation. In all, over 1000 people in a seven-county area were interviewed.

Results from the survey indicated that non-users and infrequent users are disproportionately female, older, and African American. Non-users tend to have lower levels of income. The primary reasons people mentioned that limited their use of parks included lack of time, family responsibilities, fear of crime, and activities pursued elsewhere. It was concluded that if Cleveland Metroparks were to attract would-be visitors, these barriers must be thoughtfully addressed. Particular attention needs to be paid in convincing would-be visitors that time spent in a park is an efficient use of time.

[1]From *Metroparks 2000: Conserving Our Natural Heritage* by S. Coles, 1992, pp.1-4. Adapted with permission of the author.

- Revelation that results from divine experiences, prayer, spiritual encounters, written words, mystical experiences, magic, etc.
- *Intuition*, or something we feel.
- *Everyday experience* and *common sense*, or consulting our own memory of things we have experienced or observed in the past.
- An authority telling us something. This authority can emerge due to position (e.g., teacher, parent) or by knowledge (which can be gained by training, experience, or reputation).
- *Science*, a topic that will be discussed momentarily, seeks the truth about the world around us. Admittedly, our bias in the book is to monitor and manage leisure services and program operations by using knowledge that is acquired the "scientific way."

Definitions

Evaluative research moves beyond simple evaluation insofar as there is reliance on the use of the scientific process and methods. This method is different from evaluation, which relies on judgments that are arrived at in an unsystematic and subjective manner. The evaluative researcher uses a scientific perspective and chooses from among scientific methods the tools he needs to design and execute a study that will yield objective and useful information. In a nutshell, evaluative research attempts to supplement subjective opinions with objectively acquired truth. Evaluative research can be thought of as scientific evaluation (Scriven, 1991, p. 3).

Since evaluative research hinges on science, one needs to have a fundamental understanding of what science and the scientific process mean. Wallace (1971, p. 11) defined *science* as a way of generating and testing the truth of statements about events in the world of human experience. More definitively, Lastrucci's (1963) short definition of science is the "objective, logical, and systematic method of analysis of phenomena, devised to permit the accumulation of reliable knowledge" (p. 6). Elaborating further, Lastrucci (1963, pp. 6-15) characterized science as:

- A gathering of factual, descriptive, and analytical evidence (rather than by conjecture) that is devoid of value judgments;
- Guided by the accepted rules of standardized reasoning;
- Proceeding in an orderly manner in its organization of a problem and in its methods of operation;
- Objectively demonstrating attributes or consequences in an orderly arrangement of factual knowledge and ideas about reality;
- Using a systematized form of analysis;
- Construction of an integrated system that is orderly wherein each fact, principle, theory, law, etc. supports other facts, theories, laws, etc.;
- Permitting replacement of complex explanations or methods with simpler formulations; and,
- The kind of knowledge one can depend upon because of its predictive ability.

The *scientific process* is structured inquiry using applied logic that provides us with reasoned knowledge. The scientific process is used in the pursuit of science. When we talk about using the scientific process, we mean a study has used objective and systematic inquiry. It is, however, important to note what Walizer and Wienir (1978, pp. 7-8) have referred to as the *paradox behind science*, "to be continuously questioning and criticizing research and yet to respect and use it as effectively as possible. Science demands that evaluators never be satisfied, always find flaws, criticize, and never permanently accept anything." Science provides us with a tentative way of knowing. The *uncertainty principle of science* is that every fact, no matter how certain, is always open to question.

The scientific process can be undertaken in various ways. One type of scientific inquiry is applied research, a branch of scientific inquiry that evaluative research falls into. *Applied research* uses scientific methodology to develop information aimed at clarifying or confronting an immediate societal problem (Hedrick, Bickman, & Rog, 1993, p. 2). An example of applied research is examining factors that contribute to automobile accidents among young drivers.

Evaluative research uses the scientific process, methods, and techniques to make an objective judgment about a social intervention (Babbie, 1998, p. 334). Recreational programs, activities, or services are all examples of social interventions.

The information yielded from evaluative research should enable decision makers to arrive at intelligent and rational conclusions. After reviewing the accumulated evidence and logical interpretation of the evidence that have been collected in an evaluative research inquiry, decisions should be reached that are intelligent and rational. Every evaluative research undertaking will be unique because it should be tailor-made to "fit" the situation under examination.

Please note as well that for the remainder of the text evaluation, evaluative research and scientific evaluation will be used as synonyms. We decided on this economy in word choice in order to make the text read at a faster pace. A review of the terms and their interrelationships appear in Figure 1.2.

Figure 1.2: Definition of terms and interrelationships among these terms.

Evaluation = making a subjective judgment about worth or value.

Science = way of generating and testing the truth of statements about events in the world of human experience.

Scientific process = structured inquiry using applied logic, resulting in reasoned knowledge.

Applied research = uses scientific methodology to develop information aimed at clarifying or confronting an immediate societal problem.

Evaluative research = uses the scientific process and methods to collect information systematically that will be used to make an objective judgment about a social intervention.

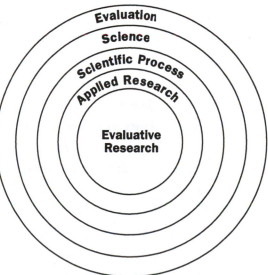

How Evaluative Research Can Help Practitioners

Leisure services are designed to benefit the human condition. The recreation profession is constantly challenged to devise ways to affect some aspect of physical, social, and/or psychological well-being positively. The importance of evaluating leisure services should not be underestimated in its role toward achieving this goal.

Recreation services are purposeful, deliberate, and organized efforts. As Weiss (1972, p. 6) noted, evaluation is "conducted for a client who has decisions to make and who looks to the evaluation for answers on which to base his [sic] decisions." Evaluative research needs to be viewed as an integral part of policy and administrative efforts.

Formal evaluations, or evaluative research, can be conducted for a variety of reasons on a broad range of topics (House, 1980; Patten, 1997). The results of these evaluations provide information that can be used to make decisions about some aspect of a service or program operation.

From the point of view of an organization, evaluative research may be undertaken to:

Determine whether or not the service achieves what it was set up to do, or the *behavioral objectives approach.* This approach focuses on determining if and to what extent clear, specific, and measurable program objectives have been met. For instance, did the children enrolled in the "Little Mermaid" class learn how to float on their backs for two minutes at a time? Did the social skills training program teach developmentally disabled participants how to order and consume food successfully inside a fast foods restaurant? Were tennis clinic participants satisfied with the quality of instruction?

Improve a program, or the *formative evaluation or management–oriented monitoring approach.* This approach focuses on identifying ways a program can be improved. The emphasis is on determining which aspects of the intervention (such as personnel and/or public relations) are effective and which are ineffective and hence in need of change. In order to eliminate unexpected results and unwanted side effects, corrective measures or steps are taken on how the program or service is implemented. Managers use formative evaluation results to make changes in their program operations. For example, evaluative research results may reveal: how a concession stand operation at a fitness club can be made more efficient or marketing strategies that can be used to maximize enrollment in classes offered at the fitness club.

Determine the costs of a service. These costs can be measured either in terms of human effort (the *effort approach*), or money (the *inputs approach*). An example of the former is how many staff are needed and scheduled to operate seasonal recreation programs in a neighborhood park? An example of an inputs approach is determining how much money is spent annually in a neighborhood park on program staff, maintenance staff, and supplies.

Quantitatively measure program inputs and outcomes, the *systems analysis pproach.* A systems analysis can be done two ways. First, a recreation service can be analyzed in terms of its cost relative to its effects. This is known as a *cost-effectiveness analysis.* These effects are usually measured in non-monetary terms (see Chapter 15). An example of a cost-effectiveness study would be to determine the cost of offering community CPR classes relative to the number of lives saved or number of resuscitation attempts made within a year of receiving training.

Second, a program can also be analyzed in terms of its cost relative to its benefits (typically measured in dollars), which is technically known as a *cost-benefit analysis*. An example of a cost-benefit analysis would be to examine the costs of operating a lunchtime fitness program relative to cost savings associated with changes in morbidity (such as number of sick days experienced).

Examine how two or more programs rank on specific indicators, outcomes, or criteria, or the *comparative focus approach*. In actuality, such a focus can also be considered a cost- effectiveness analysis. An example of an application of the comparative focus approach is examining which of three programs (such as an after–school art and space camp, a tattoo–removal program, and a sports program) leads to the biggest gain in self-worth among youth-at-risk (Witt & Compton, 1997).

Examine services, methods or approaches in terms of actual effects, or the *goal-free evaluation approach*. In other words, the extent to which the client or participant needs are being met by the program is examined. For example, how does participation in a residential, outdoor, high risk camp experience affect each camper?

Make a judgment about the success of a program, or the *summative evaluation approach*. Sometimes summative evaluation results are used to make decisions to continue a program or replicate it elsewhere. An example of a summative evaluation was one done of a pilot program sponsored by the Lighthouse Association of the Blind (see Riddick & Fleegal, 1986). The evaluation focused on determining the social-psychological gains experienced by visually impaired adults participating in a hands-on sailing instructional program.

Determine the extent a program meets professional standards for a given type of program, or the *accreditation model approach*. In other words, an authority has demanded evidence that the service or organization operates according to pre-prescribed standards. Evidence is needed to satisfy accountability requirements of program sponsors, or accreditation, licensor, or regulatory entities. Examples of such authorities are the American Camping Association, the Joint Commission on the Accreditation of Hospitals, and the National Recreation and Park Association's Agency Accreditation Program.

Difference Between Evaluative Research and Other Types of Research

Evaluative research can be distinguished from other kinds of research any number of ways. Perhaps the most dramatic distinctions revolve around purposes, contexts, and research methods (adapted from Hedrick, Bickman, & Rog, 1993, pp. 4-9).

Purposes

As already mentioned, evaluative research is a form of applied research. Applied research is usually compared to another kind of inquiry—basic research. One fundamental difference between evaluative research and basic research is the purpose or intention of the research. *Basic research* is driven by an anchoring with theory and a desire to add to the knowledge base of a substantive area. In other words, a basic research study is conducted in order to test or develop a theory—to find out if gathered evidence supports the theory being tested or leads to the establishment of a theory. Usually the basic researcher is investigating a very specific topic or question (for example, what motivates adults to play?), and thus it is knowledge, as an end in itself, that drives the researcher.

On the other hand, as an *applied* enterprise, *evaluative research* focuses on a program or some component of the service (such as facility, equipment, personnel, public relations activities, etc.). In other words, evaluative research is not triggered by a desire to examine a theory *per se*. Instead, evaluative research is set up to provide information that will enable determination of a future course of action about a program or service intervention. Evaluative research answers questions of immediate, practical concern.

Contexts

A second difference between evaluative research and basic research deals with the research contexts. Basic research typically is self-initiated, isolated from the real world (typically carried out in a lab or university classroom setting), funded by internal (university–sponsored research) or external grants, executed over several years, and has low sensitivity to cost overruns. In comparison, as an applied form of research, evaluative research is done for a specific agency or organization in an action setting (Weiss, 1972, p. 92), has a shorter–term time line, and is relatively inflexible in terms of deadlines and cost over-runs.

Another contextual difference is that in evaluative research contract monies typically are awarded to a person(s) with a multi-disciplinary background (which is needed to answer multiple questions across different areas of inquiry, such as psychology, sociology, economics, political science, etc.). Contrastingly, basic researchers are generally trained in a single discipline. They typically rely on one or a limited number of methods to execute studies that are related to the same substantive area.

Methods

A third difference between evaluative research and basic research deals with research methods. Basic research concentrates on the *construct of cause*, whereas evaluative research concentrates on the *construct of effect*. In basic research the "causal" (or independent variable) is clearly explicated and not confounded with any other variables (for further explanation see Chapter 15). If, for example, the investigator in a laboratory study is examining how shoe design affects 10K marathon performance, the precise ways the shoe's design (weight, balance, etc.) has been altered will be detailed down to the *n*th degree and probably chronicled using computer technology.

On the other hand, in evaluative research settings, control over an independent variable is seldom so clear-cut. For instance, a researcher cannot typically or fully identify the specific aspects of a program that are responsible for the noted effects. Hedrick, Bickman, and Rog (1993, p. 9) remind us we "often must treat the program as a 'black box,' providing as much descriptive information as possible to enable others to replicate the entire program and its context at a later date." Thus, evaluative research concentrates on the *construct of effect*.

Other methodological differences between basic and evaluative research relate to the unit of analysis, design, and types of data collected. Basic research often is focused on a single level of analysis or the individual. Evaluative research typically examines a specific problem at more than one level of analysis—studying individuals, groups, and/or the entire organization (Chapter 15). Basic research relies on experimental design whereas evaluative research turns to quasi-experimental or non-experimental designs. Applied researchers are often called in after a program or intervention is in place, thus precluding the possibility of using random assignment in the design adopted for the study (Chapter 7). And finally, data collection methods often differ in basic and evaluative research settings. In the controlled environment of the lab, observational data is often used (e.g., videotaping the running of toddlers in order to study the biomechanics of running in the early years of life). In real-world settings, direct observations are sometimes economically unfeasible; reliance instead is placed on self-reports, administrative records, and/or key informants (Chapter 10).

Situational Responsiveness and Social Ecology of a Formal Evaluation

Theobald (1979) makes two observations about the use of formal evaluation studies in our profession. First, he notes that formal evaluations are rarely conducted in parks and recreation settings (p. 19). Second, he observes that the majority of evaluation studies that are done in our field are seldom implemented or used (p. 167).

To us, this is a rather sad and unnecessary state of affairs. Leisure service professionals are confronted with lots of questions that can be answered with carefully crafted evaluative research. The critical challenge before us is to design evaluations that have utility or are "situationally responsive." Patten (1987, p. 73) underscores the wisdom of this advice by stating, "Evaluation use is not something to be concerned about at the end of an evaluation; how the evaluation is to be used is a primary matter of concern from the very beginning of the evaluation and throughout every step of the evaluative process."

How then do we design evaluative research that is useful or relevant? Patten's (1987) simple formula is that the evaluative researcher embark on an "active-reactive-adaptive" mode of operation. That is, the evaluative researcher should *actively* solicit information about the questions of real interest to the primary information users. The evaluative researcher then *reacts* to the information needs by designing a useful, practical, and accurate evaluation. Finally, in the course of designing or conducting an evaluative research study, new information emerges that necessitates the evaluative researcher to become *adaptive* to the changing situation.

The uniqueness of the situation that evaluative research is operating in must be considered on a case-by-case basis. Otherwise, the likelihood that the results will be used diminishes. Rossi and Freeman (1993, p. 406) dub this heightened sensitivity as assessing the social ecology of the evaluative research study. We maintain that in order to be responsive to the social-political environments surrounding the evaluative research project, one needs to adapt an active-reactive-adaptive style of operation.

The *social ecology*, or the social and political contexts, of the evaluation must be astutely appraised if one wants to improve the likelihood the results of an evaluation will be used. Evaluative research should have application value to someone. Rossi and Freeman (1993, p. 30) remind us, "evaluations need to be designed and implemented in ways that recognize the policy and program interests of the sponsors and stakeholders, and that will yield maximally useful information for decision makers given the political circumstances, program constraints, and available resources." Evaluative research is conducted in real-world settings. Thus, some questions need to be asked and answered in order to increase the likely use of the evaluation results. These questions deal with stakeholders, motive, staff commitment, and time frame.

Stakeholders

Who initiated the request for conducting the evaluative study? Rossi and Freeman (1993, p. 408) view such individuals as belonging to any possible number of stakeholder groups. *Stakeholders* can hold competing and sometimes combative views on the evaluation. Examples of stakeholders are policymakers and agency managers, program sponsors, target participants, program management, program staff, and contextual stakeholders (see Figure 1.3). Fletcher, Kaiser, and Groger (1992), for example, identify the differing values of multiple stakeholders involved in funding public park and recreation departments.

Having multiple stakeholders has several consequences for the evaluation. First, the professional evaluator must recognize that her evaluation report will be but one piece of the input that will be used to make decisions and take action. Decision making is often done in a social political arena. Findings from formal evaluations can and do become part of the political process. Sometimes a program is continued, expanded, or dismantled without regard to information provided by the evaluative research. Any one of the multiple stakeholders can exert pressure that overrides the objective results of an evaluative research study. Decision making involves weighing, assessing, and balancing the conflicting claims and interests of a variety of constituencies. The professional evaluator's role can be viewed like an expert witness at a trial. The professional evaluator is called upon to share the results of detective-like information gathering. The jury is the decision maker that decides how much weight to give the professional evaluator's input relative to others parading in front of her. It simply would be a mistake to elevate the evaluator to a role, coined by Aristotle, as the "philosopher king." It must always be remembered that the evaluator provides objectively sought-after findings that can be used in making judgments. There is an important distinction between making judgments and providing information upon which judgments can be based! Evaluative research should be approached as an undertaking to provide objective information to a decision maker or stakeholder group.

Figure 1.3: Stakeholders in an evaluation.

Policy makers and agency managers = Persons who decide whether a program is to be initiated, (dis)continued, expanded, or curtailed (e.g., Recreations Board, the president or chief executive office of a private recreation business, or the municipal park and recreations director).

Program sponsors = Organizational entities that initiate and fund the program (such as local businesses that support the marathon, county council, etc.).

Target participants = Program recipients, persons or other units who participate in the program or receive the intervention service (e.g., users of the county's aquatic center and visitors to the state park).

Program management = Group responsible for overseeing and coordinating the intervention program (e.g., therapeutic recreations supervisor of the head and brain injury unit or the manager of the local fitness club).

Program staff = People responsible for actual delivery of the intervention (e.g., teen leaders or lifeguards).

Contextual stakeholders = Individuals, organizations, groups, and other units in the immediate environment of a program (e.g., local governmental officials or persons who are influential in local politics).

Examples of how politics affect decision making are replete in recreation. The USDA Forest Service's changing policies on logging in parklands and wolf control in the national parks are two examples of stakeholder politics at work. Typically a good barometer that multiple stakeholder politics has been interjected is when policy vacillates back and forth.

Second, invariably strains will result from the varying and conflicting interests of the stakeholders. The professional evaluator will need to identify which stakeholder's perspective is used when designing the evaluation. The perspective that is used may be one imposed on the professional evaluator, one that was arrived at through consensus, or one "freely" chosen by the evaluator. It must be decided and publicly announced which perspective was used for the formal evaluation study, along with additional acknowledgment of the other perspectives. For instance, in reporting the results of a formal evaluation the evaluator should state, "The evaluation study was conducted from the perspective of the Recreation Center's Advisory Board. Nevertheless, it is acknowledged that program clients and program staff have alternative viewpoints."

Motive

Professional evaluators need also to be cognizant of something called *policy space* or "the context in which they are working" (Rossi & Freeman, 1993, p. 27). That is, what is the purpose(s) or motive(s) behind conducting the evaluation? Is the evaluation being motivated because of impending resource constraints? Changes or shifts in priorities? Suspicions that the program is ineffective or inefficient? Or other reasons? Professional evaluators must design studies that are relevant to policy, planning, and/or managerial action—evaluations need to be appropriate to the policy space.

Staff Commitment

Is there a real commitment among the organization's administrators and/or practitioners to use or apply the results of the evaluative research? These entities need to be involved in planning the evaluation—their insights can add to greater appreciation of the final results (see Chapter 2). For example, staff at a racquet sports facility may not initially understand the importance of conducting a study on the social psychological needs of users. On the other hand, a study on how to increase membership enrollments may be more embraceable. Staff input can be invaluable in shaping the topic for the study as well as providing feedback on the logistics of executing the study.

Time Frame

Evaluative research can take time, whereas the political and program worlds often move at a faster pace. It is important to know at the onset what the time frame is for the completion of the formal evaluation. It may be that the different time schedules of evaluators and decision makers are so far off it is ill-advised to undertake the evaluation.

In closing, every evaluative research project should be unique—tailored to the service, organization, or operation under examination. Nevertheless, we maintain that recreation organizations should conduct evaluations that use the scientific process and methods in order to collect information systematically. An essential ingredient to the success of an evaluation is designing a project that produces information that will be useful to stakeholders or decision makers who are poised to make informed judgments.

Main Points

- Evaluation is a common human activity.

- When evaluation is done on a subjective basis, mistakes can be made. Undertaking a formal evaluation that relies on the scientific inquiry process can help protect us against such mistakes.

- The scientific process is used in evaluative research.

- Evaluative research results can provide objective information that can be used to arrive at intelligent and rational decisions.

- The goals of recreation include affecting the physical, social, and/or psychological health of individuals. In other words, our services are aimed at positively affecting some facet of human life.

- Topics that can be examined using evaluative research include: determining the worthwhileness of a program; improving program operations; calculating program cost efficiency; appraising personnel performance; determining public relations effectiveness; or ascertaining compliance of facility design, program operations, and/or risk management with regulatory standards.

- Evaluative research should be both tailor-made and responsive to the agency, organization, or operation under study. The evaluator needs to design and implement an evaluation from the perspective of the "active-reactive-adaptive" mind-set.

- Evaluative research takes place in social and political contexts (or the social eco logical setting). The design and implementation of an evaluative research plan should reflect social responsiveness. It is important that the evaluator know: Who are the stakeholders? Why do they want the evaluation performed? What is the staff's commitment to the proposed evaluation? And the time frame being imposed to complete the evaluation?

Study Questions

1. What is meant by the term *"evaluation?"* Cite some examples of day-to-day evaluations you do.

2. What are the five ways you "know" something? Which way do you tend to use the most? The least? Why?

3. What are the relationships among *science*, the *scientific process*, and *evaluative research*?

4. Do you believe in the *"paradox behind science?"* The *"uncertainty principle of science?"* Explain/illustrate your answers.

5. Cite several reasons evaluative research is undertaken in recreation, park, and sport settings.

6. Distinguish between *evaluative research* and *basic research* in terms of (a) purposes, (b) contexts, and (c) methods.

7. How can an evaluative research undertaking be designed so it is situationally responsive?

8. What is meant by appraising the *social ecology* surrounding the initiation of an evaluation project? Explicate how stakeholders, motive, staff commitment, and time frame affect the social and political contexts of the evaluation.

References

Babbie, E. (1998). *The practice of social research* (8th ed.). Belmont, CA: Sage Publications.

Coles, S. (1992, April 22). *Metroparks 2000: Conserving our national heritage, 4,* 1-4.

Dressel, P. (1968). Measurement and evaluation of instructional objectives. In N. Gronlund, *Readings in measurement and evaluation* (pp. 11-17). New York: Macmillan.

Fletcher, J., Kaiser, R., & Groger, S. (1992). An assessment of the importance and performance of park impact fees in funding park and recreation infrastructure. *Journal of Park and Recreation Administration, 10,* 75-87.

Hedrick, T., Bickman, L., & Rog, D. (1993). *Applied research design: A practical guide.* Newbury Park, CA: Sage Publications.

House, E. (1980). *Evaluating with validity.* Beverly Hills, CA: Sage Publications.

Lastrucci, C. (1963). *The scientific approach: Basic principles of the scientific method.* Cambridge, MA: Schenkman Publishing.

Patten, M. (1987). *Creative evaluation* (2nd ed.). Newbury Park, CA: Sage Publications.

Patten, M. (1997). *Utilization-focused evaluation: The new century text* (3rd ed.). Thousand Oaks, CA: Sage Publications.

Riddick, C. & Fleegal, W. (1986). Instructional sailing program in an adult camping and vacation setting. *Journal of Blindness & Visual Impairment, 80,* 748.

Rossi, P., & Freeman, H. (1993). *Evaluation: A systematic approach.* Newbury Park, CA: Sage Publications.

Scriven, M. (1991). *Evaluation thesaurus* (4th ed.). Newbury Park, CA: Sage Publications.

Suchman, E. (1967). *Evaluation research: Principles and practices in public service and social action programs.* New York: Russell Sage Foundation.

Theobald, W. (1979). *Evaluation of recreation and park programs.* New York: John Wiley & Sons.

Walizer, M., & Wienir, P. (1978). *Research methods and analysis: Searching for relationships.* New York: Harper and Row.

Wallace, W. (1971). *The logic of science in sociology.* New York: Aldine Publishing.

Weiss, C. (1972). *Evaluation research: Methods of assessing program effectiveness.* Englewood Cliffs, NJ: Prentice-Hall.

Witt, P., & Compton, J. (1997). The at-risk youth recreation project. *Parks & Recreation, 32,* 54-61.

CHAPTER 2

Developing an Organization Evaluation System

What Will I Learn in This Chapter?
I'll be able to:

1. Explain what is meant by using an in-house evaluator, outside evaluator, and an internal and external staffing blend for an evaluator.

2. Identify trade-offs of having internal versus outside evaluators.

3. Recall sources of friction that arise between program personnel and evaluators during the execution of an evaluation.

4. Identify ideas for reducing friction between practitioners and evaluators in the planning of an evaluation.

5. Recall sections that need to be included in a written evaluation proposal.

6. Distinguish between clock time and calendar time in an evaluation project.

7. Define direct costs, fringe benefits, and indirect costs.

8. Explain what is meant by an organizational review of an evaluation proposal as well as purposes served by such a review.

9. Describe how each of the following contribute to keeping an evaluation project going: recruiting respondents, handling logistics, and conducting a mid-point review.

10. Define the national agency accreditation program and explain how it helps public leisure service organizations develop a comprehensive evaluation system.

In an ideal world it would be nice if leisure services and all the components used to deliver these services (such as personnel, facilities and the like) were periodically evaluated. Recreation organizations that proactively engage in formal evaluation activities can be considered both progressive and accountable. Think about it, what is a better mind set for managing a recreation organization? Using a model in which the organization is continuously striving, in a formal manner, to improve its programs or operations or using the philosophy that only complaints are pursued? Somehow, what appears to be the impossible dream of incorporating regular systematic evaluations into the entire operation of a leisure service system will eventually evolve as a reality for many organizations. We hope that such a mind set will be adopted from the top down (i.e., by policy makers and managers) as well as from bottom up (i.e., from front line staff). Furthermore, we envision service staff having the primary responsibility for planning such evaluations or, at the very least, being consulted with by evaluation specialists within their organization.

Our premise behind this chapter is that leisure service organizations need to devote increasing attention to developing a plan for regular, thorough, and systematic evaluations of all aspects of operations. This chapter begins by discussing issues surrounding who does the evaluation. Next, some ideas for getting and keeping an evaluative research project going are shared. The chapter ends by reviewing a voluntary, pubic agency accreditation program that essentially evaluates an agency's performance in terms of operational efficiency and operational effectiveness.

Staffing Related Issues Surrounding Evaluation

For each evaluation project a number of issues surround the person(s) doing the evaluation. More specifically, there are the matters of: whether to use someone inside and/or external to the organization to conduct the evaluation; to whom the evaluator reports; and, the evaluator's relationship with program personnel.

In-House or Outside Evaluators?

An evaluation study can be staffed three ways: internally, externally, or a blend of both. *Internally*, a study may be performed by staff affiliated with the program or service or by a research unit or department within the agency organization. An evaluation study might also be undertaken *externally* or entirely independently of either program or planning staff. That is, an agency such as a private or non-profit consultant group or a social science research institute affiliated with a university could be contracted to conduct the evaluation. Sometimes, recreation organizations may use an internal and external staffing *blend*. That is, a consultant (usually a university faculty member) may be hired to advise "in-house" staff about what and/or how to conduct the evaluation.

Regardless of whether the evaluator is internal or external to the leisure service organization, it is important to know and remember that systematic evaluation studies are grounded in social science research techniques. Thus, the person conducting the evaluation should have some social research training, be somewhat familiar with the full repertoire of social research methods, and have previous experience in conducting evaluation studies (Rossi & Freeman, 1993, p. 52-53).

Weiss (1972, p. 20) points out there are advantages and disadvantages associated with both in-house and outside evaluators. Some of the issues to consider in choosing who to turn to to do an evaluation are: confidence, objectivity, and utilization of results. In the final analysis, each organization will need to weigh the advantages and disadvantages of using an in-house versus an outside evaluator.

1. Confidence. The competence of those conducting the evaluation must be examined. Sometimes, outside evaluators are too abstract or esoteric—thus, the information produced by the evaluation has little practical value. Rossi and Freeman (1993) characterized this reality as "...the strain between a press for evaluations to be 'scientific' on the one hand and 'pragmatic' on the other (p. 27)." External evaluators may not be able to understand fully the "issues" confronting the agency. Conversely, in-house staff may not have the technical skills to conduct the evaluation.

2. Objectivity. Those doing the evaluation should not be biased in what they look for, find, and/or report. Decision makers or the public often want or demand an "impartial" judge—someone who has no stake in the program—to be involved in conducting the evaluation. An external evaluator, because there is less risk of job loss or personal retribution, can speak more frankly. Nevertheless, outside evaluators can also "lose" their objectivity if tempted by the desire to ingratiate themselves to organization staff. This tainted perspective may be fueled by the desire for future contracts ("After all, they ultimately found our program sound") and/or referrals.

3. Utilization of results. Again, results from an evaluation should be used to make decisions about a program. Sometimes, organization staff are better equipped, due to their knowledge about program operations, to make useful recommendations. That is, inside evaluators can have the edge on conjuring up recommendations that are realistic and can result in positive change. These ideas can be promoted in staff meetings and sometimes in-house evaluators are perceived as having more credence than "outsiders." On the other hand, outsiders by virtue of their credentials, may be in a better position to get the agency to pay attention to the evaluation results. Outside evaluators also might have a wealth of experiences with other programs, enabling him/her to meaningfully relate to the service or program under scrutiny.

Before moving on, it is important to point out evaluators are not licensed or certified. In 1978 the American Evaluation Association was begun and although it is the major organization for professional evaluators it has only a membership of about 2,500. Similarly, *Evaluation Review*, a cross-disciplinary international journal, has less than 3,000 subscribers. All this underscores the emerging nature of "professional" evaluators as well as the shared responsibility for evaluation by all leisure service professionals.

Evaluators Should Report To Whom?

Regardless of whether in-house or outside evaluators are used, one pressing question that needs to be addressed early on in the planning of the evaluation is the matter of, "To whom should evaluators report?" The answer to this question should rely on the focus of the evaluation (see Figure 2.1). If the focus of the evaluation is assessing demand, need or interest, the evaluator should report to both policy makers and the organization's managers. If the merit of the service is unchallenged, and the evaluation centers on the effectiveness of comparative strategies, the evaluator should probably be responsible to managers or directors. If the focus of the evaluation is to answer the questions, "Is the service worthwhile? Should it be continued? Should it be expanded?," the evaluator should report to policy makers (the board of directors, etc.). If an impact evaluation is performed, results should initially be shared with managers and program staff. Depending on which aspect of operational efficiency is being monitored (see Chapter 15), the evaluator should report to policy makers, managers, and/or staff. Findings dealing with personnel evaluations should be shared with the organization's managers and the particular staff undergoing performance appraisal. Evaluations of other non-personnel resources should be shared (depending on what is studied), with policy makers, agency managers, program staff, and/or clientele. And evaluation reports dealing with public relations and promotional related activities need to be shared with managers and clientele.

In the real world, evaluators typically serve primarily both policymakers and the organization's managers. It takes an adept evaluator to be sensitive to both groups. Managers can perceive evaluators as "checking up" on them and divulging information that reflects poorly on their management. On the other hand, policymakers may not appreciate the need to examine comparative service methods or approaches in terms of their relative effects. In the final analysis, in order to produce timely and unambiguous findings, the evaluator must also cultivate the cooperation of policymakers, the organization's managers, and program staff, as well as participants.

Evaluator's Relationship with Program Personnel

When conducting evaluative research, the evaluator's relationship with program staff can range from congenial, coexistence, to downright hostility. The interpersonal relationships that are forged between program staff and evaluator (especially researchers external to the organization or individuals working full-time within the organization but whose job description requires them to spend most or all their time engaged in research related activities) will depend on a number of factors. Some of the sources of friction and ideas for averting or lessening the friction between the evaluator and service staff will be identified (Weiss, 1972, pp. 98-107).

Sources of friction. Friction between program staff personnel and evaluators can be due to any number of things. The most common causes of friction—or personality differences, role differences, and institutional characteristics—will now be reviewed.

1. **Personality differences.** One of the contributing factors to friction can be personal-

Figure 2.1: Whom evaluators should directly report to based on the decision being made.

Decision To Be Made	Evaluator Reports To			
	Policy Makers	Managers	Staff	Clientele
Defining demand, need, or interest	X	X		
Specifying service delivery-related methods, techniques, and/or procedures		X		
Continuing program?	X			
Expanding program?	X			
Determining impact		X	X	
Assessing efficiency	X	X	X	
Managing personnel		X	X	
Monitoring other (non-personnel) resources	X	X	X	X
Monitoring public relations/promotions		X		X

ity differences between the evaluator and program staff. It has been noted that personality differences exist between people who choose a practitioner's career versus those who go into evaluative research. The practitioner has been described as a people-oriented person—concerned about people, the here and now, and action oriented. In contrast, the evaluator has been profiled as a detached questioning individual, interested in the abstract and generalizations, and without undue personal loyalties to the program or organization. In short, the evaluator's interest can lay primarily in the acquisition of knowledge; this compares to the practitioner's bent on day-to-day issues of program operation. The practitioner typically finds the evaluator's skepticism as strange and hence can have a difficult time "warming up" to the researcher as a human being.

2. **Role differences.** The practitioner can view evaluation as a threat. The evaluative research study is perceived as diverting money, time and administrator's attention in return

for the issuance of a "report card." The evaluator, under these circumstances, is seen as judging the value of the staff's work, thus challenging the professional competence and integrity of those being evaluated. One does not need to be a rocket scientist in order to understand that if evaluation results are used in decision making, the future of the program and even perhaps the person's job will be called into question! Although the rhetoric may be that the "evaluation is to add to knowledge and rational policy making" the staff person knows (s)he will in all likelihood bear the consequences if the results show program failure.

Sometimes an evaluation effort can be interpreted by the practitioner as violating cherished service concepts and traditions. For example, suppose the traditional organization value has been to stress physical activity in an effort to improve the health of its clientele. Thus, if a new program is set up under the premise that social activity should be stressed, practitioners might undermine the program and consequently the evaluation. This situation can evolve because staff feel the new emphasis (i.e., promoting social activity) runs counter to the organization's traditional values.

Another rub or source of role difference deals with frame of reference. The practitioner, as a human service provider, deals with individuals. Thus, practitioners envision themselves as being aware of individual differences. Indeed, the practitioner is acutely sensitive about differentiating one human being from another and planning programs or services that are tailored to individual needs.

Contrastingly, the evaluator's frame of reference is typically the group. Thus, the evaluator's perspective drives him/her to "lump" people together in order to calculate statistical averages, etc. The practitioner views the evaluative data as being spewed or churned out with the subsequent conclusions made from the data deemed not particularly relevant. In short, from the vantage point of the practitioner, conclusions stemming from a formal evaluation typically relate to some collective group and do not address the specific clientele with whom the practitioner is involved.

Furthermore, practitioners typically view themselves as doing all the work, in the "trenches" everyday, the Sancho Panzas of the world. The evaluator arrives, much like the galloping Don Quixote of La Mancha, ready to collect all the rewards and accolades that follow the publication of the final report. Like the criticism lodged at many architects, the evaluator (especially one external to the organization or a full-time evaluator within the organization) does not stick around very long—(s)he produces a draft, turns it in, and goes away without acknowledging any further obligation to revisit the program. Could it be the evaluator is "milking the program" of opportunities to further his/her own career without having to give much in return?

3. Institutional characteristics. Who is supervising the evaluator as well as to whom the evaluator reports are two points that must be clear to the evaluator and service staff alike. If these administrative details are ambiguous, then frictions can and do develop.

Additionally, when an organization has a history of internal conflict, evaluation may be viewed with suspicion. Evaluators may be viewed as "hatchet" men or women out to do the dirty work of the other faction. Thus, it is important that the professional evaluator possess good communication and interpersonal skills.

Ideas for reducing the friction. Schisms between practitioner and evaluator might be averted or reduced any number of ways. Adopting the thoughts of Hedrick, Bickman, & Rog (1993, p. 36) and Weiss (1972), there are a number of strategies that can aid the evaluator in achieving sound and credible results while at the same time fostering positive relationships between the evaluator and the practitioner. Some of the workable strategies include: gaining support from administrators, involving practitioners in the evaluation, defining roles and clarifying authority structure, minimizing disruptions, providing useful feedback information, and publicizing study limitations.

1. Gain administrative support. For several reasons the evaluator is prudent to involve project administrators and managers in planning the evaluation. An advisory committee may also be useful in helping with the evaluative research project. Interactions with administrators and/or an advisory group can help the evaluator develop insights and gain commitment to the study resulting, hopefully, in the eventual use of evaluation results in decision making. Still another reason to solicit dialog with administrators is that they in turn are crucial to getting and maintaining the cooperation of program staff for the evaluation effort.

2. Involve practitioners in the evaluation. There are numerous rationales for involving the practitioners or colleagues throughout the evolution of the entire evaluation. Having the practitioners involved early on can help them gain understanding of what the evaluation is all about, ultimately resulting in their support for the study. Practitioners can learn why the evaluation is being conducted and how it will proceed, thus they will probably feel less threatened. More importantly, fellow staff have keen insights and can share information and ideas that can contribute to the evaluation effort. Shared insights and inputs by practitioner colleagues can vastly improve the evaluator's level of understanding, even when the evaluator is from within house. For example, the evaluator might learn from a life guard that her intention of asking exiting pool users a three page questionnaire dealing with impressions regarding pool operations is unreasonable. The staff person astutely predicts that very few, if any persons, will agree to stand around in wet suits to answer so many questions.

Human relations skills also dictates that each person whose work will be affected by the evaluation should be kept informed as well as be given a chance to have input and otherwise express ideas and concerns. Practitioners, in particular, can have keen insights regarding the interpretation of results and the conclusions that can be drawn for future action considerations (see Chapter 14). The ideal would be to have a symbiotic relationship evolve between the practitioner and the evaluator. Collaboration between the evaluator and the practitioners should happen in order to gain insights regarding: understanding the causes of past successes and failures, the process by which the program got where it is, what should be done in the future, and how to make future directions acceptable and obtainable to and by interested parties.

3. Define roles and clarify authority structure. At the very onset, the evaluators and practitioners should be very clear about what is expected of both groups. That is, the scope and limits of their roles must be delineated, ideally in the form of a written contract. Practitioners may feel some of their prescribed obligations are incompatible with the demands placed upon them related to implementing the evaluation. For example, normally the practitioner uses an array of teaching techniques. Then (s)he is confronted by a directive from the evaluator to use one prescribed instructional technique—in order that the technique can be evaluated for its effectiveness. Suppose this directive is not acceptable to the practitioner. What are his/her options? To whom does the practitioner direct his/her appeal? Has the evaluator been given authority to change program operations?

Furthermore, lines of authority should be delineated at the very beginning of the evaluation study. When differences arise between evaluation and program personnel, and these differences cannot be reconciled by negotiation, then all parties should be clear about what channels are open for appeal; as well as the person(s) who will listen to and decide upon the appeal.

4. Minimize disruptions. The golden rule, "treat others as you wish to be treated" can help guide expectations placed by the evaluator on staff. One of the major criticisms lodged against evaluations is that program staff perceive them as the proverbial nuisance or pain. Requests, made in conjunction with executing an evaluation study, should be limited to indispensable issues in order not to disrupt program operations any more than absolutely necessary. The evaluator needs to know what issues are open to negotiation (after all, there should be a spirit of give and take) and those that are not. Why ask program staff to pose a 100 question questionnaire to clients when a 20 question version is available and will suffice? When unrealistic demands are placed on staff, at the data collection phase, it is often because the evaluator is foggy about what he is looking for and thus decides to ask everything so as not to miss anything that may turn out to be important.

5. Provide useful feedback information. The evaluator can ingratiate him/herself to staff when (s)he poses research questions that will yield information perceived by front-line staff as valuable to know. In defining the scope of the evaluation (see Chapter 6), it may prove prudent to add an emphasis that determines ways staff can do their job more efficiently. For instance, suppose the state division of parks decided to determine the satisfaction levels of state park cabin users. Some representatives of front line workers were asked to review and comment on the proposed mail questionnaire. Comments were made along the lines of revising the proposed questionnaire away from soliciting general reactions to obtaining more specific feedback on: (i) satisfaction with specific design features and elements considered important as part of the park cabin experience (e.g., cleanliness, linen service, registration system, furniture, kitchen appliances); and, (ii) important features that should be found in the park and the users' performance rating of the noted feature (such as scenic qualities, hiking trails, etc.). These suggestions in turn were incorporated in the revised questionnaire. Thus, the planned results moved away from being general, non-specific, and esoteric findings to an evaluation product perceived as useful to front line workers and managers as well as designers of future cabins. For a study conducted along the lines just described, see Hollenhorst, Olson, & Fortney (1992).

6. Publicize study limitations. In the earliest phases of planning the evaluation, it is important to make the stakeholders aware of the study's limitations. Limitations are inherent in any evaluation and emerge at a number of junctures, including the adoption of a focus (Chapter 15), framework (Chapter 5), design (Chapter 7), and data collection (Chapter 10). These limitations should be immediately recognized and be made known throughout the life of the study. By publicly recognizing and acknowledging every step of the way the limitations associated with the evaluation study, the evaluator lessens the likelihood of his/her objectivity being questioned.

Getting and Keeping an Evaluative Research Project Going

Successful evaluation projects are those that start out well organized and stay on track through to the finish. The responsibility for this is the project's director. This is usually the person who had the idea for the evaluation in the first place, or the staff member whose job description requires assumption of the responsibility. Usually it is the person who develops the evaluative research proposal who takes charge of the study. No matter how many people are involved in the project, one person must agree to supervise its progress. If this person is you, you need to be concerned with a number of things including: preparing an evaluation proposal, seeking a review of the proposal, recruiting respondents, handling logistics, and conducting a mid-point review.

Preparing an Evaluation Proposal

The initial decisions about the purpose of the evaluation and how it will be carried out are recorded in a proposal. The *proposal* is a written description of the intentions of the evaluator. It is not only useful for communicating your plans for evaluation to such interested parties as the organization's director or governing board, but the process of writing a proposal helps you to think through the research design and methods. Such clear-headed thinking, via the proposal writing process, will ultimately help you be more efficient in carrying out the study. It is much easier to find flaws in the project and correct them before beginning to collect information, than it is to discover and correct them after you have started!

More specifically, writing a thorough, well-reasoned evaluation proposal has four advantages (Gall, Borg & Gall, 1996):

• A proposal requires you to state all your ideas in written form so they can be *evaluated and improved* upon by you and other colleagues.

• The proposal can serve as a *guide* to keep you on track while conducting the study.

• A thoroughly written proposal provides a *jump start* on writing the final evaluation report. As we explain later in the book, the evaluation proposal has much the same organization and content as an evaluation report.

• Ultimately the evaluation proposal becomes part of a "*contract*" between an organization and the evaluator. As such it is used to monitor the progress of the work and to ensure accountability for the expenditure of time, staff resources, and perhaps funds.

An evaluation proposal usually contains the following sections: introduction, literature review, study procedures and methods, time line, personnel, budget, and dissemination plan. While some of these sections are identical to those required in the final evaluation report (discussed in Chapter 13), a few are unique to the evaluation proposal.

Introduction. Evaluation proposals usually begin with an introductory section that states the purpose statement, significance of the study, and the research questions, objectives, or hypotheses (see Chapter 6). Your aim in the introduction is to lead the proposal reader unyieldingly towards the same decision you have made: that a study must be done now, and with these aims.

Literature review. The point of this section, in an evaluation study, is to present a summary of related work. You are trying to show here that you are familiar with previous research on the topic of your study, as well as provide both a rationale and a context for how your study will fill knowledge gaps (see Chapter 4). In the proposal the *literature review* is relatively brief. Later, in the final report, it will likely be expanded, but in the proposal it needs to be only long enough to ground your study in an understanding of the existing knowledge base.

Study procedures and methods. This section of a proposal outlines the plan of work. Here you go into some detail about the *procedures and methods* you propose to use. Regardless of whether you are using a qualitative, quantitative, or combination approach, the proposal should include your intentions for the research design, the sample, instrumentation, data collection procedures and methods, and data analysis plan (see Chapters 7 through 10). A *data analysis strategy* must be planned before starting the study, as sample size, procedures and other decisions hinge on your intended data analysis. If you give no thought to data analysis until after the information is gathered, you may discover it is impossible to analyze it in the way you wish. There are a variety of data analysis options, which will be discussed in Chapters 11 and 12. It is critical that the proposal addresses how the data analysis ties into each of the evaluation questions, objectives, or hypotheses that have been posed for the evaluation.

Time line. Another part of the proposal that provides a basis for accountability is the projected timetable. Time becomes relevant from two perspectives. First, the nature of the study (or the research question) can have profound ramifications for how much *calendar time* is needed to conduct the study. For example, if you are studying how aging affects leisure preferences and behaviors, a long period of calendar time is needed to capture the phenomena under study. Or if you are interested in assessing downhill skiers' satisfaction with operations at a ski resort, then such an evaluation is best initiated only in winter time. In planning an evaluation, the investigator must have some familiarity with the phenomena under scrutiny; otherwise, the evaluator may fail to implement a good study if the relationship between time and the topic studied is not considered.

Time also should be considered in terms of *actual clock time* (or clock hours) needed to accomplish tasks related to the evaluation. For example, one could estimate how much time is needed for recruitment of study participants, data collection and analysis, preparation of final report, etc.

Preparation of a *time budget* can assist in resource allocation. Both calendar and clock time need to be budgeted. In order to budget calendar time, the duration of each step in the entire project must be known. Duration typically is set at the start of the project and the evaluator tailors the evaluation to fit the length of time available. There may be little flexibility in total calendar time due to an imposed project deadline. Indeed, a mistake many evaluators make in estimating the time budget is to underestimate the time needed, resulting in late delivery of written and oral reports.

In order to get a handle on clock time that should be budgeted for the evaluation, it is best to identify the major steps that are needed to be performed to complete the project (Figure 2.2). This long list can become a useful tool in: determining the staffing needs and clock time needed to complete a project, guiding the implementation of the project, and budgeting money needed to complete the evaluation.

Personnel. After the tasks necessary to complete the evaluation have been identified, the next step in preparing the proposal is to decide what kinds of people are needed to complete the requisite tasks. To assist the investigator in matching kinds of people needed for task completion, a *skills matrix* should be completed (see Figure 2.3 for an example of the skills that could be needed to evaluate a youth swim club at a YMCA). Typically a team of persons are used to design and execute a study—most individuals do not possess all the skills (let alone have the time) needed to complete a project! Thus, one consideration that needs to go into the construction of the matrix is deciding if a specific task needs one person to complete it or is it better to have several persons working on the same task. For instance, it might make sense to have multiple interviewers but only one person assigned to data analyzes.

Once the tasks have been specified and assigned to individual(s), then the amount of time required to complete each task must be estimated (Figure 2.4 highlights how this might be done with the task of choosing and designing instruments to carry out an evaluation of a YMCA youth swim club). A number of considerations go into calculating "*person loading* (or

Figure 2.2: Major steps associated with an evaluation research project.

Step

1. **Literature** review

2. Choose a quantitative, qualitative, or triangulation **framework**

3. Define **scope** (including identifying purpose of the study and explaining significance of the study)

4. Choose research **design**

5. Select **sampling** frame and sampling size

6. Specify study **procedures**

7. **Data collection**

8. **Analyze** data

9. **Write** and **present** report

amount of time required to complete each task by position)," including: nature of the task, skills and training of the person assigned the task (for example, an experienced person at data entry on a computer keyboard will take a lot less time compared to an entry level person), and time available to complete the noted task.

In budgeting personnel resources, the amount of calendar or real time must be estimated for each evaluation task and sub-task. The allocation of calendar time to each task and sub-task is portrayed in something called a "*Gantt*" *chart* (see Figure 2.5 for a Gantt chart set up for the task of choosing and designing instruments for an evaluation of the YMCA youth swim club). The Gantt chart shows not only how long (in calendar time) each activity takes but also the approximate relationship, in calendar time, among the various tasks. The Gantt chart basically serves as a management tool to help the evaluator stay on tasks so a project can be completed within a specified time period.

Budget. A proposed budget for accomplishing an evaluation study is typically needed

Figure 2.3: Skills matrix for an evaluation of a youth swim club.

Person	Literature Review	Define Scope	Research Design	Sampling	Instrumentation	Institutional Development	Statistics
Director YMCA		X	X		X	X	
TR Sports Coordinator		X		X	X	X	
Business Manager		X					X
Lifeguard		X		X	X		
Consultant	X	X	X	X	X		

Figure 2.4: Person–loading chart (in hours) for an evaluation of a youth swim club.

Task & Activity	Director	Youth Sports Coordinator	Business Manager	Lifeguard	Consultant
			Personnel		
Task 6. Choose/Design Instruments					
6.1 Specify data needs	10	5	2		20
6.2 Review existing instruments					
6.2.1 Locate instruments					30
6.2.2 Evaluate instruments	20	5		2	20
6.3 Develop new instruments					
6.3.1 Develop interview schedule	4	4		2	20
6.3.2 Pilot interview schedule		4		4	4
6.3.3 Analyze and revise interview schedule	2	2			10
Total	36	20	2	8	104

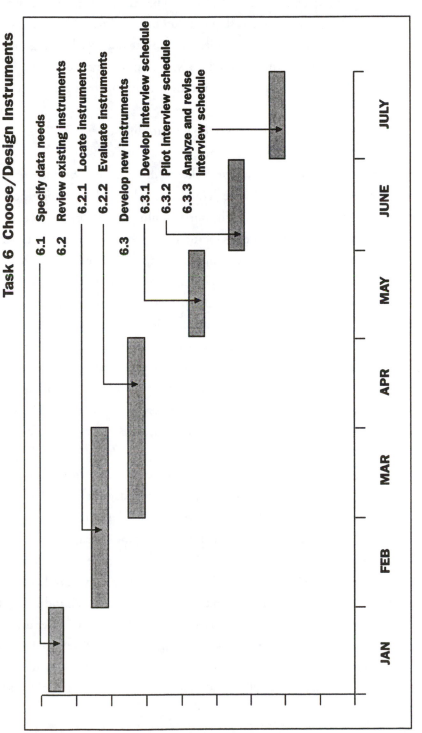

Figure 2.5: Gantt Chart for an evaluation of a youth swim club.

regardless of whether the evaluation is being performed by in-house or outside personnel. Whoever has requested the evaluation and/or whoever is going to receive the final report frequently wants to know the projected total cost of completing the evaluation.

Before moving on, it is important to note there is a general tendency to underestimate the costs of an evaluation project. Thus, care should be taken to think through all the financial implications. Cutting corners and skimping on needed financial resources might compromise the integrity of the study or render the project not worth doing. Such financial "thoroughness" may be hard to do in situations where funds are extremely limited. The best advice is to be as realistic as you can, because the important purpose of the budget is to provide a basis for fiscal accountability.

Evaluation budgets are usually broken down into three categories. These categories are direct costs, fringe benefits, and indirect costs.

1. Direct costs. A number of things make up direct costs. *Direct costs,* that typically appear as separate categories in the budget, are: personnel, travel, telephone, postage (associated with mail questionnaires including the initial mailing and return mail pre-paid postage, direct mailings, etc.), duplication (such as for interview schedules), computer (personal computer hardware or software, mainframe computer time, etc.), supplies (stationery, pencil and pens and the like) and equipment (for example, television and video cassette recorder needed to show educational materials), and other related expenses associated with conducting the evaluation (for instance, financial remunerations or scholarships awarded to study participants).

Usually the largest part of any evaluation budget is personnel. Figure 2.6 illustrates how to begin to estimate personnel costs related to the execution of an evaluation study. Again the YMCA example is used—salaries, however, have been left blank due to the realization that any quoted figures could vary by region of the country and/or would soon be out-of-date. Based on the person-loading chart (Figure 2.4), the investigator can compute total anticipated personnel costs for the project.

As mentioned above, direct costs cover a number of non-personnel items, including travel. Figure 2.7 shows the non-personnel part of a budget associated with the YMCA evaluation example dealing with the task of choosing and designing instruments needed to execute the study. *Travel costs* can include reimbursement for mileage in one's private auto to conduct interviews, attend meetings, etc. In 1998, the Internal Revenue Service's established reimbursement rate was 32.5 cents per mile driven. Additionally, travel costs also can encompass per diem costs or allowances for meals and lodging while an individual is working. The federal government as well as most university and public agencies' per diem reimbursement rates depend on the travel site location. For instance, in 1998 the federal government daily lodging and meal rates for travel to Champaign, Illinois were established at $56 and $34, respectively; for Chicago $120 was allocated for each lodging night and total meal charges for a day were set at $42.

Figure 2.6: Personnel costs for an evaluation of a youth swim club.

	Director	Youth Sports Coordinator	Business Manager	Lifeguard	Consultant
Total (hours)	36	20	2	8	104
Hourly rate/salary					
Total wages					
Fringe benefits					
Total Personnel Costs					

[a]Position is occupied by a full-time employee, thus specified salary wage is based on percentage of job that will be devoted to the evaluation (or percentage of full-time equivalency). Fringe benefits are calculated at 35% of salary.

[b]Position is occupied by part-time employee, thus specified wage is based on number of hours to be worked on the evaluation times a specified hourly rate. Fringe benefits are calculated at 25% of wages earned.

2. Fringe benefits. Personnel costs not only include salary and wages, for those paid on an hourly basis, but also include fringe benefits. *Fringe benefits* are what the employer pays, on behalf of the employee into social Security, workman's Compensation, disability insurance, life insurance, and health insurance. As a rule of thumb, fringe benefits in 1998, averaged about 21.5% to 26.5% (depending if the person was a part or full-time worker and was classified as a clerical or non-clerical worker) of the total costs calculated for salary and wages.

In budgeting for personnel, hourly wages and salaries can be combined with fringe benefits and reported on the same line within the budget. Or salary and wages can be re-

Figure 2.7: Sample budget (non-personnel costs) by specified tasks for an evaluation of a youth swim club.

	Travel	Telephone	Postage	Duplication	Computer	Supplies	Equipment	Other
Task 6. Choose/Design Instruments								
6.1 Specify data need								
6.2 Review existing instruments								
6.2.1 Locate instrumetns		25	10	20				
6.2.2 Evaluate instruments								
6.3 Develop new instruments								
6.3.1 Develop interview schedule				10		5		
6.3.2 Pilot interview schedule	50 miles@ 31¢ = $15.50							
6.3.3 Analyze and revise interview schedule								
Subtotal	$15.50	25	10	30		5		

Total Non-Personnel Other Direct Costs = $85.50   Total Personnel Costs =   Total Direct Costs =

Overhead/Indirect=   TOTAL

ported as one line item and fringe benefits can be broken out as a second line item (as demonstrated in Figure 2.6). If the evaluation project takes place over more than one year, salaries and wages then should be calculated so they reflect adjustments made for salary increases due to merit increases and cost of living adjustments.

3. **Indirect costs.** Budgets can also include *indirect costs* or overhead costs, especially if the evaluation is being performed by individuals outside the leisure service organization. Indirect costs represent costs associated with doing business (in this case planning and executing the evaluation) and is factored into the budget in order to recoup expenses associated with: office space needed to house the personnel responsible for the evaluation, utilities (electricity, water, and sewage); maintenance or custodial services (to keep the office area clean); and, general wear and tear on office furniture etc. Indirect costs are added to the total expenses of completing an evaluative research project (see Figure 2.7).

The rate used to calculate indirect costs varies by whether the institution the evaluator is associated with is under a short or long form wage agreement as defined by the Federal Office of Management and Budget (regulation A-21 circular). In 1998, the typical indirect cost ratio ranged from approximately 38% (based on salary and wages calculated for conducting the evaluation by an agency or business classified under the short form wage agreement) to 60% based on *all* costs associated with the evaluation (for an institution classified as under the long form wage agreement).

Dissemination plan. The proposal should include a plan for dissemination. A *plan for dissemination* indicates how the results and recommendations are to be communicated and implemented. Without dissemination your efforts will remain entombed in a very formal, and often seldom-read, document (Moore, 1987, p. 76)."

A rather obvious point of dissemination is within the organization or service evaluated. Yet, for every evaluation project it is worth asking whether this is sufficient. Perhaps the results ought to also be passed along more broadly. In a later chapter we discuss this more fully, but at the proposal stage you should also consider submitting the results for publication in a professional journal or magazine article, and/or delivering a paper at a seminar or conference.

After completing a draft of a proposal, you should critically read it again yourself before presenting it to the organization's board or your supervisor. To help you with this self-criticism, the most common weaknesses of proposals presented in Figure 2.8 could be used as a check list for comparison with your proposal.

Seeking Organizational Review of the Proposal

While writing an evaluation proposal is valuable in helping you clarify and reason out your thinking about how the study will be conducted, it usually is also used as a communication tool. That is, the proposal can be useful for communicating with other people inside your organization (sometimes referred to as *institutional development*) as well as with people external to your organization.

First, the proposal can be a way of fostering communication among research partners. If you are proposing to carry out a group project with colleagues, it is useful to prepare the proposal by having people on the study team independently think about, and write down their ideas for the study. Because each member of the group has some input into the study planning process, collaboration and negotiation get built in at an early stage (Robson, 1993).

In some situations the plan for an evaluation is given to you. Your supervisor may request an evaluation addressing a particular question, or in an annual evaluation protocol it may be necessary to repeat the same methods used in previous years in order to make year-to-year comparisons. The proposal serves a clarifying function, addressing precisely what needs to be done. It translates the present situation, with its parameters of time and money resources, into the mandate given.

The proposal also becomes a "sales" tool. It is used to convince the people who have approval authority or financial backing that this study is worth doing. Particularly when applying for government grants, competition is keen. In some cases, thousands of proposals are submitted, and these are read and evaluated usually by a selection committee. In the end, most of the proposals submitted to external funding sources are not funded. The usual reason that proposals are not funded typically does not deal with the quality of the proposal itself, rather a good argument for the importance of the proposed study is lacking. Many proposals simply do not measure up to the standards that the funding agency expects. Again, Figure 2.8 identifies the common detractors from a proposal's effectiveness.

Recruiting Respondents

Crucial to many evaluative research projects is seeking and obtaining respondent cooperation. Thus, preparing respondents for the study is an important procedural step. If questionnaires are to be administered to a group, arrangements will have to be made ahead of time for getting people together. Once a group of recruits has been convened you can: tell them why the study is being done, review how the results will be used, inform them how much of their time is needed to complete the questionnaire, provide directions on how the questionnaire is to be filled out, and answer questions. Remaining present to answer their questions will also serve to increase the response rate to the questionnaire—an advantage over a mailed questionnaire.

For telephone interviews, potential respondents could be readied by sending them a preliminary letter. The letter could outline the purpose of the interview and the kinds of questions that will be asked so the recruit will have time to consider their involve-

Figure 2.8: Common weaknesses of evaluation proposals.[2]

1. **The evaluation question is trivial.** Questions or problems that are on only peripheral interest to the organization or the constituents will have little likelihood of adding to knowledge and thus improvements in service delivery. The evaluation question should be timely and central to the situation; the information produced needs to be useful.

2. **The evaluation question is not sufficiently delimited.** The evaluation must be focused. The research design cannot yields valid information for every possible question. We must be able to rationally (if reluctantly) delimit the inquiry question. The research questions or problems are stated directly and clearly.

3. **The data collection methods do not match the questions.** Proposals should be detailed sufficiently in terms of respondents, instrumentation, and data analysis. Further, it should be clear from reading the proposal exactly how theses methods will answer the evaluation question(s). The specification ensures a review committee that the evaluator has properly prepared for the study.

4. **It is not demonstrated that the evaluator has the ability to conduct the study.** Portraying this ability in the proposal—either by citing your training, experience, or both—builds confidence in the trustworthiness of the results.

5. **An explicit budget statement is lacking.** The study must not be too ambitious for the funds available. Further, items of expenditures in the budget must not be ambiguous or indefinite.

[2]From *Research in education: A conceptual introduction* (p. 582) by J. McMillan and S. Schumacher, 1993, New York: Harper Collins. Adapted with permission of the authors.

ment in the study. The letter should also inform them of how long the interview is expected to take. These preparations help to secure their participation, as well, because they know that the call is legitimate.

Handling Logistics

The details of supporting the evaluation project need to be thought through in advance. These details often get overlooked! For example, are there extra phone lines needed to support phone interviews or data transmittal? Are there any special printing needs? If questionnaires need to be printed, it makes sense to alert the printing department or outside printing vendor ahead of time so they can program the work into their schedule. Similarly the computing/statistics department or staff persons in your organization need plenty of notice if the results are to be processed by them. All the details can and should be sorted out early on, otherwise problems can arise otherwise that may cause delays in the project, or worse, compromise the research plan.

Conducting A Mid-Point Review

The written evaluation proposal serves as the basis for the *mid-point review*. The proposal reminds the evaluator of the overall purpose and specific questions, objectives, or hypotheses of the project; it helps put the project back into its proper context. Specifically, the research questions from the proposal will provide a marker of what has been completed. A review of the time line should indicate whether the rate of progress originally planned has been maintained.

After beginning the evaluation project the first thing you will realize is how difficult it is to stay with the projected timetable. While it is important not to get behind schedule, it is typical that delays will occur. Respondents for an interview may take longer than expected to contact, or bad weather conditions may require that the focus group session be postponed. The best solutions, of course, are to build in slippage time in the proposal's time line, and get everything right the first time. If the work does fall behind schedule, however, do not ignore it. If the delays cause considerable concern it may be sensible to make adjustments to the time line or to review what is not getting done and consider changing the research plan or reducing the scale of the study itself. Hurrying up the pace is usually not a good solution to time constraints.

Mid-point reviews should trigger a written *interim report*. This could be quite brief, and even in an extended outline form. The goals are to communicate what has been implemented along with sharing early results. As well, the purpose of an interim report is to provide a framework for making decisions about modifying the rest of the evaluative research plan, and adjusting the time line. If the project has an advisory committee, the members almost always need to be involved in the review, as do the study's stakeholders (such as program administrators). Also, if the study is based on a qualitative framework, the interim report could be discussed with the research participants. A workshop or seminar during the course of the project to review progress and decide upon future directions might be appropriate. This session could include a group of other staff from your organization, or evaluators from other organizations, as well.

Additionally, as all researchers will tell you, around the half-way point, you and your staff may experience disillusionment, frustration and general inertia. This is normal. Sometimes this is caused by concerns over whether the evaluation question, objective, or hypothesis is actually being answered in the study; or you may feel that the whole evaluation endeavor is so overwhelming that it will be impossible to finish. Unfortunately, our best advice is that you will just have to push through it. Keep going. As you get nearer the completion of the project your initial enthusiasm should return.

Agency Accreditation

One way to develop a systematic and comprehensive evaluative research plan for public leisure service organizations is to participate in the national *agency accreditation* program. Administered by the Commission for Accreditation of Park and Recreation Agencies (CAPRA), in cooperation with the National Recreation and Park Association and the American Academy for Park and Recreation Administration, agency accreditation is a standards based program. This means that a public leisure service organization is reviewed in terms of the extent it meets specific standards. Organizations that meet the standards are awarded "accredited" status.

The CAPRA standards focus solely on operational practices of the organization, rather than availability of funds, lands, personnel, etc. (CAPRA, 1996). The 153 standards cover every aspect of an agency's operation according to ten categories: (i) authority to operate, (ii) administration, (iii) program and services management, (iv) facility and land use management, (v) planning, (vi) human resources, (vii) finance, (viii) safety and security, (ix) risk management, and even (x) evaluation and evaluative research. Within these categories standards have been set up to evaluate everything from policies related to: agency mission statements, community relations, program content, policies for volunteers, employee training and education, accounting procedures, and traffic control.

Of the 153 standards, 36 are designated as fundamental to quality operations and thus organizations must satisfy these standards. Each of the ten categories includes at least one of these fundamental standards. Some of the remaining standards may not apply, since some organizations have only parks, some only recreation, etc. Of the applicable standards, each accredited organization must comply with 85% (CAPRA, 1996).

Regarding "Evaluation and Evaluative Research" there are four specific standards an organization must achieve in order to be awarded accreditation (CAPRA, 1996):

1. **Systematic program evaluation.** There shall be a systematic evaluation plan to assess outcomes and the operational efficiency and effectiveness of the organization.

2. **Demonstration projects and action research.** There should be, each year, at least one experimental or demonstration project or involvement in some aspect of research, as related to any part of park and recreation operations.

3. **Evaluation personnel.** There should be personnel either on staff or a consultant with expertise to direct the technical evaluations dealing with various facets of an organization's operations.

4. **Employee education.** There should be an in-service education program for professional employees to enable them to carry out quality evaluations of programs.

The accreditation process consists of four steps. First, the organization conducts its own *self assessment* of how well it meets the standards. This phase concludes with a comprehensive written report documenting compliance with each standard. Then, a *site visitation team* of reviewers, selected by the Commission, spends two to three days at the agency reviewing the written documentation, and interviewing staff, board members, and users of a variety of services. The team also inspects the organization's facilities. The team is usually made up of experts from similar organizations as that being reviewed. The site visitation team's purpose is to make an independent verification that the standards have been met. Following its visitation, the site visitation team prepares a written report to CAPRA detailing its findings. *CAPRA reviews* the report to decide whether the organization should be endorsed as accredited. To maintain the accredited status, organizations must submit a brief *annual update report* to CAPRA, and apply to renew accreditation every five years.

Agency accreditation is not inexpensive. As of this writing the organization seeking accreditation pays a preliminary fee ($100), an application fee (up to $3,000) based on its annual operating budget, an annual maintenance fee (up to $500), and all costs associated with the on-site visit. The publications explaining the program range in cost from $15 to $105. For a copy of these publications or questions about the agency accreditation program, contact the National Recreation and Park Association (phone 703- 858-0784).

In spite of the costs, many consider agency accreditation quite valuable. In addition to adopting national standards regarding the structure for on-going evaluation in an organization, conferral of accreditation offers the secondary benefit of positive public relations. Publicizing the organization's achievement frequently produces public and political recognition. For example, one agency director commented, "This achievement provided valuable public relations and reinforced the fact that our park district is at the forefront of the recreation profession. We feel the benefits of the assessment far outweigh the costs (Capra, 1996)."

Main Points

- Any aspect of an organization evaluation can be performed by an in-house and/ or outside evaluator.

- There are trade-offs in having an in-house versus outside evaluator—these issues include confidence, objectivity, and utilization of results.

- To whom evaluators report to will depend on what kind of decision is being made with the evaluation results.

- Sources of friction that can arise between the evaluator and program staff personnel include personality differences, role differences, and institutional characteristics.

- Ideas for reducing friction between the practitioner and evaluator include:

gaining administrative support, involving practitioners in the evaluation, defining roles and clarifying the authority structure, minimizing disruptions, providing useful feedback information, and publicizing study limitations.

- Written evaluation proposals are used as a communication as well as a sales tool. The proposal usually contains an: introduction, literature review, study procedures and methods, time line, personnel, budget, and dissemination plan.

- In planning an evaluation project attention needs to be given to developing a time line, considering both the calendar time and actual clock time needed to accomplish evaluation related tasks.

- Budgets for an evaluation typically consist of direct (with personnel and ensuant fringe benefits typically comprising the largest part of the budget) and indirect costs.

- In order to keep an evaluation project going, thought also needs to be given to recruiting respondents, handling logistics, and conducting a mid-point review.

- One way to develop a systematic and comprehensive evaluative research plan is to participate in the national agency accreditation program. Agency accreditation is a standards based program that evaluates how well a public organization meets specific standards.

Study Questions

1. What is meant by an internal evaluator? External evaluator? Internal and external evaluator staffing blend?

2. Identify issues to consider in choosing to use in-house versus outside evaluators.

3. Identify sources of friction that can emerge between practitioners and evaluators.

4. What are some ideas for reducing friction between the practitioner and the evaluator? Which idea would be number one on your list, as a practitioner, for averting conflict with an evaluator?

5. Identify sections typically found in a written evaluation proposal. How can the proposal be used?

6. What are the two ways time should be factored in when planning an evaluation project?

7. When budgeting for an evaluation, what is meant by: Direct costs? Indirect costs? Fringe benefits?

8. What is agency accreditation? How does it provide a way to maintain an evaluative research system in a public leisure service organization?

References

Commission for Accreditation of Park and Recreation Agencies. (1996). *Agency accreditation fact sheet*. Arlington, VA: National Recreation and Park Association.

Gall, M., Borg, W., & Gall, J. (1996). *Educational research: An introduction*. White Plains, New York: Longman.

Hedrick, T., Bickman, L., & Rog, D. (1993). *Applied research design*. Newbury Park, CA: Sage Publications.

Hollenhorst, S., Olson, D., & Fortney, R. (1992). Use of importance-performance analysis to evaluate state park cabins: The case of the West Virginia park system. *Journal of Parks and Recreation Administration, 10*, 1-11.

McMillan, J., & Schumacher, S. (1993). *Research in education: A conceptual introduction*. New York: Harper Collins.

Moore, N. (1987). *How to do research*. London: The Library Association.

Robson, C. (1993). *Real world research: A resource for social scientists and practitioner-researchers*. Oxford, UK: Blackwell.

Rossi, P., & Freeman, H. (1993). *Evaluation: A systematic approach*. Newbury Park, CA: Sage Publications.

Weiss. C. (1972). *Evaluation research: Methods of assessing program effectiveness*. Englewood Cliffs, NJ: Prentice-Hall.

CHAPTER 3

Ethics of Evaluation

What Will I Learn in This Chapter?

I'll be able to:

1. Distinguish the four goals of ethically conducted evaluation research.

2. Recall how professional associations and the federal government have had an impact on ethical standards in the United States.

3. List the components of an informed consent statement.

4. Design and implement evaluation studies that honor the rights and dignity of the individuals and organizations evaluated.

5. Review proposed studies and determine if acceptable ethical practices have been followed.

The conduct of evaluative research gives rise to a myriad of ethical issues. Ethical concerns emerge at all stages of the research, from identifying the problem to study, to designing the study, to collecting information, to reporting of findings and conclusions. There are inherent moral pitfalls in all forms of research, and evaluative research studies are no exception.

Some issues, such as falsifying results, involve an intent to deceive—purposeful dishonesty—and are relatively straightforward. Others, however, are more subtle. What should we do about a teen who mentions during an interview that (s)he uses drugs at the recreation center? Should the police be notified? Or, is it fair in testing the effectiveness of a new aquatics treatment program in the rehabilitation center, that some individuals are initially denied access to the aquatics program? Or, what if evaluation results reveal a stress reduction program for a corporation's employees has failed? Are we obligated to report all the data from the study to the company CEO, even if it means potentially cutting a program we still believe in, or costing us our job?

While questions such as these are by no means new, national attention has been drawn to research ethics. There is concern for what seems like an alarming increase in the number of reported ethical misconduct cases associated with research (Penslar, 1995). Some of the cases have involved important civic leaders and research with life and death implications. There are some quite notorious illustrations of the latter. In medical research, for instance, actual physical harm was done when live cancer cells were injected beneath the skin of nonconsenting elderly people (Punch, 1994). An example of unethical research in our field has been related by Dr. Robert Bixler, Manager for Research and Program Evaluation of Cleveland Metroparks:

> Something my wife and I saw while I was on vacation got me thinking about cheating in research. We were interviewed as part of a tourism study at the entrance to a museum. The interviewer did a good job interviewing us and used an Apple Newton Pad for data entry. Being a typical male, I finished the museum almost 30 minutes ahead of my wife. I sat down and watched the interviewer as I waited. Since I knew the interview routine, which involved having the interviewee choose from lists on sheets of paper, it was quite clear that she was now sitting on a bench filling out surveys herself instead of doing other interviews. I suspect much of this sort of behavior comes from the social discomfort of approaching strangers, laziness, and the lack of understanding of the implications of such behavior for decision making. (Bixler, 1997)

Whether our evaluation project involves public figures or "people on the street," is national or local, or is of large or small scope, it is essential to consider the rights and dignity of the individuals and organizations being studied. Yet, while it is easy to identify what was unethical about the illustrations above, many of the ethical questions we face in leisure services evaluation studies are not so obvious. To help put our commitment to being ethical into practice, let us turn our attention now to what ethical research means, and how it can be applied to conducting ethical evaluations in recreation, park, and sport services.

What Is Ethics?

Ethics (derived from the Greek *ethos*, meaning character or custom) is the philosophical study of normative behavior—in other words, the "shoulds," "oughts," "rights" and "wrongs" of conduct or behavior. *Research ethics* is applying ethics in the execution of research. That is, acceptable research decisions are made and acceptable actions taken during the design, implementation and reporting phases of an evaluation study.

Making "acceptable" research decisions and taking "acceptable" research actions mean that everything within our power is done to treat the people and organizations studied graciously, and that the information collected and reported is honorable. A more precise definition of acceptable evolves around five qualities. The qualities of ethical evaluative research are: beneficence, respect, honesty, fairness, and competence (Figure 3.1). The discussion below is based on the writings of House (1990), Sieber (1992), and the American Association for Public Opinion Research (1996).

Figure 3.1: The qualities of ethical evaluative research.

Beneficence = Evaluators must ensure that participants in a study are protected from harm (including discomfort and danger) and labeling.

Respect = Study respondents have a right to self-determination, privacy, and confidentiality.

Honesty = As evaluators we should be truthful, avoid deception, and not cheat in collecting and reporting data.

Fairness = Ethical evaluation research does not sacrifice equality.

Competence = Evaluators are well-trained and thoroughly practiced in research methods and tools.

Beneficence

Beneficence is a term meaning "doing good." In the context of evaluative research, it means maximizing accurate outcomes for the evaluation project, while avoiding or minimizing unnecessary harm to participants in the study.

Doing no harm is a strong ethical obligation in any realm of human relationship, and is especially critical in evaluative research. An evaluator is many things including a researcher and administrator, but from the stand point of the ethical principle of beneficence, the evaluator is also a member of society. An evaluator brings to the endeavor socially acceptable behaviors and attitudes. The evaluator is beneficent not so much in the philanthropic sense of the word, but what the evaluator accomplishes is "for the good of the community."

Applying beneficence in the ethical practice of evaluation requires having a concern for the welfare of the study's participants. A fundamental responsibility of all evaluators is to do everything in their power to ensure that participants in a study are protected from harm (including danger and discomfort) that arises from the research procedures.

Harm can be both physical and psychological. While *physical harm* is simple enough to understand and moderately easy to predict and guard against, *psychological harm* is more difficult to define. For example, we can readily determine that asking respondents to ski down a slope as fast as they can in order to measure the quality of snow produced by newly purchased snow making equipment increases the risk that people will break a leg or worse. But suppose we are studying the effectiveness of the leisure education program in a local group of Alcoholics Anonymous. During a focus group session we ask participants whether their previous use of illegal substances was recreational. Is such a question likely to cause the focus group participants emotional discomfort? At the very least there is the potential that this question may bring to the surface quite painful memories of difficult situations that are hurtful to the study participants' feelings. There is also the concern that this question may actually produce inaccurate information in as much as they try to "protect" themselves. Thus, our attempt to gather accurate data is not only compromised, but we have risked harming participants too. While, it is often difficult to predict that a study will cause psychological harm, one must be as vigilant and provide as many safeguards as possible.

Another illustration of an ethical dilemma of the beneficence type involves the *labeling effect* (Kimmel, 1988). In therapeutic, municipal, fitness and other recreation organizations it is a common strategy to identify persons at-risk. This labeling occurs so that interventions can be developed to prevent or rectify problems. The at-risk label is then used as the basis for qualifying people for special programs. The ethical dilemma that emerges is the conflict between assigning a negative label so as to help the at-risk individual versus not qualifying that person for help by not assigning a label. While the evaluator may not always be the labeler, it is his or her responsibility to protect participants involved in an evaluative research project from labeling effects. The tradeoff is determining whether the potential for emotional harm from being labeled outweighs the special interventions that will be received? Children in city recreation programs who are labeled as high risk truants, may become victims of self-fulfilling prophesies because of stereotyping. Designing intervention studies that minimize or avoid labeling is a way for the potentially negative and unintended effects to be averted.

In summary, the concept of beneficence has multiple ethical issues. The core of ethical practice, however, is doing no harm. A research respondent should be able to expect that the evaluator has a high degree of skill in carrying out the study so that potential risks or discomforts are minimized. This is, in part, what it means to be ethical. Read, now, the research situation posed in Figure 3.2 and consider the ethical concerns related to the possibility of harm to the participants.

Respect

Another characteristic of ethical evaluative research is respect. *Respect* refers to protecting the self-esteem of participants, treating these persons with courtesy. Respect encompasses three rights, or the right to self-determination, privacy, and confidentiality.

First, the *right to self-determination*—to be able to make choices and to act independently- -could also be labeled an *autonomy* right. Let us consider the question of securing participants for a study. Do they have the right to decline to participate or withdraw after the

Figure 3.2: An example of ethical concerns in evaluation.

The Downtown Fitness Club evaluates the effect of a healthy life-styles workshop for teens. The workshop consists of three two-hour sessions in which fitness, nutrition, coping with stress, and interpersonal relationships are the topics. Volunteers for the study are from the club's teen program. One half of the volunteers are assigned to participate in the workshop and one half of them are assigned to a comparison group, and do not participate in the workshop. The workshop's success is determined by whether the attendees experience more positive change in healthful life-style attitudes.

Possibility of Harm to the Teens
It is possible that the material presented in the workshop could place a teen participant at risk by stirring up negative emotions. Some participants could feel their self esteem is compromised or threatened, or they could begin to feel they have fallen short of adult expectations. The evaluator must inform the teens and their parents or guardians about the nature of the study and the possible risks, and obtain both the teens' and their guardians' written consent to participate.

Respect for the Teens
While no problem is foreseen for the confidentiality of the teens, an unexpected issue might occur during the workshop. For example, a few teens might reveal they regularly use drugs, or someone could confide to the evaluator that the teen program advisor uses profane language. In the former case of illegal behavior, the evaluator is required to report the incident to authorities. In the latter case of unprofessional behavior, the evaluator must weigh the ethical dilemma involved in not reporting the incident against breaching participant confidentiality. Besides, what if the teens were making it all up as a way of bragging? One way to circumvent this dilemma is to tell the teens before the workshops begin what will happen if illegal behaviors are disclosed.

Honesty of Procedures and Results
From what we can tell, there does not seem to be a deception issue, and we hope the evaluator analyzes and reports the data truthfully. Given the evaluator's likely strong desire to demonstrate the workshop was effective, however, he/she will have to be careful not to attribute more success to it than the data will truthfully support.

Competence of the Evaluator
We cannot judge from the case presented that the evaluator is well trained and practiced for conducting this study. Since an experimental design is being used, the evaluator will particularly need competence in statistical procedures.

study is underway? And, even if it is officially announced that they do have these rights, are there any covert penalties for non-participation? For example, will they be made to feel left out or sense the evaluator's disappointment if they withdraw? Having the right to participate or not participate in an evaluation study is an important basic human right.

Making choices and acting as a free agent are dependent on rational decision-making and competence. For example, it does not make sense to suggest that young children, or persons with developmental disabilities, have the capacity to understand the consequences of their actions. But does it accordingly make sense to ignore their right to make their own choices? In this situation, usually the consent of their parents or guardians is sought. Competence is difficult to determine, nonetheless we must take great caution in choosing or acting in behalf of other people.

Some of you may be interested in carrying out evaluations in what could be considered "risky" projects. Evaluation studies in recreation, park, fitness, and sport organizations that are risky are typically those designed to investigate psychological or emotional characteristics. Perhaps, in order to refine program practices, you would like to determine the type and extent of emotional stress a two week Outward Bound canoe experience produces on participants. What is risky in this study is not that it is about a canoeing program, but rather that inquiries will be made about people's emotions. Evaluation studies can also involve individuals-at-risk, or people who by virtue of some factor (mental ability, physical illness, economic situation, etc.) are relatively powerless to exercise free will in choosing whether or not to be in a study. Many types of leisure service users—residents of nursing homes, as well as campers in a residential camp—may be at risk of being coerced into participating in evaluative research. Because of an implied attribute of superiority often given to researchers, less powerful people may feel too intimidated to say no to participating in a study. Later in this chapter we discuss the tool of informed consent as a way of ensuring study participants' right of self-determination.

The goal of respect includes not only the right of self-determination, but also the rights to privacy and confidentiality. The *right to privacy* means that people are reasonably shielded from public view. Individuals involved in an evaluation study have the right to determine when, how, and to what extent information about them is communicated to others.

It is certainly acceptable to make observations of public acts that would normally be viewed by others (e.g. performance in a baseball game). Secretive observations, or observations of activity that would be considered personal or sensitive, however, would not be appropriate, and are considered an invasion of privacy. While this sounds clear enough, it is not always so easy. For example, more accurate information on the conflict resolution strategies used by children might be obtained by hiding a video camera in a trash can centrally located on the playground. But might this also be an invasion of their privacy? How will the children feel when they discover or are told they have been spied on? If adults were videotaped, instead of children, would we think their right to privacy had been violated?

Privacy has become a right that is highly treasured in our society. In evaluative research observing or asking people about their attitudes, beliefs, opinions, and behaviors may be in conflict with their right to privacy. To be ethical the evaluator must consider how sensitive the questions posed, or behaviors observed, are to the individual or group being studied. Certain types of information may be considered sensitive under any circumstance. For example, some people want to keep private information about their sexual experiences. Additionally, there are other types of information, such as weight and personal income, that individuals could perceive as being sensitive in nature.

Finally, the *right to confidentiality* is also encompassed in demonstrating respect for study participants. Confidentiality can be considered an extension of privacy. Whereas privacy refers to persons, confidentiality refers to information. Once we have collected information in an evaluation study, we have an ethical responsibility to protect it. This means such things as the names of the respondents are removed from the questionnaires (which can be done by assigning a number or letter to each form), or respondents are requested to furnish the information anonymously. Ideally, not even the evaluator should be able to link the data to a specific individual. Also, respondents should be assured that any information collected from or about them will be held in confidence. This includes never revealing their identity in written reports.

There are aspects of confidentiality that, like all ethical behavior, require judgement. This point is also related to the privacy discussion above. First, concern for the privacy of the study participants and the protection of their collected information involve how "exposed" the information is going to be. As a study participant, for example, you may not consider your privacy threatened if only one or two people know your opinions. Yet it is probably a very different story if the evaluator publishes your personal opinions in the local newspaper.

Judgement is also required when trying to safeguard the privacy of public figures and institutions. Many organizations and their staff, as well as other population groups, are almost impossible to disguise, and if they cooperate in the evaluation study, may have to accept a considerable measure of exposure, particularly if the media picks up on the study. For example, a study of Italian Americans in North Boston (Whyte, 1955) done some 50 years ago recently faced new controversy when the researcher was accused of misleading respondents about the publication of the study (Boelen, 1992). Study respondents had been surprised by the long-lasting notoriety created by the study and felt their right to confidentiality was consequently compromised. Perhaps more to the point, the legitimacy of revealing information about others depends on the context in which the breach of confidence occurs (Kimmel, 1988). Gossiping about study respondents at a staff meeting or a party is clearly unethical.

Being respectful to study participants does not end with upholding their rights to self-determination, privacy, and confidentiality. As evaluators we have a professional obligation to provide respondents with *feedback* about their own results and/or the general results of the study. When feedback information is not provided back to respondents an impersonal message about their unimportance is conveyed. In simple terms, common courtesy has been breached. In reexamining Figure 3.2, are there any ethical concerns related to respect?

Honesty

A third ear-mark of ethical practice is conducting research with *honesty* or *integrity*. As evaluators we are truthful, straightforward, and keep our promises. Another label for this goal might be *fidelity*. Professionals in a human service profession have a special obligation to be trustworthy. In being described as a "professional" we have made an implicit agreement not to exploit, lie to, or deceive those in our "care." Without such an agreement, outdoor recreation, sport and fitness, tourism, therapeutic recreation, and other leisure services would be ineffective. One illustration of what we mean by honesty in evaluative research is deception.

Deception in evaluation involves a misrepresentation of the purpose, nature, or consequences of the study. Deception might mean that the evaluator simply does not inform respondents, either completely or at all, about important aspects of the study. For example, if study particiants are not told beforehand they will experience muscle soreness during the conduct of an experiment on the effect of fatigue on reaction time, a form of deception has been committed. Deception also can involve a situation in which the evaluator gives false information about the study. For example, telling subjects they are being measured on how well they serve and return a tennis ball, when they are actually being observed for their loss of temper is deception.

Either way, deception is troublesome, because some studies cannot be carried out unless some deception takes place. If people know we are measuring their loss of temper, might they not loose their temper in situations where they usually do? Or, suppose we are conducting an evaluation of the leadership styles of playground leaders and the children's responses to these styles. The leaders and children are unobtrusively observed as they go about the day's program. Although no outright deception is involved, we are going to have to give the leaders a rationale for observing them, and if the leaders know their leadership styles are being watched they may alter, even unintentionally, their style.

Thus, whenever possible, conduct the evaluation using methods that do not require deception. If this is not possible, determine whether the use of deception is justified and proceed only with caution, providing the participants with sufficient explanation as soon as possible.

Another aspect of honesty in evaluation has to do with *integrity of results*. By this we mean ensuring truthfulness in data collection procedures, analyses, and reporting. This principle is violated when errors or inaccuracies in the data occur. These could happen by actions ranging from minor unintentional mistakes to outright falsification of the results. One factor influencing intentional breaches of honesty is social pressure. Such pressure may occur when evaluators believe that positive results must be obtained in order to protect a program or their job. The case study in Figure 3.3 illustrates this.

Figure 3.3: Case Study—Cheating in Research.

Several years ago a study of visitors to several local tourist attractions was conducted. Managers were instructed on how to select visitors at random, controlling for time of day, day of week, and season of year. One manager was intimidated by the study because the questionnaire asked evaluation questions. He was afraid someone might criticize him and his staff. He decided he would ignore the random selection process and only give the questionnaires to his friends and people who visited often, assuming they were happy about the services at the site.

Just recently, a budget crunch occurred. Due to lack of funds one of the attractions needed to be closed down. The administrators used the earlier study as the basis for their decision. Sensitive to economic issues in the area, they decided to close the site that attracted the fewest number of tourists. They turned to the results of the study as a key indicator of how much tourist traffic was occurring. Since the manager had entirely local visitors in his sample, the data from the questionnaire indicated the site was not attracting any out-of-region visitors.

1. Guess which site was closed down? Why?

2. If you were the evaluator for this organization, how might you have better prepared the managers to ethically carry out their part in data collection?

(Bixler, 1997; used with permission)

Integrity of the results also involves decisions about publishing. One way in which leisure services are developed and improved is through the communication of the results of evaluation studies. Thus, publishing the results in professional magazines and journals is important, and as we will explore in Chapter 13, a written report closes the evaluation plan loop. One of the ethical issues that may arise in this respect is the temptation to report the evaluation in a somewhat different way than the information collected would indicate. This may be the situation when the study produces data that "are close" to showing significant changes as the result of a program. Obviously yielding to the temptation of fudging the data is a serious breach of professional integrity. Try out your understanding of the ethical goal of honesty in the research situation posed previously in Figure 3.2.

Fairness

Fourth, evaluators have a responsibility to treat study respondents fairly and justly. Ethical evaluative research procedures must not sacrifice fairness. Referring again to Figure 3.2, can you tell from the scenario what the quality of fairness might entail? There are two criteria for fairness that serve as the basis for ethical research (Rawls, 1971): equality and inequality.

1. Equality - all persons have an equal right to all the benefits and opportunities available. In evaluative research the application of this criterion is that to be fair, all respondents should have access to all the benefits of the study. For example, equality can and does become an issue when quasi-experimental designs are used. Some would argue that being assigned to a control group equates to being denied the right to participate in the service or program being evaluated.

2. Inequality - inequalities should be open to everyone. In evaluative research applying this criterion means that to be fair, the negative aspects of the study are also equally distributed to all respondents. For example, in an evaluation of adventure challenge programs, the weather should be bad for all participants!

While both criteria express the totality of the concept of fairness in evaluative research, we feel that evaluators in leisure service organizations have a particular responsibility to uphold the first—equality. There is an example of this in Figure 3.4. Can you identify what the researchers need to do to be fair in this study?

Competence

Finally, no matter how beneficent, respectful, honest, and fair an evaluator might be, incompetence in conducting the evaluation renders these other ethical principles meaningless. To be ethical the evaluator must take care in choosing research designs, data collection tools, and data analysis protocols that assure the reliability and validity of results. In other words, we must be competent when we are conducting evaluation studies. In this sense, this entire book is devoted to teaching evaluative research competence.

The bottom line for the discussion in this section is that we are morally bound to plan and conduct an evaluation ethically. This means that our research should be characterized as having beneficence, respect, honesty, fairness, and competence. Evaluators must know the rules of evaluative research, apply these rules throughout the conduct of the study, and understand their own limitations and seek assistance accordingly. Evaluators must be continually alert to doing the right thing. Our profession offers us help with this; here's how.

Ethical Standards

The concern for harm, respect, honesty, fairness and competence has led professional associations and governmental agencies to insist on ethical research. In fact, today the ethical standards to which evaluators subscribe are largely those of their professional associations

Figure 3.4: Video games in the nursing home: Fairness.

Here's an actual study that illustrates the ethical quality of fairness. Researchers Riddick, Spector and Drogin (1986) wanted to determine what sort of recreation program would improve the emotional states of pleasure, arousal, and dominance, as well as the affiliative behavior of patients in a nursing home. By affiliative behavior they meant the extent to which the patients feel friendly and talkative to strangers versus trying to avoid being with and talking to other people.

The recreation program they evaluated was playing video games. Ten volunteers from one nursing home played PacManthree times a week for up to three hours per session for a total of 6 weeks. Twelve volunteers from another nursing home did not play any video games. All participants in the study were at least 60 years old and not bedridden or blind.

By comparing the results for the group that played the video game with the group that did not, the evaluators found the video game players had significant changes to their arousal emotional state and affiliative behavior. That is the stimulation of playing PacMan raised the elderly nursing home patients' stress, and hence their need for social interaction. For example, players were typically overheard saying, "Help! That pink critter is out to get me. What can I do?" (p. 105).

Ethical Issues of Fairness

Is there a concern for equality in this study? Is it unfair that only half of the nursing home residents who volunteered to play PacMan actually got to? To remedy this concern, particularly because we know from the results there are benefits from playing the game, the comparison group should become a delayed experimental group. That is, they could be given the opportunity to play PacMan at a later time—as a program service that immediately follows the conclusion of the study. What should the researchers have done if results indicated there were negative consequences to the elderly patients from playing the game?

In the actual situation, after the study was completed, the video game was left in the nursing home for three months for all patients and staff to play. The researchers wanted to offer the same opportunity for the patients and staff in the control nursing home, but the realities of time and money prevented this.

and their federal and state governments. Having replaced the so-called unwritten professional ethic that presumed we would act in fair, considerate, and compassionate ways toward others, written and codified ethics documents now guide us. For example, virtually every journal that publishes research involving humans has a policy statement dealing with the canons of their ethical treatment. Ultimately what evaluators consider to be morally ethical is largely a matter of agreement among them. Often this agreement is codified by professional organizations.

Professional Organization Codes

Sociologists and anthropologists in the 1950s developed codes of research ethics in their respective fields (Kimmel, 1988). These early professional association-based research codes presented a few simple guidelilnes that were quite general and largely unenforceable (Kimmel, 1988). But the rise in social conscience and emphasis on the protection of individual rights ushered in during the late 1960s brought about a concern for more specific guidelines for the ethical treatment of research participants. For the United States, Congress codified the establishment of written professional codes for conducting research when in 1974 it formed the National Commission for the Protection of Human Subjects of Biomedical and Behavioral Research (Berg & Latin, 1994).

Today, various professional organizations (such as the American Sociological Association, the American Anthropological Association, and the American Educational Research Association) have published lists of ethical principles specifically addressing the conduct of research. Leisure-related professional organizations, such as the National Recreation and Park Association and the American Therapeutic Recreation Association, have general professional ethics documents that include codes applicable to research. Figure 3.5 contains excerpts from the professional codes of the National Intramural-Recreational Sports Association, Society of American Foresters, and the American Psychological Association.

Government Regulations

Some of you will conduct evaluative research while affiliated with organizations (such as universities) that have their own institutional review procedures. An *institutional review board* (IRB) is a panel of research experts, usually representing various academic disciplines on campus, who pass judgment on the ethical safeguards of studies before they can be conducted. The board's review serves as a means of protecting the rights of research participants. It also provides a way to protect researchers and the institution.

Additionally, United States government regulations specify that any organization receiving federal money to support research must have a committee (such as an IRB) that is competent to review research proposals that involve human subjects. Technically, then, any agency that is not receiving federal dollars is not legally required to have an IRB. However, it would seem wise for an organization that allows human subject research to be conducted has an ethical responsibility that might be best supervised by such a committee.

Figure 3.5: Excerpts from codes of ethics.

Following are ethical standards relating to research from the codes of ethics of three professional associations:

From the National Intramural-Recreational Sports Association (NIRSA) Code of Ethics:
Article I

The NIRSA member in fulfilling professional obligations shall:
....2. Be true in writing, reporting and duplicating information and give proper credit to the contributions of others.   (NIRSA National Office, nd)

From the Society of American Foresters Code of Ethics:
Canons

.....4. A member will base public comment on forestry matters on accurate knowledge and will not distort or withhold pertinent information to substantiate a point of view. Prior to making public statements on forest policies and practices, a member will indicate on whose behalf the statements are made.
.....13. A member will give credit for the methods, ideas, or assistance obtained from others.   (Society of American Foresters, 1996)

From the American Psychological Association (standards dealing specifically with the reporting and publishing of research):

6.21 Report of Results
a) Psychologists do not fabricate data or falsify results in their publications.
b) If psychologists discover significant errors in their published data, they take reasonable steps to correct such errors in a correction, retraction, erratum, or other appropriate publication means.

6.22 Plagiarism
Psychologists do not present substantial portions or elements of another's work or data as their own, even if the other work or data source is cited occasionally.

6.23 Publication Credit
a) Psychologists take responsibility and credit, including authorship credit, only for work they have actually performed or to which they have contributed.
b) Principal authorship and other publication credits accurately reflect the relative scientific or professional contributions of the individuals involved, regardless of their relative status. Mere possession of an institutional position, such as Department Chair [or Laboratory Director], does not justify authorship credit.

Figure 3.5: Cont.

Minor contributions to the research or to the writing for publications are appropriately acknowledged, such as in footnotes or in an introductory statement.

c) A student is usually listed as a principle author on any multiple-authored article that is substantially based on the student's dissertation or thesis.

6.24 Duplicate Publication of Data

Psychologists do not publish, as original data, data that have been previously published. This does not preclude republishing data when they are accompanied by proper acknowledgment.

6.25 Sharing Data

After research results are published, psychologists do not withhold the data on which their conclusions are based from other competent professionals who seek to verify the substantive claims through re-analysis and who intend to use such data only for that purpose, provided that the confidentiality of the participants can be protected and unless legal rights concerning proprietary data preclude their release.

6.26 Professional Reviewers

Psychologists who review material submitted for publication, grant, or other research proposal review respect the confidentiality of and the proprietary rights in such information of those who submitted it.

(American Psychological Association, 1992)

Informed Consent

Beyond generally understanding and appreciating the importance of ethically planned and conducted evaluative research, is there a single "best practice" we should always do in every study? Voluntary and written *informed consent* is considered by many as the central key in an ethically sound relationship between the evaluator and the research participant (Kimmel, 1988). This concept has become a requirement for government sponsored research, and a mainstay in professional association codes of ethics.

The concept of informed consent is based on the assumption that an evaluator has an ethical commitment to ensure that a potential study participant is able to comprehend enough information about the study to make a sound decision about participating. Typically, the informed consent process is that the prospective study participants, and/or their guardians, read and sign a document that provides the essential details of the study.

Informed consent statements vary in language, length, and detail. Studies that pose little risk may use very simple and brief consents. Studies involving greater risk need to provide consent statements that contain more elaborate explanations. Of course it is important that the writing level of the consent statement is at a comprehension level appropriate to the prospective respondents.

What follows is a description of some of the basic elements of an informed consent document (Berg & Latin, 1994). Figure 3.6 also illustrates how these elements might look when made into a form.

Figure 3.6: Example of an Informed Consent Form.

You are invited to participate in an evaluation study. The purpose of this study is to determine perceived barriers to promotion among women middle managers of the city's recreation and parks department.

General Information: As a participant in this study you will be asked to complete a background questionnaire about yourself. You will also be asked about your perceptions on the promotion of middle management women within the department. A total of about 15 minutes will be needed to complete both questionnaires. There is no monetary compensation for participating. A copy of the final report will be distributed to all employees of the department.

Risks: While no foreseeable risks or discomforts are expected for your participation, you are free to withdraw from the study at any time without any reprisal whatsoever.

Benefits: Your participation in the study will help the recreation and parks department make decisions about general employee promotion policies. The determination of specific and individual promotions are not part of the study.

Confidentiality: The information in the study records will be kept confidential. Data will be stored securely and will be made available only to the evaluation project director. No reference will be made in oral or written reports that could link you to the study.

Consent: I have read and understand the above information. I agree to participate in this study.

Respondent's Signature _____ Date _____

Evaluator's Signature _____ Date _____

---

1. **Study background and invitation to participate.** This is a brief statement that provides the purpose behind the study, the need for it, and why the respondent is being asked to participate.

2. **Explanation of procedures.** The procedures that the respondent will be asked to do are described in this section. Failing to provide all information about this could be regarded as unethical deception. Depending on the study, this should include the potential risks and discomforts if there are any. Such risks might be physical (nausea), psychological (anxiety, fear), economic (costly in time or money), or social (embarrassment).

3. **Potential benefits. In this section, the two types of benefits that may result from the study are mentioned.** First are the possible benefits to the respondents themselves (such as having fun, meeting new people). Second, possible benefits to the agency, community, or society in general (such as improved recreation services) are enumerated.

4. **Rights of inquiry and withdrawal.** Respondents must be informed that, at any time during the course of the study, they have the right to ask questions and have them answered by the evaluator. They also must be told they have the right to withdraw from the study whenever they desire with no retribution. A statement must also be made that clearly states how they can receive a copy of the final report if they wish.

Actually, the consent form serves only to "assist" the evaluator in securing from the respondents a valid consent to participate in the study (Berg & Latin, 1994). A signature from them does not automatically mean a valid consent was obtained. In being sure they are perfectly clear on what they have consented to, we recommend that you ask several questions about the statement before obtaining their signatures, in order to be sure they understand.

Main Points

For each evaluation project you should be able to account for each item on the following ethical practices checklist:

- Evaluators must protect the study participant from physical and emotional discomfort, harm, embarrassment, and danger that may arise from research procedures.

- Participants have the right to be free of coercion to be in the study. Evaluators respect their freedom to decline to participate in or to withdraw from the study at any time.

- A signed informed consent to participate should be obtained from the potential study respondents, or their parent or guardian. It is an important way to assure that participation is voluntary and that participants understand the nature of the study and how data will be collected and used.

- If methodological requirements make the use of deception necessary, evaluators have a special responsibility to determine whether the use of such techniques is justified, use alternative procedures when available, and provide participants with sufficient explanation as soon as possible.

- Participants have a right to privacy and confidentiality. Their responses should not be made public or linked specifically to them in maintaining and reporting the results.

- Results should be collected, analyzed and reported as honestly and accurately as possible.

- Evaluators have an obligation to honor all promises and commitments made to study participants, including providing them with feedback on the results.

- Take care that appropriate agency committees and authorities have been consulted and given approval for the evaluation study. Obtain explicit authorization before you collect any data.

Study Questions

1. What are the five principles of ethical evaluative research?

2. The principle of beneficence in ethical evaluative research contains multiple ethical issues. What are these?

3. What are the three rights to be assured when conducting evaluative research respectfully?

4. The principle of fairness refers to the goals of both equality and inequality. Explain this contradiction.

5. How might deception in evaluative research harm study participants, the evaluator, and the organization?

6. Explain the principle of competence.

7. How does our profession offer us help in maintaining ethical principles?

8. What is informed consent, and how does it serve as a tool for ethically planned and conducted evaluative research?

9. How does a "research review board" serve as a tool for ethically planned and conducted evaluative research?

References

American Association for Public Opinion Research. (1996). *AAPOR code of professional ethics and* practices. Ann Arbor, MI: American Association for Public Opinion Research.

American Psychological Association. (December 1992). Ethical principles of psychologists and code of conduct. *American Psychologist, 47,* 1597-1611.

Berg, K.E. & Latin, R.W. (1994). *Essentials of modern research methods in health, physical education, and recreation.* Englewood Cliffs, NJ: Prentice Hall.

Bixler, R. (15 July 1997). E-mail correspondence.

Boelen, W.A. M. (1992). Street corner society: Cornerville revisited. *Journal of Contemporary Ethnography, 21,* 11-51.

House, E.R. (1990). An ethics of qualitative field studies. In E.G. Guba (Ed.), *The paradigm dialog.* Newbury Park, CA: Sage Publications.

Kimmel, A.J. (1988). *Ethics and values in applied social research.* Newbury Park: Sage Publications.

NIRSA National Office. (nd). *National Intramural-Recreational Sports Association: Code of ethics.* Corvallis, OR: NIRSA National Office.

Penslar, R.L. (1995). *Research ethics: Cases and materials.* Bloomington, IN: Indiana University Press.

Punch, M. (1994). Politics and ethics in qualitative research. In N. K. Denzin and Y.S. Lincoln (Eds.), *Handbook of Qualitative Research.* Thousand Oaks: Sage Publications.

Rawls, J. (1971). *A theory of justice.* Cambridge, MA: Harvard University Press.

Riddick, C.C., Spector, S.G., & Drogin, E.B. (1986). The effects of video game play on the emotional states and affiliative behavior of nursing home residents. *Activities, Adaptation and Aging, 8,* 95-107.

Sieber, J.E. (1992). *Planning ethically responsible research: A guide for students and internal review boards* (Applied Social Research Methods Series, Vol. 31). Newbury Park, CA: Sage Publications.

Society of American Foresters. (1996). *Ethics guide for foresters and natural resource professionals.* Bethesda, MD: Society of American Foresters.

Whyte, W.F. (1955). *Street corner society: The social structure of an Italian slum* (2nd ed.). Chicago: University of Chicago Press.

PART II: EVALUATION PLANNING MODEL

Stage One: Focus

Chapter 4: Literature Review

Chapter 5: Quantitative and Qualitative Frameworks

Chapter 6: Defining the Scope of the Evaluation

Stage Two: Approach

Chapter 7: Designs Used in Evaluative Research

Chapter 8: Sampling & Sampling Size

Stage Three: Implementation

Chapter 9: Procedures

Chapter 10: Data Collection

Chapter 11: Making Sense of Quantitative Data

Chapter 12: Making Sense of Qualitative Data

Stage Four: Accountability

Chapter 13: Writing and Presenting Reports

Chapter 14: From Results to Policy and Practice

Evaluation research is both a science and an art. There is, on the one hand, a general order of activities in planning a study that one must follow in order to avoid mistakes. Yet, good research planning also requires creativity and responsiveness. That is, the development of an evaluation plan is an iterative process infused by new information that typically necessitates changes to earlier decisions made in the plan. Thus, evaluation research demands

61

paying attention to the tenets of best practice in conducting the study (the science of the effort), as well as remaining open to the necessity of modifying this best practice according to the unique situation of the study (the art of the effort).

The basic model of an evaluation research plan has four stages. The first stage defines the focus of the evaluation. Stage two determines the evaluation's approach. Then stage three is the actual implementation of the study. This is followed by stage four, which, through reporting and applying the results, links the research to agency accountability and management decisions.

Stage 1 ——>   **Stage 2 ——>**   **Stage 3 ——>**   **Stage 4 ——>**

Focus   **Approach**   **Implementation**   **Accountability**

To help you become competent in these four stages, they have been sub-divided into smaller steps. Within the first stage there are three steps for defining the focus of the evaluation: conducting a literature review (Chapter 4), understanding quantitative and qualitative research frameworks (Chapter 5), and defining the scope of the evaluation (Chapter 6). Likewise, breaking down the second stage, there are two steps needed to determine the evaluation approach: choosing a research design (Chapter 7) and sampling (Chapter 8).

Stage three, implementation, has three steps: procedures required in carrying out the study (Chapter 9), gathering information or data collection (Chapter 10), and data analysis. Data analysis can be broken down two ways: quantitative data analysis (Chapter 11) and qualitative data analysis (Chapter 12). Finally, stage four, consists of two steps: writing and presenting the report about the study's conclusions (Chapter 13) and converting the conclusions into decisions about agency policies and personnel practices (Chapter 14).

CHAPTER 4

Literature Review

What Will I Learn in This Chapter?

I'll be able to:

1. Describe the functions of a literature review.

2. Identify the steps for getting to primary literature sources.

3. Explain when and for what reason to use a secondary source, general reference, and primary source.

4. Define the phrase *"search term"* and explain how search terms are used in a literature search.

5. Conduct both manual and computer searches on a topic of interest.

6. Recall tips for sorting and making sense out of literature read.

7. Use a summary sheet to synthesize an empirical article located with a literature search.

8. List the approaches to organizing the literature section in a written report of a quantitative study.

9. Identify the ways a literature review can be used in a qualitative study.

_____

Within the first stage of evaluative research planning, the first step is to conduct a literature review. An important point sometimes overlooked or not appreciated is that evaluative research should build on the work of others. When embarking on an evaluation, the relevant work of others needs to be identified in order to gain a clearer understanding of how to proceed with one's own evaluation in terms of focus, approach, and implementation. While previously done studies and writings may be imperfect, it is important to review this literature because you can build on the work of others. Conducting a literature review means culling through publications, such as professional journals and academic books, to find writings similar to or related to your evaluation topic. Admittedly, this is a time-consuming process but it is a task, if done thoroughly, which yields huge dividends! Our collective experience is that all too often investigators (from the novice to the "seasoned" veteran) rush through this step, ultimately detracting from the quality of their own evaluative research project.

Functions of a Literature Review

So what are the dividends associated with identifying and reviewing earlier writings? The literature review can assist with:

1. Becoming familiar with the historical background and conceptual approaches or perspectives for understanding a problem. Reading about the problem and the ways others have examined it allows us to learn about the changing ways the problem has been addressed over time. For instance, the studies undertaken in the 1970s that deal with the mental health of older persons could be described as simplistic. This is because most of these investigations only examined a couple of things that might factor into the psychological well-being of older persons. In contrast, in the last few years, gerontological research inquiries reflect more sophisticated theory and have detected an array of factors affect one's well being.

2. Finding or honing in on a suitable and practical problem or approach that is germane to your situation. You might find an earlier work that acts as a springboard to your study. That is, you might modify an earlier work found in a journal article for your own purpose by using the same question, problem, or hypothesis but adapting it to your own population. An article, for example, on the impact of a fitness program on men might be replicated using instead a group of females.

Sometimes in the literature you learn about aspects of a situation you had not previously considered. The evaluator might report about something that happened during the course of her study that did not work out and ideally shares ideas concerning why the problems occurred, highlighting procedures to avoid. For instance, the writer based on his/her experiences, might advise against assigning selected individuals to receive a novel, innovative, and free recreation service or no service at all. Such insights can help in planning an evaluation study.

The background reading done in a literature review will also be useful in shedding light on how others have thought about the problem. Sociologists, psychologists, and anthropologists have studied individual or group behavior and produced formal theories or conceptual approaches or perspectives that can be used to represent most situations that occur in recreation. Individuals who are unfamiliar with these theories and associated research may initially think that little or no previous work exists that is relevant to the problems at hand.

Depending on the nature of the problem being examined, evaluators may need to identify a conceptual foundation or perspective to how she approaches a problem. For example, as Chapter 17 reveals, a number of different approaches to evaluating personnel performance exist. A literature review can reveal a perspective about the relevant or important variables that should be included in a study. For example, Fletcher, Kaiser, and Groger (1992, p. 78) surveyed a group of municipal park and recreation directors about their satisfaction with park impact fee programs. The acknowledged first step in conducting this study involved reviewing the literature in order to identify the important characteristics or attributes of park impact fees. What was found by this literature review was then listed in a questionnaire format and sent to the queried directors.

3. Providing rationale for establishing the importance of the study. Other works might cite statistics regarding the magnitude of the problem you are studying, eloquently criticize earlier studies (due to, for example, mistakes in how these studies were executed), or point out in testimonial fashion the need for the kind of research you are proposing. Additionally, many persons embarking on an evaluation all too often have tunnel vision and are not able to identify a societal or organizational issue or state the significance surrounding the specific problem (Chapter 6 will go into this point in greater detail).

4. Providing a context by which the gaps to earlier works can be filled. Such gaps could be problems with conceptualization (maybe the earlier works were atheoretical or did not identify a conceptual framework or perspective), sampling, and/or measurement. When reviewing related literature, we must develop the ability to identify the relative weaknesses or shortcomings of previous research. Sometimes an author in her concluding remarks will be savvy and nice enough to identify the limitations of the study. Often times, however, this does not happen. Regardless, identified weaknesses of earlier studies can then be reflected upon and addressed in the study being contemplated.

It is important to note, that related, empirical studies centering around the same problem are never in perfect unison or harmony when it comes to findings. Congruence in findings seldom happens. Relying on knowledge of the technical aspects of research methods, you should be able to begin to discern possible sources for noted conflicting results. For instance, the literature on the life satisfaction of older persons is replete with inconsistencies regarding the role of leisure and leisure activity in affecting the mental health of elders. A lot of these inconsistencies can be traced to differences in sampling and instruments used by the reporting investigators.

5. Comparing the results of previous studies to the evaluation study being planned or reported. It is helpful to provide a perspective of how your evaluation approach or results fit in the context of these earlier works. Is the approach you have chosen to use for evaluating the organizations's marketing defensible in terms of current writings? Are the evaluation findings of your organization's physical plant consistent with other organization's reports, or does your organization operate at a higher or lower level?

Furthermore, it may be important to point out the similarities or dissimilarities of the group or population you are studying relative to previously studied groups. For example, suppose you are designing a study to determine the need for a leisure education program for adults who have been long-term residents in a private psychiatric hospital and who are soon facing community discharge (see Wolfe & Riddick, 1984). You use a leisure attitude instrument for which published normative data exist for non-institutionalized adults. In comparing your results to this normative data you find substantial and significant differences between the two groups. Voilà—you now probably have enough information to rationalize the need for your leisure education program intervention!

In summary, a major purpose in doing a review of literature is to be able to draw ideas from earlier evaluations about how to conceptualize, plan, and carry out your proposed study. You should selfishly review a study in terms of discovering insights on:

- Conceptual perspectives for approaching, understanding, or explaining a problem (see Chapter 6).
- Phenomena or variables that should be included in the study (see Chapters 6 and 15).
- Research designs that are promising for studying the problem at hand (e.g., survey, case study, quasi-experimental, ethnographic—see Chapters 5 and 7).
- Ideas that relate to sampling, instruments, or procedures that could be used to carry out your study (Chapters 8-10).

Steps for Getting to Primary Literature Sources

A literature review can be done by a manual search or a computer search. The steps are basically the same, the only real differences are that the computer search is faster, may cost something to perform (the cost of an on-line search will depend on the length and complexity of the search), provides a printout of the search, and can have more than one search term or descriptor invoked during the search.

There are basically six steps involved in a literature search (adapted from Fraenkel & Wallen, 1993, pp. 59-60):

1. Begin by identifying the subject matter, problem, or question. This step receives in-depth coverage in Chapter 6. One approach for identifying the subject matter, problem, or question is to observe the world around you and juxtapose professional readings or research presentations related to the subject of inquiry. Sometimes ideas for inquiry can be triggered by a review-synthesis-type article or a pertinent single study journal article. Other times ideas begin to germinate when reading a relevant book or monograph or listening to research reported at a recent conference or professional meeting.

Identifying an evaluative research problem typically begins with crafting a general question and then refining or narrowing this question down to a specific area of concern. For instance, you might initially have begun with the question, "What sorts of teaching methods work well in the camp setting?" Narrowing this question down so it focuses on a specific issue might be "Is videotaping a more effective technique than group instruction to teach canoeing skills?"

2. Locate and review a relevant secondary source(s). A *secondary source* is a publication in which the author(s) describes the work of others. Common secondary sources are textbooks, encyclopedias, and research reviews. *Research reviews* are specialized and detailed literature summaries published either as monographs or by an existing professional journal. The author(s) of these reviews critically synthesize what is known about a topic, provide an integrated summary, and suggest areas of needed research (see Figure 4.1).

Figure 4.1: Research reviews containing topics related to park, recreation, and sport fitness topics.

Annual Reviews of Medicine

Annual Review of Physiology

Annual Review of Psychology

Annual Review of Public Health

Annual in Therapeutic Recreation

Benefits of Therapeutic Recreation: A Consensus View (Note: This is a publication edited by C. Coyle, W. Kinney, B. Riley, & J. Shank. (1991). Ravensdale, WA: Idyll Arbor, Inc.)

Exercise and Sport Science Reviews (published annually)

Physiological Reviews (published quarterly)

Psychological Review (published quarterly)

Review of Educational Research (published quarterly)

Review of Research in Education (published annually)

One warning is never to depend entirely on what is read in a secondary source. As Eichelberger (1989, p.86) states, "Authors who write about the research or theories of others usually have different interests or backgrounds that lead them to overemphasize certain aspects and de-emphasize or leave out other aspects of the work." In short, if you are relying heavily on information presented in a secondary source, find the original article and confirm that the secondary source has reported it accurately.

3. **Refine the subject matter, problem, or question again and then identify a search term(s) or key words or phrases related to the chosen problem.** Looking through one or two secondary sources gives you an overview or "feel" of previous work that has been done on the subject matter, problem, or question you are interested in evaluating. Many times reviews of secondary sources provide you with a clearer idea of exactly what to investigate. For this step, we advise you to look again at the selected subject matter, problem, or question to determine if it needs to be rewritten to make it more focused.

Now you are at the juncture of identifying a search term(s). A *search term* is a descriptor word(s) used to locate primary sources. The search term should include the most important word(s) found relevant to the problem, subject matter, or question being examined. Take, for instance, the research question "Do surfaces used on a children's playground have any relationship to the amount and severity of injuries experienced in this setting?" What are the most important words or key terms used in this question? "Playground surface" is the answer. This term, plus other critical terms that are found in the question (such as "injuries") should be listed as the search terms.

4. **Consult one or two general reference works.** A *general reference* locates sources such as articles, books and other documents related to the evaluative research problem. Most general references are either *indices* (that list author, title, and place of publication of articles and other materials) or *abstracts* (that give a brief summary of various publications as well as their author, title, and place of publication).

An *index* publication reviews selected professional journal holdings and classifies articles by subject(s) or topic(s) (see Figure 4.2). A number of indices can be retrieved via the Internet [such as Accessible Library Catalogs and Databases and CARL (Colorado Alliance of Research Libraries)].

Figure 4.2: Indices with holdings related to park, recreation, and sport/fitness topics.

ABI/Inform: Indexes articles from over 1,400 business journals (covering a variety of topics including personnel issues, consumer behavior, organizational behavior, and human resource management).

Current Contents: Contains tables of contents from over 7,000 journals and 2,000 books related to the social and behavioral sciences (divided by subareas).

Chicano Index : Contains citations with abstracts written by and about Chicanos and other Latinos in the United States.

Current Index to Journals in Education: Indexes an average of 1,500 journal articles in about 800 publications (including foreign countries); published by ERIC.

Education Index: Indexes articles appearing in over 400 educational publications; gives only bibliographic data (i.e., author, title, and place of publication).

Exceptional Child Education Resources: Contains articles (by author, subject, and title indexes), related to exceptional children (both disabled and gifted) from over 200 journals and selected dissertations.

Expanded Academic Index: Abstracts articles in more than 1,500 scholarly (for example, in social science and humanities) and general interest journals.

FastDoc: Contains citations to more than 340,000 articles from more than 1,000 general interest and business serials, many of which are in the social and behavioral sciences.

Figure 4.2: Cont.

GENMED: Collection of full text databases covering the entire textual contents of more than 66 journals (including biomedical, journals).

Hispanic American Periodicals Index: Reference annual that indexes by subject and author in over 360 scholarly journals (in social sciences and the humanities); topics deal with Latin Americans in the U.S.

Index to Black Periodicals: Cites articles appearing each year in major black American journals.

Index Medicus (available in MEDLINE computer database): Accesses 3,600 biomedical journals (national and international).

ISI Document Solutions: Lists cited authors (from articles, reviews, meeting abstracts) with those who discussed the cited work; using this list you can quickly build a collection of references that are likely to be specific to your topic.

Physical Education Index: Subject index to literature (in coaching, dance, health, physical education, physical fitness, recreation, physical therapy, sports, and sports medicine) to 180 journals (national and international).

PsychINFO: Computer search providing citations and abstracts to 1,300 international periodicals as well as technical reports and dissertations dealing with psychology and behavioral sciences.

Science Citation Index (available in SCISEARCH computer database): Citations and abstracts to more than 4,600 international social science and scientific journals.

Social Science Citation Index (available in SOCIAL SCISEARCH computer database): Lists cited authors and their works together with all authors who have discussed the cited works in articles; using this list you can quickly build a collection of references that are likely to be very specific to your topic.

Social Sciences Index: Index to articles in more than 415 periodicals in the social sciences (such as sociology, psychology, anthropology, environmental science, etc.).

SPORT (on line version) and SPORT DISCUS (CD-ROM version): International data base (spanning from 1975 to the present) that contains 320,000 citations on sports medicine, exercise, physiology, biomechanics, psychology, training techniques, coaching, physical education, physical fitness, recreation, and facilities and equipment.

TourCD: Contains 20 years of information from 280 journals published worldwide covering such subjects as leisure and tourism policies and industries, facility management and planning, natural resources and environment, and recreation activities.

Abstracts are succinct summaries of research published in refereed journals or as dissertations, or presented at professional conferences (see Figure 4.3). An increasing number of abstracts are also available in computer database form.

Figure 4.3: Abstracts containing holdings related to park, recreation, and sport fitness topics.

I. Abstracts of Research Published in Journals

Biological Abstracts (available in BIOSIS PREVIEWS computer database): References and indexes to the world's biological and biomedical reports, reviews, and meeting literature; covers articles from nearly 7,000 periodicals.

Child Development Abstracts: Contains abstracts and reviews research literature in journals, technical reports, and books related to the growth and development of children.

Index of Abstracts of Foreign Physical Education Literature: Abstracts of research in journals published outside the United States.

Medical Abstracts Newsletter: Summarizes, in plain English, studies reported in over 140 medical journals.

MEDLINE: Abstracts articles in more than 3,400 international journals in medicine (including psychology and psychiatry).

Psychological Abstracts (available in PSYCHINFO computer database): Published by the American Psychological Association, this covers over 1,300 journals, plus reports, monographs, and other documents (including books and other secondary sources); abstracts are presented in addition to bibliographical data.

PsycLit: Contains *Psychological Abstracts* or abstracts to psychological journals that have been published worldwide since 1974.

Social Works Abstracts: contains more than 28,000 citations, with abstracts, to journal articles, doctoral dissertations, and other materials on social work and related areas.

Sociofile: Contains *Sociological Abstracts* and *Social Planning/Policy & Development Abstracts;* abstracts to over 1,900 journals.

Sociological Abstracts (available in SOCIOLOGICAL ABSTRACTS computer database): Similar to *Psychological Abstracts,* it provides bibliographic data plus abstracts.

Women's Studies Abstracts: Abstracts 78 American and international journals.

Figure 4.3: Cont.

II. Abstracts of Research Presented at Professional Meetings

Abstracts from the Annual Meeting of the American College of Sports Medicine: Published annually as a supplement to *Medicine and Science in Sports and Exercise.*

Abstracts from Annual Meeting of the Research Consortium of the American Alliance of Health, Physical Education, Recreation, and Dance: Published annually as a supplement to the *Research Quarterly for Exercise and Sport.*

Abstracts from the Annual Meeting of the Gerontological Society of America: Published in October as a supplement to the *Gerontologist.*

Abstracts from the Annual Meeting of the Leisure Research Symposium: Published annually by National Recreation & Park Association.

III. Other

Dissertation Abstracts (available in DISSERTATION ABSTRACTS ON DISC, this computerized version also contains masters' theses): Contains doctoral dissertations produced at the approximately 500 American and Canadian universities; Section A contains dissertations in the social sciences and education, and Section B contains dissertations in the physical sciences (including physical education and psychology).

Dissertation Abstracts International: Contains dissertations produced outside the United States.

A *bibliography* is also considered a general reference. A bibliography contains a list of books and articles relevant to a specific topic. Usually, the best starting point for using a bibliography is to review the latest entries in order to locate the most recent theories, research, etc. on the selected topic. *Focus on Sports Science & Medicine* is a new monthly bibliographic service (produced by the Institute for Scientific Information, the same organization that does *Current Contents*) that reviews 900 source items related to biomechanics, conditioning, exercise, physiology, orthopedics, rehabilitation, sport psychology, and training.

5. **Review selected general references to identify relevant primary sources.** In this step we find the most recent issue of the general reference and work backwards (monthly issues are typically combined every quarter, and quarterly issues are combined into a yearly volume). Determine if any of the current issues cite any articles listed under the chosen search

term(s). If so, list on an index card the bibliographic data (e.g., author, title, publication source, see Figure 4.4) about the located article. It is a good practice to record somewhere on this card the general reference that was used to locate the article. That way, if you inadvertently copied something wrong in the citation you can go back and record, from the general reference, the correct information. Lastly, a "Category" entry line on the card will permit you to jot a note to yourself regarding initial thoughts on where you think you might use the primary source (e.g., problem statement, theory, methods).

Figure 4.4: Sample bibliographic card.

Category: _____ Library Call No. _____

AUTHOR: _____

TITLE: _____

Place of Publication: _____

Publisher: _____

Year: _____ Volume: _____ Page Number: _____

Reference:

Notes:

The question frequently arises as to how far back in time to go in conducting a literature review. The answer is not etched in stone; answers to the question will vary. Nevertheless, the common standard practice is that materials up to five years past should be reviewed.

6. Obtain and review (by recording and summarizing key points) relevant primary sources. *Primary sources* are publications that contain the reports of actual studies. Findings of studies are communicated directly to readers. Most primary sources in recreation are journals. *Journals* are usually published monthly or quarterly, and the articles published in them typically report on a particular research study that has undergone peer review (Figure

4.5). *Peer review* entails the editor of the journal soliciting generally two or three persons to read the manuscript. In order to judge the value and merits of publishing an article, these individuals usually are asked to perform a *blind review*—that is, the identity of the authors is not given in the manuscript sent to them. Additionally, these reviewers critique the manuscript, identifying ways the manuscript could or should be revised prior to publication.

Figure 4.5: Journals related to park, recreation, and sport fitness services.

Activities, Adaptation & Aging

Adapted Physical Activity Quarterly

American Educational Research Journal

Annals of Tourism Research

Anthropology and Education Journal

Applied Behavioral Measurement

Behavior Assessment

Behavior Therapy

British Journal of Educational Studies

Camping Magazine

Canadian Education and Research Digest

Child and Adolescent Social Work Journal

Child Development

Dance Research Journal

Educational Administration Quarterly

Educational and Psychological Measurement

Educational Gerontology

Educational and Psychological Measurement

Evaluation Family Practice

Gerontologist

International Journal of Aging and Human Development

International Journal of Behavioral Development

International Journal of Rehabilitation Research

International Journal of Sport Sociology

International Review of Education

Journal of Adolescent Research

Journal of the American School Health Association

Journal of Applied Biomechanics

Journal of Applied Recreation Research

Journal of Behavioral Assessment and Psychopathology

Journal of Biomechanics

Journal of Clinical Psychology

Journal of Consulting and Clinical Psychology

Journal of Counseling and Development

Journal of Cross-Cultural Psychology

Journal of Educational Measurement

Journal of Educational Psychology

Journal of Educational Research

Journal of Experimental Education

Journal of Gerontological Social Work

Journal of Health Education

Journal of Health, Physical Education, Recreation, and Dance

Journal of Health Promotion

Journal of Leisurability

Journal of Leisure Research

Journal of Marriage and the Family

Journal of Motor Behavior

Journal of Music Teacher Education

Journal of the National Intramural-Recreational Sports Association

Figure 4.5: Cont.

Journal of Park and Recreation Administration

Journal of Personality Assessment

Journal of the Philosophy of Sport

Journal of Psychology

Journal of Research and Development in Education

Journal of Research in Science Teaching

Journal of Social Psychology

Journal of Sport Behavior

Journal of Sport and Exercise Psychology

Journal of Sport and Social Issues

Journal of Sport Management

Journal of Sports Medicine and Physical Fitness

Journal of Sport Psychology

Journal of Sports Sciences

Journal of Strength and Conditioning Research

Journal of Swimming Research

Journal of Teaching in Physical Education

Leisure Sciences

Leisure Studies

Loisir et Societe/Society and Leisure

Measurement and Evaluation in Counseling and Development

Medicine and Science in Sports and Exercise

Parks and Recreation

Perceptual and Motor Skills

Psychological Assessment

Psychological Bulletin

Psychological Review

Research Quarterly for Exercise and Sport

Sociology of Education

Sport Science Review

Sports Medicine

Therapeutic Recreation Journal

Theory and Research in Social Education

Primary sources can also be reports, published by the United States government or private organizations, papers presented at professional meetings, final reports of federally funded research projects, commissioned papers written for government agencies, and commissioned papers that contain research findings. Excellent primary sources are the on-line Educational Resources Information Center (ERIC)'s database; as well as microfilms of theses and dissertations. Annually, the College of Human Development and Performance at the University of Oregon produces *microfilm* (complete pages are photographed and reduced for storage purposes) on dissertations and theses that relate to sport science, exercise science, and physical education.

When you have identified all pertinent primary sources, the full-fledged review can begin. It is a good idea to begin with the most current or recent articles and references and work backward. The rationale for this advice is that most of the more recent writings will have noted and incorporated earlier studies as a foundation. Thus, reading these most recent works can provide a quicker understanding of previous work.

Finally, it is a good practice to take a moment or two to glance over references cited in each primary source. Sometimes, especially when an excellent journal article has been located, reviewing the reference section gives you leads or acts as a cross-check to other possible references on the topic at hand.

What to Record From a Primary Source

In the course of conducting a literature review, hundreds of research-related articles are encountered. What is the essential information that should be included in a review of this literature? Knowing what to look for when reading and what to extract and summarize from these sources is critical. Figure 4.6 presents one notational format that relies heavily on a checklist approach for summarizing *empirical* (or data-based) articles. Basically, this form records information about the study's problem statement, data characteristics, data analysis, and conclusions. The form also contains a summary section to record an overall rating regarding the methodological adequacy of the reported research (the scoring of each of these headings is detailed in Riddick, DeSchriver, & Weissinger, 1991).

It also should be noted that some people prefer to record summaries of research on four-by-six-inch cards. Regardless of which system is used, record no more than one article on each paper/card since in organizing the literature search results, inevitably studies will be shifted around.

Sorting and Making Sense Out of Literature Read

When reviewing the primary source literature, one is confronted with two tasks. First, the reader must analyze the literature in terms of relevance and quality. Next, one is confronted with the task of synthesizing what has been read.

Analysis of Literature

When conducting a literature review, one should be able to assess the *relevance* of each study or source. Relevance of a study or source is determined by the degree of similarity between the study under review and the study being planned. The connecting link could be on any number of dimensions (e.g., similar problem, subject matter, topic, study population, and/or setting).

Furthermore, when reviewing the literature, one needs to assess the *quality* of a study. Quality of the study is determined by the confidence one has about the conclusions reached in the study (Eichelberger, 1989, p. 74). Many problems can exist that raise doubts about the conclusions reached in a study, thus calling into question the quality of the study. Some of the problems encountered can relate to:

Figure 4.6: Review of literature summary sheet.[1]

YEAR: _____ VOL. _____ NO. _____ P.P. _____

AUTHOR(S): _____

TITLE and JOURNAL: _____

1. SUBSTANTIVE AREA: _____   _____

2. PROBLEM STATEMENT:

   A. Objective(s) or study purpose(s) stated explicitness (circle one)   *

   0 Poor   1 Adequate   _____

   B. Theoretical bases for the study (circle one)?   *

   0 No   1 Yes   _____

   C. Hypotheses stated (circle one)?   _____   *

   0 No   1 No, but implied in statistical presentation   2 Yes

   D. Concept Operationalization (circle one)

   0 Poor   1 Adequate   _____   *

3. DATA CHARACTERISTICS

   A. Study design used (circle one)?

      Not applicable—survey research   _____

      Yes (specify) _____

   B. Primary database (circle those applicable)

      Interview   _____

      Questionnaire   _____

      Observation   _____

   C. Secondary database (circle those applicable)

      Census/vital statistics   _____

      Survey   _____

      Documents, records, reports   _____

   D. Location of study (circle answer)?   _____

      United States

      Canada

      Other (specify) _____

   E. Sampling universe defined (circle one)?   *

      0 No   1 Yes

F. Type sample used (circle one)   _____ *

   0 Not specified   2 Enumeration

   1 Non-probability   3 Probability

G. Sample size (*N*) (specify & circle): _____   _____

   100   700-899

   100-299   900-999

   300-499   1000

   500-699   No information given

H. Response rate (specify & circle): _____   _____

   1-25%   51-75%

   26-50%   76-100%

I. Validity of measures addressed (circle answer(s))?   _____ *

   0 No

   1 Yes (If so, answer "a" and "b")

     a. Discussion of validity?

     0 No   1 Yes

     b. Used stats to check?

     0 No   1 Yes

J. Reliability of measures addressed (circle answer(s))?   _____ *

   0 No

   1 Yes (If so, answer "a" and "b")

   a. Discussions of reliability?

     0 No   1 Yes

   b. Used stats to check?

     0 No   1 Yes

4. DATA ANALYSIS:

A. Criteria/justification for analytic technique(s) presented? (circle one)   _____ *

   0 No   1 Yes

B. Type of analyses (circle answer(s))?   _____ *

   0 Univariate   1 Bivariate   2 Multivariate

C. Primary analytic technique(s) employed (circle which 3 apply).

   Descriptive   _____

   Non-par. test/indep. (e.g., X^2, diff Md)   _____

   Non-par. asoc. (e.g., Parson)   _____

   ANOVA, ANCOVA, *t* and/or *z* (circle each that applies)

Figure 4.6 cont.

Regression

Factor/cluster analysis

Path analysis

Discrete dependent variable transformation (e.g., log-linear tech., logistic
regression, discriminant analysis—circle each that applies

Other (specify): _____

   D. Interaction considered (circle one)?   _____

       No   Yes   Not applicable

   E. Form of relationship (circle one)?   _____

       Linear   Non-linear   Not applicable

   F. Test of significance (circle one)?   _____

       No   Yes   Not applicable

   G. Unit of analysis (circle one)?   _____

Individual

Household

Organization

Ecological (neighborhood, communities, counties)

5. CONCLUSIONS:

   A. Are conclusions congruent with problem and objective (circle one)?   _____ *

       0 No   1 Yes

   B. Recognition of general methodological limitations (circle one)?   _____ *

       0 No   1 Yes

   C. Have implications for the practitioner been discussed (circle one)?   _____ *

       0 No   1 Yes

   D. Internal validity of study (circle one)?   _____ *

       0 Poor   1 Adequate

   E. External validity of study (circle one)?   _____ *

       0 Poor   1 Adequate

6. SUMMARY OF OVERALL METHODOLOGICAL ADEQUACY (circle one):

Inadequate

Adequate (14 pts. or more–specify): _____   _____

[1]Form used to summarize literature reported in *A Methodological Review of Research in Journal of Leisure Research from 1983-87* by C. Riddick, M. De Schriver, & E. Weissinger, 1998. Reprinted with permission of the authors.

- How the phenomena or factors under study were defined or measured.
- Which research design was adopted for the study.
- The sampling procedures used to execute the study.

Technical knowledge of measurement, research design, and statistics will typically help the individual read with what Joiner (1972, p. 1) calls a "skeptical yet sympathetic eye that is equipped with the ability to detect crap." Figure 4.6 can be used to summarize research methodology used in a evaluative research study, as well as judge the quality of the reported research.

One last thought on the subject is that learning to analyze a reported study objectively can be difficult. This difficulty arises from the fact that each of us walks around with our own sets of beliefs and biases. As has been noted, "When one interpretation of results requires major changes in the tentative plans we have for doing the study, most of us will try harder to find evidence against the interpretation in contrast to evidence that supports it" (Eichelberger, 1989, p. 75). In doing the literature review, we need to learn and then apply the technical aspects of scientific research methodology in order to arrive at a more accurate interpretation of what really was found in the reported evaluative study.

Synthesis of the Literature Review

Another difficult task confronting literature reviewers, especially novice ones, is to be able to synthesize what they have read (Eichelberger, 1989, p. 75). As with other aspects of evaluative research, experience is needed to do this task well.

As you will learn in Chapter 5, there are two (although we argue for an eclectic approach) orientations to help you focus your study, or quantitative and qualitative frameworks. Accordingly, a preview to that chapter within the context of uses of a literature review will now be discussed. You probably should re-read this section after studying Chapter 5.

Often the report from a quantitative study includes a separate section describing the review of literature. If this is done, the literature in this section can be summarized along one or more of three themes—integrative, theoretical, or methodological. An *integrative* literature review summarizes past research (see Figure 4.7 for an example of the summary sheet approach that can be used to present an integration of relevant findings). The *theoretical* review focuses on the theory or conceptual approach that is the foundation for the study. Typically this theoretical review provides the basis for the study (see Chapter 6 for additional information on organizational options of where to place or refer to theory in a quantitative study). A *methodological* review identifies the strengths and weaknesses of methods used to pursue a line of inquiry. That is, in a methodological review, the merits and drawbacks of different methodologies used in cited studies are discussed.

Creswell (1994, pp. 21-23) has identified three ways literature on other research can be used in a qualitative study. First, all qualitative studies can use literature, in the introduction

Figure 4.7: An Example of an integrative literature review: Effects of selected therapeutic recreation activities on geriatric physical health.[2]

Investigator(s)	Subjects	TR Activity	Theoretical Foundations	Focus	Measure(s)	Outcome(s)
Cutler Riddick (1985)	Older residents in a public subsidized housing complex with a senior center _N_=22 (randomly assigned to one of three groups: an aquarium group, a visitor group, or a control group)	Goldfish aquariums were placed in participants' homes; nine bi-weekly visits from the researcher (from 25-35 min./visit) for sixmonths Visitor group received 10 bi-weekly visits from the researcher, (from 30-40 min./visit) for six months	None	Blood pressure	Sphygmomanometer	Significant decrease in diastolic blood pressure in aquarium group (from the pre- to posttest)
DeSchriver & Cutler Rddick (1990)	Older residents in a public subsidized housing complex _N_=27 (Randomly assigned to one of three groups: viewed a fish aquarium, viewed a fish videotape, or viewed a placebo videotape)	Viewing of the fish aquarium, fish videotape, or placebo videotape lasted eight minutes, once a week, over a three-week period	Relaxation Theory	Pulse rate Skin temperature General skeletal muscle tension	Lumiscope Digitronic I model (beats per minute) Yellow Springs Temperature Meter Bicep Electromyography (EMG)	No significant change No significant change No significant change
Gowing (1984)	Elderly home health care recipients _N_=33 (non-equivalent control group design)	Minimal care pets (goldfish) for a six-week period	None	Blood pressure	Sphygmomanometer (assumed--not stated)	No significant improvement when comparing pre- and posttest scores
Green (1989)	Elderly community residents enrolled in a community service program _N_=24 (one-group pretest-posttest design)	Water aerobic program (two times a week for 16 weeks)	None	Blood pressure Resting pulse	Sphygmomanometer Pulse rate	Significant reduction in diastolic blood pressure (when comparing pre- and posttest scores) No significant improvement

[2]From _The Benefits of Therapeutic Recreation in Gerontology_ (p. 73), by C. Riddick & J. Keller, 1991, In C. Coule, W. Kinney, B. Riley, & J. Shank (Eds.), _Benefits of therapeutic recreation: A consensus view_ (pp. 151-204). Ravensdale, WA: Idyll Arbor, Inc. Reprinted with permission of the authors.

of the study, in order to "frame" the problem (e.g., what the study approach is and why the approach being used is appropriate—see Chapter 5.). Second, depending on the data-collection methodology (see Chapter 10) used to conduct the qualitative study, literature will be cited on the theory behind the method either cursorily or in depth. Third, the literature review can be used at the end of the study in order to make inductive conclusions or summaries (see Chapter 5). Related literature may be cited when findings are compared and contrasted in order to identify themes or categories.

Finally, we would like to close by encouraging you to take a sneak preview of what is contained in the final report (see Chapter 13). For those of you reading this paragraph and wondering if someone assembled this book on the wrong order hold on. The rationale for slipping this information in here is reflected on the quip, "If you don't know where you're going, how will you know you arrived?" Most of us know before we head out the door on a trip where our final destination is going to be. The logistics of the trip (actual dates of departure and return, how we get there, what we pack, etc.) typically can be tinkered with between the initial decision to go on a trip and the day we actually depart on our excursion.

Likewise, once a decision has been made to conduct a scientific evaluation, there is time to decide on the multitude of "how do's and how to's." What is not negotiable is the fact that a final written report must be produced at the end of the evaluation journey. Thus, it is important for the evaluator to begin early on, in the evaluation activity, to have a conceptual road map to refer to in thinking about the written report. Having an idea of the content and organization of the final written end product will prove invaluable as you move along in planning, designing, and executing the evaluation study.

Main Points

- Taking the time to review the professional literature pays huge dividends.

- Some of the ways a literature review can help you is in the provision of the study background (e.g., historical and conceptual perspectives), identification or refinement of a problem, establishment of a study rationale, provision of a context by which the gaps to earlier studies can be filled, and comparative analysis of previously published approaches and/or research results.

- There are six steps involved in conducting a literature search: (1) identify the subject matter, problem, or question that reflects the focus for the evaluation; (2) locate and review a secondary source(s) related to the subject matter, problem, or question; (3) refine the subject matter, problem, or question and then identify search terms; (4) consult a general reference(s); (5) review the general reference(s) to identify primary sources; and, (6) obtain and review primary sources.

- A *secondary* source is a publication that describes the works of others. Common secondary sources are textbooks, encyclopedias, and research reviews.

- A *general reference* locates sources (such as books and articles) via an index, abstract, or bibliography.

- An *index* reviews selected professional journal holdings and classifies articles by subject(s) or topic(s).

- An *abstract* summarizes research that either appears in a journal, was presented at professional meetings, or has been printed elsewhere (e.g., dissertation).

- A *bibliography* contains a listing (within a specified time period usually) of books, articles, and monographs on a specific topic.

- A *primary source* is a publication that contains the reprints of actual studies. Professional journals, doctoral dissertations, and masters' theses are examples of a primary source.

- Sorting and making sense out of what literature you read entails analyzing what is read in terms of its relevance to the subject matter, problem, or question under scrutiny; deciding upon the quality of the study/reading; and synthesizing what you read.

- Synthesizing quantitative studies can mean summarizing the literature around one of three themes: an integrative review, a theoretical review, and/or a methodological review.

- Synthesizing qualitative studies can mean using the literature in one or more of three places: in the introduction to frame the problem, in a separate "review of literature" section, and/or at the end of the study in order to make inductive conclusions or summaries.

- It is also important, at the literature review stage, to be mindful of the content and organization of the final evaluative research report.

Study Questions

1. How can a literature review help you when planning an evaluation study?

2. What is a *secondary source*? How can secondary sources help you with planning an evaluation study?

3. What is a *general reference*? Cite some examples. How can general references help you with drafting an evaluation study?

4. What does it mean to "analyze the literature?"

5. What are the three ways literature (i.e., primary sources) can be summarized?

References

Creswell, J. (1994). *Research design: Qualitative & quantitative approaches*. Thousand Oaks, CA: Sage Publications.

Cutler Riddick, C. (1985). Health, aquariums, and the non-institutionalized elderly. In M. Sussman (Ed.), *Pets and the family* (pp. 163-173). New York: Haworth Press.

DeSchriver, M., & Riddick Cutler, C. (1990). Effects of watching aquariums on elders' stress. *Anthrozoos, 9*, 44-48.

Eichelberger, R. (1989). *Disciplined inquiry: Understanding and doing educational research*. New York: Longman.

Fletcher, J., Kaiser, R., & Groger, S. (1992). An assessment of the importance and performance of park impact fees in funding park and recreation infrastructure. *Journal of Park and Recreation Administration, 10*, 75-87.

Fraenkel, J. & Wallen, N. (1993). *How to design and evaluate research in education* (2nd ed.). New York: McGraw-Hill.

Gowing, C. (1984). *The effects of minimal care pets on homebound elderly and their professional caregivers*. Unpublished doctoral dissertation. University of Illinois at Urbana-Champaign.

Green, J. (1989). Effects of a water aerobics program on the blood pressure, percentage of body fat, weight and resting pulse rate of senior citizens. *Journal of Applied Gerontology, 8*, 132-138.

Joiner, B. (1972). *How to read with a skeptical yet sympathetic eye*. Unpublished manuscript. Pennsylvania State University, Department of Statistics.

Riddick, C., DeSchriver, M., & Weissinger, E. (1991). *A methodological review of research in Journal of Leisure Research from 1983 through 1987*. Paper presented at the National Recreation & Park Association's Leisure Research Symposium, Baltimore, MD.

Riddick, C., & Keller, J. (1991). The benefits of therapeutic recreation in gerontology. In C. Coyle, W.B. Kinney, B. Riley, & J. Shank (Eds.), *Benefits of therapeutic recreation: A consensus view* (pp. 151-204). Ravensdale, WA: Idyll Arbor, Inc.

Wolfe, R., & Riddick, C. (1984). Effects of leisure counseling on adult psychiatric outpatients. *Therapeutic Recreation Journal, 3*, 30-37.

CHAPTER 5

Quantitative and Qualitative Frameworks

What Will I Learn in This Chapter?

I'll be able to:

1. Identify the two frameworks used in leisure service evaluation research.

2. Explain the difference between deductive and inductive logic and how each contributes to theory building.

3. Cite an example of a structured and an unstructured question-answer response.

4. Recall the points to consider when choosing between adoption of a quantitative or qualitative framework.

The first stage of focusing an evaluation also requires a determination of the research framework. An individual's conscious or unconscious perspective for looking at the world affects the decisions that person makes in designing and implementing an evaluative research study. Each of us has a mind set that helps us understand phenomena by advancing assumptions we have about the social world, defining what the problem is, directing us on how the inquiry or the evaluation should proceed, and assisting us with the identification of what constitutes a legitimate solution (Creswell, 1994, p. 1). These mind sets help us break down the complexity of the real world; tell us what is important, legitimate and reasonable; and tell us what to do (Patton, 1987, p. 23).

Two frameworks that have been discussed and debated in the recreation field are qualitative and quantitative frameworks. Bullock (1993), for example, provides an excellent overview of how these two frameworks have been applied to therapeutic recreation. The point is that an evaluative research study can typically be characterized, depending on which framework has been adopted as a qualitative study or a quantitative study.

Definitions

A *quantitative* framework is an "inquiry into a social or human problem, based on testing a theory composed of variables, measured with numbers, and analyzed with statistical procedures, in order to determine whether the predictive generalizations of the theory hold true"(Creswell, 1994, pp. 3). Through time, synonyms to the quantitative framework have emerged in the literature and include such terms as traditional, positivist, experimental, empiricist, realistic, deterministic, nomothetic, or normative perspective (Creswell, 1994, p. 4).

A *qualitative* framework is "defined as an inquiry process of understanding a social or human problem, based on building a complex, holistic picture, formed with words, reporting detailed views of informants, and conducted in a natural setting" (Creswell, 1994, pp.2-3). A qualitative framework is often turned to when existing theory and/or previous research are considered lacking (due to inaccuracy, inappropriateness, incorrectness). Synonyms that have emerged for the qualitative framework include describing a study as using a constructivist, naturalistic, interpretative, postpositivist, postmodern, nominalistic, or ideographic perspective (Creswell, 1994, p. 4).

Figure 5.1 illustrates how the two frameworks can be used in studying a problem. That is, both quantitative and qualitative frameworks are used in designing a study set up to better understand a persistent problem confronting outdoor resource managers, namely littering.

Critics have lined up for each of these approaches. Black (1993, p. 3) noted that, "Poorly conducted normative studies can produce findings that are so trivial as to contribute little to the body of research. On the other hand, interpretive studies can be so isolated, subjective, and idiosyncratic that there is no hope of any generalization or contribution to a greater body of knowledge." Rossi and Freeman captured the essence of the criticism of both sides by stating,

> critics of quantitative data decry the dehumanizing tendencies of numerical representation, claiming that a better understanding of causal processes can be obtained from intimate acquaintance with people and their problems and the resulting qualitative observations ... the advocates of quantitative data reply that qualitative data are expensive to gather on an extensive basis, are highly subject to misinterpretation, and usually contain information that is not uniformly collected across all cases and situations. (1993, p. 254)

To understand better the distinction between these two frameworks, the methodological assumptions associated with each will be summarized. For more in-depth reading on the topic consult Guba (1990). We will also share some thoughts about how one might go about choosing one framework over the other for a study.

Methodological Assumptions

It is important to recognize at the onset that the following noted differences between a qualitative and quantitative framework are a heuristic presentation. That is, a *heuristic* description is the presumed ideal; seldom will any one evaluation study exemplify all of the noted assumptions or characteristics.

Figure 5.1: Example of how quantitative and qualitative frameworks can be used to study littering behavior at a state park.

Problem: Man-made litter at a state park.

I.   **Quantitative Framework Approach**

Deductive Theory: Protection motivation theory.

Hypothesis: Individuals who receive, upon entry to the park, printed information that describes sanctions (or punishments) for littering will be less likely to break littering rules when compared to individuals who do not receive such information.

Design: Static group.

Sampling Approach: Systematic sampling.

Method of Collecting Information: Structured/closed-ended form to record observed incidents of littering.

II. **Qualitative Framework Approach**

Inductive Theory: Pattern theory as revealed from executing case studies.

Research Question: What causes people to litter at parks?

Design: Case study.

Sampling Approach: Volunteer sampling.

Method of Collecting Information: In-depth interviews with people who litter using unstructured interview question.

Quantitative and qualitative studies differ on a number of issues related to how the study is carried out. The methodological differences between the two frameworks deal with deductive versus inductive logic, structured versus unstructured inquiry, sample size, and generalizability.

1. Deductive versus inductive logic. Wallace (1971) portrays deduction and induction in a two-dimensional model. The schematic in Figure 5.2 illustrates the link between theory (derived by deduction and induction) and scientific research. It is important to remember that both deduction and induction are means to the construction and/or refinement of social theories (Babbie, 1995, p.55).

Figure 5.2: Deductive versus inductive logic.[1]

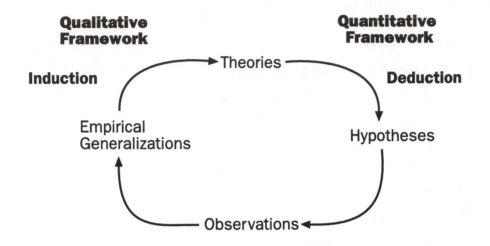

[1]Reprinted with permission from W. Wallace, (1971), *Logic of Science in Sociology*, New York: Aldine De Gruyter.

Quantitative studies are based on deductive logic. *Deductive logic* requires us to reason ***toward*** observations. The deductive approach is triggered by reviewing literature or previous research. The literature review reveals a theory that applies or "sheds some light" or helps explain what is going on. This theory is adopted for the study, and in turn a problem statement and accompanying research question, objective, and/or hypothesis will "flow" or stem from the theory and shape the direction of the study. In other words, the theory influences the research question, objective and/or hypothesis that will be "tested." Research findings will either support or reject the theory under examination. Hence, we have gone from some general theory and applied it to a particular situation or setting. This application and testing of theory is the essence of deductive logic.

Being tested means that observations will be made to find out whether there is support for what was expected theoretically. Research questions, objectives, and/or hypotheses, using the deductive logic outlined above, are chosen at the onset of the study and remain fixed throughout the study. This is also known as *a priori* or predictive explanation of phenomena.

For an application of deductive logic in designing evaluative research, suppose you are a manager of a state park and are confronted with a large annual expense related to cleaning trails of man-made litter. You want to explore a way to correct this problem that is both inexpensive to implement yet is effective in reducing the problem. A review of the literature reveals that the *protection motivation theory* might help direct you in this inquiry (Figure

5.1). This theory speculates that rule compliance is affected by being exposed to fear tactics and awareness-of-consequences information (Gramann, Bonifield, & Kim, 1995). Thus, a hypothesis that could be derived from this theory and subsequently tested is that individuals who receive probable sanction information upon park entry, (in this case, outlining the fines imposed on people who litter), are less likely to break littering rules compared to those who do not get this information. In order to test whether this theoretical conclusion is correct, littering behaviors or patterns would be observed. This technique is an example of applied or evaluative research, based on a quantitative framework, which uses deductive logic to guide the effort.

Contrastingly, in the qualitative approach, *inductive logic* is used. Inductive logic requires us to reason ***from*** observations. Observations are made and then time is taken to reflect on the information collected by articulating patterns or general principles that explain the relationship between the objects observed (Babbie, 1995, p. 54). The research problem and question that needs to be posed is then identified based on the "context-bound" information that has been collected. This style is also referred to as an *ex post facto* explanation of phenomena.

Applying a qualitative framework to the littering problem described above, the study would begin by observing or conducting open-ended, in-depth interviews with people who litter on a state park hiking trail. After interviews had been made, what had been observed and noted would be reviewed and reflected upon in order to articulate what kinds of people are more likely to litter. Once this profile was built, steps would be implemented to correct the problem (Figure 5.1).

2. Structured versus unstructured inquiry. A quantitative researcher tends to collect information by using structured, closed-ended (such as multiple choice or "yes-no" questions) questionnaires or interviews. A qualitative researcher relies on open-ended questions (e.g., "What do you think the problem is?") or observation (Figure 5.1). Chapter 10 will describe the various data collection methods associated with quantitative and qualitative frameworks.

The quantitative study uses instruments or measures with known validity and reliability. For the qualitative evaluator, ways to predetermine answers into categories cannot happen a *priori*, instead categories emerge from informants. If a question about the accuracy of information is raised, the qualitative evaluator talks about steps of verifying the information with other sources, such as informants (Creswell, 1994, p. 7).

3. Sample size. A quantitative approach to evaluative research tends to sample a large number of persons, whereas a qualitative approach is associated with selecting a small number of persons to study. Sample size is tied inextricably to the method(s) used to collect data. The quantitative researcher, for example, may use a questionnaire that requires little if anytime interacting directly with study participants. The qualitative researcher, contrastingly, tends to use interviews or observations over an extended period of time.

4. Generalizability. A characteristic of a quantitative researcher is to summarize responses with statistics that emphasize sample or group findings. This sort of approach to research typically concludes by making generalizations about the broader population studied. A qualitative researcher is not concerned with generalizing findings beyond those persons studied. Instead, *ideographic interpretation* is used. That is, data are interpreted in regard to particulars, and conclusions are limited to only individuals who were observed or interviewed.

Choosing Between Quantitative versus Qualitative Framework

Patton (1987) reminds us that evaluative research should be creative. By this, he means we must realize that we should be creative thinkers and problem solvers and remember there is more than one right answer. Patton (1987, p. 22) admonishes us, "Rather than be faithful to some model or paradigm, the evaluator can be faithful to the situation—and in so being, can be creative."

In essence, we need to realize that most of us operate on pre-programmed mental tapes that reflect the scientific paradigm in which we have been trained. Patton (1987, p. 23) points out that the scientific paradigm we have been trained in usually includes the "idea that there is a single best solution and a single right answer." This perspective, that there is one right answer, is typically embraced by our educational system. Roger von Oech notes,

> By the time the average person finishes college, he or she will have taken over 2,600 tests. . . . Thus, the 'right' answer approach becomes deeply ingrained in our thinking. . . . The difficulty is that most of life does not present itself this way. . . . there are many right answers—all depending on what you are looking for. But if you think there is only one right answer, then you will stop looking as soon as you find one. (1983, p. 21)

Rossi & Freeman (1993, p. 437) maintain that the critical points to remember in the debate of which is the better framework are: (1) appreciate the utility of each framework, and, (2) recall that the choice of framework should depend on the evaluation question at hand. This latter point, fitting the framework to the purpose(s) of the evaluation, is a critical issue.

Even so, because we embrace the use of multiple sources of information (technically this is known as *triangulation*—a concept addressed in greater detail in Chapter 10), we would argue that both approaches, whenever possible, should be used. The two frameworks should be viewed as **complementing** each other rather than competing. Whenever possible, a combination of structured and unstructured interviews should be considered. Results can be cast in both statistical reporting as well as quotations from subjects.

Scott, Witt, and Foss' (1996) evaluation of the impact of an art center's creative club on children at risk demonstrates reliance on a two-prong framework approach. The primary methods of data collection used in this evaluative study were structured observation and in-depth interviews. These choices were defended because "a mixed form of data collection yields different views or slices of data. Different methods, thus produced additional and complementary data and guarded against biases that may have emerged using a single method (p. 47)."

Rossi and Freeman (1993, p. 254) point out that qualitative observations have an important role to play in the monitoring of ongoing programs. Our own collective research experiences indeed confirm the "richness" of information derived from using a qualitative framework. Subjects oftentimes capture the truer or more poignant meaning of a recreation experience by using their own words rather than artificial categories supplied by the investigator. A case in point is the study that examined the effects of introducing a new hobby—fish aquariums—to a sample of non-institutionalized elders (Riddick, 1985). Impressive results were noted in this study using conventional quantitative tools of physiological and paper-and-pencil tests (the aquarium group, when compared to two other control groups, underwent positive changes in diastolic blood pressure, leisure satisfaction, and relaxation states). Nevertheless, the collected, personal, one-line reflections underscored, in human terms, what happened to the elders when the fish entered their lives. "They gave me a reason to get up in the morning. They depend on me to feed them. Their antics made me laugh. We watched television together. They make the apartment feel less empty, added happiness to my life, and were a way to meet or get to know other people"(p. 171).

Geiger and Miko (1995) also reflect, in a study examining the meaning of recreation activities to elderly nursing home residents, on the importance of using a qualitative framework by noting,

> If this study had been approached in a manner other than the qualitative approach, the results would likely have been quite different. The use of the exact words of the respondents and repeated interviews and observations of the residents and their activities produced credible data. The detailed explanations of the resident's perceived meaning of their leisure activities provided data that contributes to quality of life. (p. 137)

Creswell (1994, p. 9) identified a number of factors that influence the evaluator in adopting a framework. These are the:

• Training and experience of the evaluator;
• Psychological attributes of evaluator;
• Nature of the problem; and
• The audience for the study report.

Training and Experience of the Evaluator

The background of the evaluator can dictate which kind of study is used. Individuals with a background in statistics, computers, business, or economics oftentimes pursue quantitative studies. Persons with a strong literary background or who have been trained in anthropology, sociology, education, or social work often adopt a qualitative framework for the evaluation study. Occasionally, a competent evaluator will possess adequate skills in both frameworks.

Similarly, one's training or discipline typically extends itself as reductionism. As Babbie (1998, p. 97) defined it *reductionism* is "...seeing and explaining everything in terms of a particular, narrow set of concepts." In other words, our formal training almost always preprograms us into explaining human behavior from the discipline we have adopted—sociologists tend to consider only sociological variables, psychologists typically consider only psychological variables, economists normally turn to economic explainers or predictors, etc.

Psychological Attributes of the Evaluator

An individual who prefers following rules and guidelines for conducting research and/or has low tolerance for ambiguity typically will adopt a quantitative study. Alternatively, the individual who does not need specific rules and procedures to follow when conducting the research and/or has a high tolerance for ambiguity will likely adopt a qualitative study framework.

Nature of the Problem

Some research questions inherently lend themselves more to one approach than another. When little is known about a topic, qualitative research is generally the favored approach. A paucity of research or theory (that is, inadequate, incomplete, or non-existent theory) oftentimes guides the researcher to use a qualitative approach. Based on qualitative results, theories might be then induced. This could enable, at a later point in time, extension studies of a quantifiable nature. Extension studies examine hypotheses drawn from these new theories.

An example of a topic about which little is known is the effects of recreational programs on gangs. In an evaluation study of a late night basketball program for gang members Derezotes (1995, p. 39) stated, "Since the research required study of personal experiences of a relatively little-known and complex social phenomenon, Late Nite staff and the author selected together a qualitative design." Other examples of topics that lend themselves to qualitative study because not much or anything on the noted topic can be found in a review of literature include: psychological needs met by "surfing" the Internet; social psychological cues exhibited by males versus females in bars; and, factors affecting addiction to "playing" the stock market.

On the other hand, some questions inherently lend themselves to a quantifiable approach. One example of a question that is open to study using the quantitative framework is, "What is the impact of multiple recreational use at the Grand Canyon?" This question could be investigated by examining the impact of various user groups (hikers, rafters, over– head fly-by's, horseback riders, etc.) on physical as well as social carrying capacity. That is, the kinds and amount of usage could be examined in terms of effects on soil compression, noise pollution, water pollution, and perceived crowding.

Then there are questions that can use both approaches. An example of this situation is gauging the emotional impact of caring for children with AIDS on therapeutic recreation (TR) professionals working in a chronic-care setting. In this setting, a mood-state scale might be used along with in-depth, open-ended interviews that ask TR professionals to identify the "highs" and "lows" of working with this very special population.

Audience for the Study Report

Sometimes the audience (or decision makers) for the evaluative research study report are accustomed to studies containing quantifiable data and thus expect to be supplied with "hard evidence." Translated, this typically means presenting results in terms of numbers or statistics. Other times, the audience for the study may be receptive and supportive of qualitatively designed studies. We maintain, however, that the ideal is to educate the users of the evaluation report as to the merits of incorporating both frameworks into the study.

Main Points

- Our mind set or how we view the world (i.e., *reductionism*) spills over into how we go about planning and conducting evaluative research.

- Quantitative and/or qualitative frameworks can be used in conducting evaluations. These frameworks differ in regard to assumptions made.

- Differences in the two frameworks pivot around methodological assumptions related to inductive-deductive logic, structured-unstructured inquiry, sample size, and generalizability.

- *Deductive logic* requires one to reason ***toward*** observations—and hence is associated with the quantitative framework.

- *Inductive logic* requires one to reason ***from*** observations—and thus is tied to the qualitative framework.

- A number of factors can affect choosing one of the two frameworks over the other: training and experience of the evaluator, psychological attributes of the evaluator, nature of the problem, and audience for the study report.

- Since both frameworks have merit, whenever possible both (or *triangulation*) should be used when planning an evaluative research project.

Study Questions

1. What is meant by adopting a *quantitative* framework for an evaluation study?

2. What is meant by adopting a *qualitative* framework for an evaluation study?

3. What is *inductive logic? Deductive logic?* Draw a picture diagramming the interrelationships among quantitative and qualitative frameworks and inductive and deductive logic.

4. What is meant by using a *triangulation* approach to designing a study? When should it be used?

5. How does the training, experience, and psychological attributes of the evaluator affect whether he adopts a quantitative or qualitative framework?

6. How does the nature of the problem and the audience for the evaluation report affect whether the evaluator adopts a quantitative or qualitative framework?

References

Babbie, E. (1995). *The practice of social research* (7th ed.). Belmont, CA: Wadsworth Publishing .

Black, T. (1993). *Evaluating social science research: An introduction.* Thousand Oaks, CA: Sage Publications.

Bullock, C. (1993). Ways of knowing: The naturalistic and postivistic perspectives in research. In M. Malkin & C. Howe (Eds.), *Research in therapeutic recreation: Concepts and methods* (pp. 25-41). State College, PA: Venture Publishing..

Creswell, J. (1994). *Research design: Qualitative & quantitative approaches.* Thousand Oaks, CA: Sage Publications.

Derezotes, D. (1995). Evaluation of the Late Nite basketball project. *Child and Adolescent Social Work Journal, 12,* 33-49.

Geiger, C., & Miko, P. (1995). Meaning of recreation/leisure activities to elderly nursing home residents: A qualitative study. *Therapeutic Recreation Journal, 29,* 131-138.

Gramann, J., Bonifield, R., & Kim, Y. (1995). Effect of personality and situational factors on intentions to obey rules in outdoor recreation areas. *Journal of Leisure Research, 27,* 321-343.

Guba, E. (Ed.) (1990). *The paradigm dialog.* Newbury, CA: Sage Publications.

Patton, M. (1987). *Creative evaluation.* Newbury Park, CA: Sage Publications.

Oech, R. von (1983). *A whack on the side of the head: How to unlock your mind for innovation.* New York: Warner Books.

Riddick, C. (1985). Health, aquariums, and the non-institutionalized elderly. *Family Review, 8,*163-173.

Rossi, P., & Freeman, H. (1993). *Evaluation: A systematic approach*. Newbury Park, CA: Sage Publications.

Scott, D., Witt, P., & Foss, M. (1996). Evaluation of the impact of the Doughterty Art Center's creativity club on children at-risk. *Journal of Park and Recreation Administration, 14*(3), 41-59.

von Oech, R. (1983). *A whack on the side of the head: How to unlock your mind for innovation*. New York: Warner Books.

Wallace, W. (1971). *The logic of science in sociology*. New York: Aldine de Gruyter.

CHAPTER 6

Defining the Scope of Evaluative Research

What Will I Learn in This Chapter?

I'll be able to:

1. Explain unit of analysis and recall the common units of analysis.

2. Cite an example of an ecological fallacy.

3. Define a variable and specify and give an example of the three kinds of variables.

4. Draft two purpose statements—one related to a quantitative framework and the other related to a qualitative framework.

5. Draft a statement on the significance of a study.

6. State the role of a theory or conceptual model in defining the scope of an evaluation.

7. Read an evaluative research article and be able to draw a diagram of the interrelationships examined and reported in the article.

8. Write a research question, objective, and hypothesis.

The final step in stage one (focus) of evaluative research planning is defining the study's scope. As an overview, defining the scope of a study translates into identifying what you plan to evaluate and providing a context for the significance of the proposed endeavor. It has been our experience that many persons find it difficult to articulate the scope for an evaluation. One is well into the evaluation journey once: there is closure on a purpose statement; agreement has been reached regarding the significance of the study; a linkage has been made to a logical conceptual or theoretical base; and an acceptable research question, objective, and/or hypothesis has been specified.

This chapter is divided into four major parts. Ideas for developing statements about a study's purpose and significance are the first and second order of business. Third, the role of theory in evaluative research is elaborated upon. And fourth, specific ideas for framing the research question, objective, or hypothesis are shared.

Purpose Statement

A purpose statement should specify the overall intent of the study. While qualitative and quantitative purpose statements both share the conveyance of overall intent, their precise form and language differ (due to the assumptions undergirding each framework). One common denominator between quantitative and qualitative purpose statements, however, is the need to identify the unit of analysis in the purpose statement.

Unit of Analysis

Unit of analysis deals with what or whom you want to study. It is essential that no misunderstanding exists about whom or what is being studied. Four of the more common units of analysis are (Babbie, 1998):

- Individuals,
- Groups,
- Organizations, and
- Artifacts.

Other units of analysis include role, spatial, time period, institutional, community, cultural, and event units (Babbie, 1998). The most popular units of analysis in leisure research are individuals and groups (Riddick, DeSchriver, & Weissinger, 1991).

Individuals as a unit of analysis include participants, residents, patients, students, and staff. In a technical sense, these studied individuals are considered as representing a population (a term described in Chapter 8). An example of a study that used individuals as the unit of analysis would be to determine if students with a high grade-point average (GPA) received a better grade in Evaluation of Leisure Services course than those with a low GPA. In this case, students are the individuals who serve as the unit of analysis.

Groups may also be the unit of analysis. Examples of social groups are families, gangs, and friendship cliques. Suppose you want to explore if the life cycle stage of families (or those with infant, adolescent, or adult children) has any affect on the kinds of leisure activities participated in and/or the frequency of leisure activity. The unit of analysis in this example is families.

Organizations, as a unit of analysis, consist of formal social organizations. Examples of organizations are a recreation department, fitness club, church, or university. You might, for instance, want to compare municipal recreation departments in your state or region in terms of number of employees, size of budget, and breakdown of employees by gender, race, etc.

Social artifacts are products or "things" produced by humans. Examples of artifacts are books, paintings, songs, and buildings. Suppose you want to examine the editorials in a local paper regarding support for the annual recreation budget over the past few years. In this study, a social artifact, or newspaper editorials, is the unit of analysis.

Before closing out on the topic of units of analysis, there are two important reasons why you need to understand this topic fully. First, the purpose statement should clearly identify what is or has been studied, otherwise you or the person preparing the evaluative research study run the risk of making assertions about one unit of analysis based on the examination of another unit of analysis. For instance, you must decide whether you are studying gangs as a group or gang members, fitness clubs or fitness club members, municipal recreation directors or municipal recreation agencies.

Likewise, if you make assertions about individuals based on the examination of groups or other aggregates, you are committing an *ecological fallacy* (Babbie, 1995, pp. 96-97). It is incorrect to assume that patterns observed in a group apply to individuals making up the group. For example, suppose you are interested in learning about the nature of support received by a female candidate for the Society of Park and Recreation Educators (SPRE) presidency. You have access to the vote count by state SPRE membership, enabling you to know which states gave the female candidate the greatest support and which gave her the least. You also have access to demographic data by state SPRE membership. Your analysis of data indicates that states whose SPRE members were predominantly females gave the female candidate a greater proportion of votes than states whose SPRE voters were primarily males. If you concluded from these findings that female SPRE members were more likely to vote for the female candidate than male SPRE members (or that gender affected support for the female candidate), you committed an ecological fallacy. In other words, state SPRE voting patterns (a group) were the units of analysis, yet you drew conclusions about individual SPRE members. It may have been that male SPRE members in states with predominantly female SPRE members also voted for the female candidate!

Quantitative Purpose Statement

The purpose statement reflecting a quantitative study identifies one or more variables within the statement. Before proceeding, however, it is important to review what the word *variable* means and to review briefly the three kinds of variables that can be involved in a study. A *variable* relates to a discrete phenomena or concept (such as a trait or characteristic). A variable is observed or measured in **at least** two categories. Each category is mutually exclusive. That is, a person is classified into only one category, rank, or order. For instance, gender is a variable—you are either a male or female. Likewise, order of finishing a foot race is a variable—first, second, third place and so on.

Variables can be identified as either dependent or an independent. The distinction between how a variable is categorized depends on temporal order. By this it is meant that one variable precedes another in time. Because of this time ordering, one variable "influences" or "affects" another variable. This so-called "cause" variable is the *independent variable*, and it is speculated to affect a dependent variable. The *dependent variable* is the variable you are trying to understand, explain, or predict (by examining how one or more independent variables affect it). Another type of variable is known as the *intervening variable* (sometimes dubbed the "mediating" variable, though, technically, mediating variables are also independent variables, see Chapter 15). These variables intervene between an independent and a dependent variable and are statistically controlled in the analysis (see Figure 6.1).

Figure 6.1: Schematic depicting the relationship among variables in a reported study.[1]

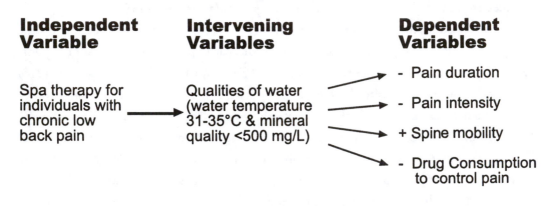

[1]Derived from "Short and Long-term Effects of Spa Therapy on Chronic Low Back Pain" by F. Guillemin, F. Constant, J. Collin, & M. Boulange, (1994), *British Journal of Rheumatology, 33.*

Principles for developing a "good" quantitative purpose statement are (Creswell, 1994, pp. 64-65):

1. Begin the purpose statement passage with the word *purpose, intent, or objective.* That is, start with "The purpose (intent, objective, or focus) of this study is (was or will be)..." The verb tense used in a problem statement, regardless of whether a quantitative or qualitative framework is being used, will depend on whether the proposal is presented as a plan for the evaluative research study (in which case the future tense is used) or if it has been completed (in which case the present or past tense is used). An example of a purpose statement is one written by Fletcher, Kaiser, & Groger (1992, p. 77), "The focus of this paper is an examination of the satisfaction of local park and recreation officials with park impact fees and alternative mechanisms for financing capital development."

2. Identify the theory or conceptual framework to be tested in the study. The identified theory might be a formal articulated theory. For instance, "The purpose of the study was to test Mehrabian's three factor theory of emotions. The effects of videogame play on the emotional states, affiliative behaviors, and pleasure state of nursing home residents were examined within the context of this theory" (Riddick, Spector, & Drogin, 1986, p. 425).

A conceptual model map that has been "pieced together" could also be posed as the basis of a study (see Figure 6.1 for an example of such a conceptual map). Another example of a conceptual model is one that Green and Chalip (1997) identified after a literature review. This model included variables to explain parents' and children's enduring soccer involvement.

3. Identify the proposed variables for the study (dependent, and if appropriate, the independent and intervening variables). An example would be to state, "The intent of this study was to determine if there was a positive relationship between amount of television adults watch and the adult viewer's weight." In this case, the independent variable was the amount of television watched and the dependent variable was the adult viewer's weight. Or, one could state, "The objective of this study was to evaluate employees' reactions to the implementation of a management-by-objectives approach to performance appraisal." In this situation, employees' reactions are the primary (or dependent variable) focus of the study.

4. If possible, specify the nature of the relationship between the variables under study. Ideally, the nature of the relationship between or among variables should be identified. This can be done in one of three ways. Typically, a positive or negative relationship between the identified variables is speculated upon. Using the television viewing and weight example noted above, by declaring a positive relationship between the variables the researcher is conjecturing that as the amount of television increases, the likelihood of weight gain will occur (perhaps the origin of the term, "couch potato"). The converse of this statement also would be examined for its truth, or as the amount of television viewing decreases, the chances of lower weight will occur.

Another strategy for identifying the nature of the relationship between variables identified in the purpose statement is to identify two or more groups that will be compared in terms of the dependent variable. An example of such a statement is one advanced by Searle and Mahon (1993, p. 13) who intended to examine if, "older adults, three months after the completion of a leisure education program, will have higher levels of leisure competence than a control group."

A third approach to drafting a purpose statement is to use a combination of comparing and relating. While this is a more sophisticated approach it can amount to, for instance, using a two-factor experiment where the evaluator has two or more experimental groups as well as a continuous dependent variable. For example, Baker and Witt (1996, p. 65) incorporated this approach by stating the purpose of the study was to determine "if children participating in an after school recreation program would differ from children who did not participate in the program in terms of better school attendance, grades, school and home behaviors, and self-esteem."

5. Order the variables in the relationship or comparison sentence from independent to dependent. For instance:

> "The purpose of the study was to test the relaxation theory by having elderly persons view an aquarium and determine whether engagement in this activity evoked a relaxational response or reduced physiological stress ... (or reduction in pulse rate, increase in skin temperature, and a reduction in muscle tension). (DeSchriver & Riddick, 1991, p. 44)

In this example, the independent variable was the intervention (a stocked aquarium) and the dependent variable was physiological stress (as measured by the three noted variables).

Drafting a quantitative purpose statement can be hard work. One way to meet the challenge is to organize your thoughts using a worksheet (see Figure 6.2).

Figure 6.2: Quantitative purpose statement worksheet.

1. The **purpose/intent** (circle one) will be to understand/explain/predict (circle one and then elaborate): _____

_____.

2. The study will (choose one):
   A. Test the (identify)_____ **theory** OR
   B. Study a **conceptual model** [diagram the variables that will be examined, ordering relationships from independent variable(s) to dependent variable(s)].

3. The research **question/objective/hypothesis**[1] (circle one) will be (specify):

_____

_____.

4. The **independent variable(s)** in the study are (specify): _____
and the **dependent variable(s)** in the study are (specify): _____.

5. The **unit of analysis** for the study is (specify individual group, organization, or social artifact): _____.

[1]Note: If stating a hypothesis, if at all possible state it in the **alternative** form, specifying the nature (ie., positive or negative) of the relationship between noted variables.

Qualitative Purpose Statement

A qualitative purpose statement implies or expresses the assumptions of the qualitative framework. Principles for constructing a "good" qualitative purpose statement include (Creswell, 1994, pp. 57-58):

1. **Call attention to the purpose statement by using such words as** *purpose, intent, goal, and objective.* This statement should be set off in a paragraph and begin with, "The purpose (or intent or objective) of this study is (was or will be)......" An example of a purpose statement using a qualitative framework to understand how participation in a late night basketball program affected gang members is, "The research goal was to help determine the impact of the program upon not only the participants but also the project staff, families, and community as a whole" (Derezotes, 1995, p. 39).

2. **Use words that convey an emerging design that is based on experiences of individuals in a natural setting and an inductive mode** (to refresh your memory, refer to Chapter 5). Such words are: *understand, describe, develop, discover,* and *investigate.* Geiger and Miko (1995, p. 132) practiced this principle when they said, "systematic research designed to study recreation/leisure as experienced by institutionalized elders remains limited. The specific purpose of this work was to investigate the perceived meaning of recreation/leisure participation among a select group of nursing home residents."

3. **Focus on the central concept or idea being explored, discovered, developed or understood in the study.** This central concept may be a single idea or several sub-ideas. For example, suppose the central idea is to explore the fitness director's roles in enhancing staff development. One could specify this central idea, as well as investigate the assumption of specific kinds of roles (e.g., advocate, catalyst, and mentor) by the fitness director, in promoting staff development.

4. **Eliminate words in the purpose statement that suggest a directional orientation to the evaluative study** (e.g., **informing, useful**). Also do not use words such as *relationship* or *comparison,* because they convey a quantitative cause-and-effect or group-comparison methodology.

5. **Identify the method of inquiry used in data collection, analysis, and the process of research.** For example, Geiger and Miko stated:

> Personal oral interview was the methodological procedure chosen for this study. This methodology appears to be one of the most productive means of collecting qualitative data. Many nursing home residents have difficulty reading and writing, consequently expecting them to fill out a questionnaire would be unrealistic. Observations and document collection were also used to supplement the data collection. (1995, p. 132)

Figure 6.3 is a worksheet for developing a qualitative purpose statement. The various points that typically are covered in such a statement are highlighted on this form.

Figure 6.3: Qualitative purpose statement worksheet.

1. The **purpose/intent/goal/objective** (circle one) is to **understand/describe/develop/discover/investigate** (circle one and then identify the concept(s) under examination]:

_____

_____

2. The **design** that will be used is (circle answer):
    Ethnographic study
    Case study
    Content analysis using:
        Public or private (circle one) records
        Relying on primary or secondary (circle one) data
    Historical study relying on primary or secondary data (circle answer)
    Other (specify): _____

3. The **method of inquiry** that will be used is (circle answer):
    Unstructured interview
    Focus group
    Participant observation
    Non-reactive meansures or (circle answer):
        Physical tracing
        Archival records/documents
    Other (specify): _____

4. The **unit of analysis** that will be used for the study (circle answer):
    Individuals
    Groups
    Organizations
    Social artifacts

Significance of the Study Statement

The significance statement establishes a context for why the study is important. Evaluative research studies, using either a qualitative or quantitative framework, need to identify clearly their significance for an organization. Evaluation projects cost money and take time, thus we must be able to answer the following line of questions, "Why bother with the study? So what? What is the importance or worthwhileness of the endeavor?"

Every evaluative research project needs a statement of significance. Since inevitably this statement must be made, our perspective is the sooner it is drafted the better! Some hints for writing a significance statement follow:

1. Discuss the importance of the study in terms of how information or knowledge gained from the study can improve an organization's operations or service delivery. One group of researchers wanted to explore public officials' reactions to park impact fees, noting such fees could infuse public coffers. The urgency for doing such a study was cogently set forth by stating,

> The 'infrastructure crisis' facing many park and recreation agencies are the result of fiscal constraints and physical deterioration of facilities. The curtailment of federal and state grant programs for capital facilities, together with declining tax bases and voter-approved tax limitations, have heightened these crises. (Fletcher, Kaiser, & Groger, 1992, pp. 75-76)

2. Craft the significance statement in the context of some societal issue or dilemma. For instance, Baker and Witt set the significance for their study by reminding us of a serious issue confronting many American youth:

> The recent Carnegie Commission's Report, *A Matter of Time: Risk and Opportunity in the Non-School Hours* (1992), indicated that youth in the United States have a lot of discretionary time. . . . After-school (as well as late-night, weekend, and summer) recreation programs can be one means of providing more structured, better supervised, and more productive use of free time. (1996, p. 60)

Grossman also sets the stage for why he penned his article on therapeutic recreation specialists' work with individuals with HIV infections by reminding us:

> The HIV/AIDS pandemic continues to grow at an alarming rate. In a decade and a half, it has transformed the world. HIV infections continue to be reported from virtually all countries, and around 23 million adults and children have become infected worldwide. . . . International, national, regional recreation and park, and therapeutic recreation organizations, as well as local leisure services providers and therapeutic recreation specialists, have a professional and social responsibility to become involved in the fight against the daunting challenges of HIV/AIDS. (1997, pp. 121-122)

3. Point out how study results can fill in some of the knowledge gaps or deficiencies in our professional literature. Many times, this angle can be combined along with how information gained from the study can be applied in a practical setting. Target an audience and note the significance of the problem to this audience in a way they can understand. A study that set forth significance in terms of both the knowledge base and practical setting application is Scott, Witt, and Foss' evaluative research on the impact of at-risk children participating in an art program.

Besides documenting the positive outcomes and benefits of such programs, studies are needed that identify key or salient program features that seemingly contribute to these outcomes. As recreation professionals know too well, some programs are better than others. Unfortunately, little research has been undertaken to discern what elements within a program contributes to its success (or failure). (1996, p. 44)

Role of Theory

A *theory* is a set of interrelated constructs, definitions, and propositions that presents a systematic view of phenomena by specifying relations among variables with the purpose of explaining natural phenomena or an aspect of life (Babbie, 1998, p. 51; Kerlinger, 1986, p. 9). A theory, then, can serve as the rationale, basis, foundation, or perspective that specifies *how* and *why* variables are interrelated (review Chapter 4). A theory helps us understand, explain or predict the world around us.

Depending on the kind of study undertaken, theory can play a critical part. As introduced in Chapter 5, for many quantitative studies, theory is identified and serves as the basis for explaining the questions, hypotheses, or objectives. On the other hand, for qualitative studies, the predominance and place of theory is often not as pronounced.

It is important to point out, though that no theory is universal. That is, there are always exceptions to the rule. Indeed, these exceptions may lead one to refine a theory in order to take into account the exceptions!

Quantitative Perspective

If a theory is used in a quantitative study it is identified *a priori* and becomes a backdrop or guidepost for directing the study. Again, under these circumstances theory is used deductively—one objective for the evaluative study is to test the theory in order to find out if it applies or explains the situation at hand. The theory becomes a framework for the entire study, an organizing model for the research questions or hypotheses (Creswell, 1994, p. 88). As has already been pointed out (Chapter 5), there are also "informal" theories or conceptual models that the evaluator "pieces together," after reviewing the literature, to identify relevant variables for understanding a problem or issue (see Figure 6.1 for an example of an informal theory or conceptual model that was examined in a study).

Theory sources. The unit of analysis (reviewed earlier in this chapter) will help determine which discipline to turn to in order to find an applicable theory. For instance, if the unit of analysis is individuals, look to the psychology literature. If the units of analysis are groups or organizations, then sociology literature may be helpful. If individuals and groups are the focus of study, then the social psychology literature should prove to be helpful.

The fact of the matter is there are myriad disciplines (e.g., anthropology, economics, business) to turn to in order to find a theory that might guide you in an evaluative research effort. Additionally, a review of literature can oftentimes divulge related prior studies that provide theoretical ideas. Some of the more popular social science theories are identified by Babbie (1995), Linzey and Aronson (1985), Marshall (1996), Sills (1972), and Webb, Beals, and White (1986). Price and Mueller (1986) review some often-used organizational theory ideas. Social, psychological, and social psychological theories related to recreation can be found in the writings of Coyle, Kinney, Riley, and Shank (1991), Dattilo and Kleiber (1993), Iso-Ahola (1980), Iso-Ahola and Hatfield (1986), and Kelly (1993).

Placement of the theory. There are a number of options regarding where theory is introduced and discussed in a quantitative study. That is, theory can be incorporated in the introduction, appear in the literature review, form a separate section that presents an in-depth discussion of the theoretical foundation for the study, or integrated with the interpretation of study results. Where to introduce theory depends on the writing style of the evaluator and the audience for the evaluation study.

Presenting theory or conceptualization visually. To help the reader or listener visualize the interconnections among independent, dependent, and intervening variables, it is helpful to recast theory or conceptual musings into a visual causal model (see Figure 6.1). Duncan (1985) and Creswell (1994, p. 85) provide us with some suggestions on how to create these diagrams:

- Place the independent variables on the left and the dependent variables on the right.
- Use one-way arrow paths leading from each determining variable to each variable dependent on it.
- Indicate the nature of the relationship between variables by inserting valence signs on the paths— positive or negative valences could be used to postulate positive or negative relationships.

Qualitative Perspective

The use of theory in qualitative studies is less clear than it is for quantitative studies. The use of theory in qualitative studies can perhaps best be described as inducing or putting forth a new theory to explain events observed.

One example is *grounded theory,* or theory that is grounded on observations or information from informants (see Glaser & Strauss, 1967). As Patten (1997, p. 27) notes, "Grounded theory is often thought of as evolutionary. That is, it usually is developed during the process of making observations, and it is regularly revised as new observations warrant."

Qualitative research portrays the everyday experiences of individuals by observing and interviewing them and relevant others, thus providing a cultural picture (Fraenkel & Wallen, 1990). Thus, these studies might use a specific causal theory (Kerlinger, 1986) or some existing theory of culture. For instance, structural functionalism theory, symbolic interaction theory, pattern theory, or social exchange theory could be used (see Goetz & LeCompte, 1984; or Neuman, 1991).

Theory bases for qualitative frameworks can be found in a number of resources. Among the primary sources for qualitative studies are the following journals: *International Journal of Qualitative Studies in Education, Qualitative Sociology, American Education Research Journal,* and *Educational Researcher.* Additionally, an excellent general reference on theories for qualitative frameworks is Denzin and Lincoln (1994). Merriam (1988) also is a useful reference tool for those choosing a case study approach.

As introduced in Chapter 5, in qualitative studies, theory is viewed as being inductive. As such, theory may emerge during the data collection and analysis phase of the research, or be identified late in the study in order to interpret the data (e.g., pattern theory, grounded theory).

Framing the Research Question, Objective or Hypothesis

A research question, objective, and hypothesis are essentially a restatement and clarification of the purpose statement. If the purpose of the study is to examine only one variable (e.g., satisfaction level of sport facility users), then inclusion in a written report of a research question, objective, or hypothesis is not necessary.

The choice between using a research question, research objective, or research hypothesis is a matter of style. A *research question* poses a relationship between variables but phrases the relationship in the form of a question (e.g., "What is the relationship between...", "Which is the better way to...", "What happens to people participating in...", " What would happen if..."). A *research objective* examines a relationship between or among variables in a declarative form (e.g., "The objective of the study is to examine the effects of social interaction on..."). And a *research hypothesis* is a declarative statement predicting how two or more variables will be found to be related to each other when they are studied.

A review of literature is replete with examples of each of these approaches. For instance:

- **Research Question:** Is there a relationship between the level of participation in the after- school program (i.e., participant or non-participant, and number of activities attended) and number of absences from school and school tardiness, school grades, self-esteem, and behavior at home and school (Baker & Witt, 1996, p. 64)?

- **Research Objective:** The two objectives of the study were: (1) to conduct additional tests of the reliability and validity of Havitz's sector bias instrument (SBI)—a measure of participants' perceptions of government agencies and commercial businesses and (2) to examine the consistency of perceptions as measured by the SBI with site choices for various recreational activities (Havitz, 1991, p. 2).

- **Research Hypothesis:** It was hypothesized that children participating in the school district and parks and recreation department sponsored after-school program would show positive changes in school attendance, grades, behavior (both at school and home), and self-esteem, and that they would significantly differ from individuals who did not participate in the after-school program (Baker & Witt, 1996, p. 64).

Which you use in a study—a research question, objective, or hypothesis— is a matter of personal choice. All three approaches are acceptable in the scientific community. Typically, research questions, objectives and hypotheses are associated with quantitative research; whereas research questions only are associated with qualitative research.

Before progressing, we feel it important to reiterate once again a point made in Chapter 1. Regarding the process for making decisions about the purpose of an evaluation, Patten (1987, p. 75) reminds us that user-focused evaluation is shaped by the information needs of the people for whom the evaluation information is being collected. The evaluator works with the stakeholders in order to determine the relevant evaluation question(s). The identified evaluation questions that emerge always should be verified to their necessity by asking, "What difference would that information make?" or "What would the decision-makers do if they had an answer to that question?" (Patten, 1987, p. 76).

Research Question, Objective, and Hypothesis in Quantitative Research

In quantitative studies, research questions, objectives, and hypotheses represent restatements of the purpose of the study. In survey research projects, these restatements typically are in the form of research questions or objectives (e.g., "Does stress affect the leisure satisfaction of university students?"); in quasi-experiments and non-experiments they are hypotheses. Research questions, objectives, and hypotheses can present a comparison between two or more groups in terms of a dependent variable such as, "Is there a difference in the self concept of individuals who participate in the midnight basketball league as compared to those who do not?" Research questions, objectives, and hypotheses can also examine the relationship between independent and dependent variables (for example, "Do individuals playing midnight basketball, over the course of six months, experience changes in their self esteem?").

Types of questions. Hedrick, Bickman, and Rog (1993, p. 25) provided a typology for classifying research questions that addresses current or past conditions into four categories: descriptive, normative, correlative, and impact questions. An adaptation of this typology to recreation is presented in Figure 6.4.

Descriptive questions are straightforward questions dealing with "What is?", "What was?", and "How?" The question being posed requires gathering data that are descriptive in nature, designed to present information on what exists or what is happening.

Normative questions require comparing *what is* to some standard. The standard may come from any number of sources including professional standards and program goals.

Figure 6.4: Types of applied research questions related to leisure.

Descriptive Questions:

What are the in-service training needs of volunteers in the Seniors Division of Montgomery County Recreation Department?

How prevalent is boredom among students at Gallaudet University?

How many latchkey children are there in Miami?

Normative Questions:

Are the methods being used to teach swimming at the Rockville community pool in conformance with American Red Cross standards?

To what extent are protocol standards being met by the Therapeutic Recreation Service of the Traumatic Brain Injury unit at the National Rehabilitation Hospital?

To what extend is the program goal of 1% loss in body fat over a three-month period being realized by enrollees of the Ponce de Leon Fitness Club?

Correlative Questions:

Is there a relationship between number of minutes of workout per week and weight of adult male members at the Coral Gables Fitness and Racquet Club?

For the pre-retirement education enrollees, what is the relationship among leisure values, knowledge of leisure resources in the community, and attitude of significant others towards leisure and the participants' leisure satisfaction?

Is there an association between offering snacks at scheduled recreational activities at Autumnfield nursing home and attendance at these events?

Impact Questions Dealing with Absolute Effects:

Does participation in a leisure education program decrease the probability of subsequent drug abuse by outpatient psychiatric patients at Chestnut Lodge?

Does lack of knowledge about litter rules and number of trash containers located along the hiking trail at Magnolia Gardens increase the likelihood of hikers littering?

Impact Questions Dealing with Relative Effects:

Which type of training, classroom, or practicum experience, is most effective in increasing gerontological knowledge of recreation majors at Indiana University?

What is the relative contribution of two factors, lack of knowledge about litter rules and number of trash containers, in leading Appalachian Trail hikers to litter?

Correlative questions ask whether certain things or entities are related. As will be discussed in Chapter 15, correlational questions examine the likelihood or chance there is a relationship between or among variables.

Impact questions examine *what causes* or *caused what*. There are two types of impact questions: absolute effectiveness and relative effectiveness. *Absolute effectiveness* questions deal with ascertaining simple effects; whereas *relative effectiveness* questions compare two or more alternatives.

Two points should be made about the typology presented in Figure 6.4. First, although this classification of questions comprises the core of applied research, it is not all-encompassing. That is, the orientation of this typology is on current or past conditions. Research questions can also be formulated that are projective in nature (e.g., "What is the forecast for next year's demand for aquatic facilities in Montgomery County?"). Second, the classification system does not involve cost questions related to simple costs (e.g., "What is the cost of keeping the La Piscina swimming pool open 12 hours on Sundays?"), cost-benefit analysis, or cost-effect analysis (the latter two costs were introduced in Chapter 1 and will be covered in-depth in Chapter 15). Both of these areas, projection questions and cost-related questions, certainly can be important areas to delve into when formulating a research question.

Principles for developing questions, objectives, and hypotheses. Principles for developing quantitative research questions, objectives, and hypotheses are (Creswell, 1994, pp. 73-77; Black, 1993, p.31):

1. **If at all possible, develop (by deducing) questions, objectives, or hypotheses from theory.** For example, based on the activity theory, it could be postulated that social interactions are positively related to life satisfaction.

2. **Hypotheses, however, might emanate from educated guess-work.** According to Kidder & Judd (1986, p.13) among the inspirational sources for such *naive hypothesis* are:

- **Authority** = Authorities or experts can provide insights on the hypotheses that could be examined. Using experts to help identify "good" hypotheses is wise as long as the person is indeed an expert in the area under consideration, can critically assess the situation, and develop creative and applicable hypotheses.

- **Consensus** = Consensus-driven hypotheses emerge from the wisdom of peers or users of our services. For instance, suppose the issue is how to curb graffiti on recreational center properties. In order to identify hypothetical approaches, help might be sought from an academic person who is an authority on the issue. Equally, if not more informative, is to ask center staff and teen users for their ideas.

- **Observation** = In this approach, initial conjectures are compared to observations. For instance, suppose it is initially believed that prejudice toward individuals with physical disabilities is caused by a lack of personal acquaintance with members of this group. To learn whether this hypothesis is accurate, you might conduct some informal interview with various acquaintances (colleagues, peers, or patrons) asking about their friendships with persons with physical disabilities. You then can find out if your initial thoughts about a person's degree of prejudice toward the special population group seem to be related to the number of friendships she had with individuals with physical disabilities. If there appears to be a correlation, you could then proceed with formal adoption of the hypothesis and proceed with the study.

3. Unless some compelling reason can be put forth, consider using variables other than demographic variables (e.g., age, income, education, socioeconomic status) for independent variables. Demographic variables, if used at all, typically are used as intervening variables. For instance, how does gender temper the benefits derived from participating in an exercise program? And what demographic factors are associated with mental improvement when bibliotherapy is used?

4. Use the same word order in writing the questions, objectives, or hypotheses. Similar to the advice given for drafting a quantitative-related purpose statement, order the variables by beginning with the independent variable(s) and concluding with the dependent variable(s). In other words, name variables in the order in which they occur. An example using this advice is, "There is a positive relationship between leisure activity participation and mental health of older women." Compare this statement to, "Lower mental health will be experienced by older adult women who are inactive." The problem with the latter statement is that temporal order is reversed. The impression given is that mental health affects activity level, when in truth the reverse is being speculated.

5. Consider using the alternative hypothesis form (instead of the null form) and make the choice of directionality based on the audience for the evaluation study. Again, a *hypothesis* is a conjectural statement, a tentative proposition about the relationship between two or more variables (Kerlinger, 1986). The traditional *null hypothesis* is written in the format that there is no relationship between or among the variables (e.g., "There is no relationship between aerobic activity and body self-image."). An *alternative hypothesis* pinpoints directionality by specifying the nature of the relationship between the noted variables (as explained earlier in this chapter). Even though it can be argued from a statistical point of view that it is better to write hypothesis from the null vantage point, the literature and/or practice typically provide insights into directionality. In between a null and alternative hypothesis is a *non-directional hypothesis* that is framed in a non-directional way. That is, it is speculated that a difference will exist but the exact nature of that difference is not made clear.

Examples of a directional (or alternative) hypothesis and non-directional hypothesis are:

- **Directional Hypothesis or an Alternative Hypothesis (based on Activity Theory):** It is hypothesized that older individuals who are more active, relative to those who are not, will experience better mental health.

  The directional hypothesis speculates a relationship exists between two variables or activity level and mental health. This is considered a directional hypothesis because it speculates which group will be higher or have more of something.

- **Non-Directional Hypothesis:** It is hypothesized that the social psychological states of nursing home residents who are involved in video game play will be different from those who do not.

6. **If making a comparison, the elements to be compared should be identified.** For instance, the hypothesis, "Female competitive collegiate swimmers, relative to other groups, have an elevated profile of moods state" is unclear. An improved version [because comparative groups are identified] would be, "Female varsity swimmers, compared to collegiate female recreational swimmers or physically inactive collegiate females, will have a higher profile of moods state"(Riddick, 1984, p. 162).

7. **Because most hypotheses deal with groups as the unit of measurement, plural forms of a hypotheses should be used.** Not applying this principle would result in the hypothesis, "There is a direct relationship between an older woman's activity level and her level of mental health." The terms *older woman's* and *her level* are singular. This problem

---

Figure 6.5: Example of a grand tour question and subquestions.

Grand-Tour Question:

What is the La Flaca fitness club doing to maximize use of its inside tennis bubble facility?

Subordinate Questions:

Is the rate charged to fitness club members to add on tennis privileges competitive?

Are rates charged for member's guests to use the tennis facility competitive?

Do fitness club members support the continued operation of the tennis bubble?

From users point of view, how can the tennis facility be improved?

---

would be corrected in the following improved version, "There is a direct relationship between older women and their level of mental health."

8. **Do not use the words "significant" or "significance" in the hypothesis.** These terms, by convention, are reserved for the results of tests of statistical significance (see Chapter 11).

Research Questions in Qualitative Research

Research questions associated with qualitative studies usually take two forms: a grand-tour question which could be considered as a guiding hypothesis followed by several sub-questions. A *grand-tour question* is a statement of the question being examined in the study. This question is cast in general or broad terms so as not to limit inquiry. Typically a study will have one or two grand-tour questions. These questions become topics that are explored in interviews, observations, and/or archival material. It is important to note that the research questions can evolve and change during the study—these questions can be under continual review and reformulation. Figure 6.5 presents an example of a grand-tour question and subquestions.

Creswell (1994, pp. 70-71) shares some hints when formulating these grand tour questions including:

1. **Begin the grand-tour question with the words *what* or *how*.** Then tell the reader that the study will do one of the following: discover, explain or seek to understand, explore a process, or describe the experience.

2. **Write questions that use non-directional wording.** The questions should describe rather than relate variables or compare groups. Do not use words that suggest or infer a quantitative study or words with a directional orientation such as *affect, influence, impact, determine, cause,* and *relate.*

3. **Remember the question format will probably relate to the specific qualitative framework used for the study.** For example:

- **Ethnographic question may relate to a proposed taxonomy.** An example an ethnographic question is, "How could the social interactions of in-line skating program participants be classified?"
- **Grounded theory question may relate to procedures in the data analysis.** An illustration of a grounded theory question is, "What are the categories to emerge from interactions between tennis clinic instructors and students?"
- **Phenomenological question is stated broadly, without reference to the existing literature or typology.** An example of such a question is, "What is it like for a therapeutic recreational practitioner to work with individuals hospitalized in a psychiatric facility?"

Main Points

- In designing the focus of a study, be clear about the unit of analysis. What is it you want to analyze—individuals, groups, organizations, or social artifacts? If you study one unit of analysis and then impute the findings to another unit of analysis, you have committed an *ecological fallacy.*

- Variables are addressed in purpose statements, as well as research questions, objectives, and/or hypotheses. A *variable* names a specific phenomena or construct (such as a trait or characteristic).

- Most evaluative research studies deal with three kinds of variables or the *dependent variable(s)* (the variable you want to understand, explain, or predict), *independent variable(s)* (the variable you believe is influencing or affecting the dependent variable), and an *intervening variable(s)* (or a mediating influence between the independent and dependent variables—technically mediating variables are independent variables also).

- A purpose statement identifies the variable(s) that will be studied. If the study uses a quantitative framework, the nature of the relationship between the specified independent and dependent variables should be stated (either by comparing and/or relating the variables under examination). If the study uses a qualitative framework, do not suggest directionality between/among the noted variables.

- The significance statement provides a context for the study by identifying how the study can improve an organization's operations or service delivery, a pressing societal issue or dilemma, and/or how the study can fill in some of the knowledge gaps or deficiencies in the professional literature.

- A theory or conceptual road map can provide a perspective of how and why variables are interrelated.

- Research questions, objectives, and/or hypotheses are restatements to the purpose of the study and take on unique forms. That is, in quantitative studies, a research question poses the relationship between variables in the form of a question, an objective identifies a relationship between two or more variables in declarative form, and a hypothesis is a declarative statement predicting how two or more variables are related.

- A hypothesis can be written in one of three forms: null, non-directional, and alternative. Whenever possible, consider using the latter form because the literature and/or practice typically provide insights into directionality.

Study Questions

1. What should be specified in a *purpose statement*?

2. What is meant by *unit of analysis*? What are the common types used in recreation research?

3. If the leisure behaviors of students enrolled in your measurement and evaluation class were used to make generalizations about the leisure behaviors of students at your university, would an *ecological fallacy* be committed? Why or why not?

4. What is a *variable*? *Independent variable*? *Dependent variable*?

5. What is a principle for writing a "good" quantitative purpose statement? A "good" qualitative purpose statement?

6. What is a *theory*? How does it help us in conducting evaluative research in recreation settings?

7. Why is a significance statement important?

8. Write examples of a *research question* (for a quantitative study and a qualitative study) and a *research objective*.

9. What is a *hypothesis*? Give an example of a *null hypothesis* and an *alternative hypothesis*.

References

Babbie, E. (1998). *The practice of social research* (8th ed.). Belmont, CA: Wadsworth.

Baker, D., & Witt, P. (1996). Evaluation of the impact of two after-school programs. *Journal of Park and Recreation Administration, 14*(3), 60-81.

Black, T. (1993). *Evaluating social science research: An introduction.* Thousand Oaks, CA: Sage Publications.

Coyle, C., Kinney, W.B., Riley, B., & Shank, J. (Eds.). (1991). *Benefits of therapeutic recreation: A consensus view.* Ravensdale, WA: Idyll Arbor, Inc.

Creswell, J. (1994). *Research design: Qualitative & quantitative approaches.* Thousand Oaks, CA: Sage Publications.

Dattilo, J., & Kleiber, D. (1993). Psychological perspectives for therapeutic recreation research: The psychology of enjoyment. In M. Malkin & C. Howe, *Research in therapeutic recreation: Concepts and methods* (pp. 57-76). State College, PA: Venture Publishing.

Denzin, N., & Lincoln, Y. (1994). *Handbook of qualitative research.* Thousand Oaks, CA: Sage Publications.

Derezotes, D. (1995). Evaluation of the Late Nite basketball project. *Child and Adolescent Social Work Journal, 12*, 33-49.

DeSchriver, M., & Riddick, C., (1991). Effects of watching aquariums on elders' stress. *Anthrozoos, 4*, 44-48.

Duncan, O.D. (1985). Path analysis: Sociological examples. In H.M. Blalock (Ed.), *Causal models in the social sciences* (2nd ed.),(pp. 55-79). Hawthorne, New York: Aldine De Gruyer.

Fletcher, J., Kaiser, R., & Groger, S. (1992). An assessment of the importance and performance of park impact fees in funding park and recreation infrastructure. *Journal of Park and Recreation Administration, 10*, 75-87.

Frankel, J.R., & Wallen, P.E. (1990). *How to design and evaluate in education (2nd ed.)*. New York: McGraw-Hill.

Geiger, C., & Miko, P. (1995). Meaning of recreation/leisure activities to elderly nursing home residents: A qualitative study. *Therapeutic Recreation Journal, 29*, 131-138.

Glaser, B., & Strauss, A. (1967). *The discovery of grounded theory*. Chicago: Aldine.

Goetz, J.P., & LeCompte, M.D. (1984). *Ethnography and qualitative design in educational research*. New York: Academic Press.

Green, B., & Chalip, L. (1997). Enduring involvement in youth soccer: The socialization of parent and child. *Journal of Leisure Research, 29*, 61-77.

Grossman, A. (1997). Concern, compassion, and community: Facing the daunting worldwide chalenges of HIV/AIDS. *Therapeutic Recreation Journal, 31*, 121-129.

Guillemin, F., Constant, F., Collin, J., & Boulange, M. (1994). Short- and long-term effects of spa therapy on chronic low back pain. *British Journal of Rheumatology, 33*, 148-151.

Havitz, M. (1991). Measuring sector biases in recreation participants. *Journal of Park and Recreation Administration, 9*, 1-17.

Hedrick, T., Bickman, L., & Rog, D. (1993). *Applied research design: A practical guide*. Newbury Park, CA: Sage Publications.

Iso-Ahola, S. (1980). The social psychology of leisure and recreation. Dubuque, IA: Wm. C. Brown.

Iso-Ahola, S., & Hatfield, B. (1986). *Psychology of sports: A social psychological approach*. Dubuque, IA: Wm. C. Brown.

Kelly, J. (Ed.) (1993). *Activity and aging: Staying involved in later life*. Newbury, CA: Sage Publications.

Kerlinger, F.N. (1986). *Foundations of behavioral research (3 rd ed.)*. New York: Holt, Rinehart, & Winston.

Kidder, L. &, Judd, C. (1986). *Research methods in social relations*. New York: Holt, Rinehard, & Winston.

Linzey, G., & Aronson, E. (Eds.) (1985). *Handbook of social psychology (3rd ed.)*. New York: Random House.

Marshall, V. (1996). The state of theory in aging and the social sciences. In R. Binstock & L. George (Eds.), *Handbook of aging and the social sciences* (pp. 12-30). New York: Academic Press.

Merriam, S. B. (1988). *Case study research in education: A qualitative approach*. San Francisco: Jossey-Bass.

Neuman, W.L. (1991). *Social research methods: Qualitative and quantitative approaches*. Boston: Allyn & Bacon.

Patten, M. (1987). *Creative evaluation* (2nd ed.). Newbury, CA: Sage Publications.

Patten, M. (1997). *Understanding research methods: An overview of essentials*. Los Angeles: Pyrczak Publishing.

Price, J.L., & Mueller, C.W. (1986). *Handbook of organizational measurements*. New York: Longman.

Riddick, C. (1984). Comparative psychological profiles of three groups of female collegians: Competitive swimmers, recreational swimmers, and inactive swimmers. *Journal of Sport Behavior, 7*, 160-174.

Riddick, C., DeSchriver, M., & Weissinger, E. (1991, October). *A methodological review of research in Journal of Leisure Research from 1983 through 1987*. Paper presented at the National Recreation & Park Association's Leisure Research Symposium, Baltimore, MD.

Riddick, C., Spector, S., & Drogin, E. (1986). The effects of video game play on the emotional states and affiliative behavior of nursing home residents. *Activities, Adaptation & Aging, 8*, 95-108.

Scott, D., Witt, P., & Foss, M. (1996). Evaluation of the impact of the Dougherty arts center's creativity club on children at-risk. *Journal of Park and Recreation Administration, 14*(3), 41-59.

Searle, M., & Mahon, M. (1993). The effects of a leisure education program on selected social-psychological variables: A three-month follow-up investigation. *Therapeutic Recreation Journal, 27*, 9-21.

Sills, D. (Ed.) (1972). *International encyclopedia of the social sciences*. New York: MacMillan.

Webb, W.H., Beals, A.R., & White, C.M. (1986). *Sources of information in the social sciences: A guide to the literature* (3rd ed.). Chicago: American Library Association.

CHAPTER 7

Designs Used in Evaluative Research

What Will I Learn in This Chapter?
I'll be able to:

1. Define internal and external validity.

2. Identify threats to internal and external validity.

3. Distinguish among the quantitative affiliated designs or experimental, quasi-experimental, pre-experimental, and non-experimental designs.

4. Recall the broad classes of questions surveys can address.

5. Explain criteria used to judge rigor in qualitative designs.

6. Distinguish the appropriate uses of such qualitative designs as ethnographic study, case study, content analysis, and historical study.

Similar to pie making, where more than one good recipe exists, there is also no one "best" or most suitable way of designing an evaluative research study. Many designs are used in parks, recreation, and sport service settings. For example, there are quasi-experimental designs and pre-experimental designs, as well as such non-experimental designs as surveys, correlational designs, ethnographic study, case study, content analysis, and historical study. Factors to consider in choosing a design include (Weiss, 1972, p. 4):

- Information needs of the users of the study.
- Program setting constraints—time, people, and money.
- Protection of respondents.

When assessing leisure service outcomes or impacts, one overriding principle assists with choosing a design. That is, the more rigorous the research design, the more plausible the resulting estimate.

This chapter is divided into two major sections. That is, the first section addresses designs associated with a quantitative frameworks. The second section discusses designs related to a qualitative framework.

Designs Related to a Quantitative Framework

This section is divided into three parts: internal validity, external validity, and the designs related to a quantitative framework and typically used in evaluative research are reviewed.

Internal Validity

Most evaluative research studies in our profession center on examining a form of rigor known as internal validity. If a decision is going to be made on whether a recreation program has any merits or desirable effects, the focus is said to be on internal validity. Basically, *internal validity* studies focus on determining whether or not a program works (its *efficiency*, or *summative or behavioral objectives approach*). Internal validity also can determine whether a recreation program achieves a certain standard (*quality assurance or accreditation approach*) or how it compares to other programs (*comparative focus or a systems approach*). The issue in internal validity is correctly relating a program to noted outcomes.

Another perspective for deciding on which design to use is to examine where the program is in its life cycle. It has been suggested that in the early stages of a program, the evaluation emphasis should be on internal validity—that is, to identify programs that work under at least some conditions. Later on in the life cycle of a program, the evaluation can shift to examining generalizability, and thus a design that comes closest to maximizing external validity should be used (Rossi & Freeman, 1993, p. 257).

If internal validity is the focus of a study, then it is not imperative that the design chosen be one that maximizes ability to generalize to a larger population. In essence, a study focus on internal validity is being done in order to have reason to believe that the program accounts for the observed change(s). Internal validity addresses the degree that changes noted in the respondents are due to the program. When these changes emerge due to something else, then the internal validity of the study is "threatened." At the very least these threats can be thought of as becoming *confounded* with the treatment as an explanation for the noted changes. The worst case scenario is that these threats single-handedly become potential explanations for the observed changes. Internal validity hinges upon primarily the design of the study and, to a lesser degree, issues related to the collection of data.

Threats to internal validity. When something other than a true experimental design (a design described later on) is used, then threats to internal validity exist. Campbell and Stanley (1963) have identified eight kinds of "outside" or non-program variables that can affect the outcomes of quasi-experimental, pre-experimental, and non-experimental designs. In essence, any one of these sources (technically known as *sources of confounding influence*) can be responsible, rather than the leisure service under study, for any changes that are noted in the participants. These sources of confounding influence are known as *threats to the internal validity* of the study. The threats that exist to the internal validity of the designs commonly used in leisure research are identified in Figure 7.1.

1. **Maturation.** People change due to natural development—they become older, wiser, experience weight change, etc. These *endogenous, maturational* changes happen with or without program participation. For example, did the aerobic program really improve teenage girls' self-concept or did the noted changes occur due to a natural age-related transition or some other factor—like receipt of a "glowing" report card or having a new boyfriend? Or perhaps participation in a "Post Heart Attack Recovery Club" is being attributed to noted physiological improvements. Then, again, the noted changes could have been brought about by natural recovery. If nature is responsible for changes, then these maturation factors have become a threat to the internal validity of the study's findings.

2. **History.** Outside or environmental events can affect change between the pretest and the posttest (terms that will be described more in depth later on). Something other than what was intended happens to the participants between the first test or observation (*pretest*) and the posttest. This "something" produces an effect(s) that can be confused with that produced by the program and/or other independent variable(s). An example of historical events could include member(s) of the experimental group watching a television program on a subject related to the program intervention. Suppose, for example, individuals are enrolled in a stress–reduction class and several weeks after the class many of these persons watch a series of television programs on the same topic. The question arises whether the class or the television series is responsible for attitude and/or behavioral changes in how the participants handle stress.

3. **Testing.** Testing can be a threat to either the internal or external validity of a study. Taking a test for the first time can affect performance the next time the same test is taken (technically known as *pretest sensitization*). Respondents become aware and sensitized to the questions—by the second time around they have "learned" the answers as a result of this increased sensitivity. For instance, suppose a group of persons receive a pretest on prejudice towards individuals with a physical disability. Then this group experiences a treatment that is designed to lessen this sort of prejudice. How the respondents act to the treatment may be affected by the experience of taking the pretest. That is, having to think about prejudice while taking or even after taking the pretest might change respondents' sensitivity and receptivity to the treatment. Such a *testing effect* becomes a problem if we want to generalize about how the treatment will work in the population if the population will not be given a pretest.

4. **Instrumentation.** Changes in the calculation of measuring instruments (an unreliable scale or skin–fold caliper, for example) can occur between pretest and posttest. Additionally, changes in the observers can become a threat to internal validity. For instance,

perhaps the judges' observation abilities changed (as opposed to the individual participants chang-ing) from pretest to posttest. In other words, the judges have become more or less skilled at judging.

5. **Statistical regression.** If groups have been selected on the basis of extreme scores (the "best" or the "worse"), then the likelihood of change is inevitable (i.e., they cannot get any "better" or "worse").

6. **Experimental mortality.** Experimental mortality is differential loss (or *attrition*) of respondents or study participants from the *experimental group* (the group offered the recre-ation program) and the *control group* (the group the recreation program is being withheld from—both of these terms will be addressed later on). "Drop-outs" from one group can be markedly different from those remaining in the group and/or the other comparison group. One seldom knows whether those staying with a program to its end are those who may have needed the program most or least.

7. **Selection bias.** People involved in the study have been chosen not on the basis of randomization; instead, "intact" groups are chosen. For example, suppose the efficacy of a consumer–relations training program is being evaluated. Staff at the Aspen Hill Fitness Club have been chosen to serve as the experimental group, whereas staff at the Takoma Park Fit-ness Club serve as the control group. Using these intact groups results in the strong possibil-ity that the two groups are not initially the same in all important respects. The nagging question becomes whether any significant changes noted in the experimental group are due to the consumer-relations training program or original group characteristics. Maybe staff in the experimental group had higher educational attainment, or maybe staff as a whole had worked longer at a fitness center relative to the staff in the control group.

8. **Selection can interact with all the other threats** (noted in points 1 through 7 above). For example, there is selection-history interaction when members of the experimental and control group are not chosen randomly and the two groups are not alike in background. Maybe the camp counselors at Camp Ton-A-Wanda (the experimental group) are all returning counse-lors, whereas most of the counselors at Camp Carolina are first time counselors.

Hierarchy of design options to maximize internal validity. When the overall purpose of the study is on the internal validity of findings, then a number of designs can be used (Note: The various kinds of designs will be discussed in the latter half of this chapter). The follow-ing designs, listed in order of preference for maximizing internal validity, are (Green, 1976):

Choice 1: True experimental design.
Choice 2: Experimental design in a convenience sample.
Choice 3: Experimental design minus pretests.
Choice 4: Experimental design minus pretests in a convenience sample.
Choice 5: Quasi-experimental design with matched comparison group rather than

random assignment to obtain a true control group.

Choice 6: Quasi-experimental design with matched comparison groups without pretests.

Choice 7: Quasi-experimental design with pretests but no control group.

Choice 8: Choice 7 in a convenience sample.

Choice 9: Quasi-experimental design with no pretests and no control group.

Choice 10: Choice 9 in a convenience sample.

External Validity

Another concern dealing with rigor in quantitative designs is external validity. What is external validity? *External validity* is the ability to generalize a study's findings to the "real" world or beyond the group sampled (Babbie, 1998, p. 244). It boils down to the amount of confidence one has to be able to say, "What I found in this particular study is likely to be found elsewhere." External validity is concerned with to whom and under what circumstances can the results be generalized and replicated elsewhere (Patten, 1997, p. 83).

When should an evaluation focus on external validity? Green's advice is, "If the evaluation is intended to provide evidence for the general effectiveness of a program or method, then external validity or generalizability of findings is paramount" (1976, p. 43). Other times external validity should be the focus for an evaluation are when decisions are being made on whether to duplicate a program, continue a program, or abandon a program or educational method altogether. And external validity should be foremost in choosing a design when the program being evaluated has been designed to remedy or manage a very serious condition or when a controversial program is under scrutiny.

Being able to *generalize* is affected by a number of factors. In order to generalize, one needs to select a sample in such a way it can be characterized as an unbiased sample of the population that will be or actually are the clients for the program under scrutiny. It would make little sense to test a new method of teaching swimming in classes consisting of developmentally disabled individuals if the program is designed for use in "average" or non-disabled individuals. Similarly, evaluation of a pilot or test program administered by dedicated and skillful staff may not be generalizable to programs administered by workers who do not share the same levels of commitment and skill. A number of factors can be responsible for compromising or distorting the external validity of a study. Some of these threats to external validity are identified below.

Threats to external validity. Any number of things (or sources of confounding influence) can limit our ability to generalize noted findings to the sample's population. Seven of these *threats to external validity* are summarized below (Campbell & Stanley, 1963). External validity threats that exist for the popular designs used in evaluation research are noted in Figure 7.1.

1. **Selection bias.** If a sample is selected in a biased manner, our ability to generalize to the population from which the sample was drawn is limited. Uncontrolled selection (or self

Figure 7.1: Threats to invalidity for selected experimental, quasi-experimental, and pre-experimental designs.[1]

Sources of Invalidity
Selected Experimental, Quasi-Experimental, & Pre-Experimental Designs

Threats to Validity	Rigorous Control		Partial Control			Little Control	
	1[a]	2[a]	3[a]	4[a]	5[a]	6[a]	7[a]
I. External Validity							
Selection bias	+	-	-	-	-	-	-
Reactive effects	?	?	?	?	?	?	?
Testing	?	?	?	?	?		
Multiple treatment interference				-			
Inadequate operational definition dependent variable		?	?	?	?	?	
Hawthorne effect	?	?	?	?	?	?	?
Interaction (selection with Hawthorne effect, etc.)	+	?	?	-	-	-	-
I.I Internal Validity							
Maturation	+	+	+	+	-	-	-
History	+	+	?	-	-	-	-
Testing	?	?	?	?	?		
Instrumentation	?	?	?	?	?		
Statistical regression	+	+	?	+	?	?	?
Experimental mortality	+	+	-	-	-	+	+
Selection bias	+	-	-	-	-	-	-
Interaction (selection with history, etc.)	+	+	-	+	-	-	-

[a] Names of Designs 1 to 7 are: 1 = Pretest-Posttest Randomized Control Group (experimental design)   2 = Solomon Randomized Four-Group   3 = Nonequivalent (non-randomized) Control Group
4 = Equivalent Time Series   5 = One-Group Pretest-Posttest   6 = One-Time PostTest Shot   7 = Static-Group Comparison

Note. A minus (-) symbol indicates a lack of control, a plus (+) symbol indicates control of a factor, a question mark (?) suggests there is some source of concern, and a blank indicates that the factor is not relevant.

[1] Adapted from *Understanding educational research* (4th ed.) (p. 280), by D. Van Dalen (1979), New York: McGraw–Hill.

selection into the program) often results in preexisting differences between those enrolled in a program and otherwise eligible persons who do not enroll. Under these circumstances, outcomes of the program may be accounted for by selection and not really attributable to the intervention.

2. **Reactive effects of experimental arrangements.** If the experimental setting is different from the natural setting in which the population usually operates or lives, the effects observed in the experimental setting may not generalize to the natural setting. For instance, responses given or recorded inside a laboratory booth about footwork and strategies for winning at tennis may not be the same behaviors demonstrated outside on a tennis court.

3. **Testing.** Again, initial testing, acting as a sensitizing agent, can affect performance on subsequent testing.

4. **Multiple treatment interference.** If respondents are exposed to several different programs or activities it becomes difficult to "tease" how each program is uniquely affecting them. In other words, discerning which treatment is the determining factor to the noted changes will be difficult. For example, if "troubled" youth experience a two-week residential high-risk adventure program consisting of bungee jumping, repelling, water rafting, etc., it becomes difficult to monitor how each specific program element affects teenagers' mental and social health.

5. **Inadequate operational definition of dependent variable.** If the measure or instrument chosen to gauge the dependent variable under study is no good, the result noted in the experimental situation will not be seen in real life (this concept will be discussed in greater detail in Chapter 9). An example of an inadequate operational definition of a dependent variable is to ask respondents, in a paper and pencil test, if they aspire for a white– or blue–collar job in recreation. This approach for measuring career choice may not make sense to the respondent—he may not have a clue of what is being asked.

6. **Hawthorne effect.** It has been found that when individuals know they are part of an experiment their performance, behavior, and/or self-reported disclosures will be altered–the so-called *Hawthorne effect*. These kind of alterations are technically known as *contamination*. Medical research, in order to get around this problem, often uses a *double-blind design*. In this design, no one (neither the researchers collecting data nor the respondents themselves) know who is in the experimental group and who is in the control group. A double-blind design, however, in social science research, is typically impossible to adopt.

7. **Selection can interact with any of the extraneous variables (noted in 1-6 above for external validity).** For example, there can be a selection-Hawthorne interaction effect when lifeguards volunteer to be in a study set up to evaluate the effectiveness of a new lifeguard training program. If observations are made of lifeguards (both those in the experimental and control groups) while on duty, it will be difficult to ascertain if any noted changes over time are due to self-selection into the study, changed behaviors because the lifeguards know they

are being studied, or because of what was learned in the new course.

Hierarchy of design options to maximize external validity. According to Green (1976, p. 44), when the study's emphasis is on maximizing external validity, the two elements that must be present in the design chosen are posttest and representative sample (terms that will be discussed shortly). Thus, the following designs, in descending order of preference, will help obtain external validity in terms of study findings:

Choice 1: True experimental design.

Choice 2: Experimental design minus pretests.

Choice 3: Quasi-experimental design with matched control group(s).

Choice 4: Quasi-experimental design with no control group.

Choice 5: Quasi-experimental design with no pretest and no control group.

Choice 6: The foregoing choices without a representative sample.

Quantitative Designs

Designs related to a quantitative framework can fall into one of four categories. That is, there is the experimental research design, quasi-experimental designs, pre-experimental designs, and non-experimental designs.

Experimental research design. One of the fundamental distinctions in research is whether the design is an "experimental," "quasi-experimental," "pre-experimental," or "non-experimental" design. The *sine qua non* or grand master design in science is the classic experimental design or the pretest-posttest randomized control group design. There are five elements that comprise an experimental research design:

1. *Random selection* **from the study population study.** Essentially, this means everyone in the population has an equal chance of being selected for the study. For example, if a school district were interested in evaluating a new aerobics program for senior-high-aged students, then all students enrolled in the district's high schools would have an equal chance of being selected for involvement in the study (Chapter 8 explains random selection in greater detail).

2. *Experimental group* **(or the group offered or exposed to the program) and** *control group* **(or the group that does not participate in the program).** The program is viewed as being physically manipulated or administered.

3. *Random assignment* **to either the experimental group or the control group.** That is, everyone selected for the study has an equal chance of being assigned to either the experimental or control group.

4. **Pretest.** *Pretest* or baseline data are collected on the two groups (experimental group and control group) before the intervention is introduced or experienced.

5. **Posttest.** *Posttest* data are collected on members of both the experimental and

control groups after the program is completed by the experimental group. Pretest data are then compared to posttest observation to find out if the treatment "caused" or affected change in the individual.

Any combination of these five elements associated with experimental research design may or may not be present in a design chosen for an evaluation study. Figure 7.2 summarizes notations that are used schematic representations of the various designs.

In truth, evaluators seldom are able to adopt and execute an experimental design. Typi-

---

Figure 7.2: Summary of notation rules used to schematically represent a design.

RS = Random selection

RA= Random assignment to separate groups

X = Program intervention

O = Observation or measurement that is recorded on a time line; for instance, OXO means a pretest occurred before (or to the left of) the program intervention and a posttest occurred after (or to the right of) the program intervention

---

cally, random selection or random assignment are two stumbling blocks. To a lesser extent, getting or asking people to serve as a control group can also be an obstacle. For instance, there may be no "extra" people to serve in this capacity (all the eligible people want or demand to be in the experimental group) or individuals will not accept *delayed acceptance* into the program (that is, in phase 1 they serve as part of the control group, and later on in phase 2 they become part of a second experimental group and receive the intervention). Or it may be that program administrators or managers feel, from an ethical or political viewpoint, they cannot "deny" or "delay" service to anyone.

Besides being virtually impossible to execute, there is one other criticism of the classical experimental design. That is, the changes observed in the experimental group may be the result of a combination of the pretest and treatment (known as *pretest sensitization*) rather than solely the treatment or intervention alone.

In the final consideration, evaluators typically must bypass the "perfect" design and instead choose a "good enough" design. The alternatives to the experimental design are many though not equal. The gold standard is the classical experimental design. The use of any other design results in having to decide and acknowledge the trade-offs that have been made. Some of the designs produce more credible estimates of impact. The options also vary in practicality, cost, and levels of technical skills required to implement the design (Rossi & Freeman, 1993, p. 220).

127

Quasi-experimental designs. Unlike the experimental design, quasi-experimental designs are practical. In quasi-experimental designs control and experimental groups are used in the study, but study participants (or *subjects*) are not randomly assigned to the experimental and control groups.

One or more threats, however, to internal and external validity exist for quasi-experimental designs. It is imperative that when executing an evaluative research study with a quasi-experimental design, great care be taken in knowing what has been controlled for and what has not.

Within quasi-experimental designs, a number of choices exist. The best designs are those that control relevant outside effects and lead to valid inferences about the program (Weiss, 1972, p. 67). Some of the more popular and traditional quasi-experimental designs used in evaluation of leisure services include the Solomon randomized four-group, nonequivalent control group, and the equivalent time series.

1. Solomon randomized four group. In this design study, participants are randomly assigned to one of four groups. Two of the groups receive the intervention program and two groups do not. Two groups receive a pretest and a posttest and two groups receive only a posttest. The schematic of this design is:

<pre>
R   O   X   O
R   O   O
R   X   O

R   O
</pre>

One advantage of this design is that the first two groups can be compared in order to determine how much gain is made. Another advantage is that the last two groups can be compared in order to determine the effectiveness of the intervention. The major drawback of this design is that a reasonably large pool of persons (at least 45 individuals) is needed to execute the design (Patten, 1997, p. 80).

2. Nonequivalent control group design. In the nonequivalent control group design there are two groups, an experimental and control group, in which each undergoes pretesting and posttesting. The schematic of this design is:

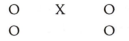

<pre>
O   X   O
O   O
</pre>

When random assignment to the two groups is impossible, the nonequivalent control group design is often chosen. Indeed, this has become a very popular design in evaluations done of recreation programs. In order to increase accuracy of results, attempts should be made to use some form of matching.

Matching can be accomplished by selecting a group as a control whose characteristics resemble the major relevant features of the group exposed to the program. For instance, an evaluation of the effects of video game play on nursing home residents (a study referred to in Chapter 3) required using a control group drawn from a second nursing home. This second home was selected on the basis that it matched the first home in terms of belonging to the same chain of homes (Riddick, Spector, & Drogin, 1986).

An extension of group matching is also to select control group members on the basis of individual matching or aggregate matching. In *individual matching* a "partner" for each experimental group member is drawn for the control group. Partners are drawn on the basis of how they match on some predetermined relevant variables. For instance, if age is considered an important matching variable, the roster of unexposed nursing home residents would be scrutinized to locate the closest equivalent elder for pairing with a resident in the experimental group. The criteria of closeness may be adjusted to make matching possible. For instance, a match would be declared if the exposed and unexposed elders are within one year of age of each other.

In *aggregate matching* the overall distributions in the experimental and control groups on each matching variable are made to correspond. Here the emphasis is not on matching individuals but variables. Thus, the same proportions of elders by age would be found in the participating and comparison groups. These results may have been obtained by including a 70- and 80-year old in the comparison group to balance the aggregate distribution of the experimental group (or a 74-year old and a 76-year old).

Individual matching is considered preferable to aggregate matching. The problems with executing individual matching, however, are that it is expensive, time-consuming, and difficult to execute for a large number of variables.

Another issue is the matter of what characteristics should be used for matching. Often times there is little *a priori* knowledge about what characteristics to use. Some general guidelines exist for generic control variables by units of analysis and appear in Figure 7.3. These generic controls should be used only when other types of controls are not available and they should be used with caution.

A number of threats to the internal and external validity of the nonequivalent control group design exist. These threats include mortality, interaction of selection with other threats such as history, and selection bias.

3. Equivalent time series. In the equivalent time series design, one group is followed over time as it experiences a program. The schematic of this design is:

X OX OX OX O

Figure 7.3: Characteristics useful in devising constructed control groups.[2]

I.   **Characteristics of Individuals**
Age
Gender
Educational attainment
Socioeconomic status
Marital status
Ethnicity
Health status

II. **Characteristics of Families**
Life-cycle stage
Number of members
Educational attainment
Income level
Employment status
Socioeconomic status

III. **Characteristics of Organized Units**

(e.g., recreation organizations, long-term facilities, schools, classes.)

Size differentiation (number of students, patrons served, etc.)
Budget
Number of employees (full-time, part-time, and volunteers)
Public, private, or non-profit status
Organizational chart or chain-of-command
Percentage of clients receiving Medicare and Medicaid

[2]From (p. 311), Adapted from P. Rossi and H. Freeman, *Evaluation: A Systematic Approach* (p. 311), (1993), by Sage Publications. Reprinted with permission of the publisher.

Study participants in this design serve as both experimental and control group subjects (technically known as *reflective controls*). Over time, various component strategies or program conditions are introduced to the subjects. A multifaceted program, such as a fitness program that introduces units on weight training, cardiovascular endurance, flexibility, etc. would be a candidate for using an equivalent time series design.

The constraints of the real-world field research (too few clients, demand for quick feedback, inadequate funds, dropouts, lack of records or access to records, changes made in the program, etc.), however, often prevent adoption or the use of this design. Additionally, a major disadvantage of this design is the multiple treatment interference. That is, if change is noted at the second or later posttest, it is not known with certainty which of earlier component or components acting together is responsible for the noted change.

Pre-experimental designs. Pre-experimental designs do not have a control group to compare with the experimental group. Thus, because of their poor control of internal validity, pre-experimental designs have little value for investigating cause-effect relationships. In other words, these designs foster differing interpretations of how much change has occurred and how much of any observed change was due to the prgram intervention itself.

Pre-experimental designs can, however, be useful when conducting a *pilot study* (pilot studies are discussed in Chapter 9). A pilot study is used when the goal is to try out new interventions and/or measurement tools in order to learn more about the acceptability and accuracy of them. In instances where a pilot study is being conducted, then a pre-experimental design is defensible (Patten, 1997, p. 83). The pre-experimental designs used in recreation evaluations are one-group pretest-posttest design, one-time posttest design, and static group comparison.

1. **One-group pretest-posttest.** In a one-group pretest-post-test design one group receives a pretest before experiencing the program and a posttest after concluding the program. The schematic of this design is:

$$O \qquad X \qquad O$$

An example of how this design could be used is monitoring body fat changes of aerobic participants. Students' body fat could be recorded the first and last day of classes. The limitations of this design are that any changes noted from pretest to posttest may not be attributed to the program but instead result from any number of factors including maturation, interactive effects, selection bias, and history.

2. **One-time posttest.** In the one-time posttest design, the group receiving the program is tested only once, or at the conclusion of the program. The schematic for this design is:

$$X \qquad O$$

A major problem associated with this design stems from selection of study participants. It is difficult to tell where these individuals stood earlier on, before their involvement in the program in terms of the dependent variable(s) under study. Sometimes evaluators try to get around this problem by asking people to judge how much they have changed as a result of participation in the program. If at all possible, the use of this design should be avoided since its use is associated with a number of threats to internal validity.

3. Static-group comparison. In the static-group comparison design, experimental and control groups are used and data are only collected once. The schematic for this design is:

X O

   O

An example of when this design could be used would be to assess how Stone Valley's environmental education program affects the environmental knowledge of middle school students. Knowledge of the environment could be assessed in both the experimental and control groups one time or when the experimental group had completed the environmental education program.

The major problem with the static-group comparison design deals with the selection of subjects and the consequent internal validity threats. By this we mean selection of the two groups has not been made in such a way that we have full confidence that they were initially the same in all important aspects (e.g., were baseline knowledge scores for the dependent variable about the same for the two groups?).

Non-experimental designs. In non-experimental studies, a program is not purposively given to one group and withheld from another. Rather, individuals are observed or surveyed in order to describe them as they exist. Two such designs, survey research and *ex post facto* design, will be covered below. It is important to note that information gleaned from a survey can also be used in a causal-comparison or *ex post facto* design.

1. Survey research. The *survey or poll* is one of the most common kinds of non- experimental research used in leisure services. Indeed, survey research is the most common design used in studies reported in recreation and leisure professional journals (see Riddick, DeSchriver, & Weissinger, 1991; and Bedini & Wu, 1994).

In a survey, individuals (called *respondents*) are interviewed or questioned in order to determine and describe attitudes, beliefs, preferences, self-reported behaviors, etc. Weisberg, Krosnick, and Bowen (1996) pointed out that surveys can be used to address four broad classes of questions. These questions are:

- *Prevalence* of attitudes, beliefs, preferences, and/or self-reported behaviors.
- *Changes* in attitudes, beliefs, preferences, and/or self-reported behaviors over time.
- *Differences* between groups of people in their attitudes, beliefs, preferences and/or self-reported behaviors.
- *Causal* propositions about these attitudes, beliefs, preferences, and behaviors. When causal propositions become the emphasis for an evaluative study, the survey becomes a vehicle to conduct an *ex post facto* design.

In executing a survey, everyone in the population can be interviewed (this is called a *census*) or a sample or some members of the population can be used (sampling is the topic of Chapter 8). If the latter approach is taken, inferences (or generalizations) to the population are made from the sample data results. For instance, to find out their thoughts about the softball league experience, we could survey all 1,000 people playing in the woman's slow-pitch softball league (the *population*) or conduct a random sample of about 275 people from the playing rosters. If the latter approach was taken, then study results based on the sample of 275 could be generalized to what would have been found if all 1,000 slow-pitch partici-pants had been surveyed.

Surveys can be conducted by mail questionnaires, face-to-face interviews, or by tele-phone interviews (Chapter 10 describes these data-collection techniques). Furthermore, sur-veys can be administered on a one-shot basis to several different groups at the same time. If age is used as the basis for selecting different groups, a one-time administration is known as a *cross-sectional survey*. If the same age cohort is surveyed at different times, this is known as a *longitudinal survey*. Several age cohorts are studied over time but with different persons being used to represent each age cohort is known as a *time-lag survey*. For more information on these varying survey designs consult Baltes, Reese, and Nesselroade (1986).

Critical to the integrity of a survey is response rate. *Response rate* is a guide to the representativeness of the sample respondents. If a high response rate is obtained, there is less chance of significant response bias than if a low rate is achieved. What, then, is a high response rate? The experts do not agree on this subject. Babbie's (1995, p. 262) rules of thumb are liberal on this issue: 50% is considered *adequate*, 60% is *good*, and 70% is *very good*. In contrast, many survey researchers state that 75% or more of the designated sample should be the norm. Interestingly, the Bureau of the Census reportedly has the highest re-sponse rate of all continuing surveys, achieving a cooperation rate in the high 90th percen-tile (Rossi & Freeman, 1993, p. 239).

Continuing with response rate, it is important to note there are two ways to calculate response rate. The first way is to determine the percentage of people in the original sample from whom completed interviews or questionnaires were obtained. Thus, if 75 persons in the original sample of 100 were interviewed or returned their questionnaires, the response rate is 75%. This response rate was calculated using the formula:

$$\text{Response rate} = \left(\frac{\text{number returned}}{\text{number in sample}} \right) \times 100$$

Another approach for calculating response rate is to use the percentage of contacts with eligible respondents that result in completed interviews or questionnaires. The difference between this approach and the first approach is that unsuccessful contacts (the individual was ineligible or unreachable) are excluded from consideration. The formula for this calculation is:

$$\text{Response rate} = \left(\frac{\text{number returned}}{\text{number in sample - (non-eligible+ unreachable)}} \right) \text{x} \quad 100$$

Using this formula, suppose if 100 people were sent a questionnaire, 10 were unreachable (they moved and there was no forwarding address) and 10 were ineligible (they were living in an institution rather than the community), the original sample of potential respondents would be adjusted to 80. Then if 75 questionnaires were completed and returned, the response rate would be 93.7% (or 75/80).

The last point we want to make about survey research deals with secondary data. Every once in a while, someone else has independently collected survey information on a topic of interest to you. When an existing archival database is used or relied on it is known as a *secondary database*. Before using a secondary database, make sure you have a clear understanding of what sampling technique (described in the next chapter) was used and the response rate was for the survey.

Sources of public-access, social-science data archives are identified by Kiecolt and Nathan (1985). Additionally, an excellent source of data sets (that typically include surveys with individuals chosen randomly throughout the United States) dealing with health, aging, and human development is available from the National Archive of Computerized Data on Aging affiliated with the Inter-University Consortium for Political and Social Research (ICPSR). Procedures and costs for obtaining data differ according to whether the requester is affiliated with one of the universities or colleges holding membership in ICPSR. For more information contact: ICPSR User Support, P.O. Box 1248, Ann Arbor, MI 48106-1248, phone (734) 998-9799.

2. *Ex post facto design*. The *ex post facto* (or correlational) design is a causal- comparative design. There are times when it is impossible or impractical to conduct an experiment, and hence this sort of design is used.

The characteristics of a causal-comparative study are that:

- A current condition or state of affairs is observed and described; and
- Attempts are made to identify the possible "cause(s)" of the condition.

For example, in an attempt to understand the background circumstances of why one adolescent is chosen over another to attend Jamboree, it might be decided to gauge the bearing, if any, of number of years one has been in scouting on Jamboree selection. It is important to note that the *ex post facto* design is descriptive, and thus it is erroneous to assume an actual cause-effect relationship. All that can truly be established is that there is an association between two or more traits or events. Instead of thinking "A is the cause of B," what really is accurate to say is "If A is introduced, B is more likely to result than if A is not introduced." The point to understand is not to think or imply B always results if A is introduced. If it is found by applying this logic to the scouting example, that number of years involved in scouting has an affect on who is chosen, then all one can accurately say is that those adolescents who have been scouts the longest are more likely to be chosen to attend Jamboree.

Evaluators do not give or offer treatments in *ex post facto* designs. Instead, the research is describing observations and trying to make after-the-fact linkages between or among variables. One example of *ex post facto* design is Riddick's (1986) survey to determine if knowledge of community leisure resources and leisure values were positively related to leisure satisfaction.

Designs Related to a Qualitative Framework

Approaching an evaluative study from a qualitative perspective offers dozens of possible research designs. These include such strategies as oral history, investigative journalism, connoisseurship, and literary criticism. For the purposes of evaluating a recreation, park, sport or fitness service, however, we will discuss the most commonly used qualitative research designs: ethnographic study, case study, content analysis, and an historical study. First, however, we discuss the very important criteria for rigor in these designs.

Rigor in Qualitative Designs

The question of rigor always plagues evaluative research. Regardless of the framework chosen, concern for a research design that is rigorous will be constant. When choosing qualitative designs, rigor means that the evaluation is not so subjective that it cannot be trusted. Rigor encompasses the satisfaction of three criteria: truthfulness, applicability, and consistency (Lincoln & Guba, 1986).

Truthfulness, or trustworthiness or credibility, refers to the "truth" value of the results from the study. (For those readers already familiar with quantitative designs, you can consider truthfulness as somewhat parallel to internal validity.) Techniques appropriate for increasing the truthfulness of results are consistent with the procedural rules in using qualitative data collection methods. These include (Lincoln & Guba, 1986, p. 77):

- **Prolonged engagement** = lengthy and intensive contact with the phenomena or respondents in the field to avoid the distortions of comprehension that can accompany concluding too quickly
- **Persistent observation** = in-depth pursuit of those themes or understandings found to be especially obvious

- **Cross-checking** = exposing yourself to a disinterested, professional peer whose role is to "keep the inquirer honest" (p. 77)
- **Member checks** = the process of continuous, informal testing of information that is acquired by soliciting reactions of the respondents themselves: asking respondents if your understanding of the phenomenon matches what they have told you.

The second criterion of rigor for qualitative designs is applicability. *Applicability*, or transferability, is a check for how useful the evaluative findings are to other situations. (For readers familiar with external validity in quantitative designs, applicability is an analog.) To enhance applicability, evaluators using qualitative designs rely on what is termed "thick description." That is, in the written report that follows the analysis of the information gathered in the study, the narrative is richly developed. The descriptions and context are so thoroughly presented that judgments about the degree of fit or similarity may be made by others who wish to apply all or part of the findings to other situations (Lincoln & Guba, 1986, p. 77).

Finally, the criterion of consistency is important to the rigor of qualitative evaluative research designs. *Consistency*, or dependability or confirmability, means that the findings from the study are reliable. (In fact, reliability is the term used to describe this concept in quantitative designs.) Consistency may be enhanced by conducting what is labeled an *external audit*. An external audit examines the process and the results of the study to be sure that the interpretations and judgments made by the evaluator can be confirmed. This requires that the evaluator leaves an audit trail, or notes and materials, that help the auditor trace how the evaluator came to the conclusions. In addition, this also requires a competent external, disinterested auditor.

With the rigor criteria of trustworthiness, applicability, and consistency in mind, we now move to a description of the common qualitative designs used in evaluative research projects in parks, recreation, and sport and fitness organizations.

Qualitative Designs

A number of designs exist that relate to a qualitative framework. The more popular ones, discussed below, are ethnographic study, case study, content analysis, and historical study.

Ethnographic study. In an *ethnographic study* the evaluator attempts to obtain as holistic an understanding as possible of a group, setting, or situation. The emphasis is on portraying the regular, everyday experiences of the group or situation by observing and/or interviewing intensely, and over a sustained period of time (Miles & Huberman, 1994). It is the extended contact with the setting and the concern for mundane and day-to-day events that characterize the ethnographic approach to evaluation. Evaluators using an ethnographic approach try to comprehend as much of what is going on as they can—to understand the "whole picture" (Fraenkel & Wallen, 1993).

To illustrate, suppose an evaluator of a retirement community wants to know about the experience of living there. The goal would be to document the daily, ongoing experiences of the residents. To accomplish this using an ethnographic study, the evaluator would regularly visit the retirement community over a lengthy period of time—perhaps actually live there. Residents would be observed and interviewed extensively in order to describe as fully as possible what their lives are like. Descriptions resulting from such an ethnographic study might depict the social atmosphere of the community, the intellectual and/or emotional experiences of the residents, the manner in which recreation administrators and staff act toward and react to the residents, how the recreational behavioral norms of the community are learned and perpetuated, and the concerns residents and staff have about the delivery of leisure services. These portrayals would be based on data collected in the form of observation notes, audiotapes of interviews, videotapes of specific activities or events, copies of weekly activities calendars, and anything else the evaluator thinks will provide an understanding of life in the community.

There are several features of an ethnographic study that are worth highlighting. First, the evaluator will not likely begin with a precise research question or hypothesis, but rather attempt to understand an ongoing situation without any advance predictions. Ethnographic study is essentially a *discovery* process (Miles & Huberman, 1994). The evaluator observes and interviews for a period of time, formulates some initial conclusions that in turn lead to additional observations and interviews, observes and interviews again, and so on.

Another characteristic of the ethnographic study is that it is largely a *descriptive* enterprise (Miles & Huberman, 1994). The idea is to reach across the multiple sources of information and to "uncover" what is typical about the setting or situation studied—not to explain or justify it, but simply to depict "this is how things are." Finally, there are times when the description that results from an ethnographic study is used to *develop a theory* or general conceptual framework that will shape the focus of additional studies (Miles & Huberman, 1994).

An ethnographic study design in evaluative research provides, then, a description of the current situation, which can serve as the basis for developing recommendations for future changes to that situation. For example, suppose the evaluator in the retirement community example above discovers, through the ethnographic study, that residents are typically the busiest in the morning hours performing personal maintenance tasks, such as getting breakfast, washing dishes, reading the newspaper, watering plants, and doing laundry. Based on this description, the evaluator may recommend to the recreation staff that programs and activities should only be scheduled in the afternoon and evening hours. Thus, the currently offered morning programs, which have not been well attended, should be re-scheduled.

Case study. A special kind of ethnographic study is the evaluation of a single individual, program, or agency. This is called a *case study*. For example, suppose there is one resident of the retirement community who seems to be particularly enjoying the resources and opportunities there. To focus on this more, the evaluator could conduct a case study on this one individual. In hopes of gaining insight into why this resident enjoys living there so much, observations could be done of her on a regular basis to discern her patterns of behavior. Also her friends, family members, and the retirement community staff might be interviewed about their perceptions or observations about her. In short, as much information as possible on this one individual would be collected. The idea is that through the study of a unique individual, insights are gained that may suggest ways to help other residents make the most of life in the retirement community.

The "case" in a case study can be identified several ways. Abstractly, a *case* can be defined as a single "phenomenon occurring in a bounded context" (Miles & Huberman, 1994, p. 25). Often, as with the retirement community resident in the case study example above, this one phenomenon is an individual. In a case study there is just one case, while in the other approaches we discuss in this chapter several cases are studied. There are many possible single cases to study. In addition to the individual case, one could study a role, small group, organization, community, event, and time period case (adapted from Miles & Huberman, 1994).

Examples of *individuals* as the case are:
- A college student's "out of class" experiences: how does he spend his free time?
- The aerobics leader's teaching style: what teaching technique does she use for cardio-boxing?

Examples of a *role* as the case are:
- The role of a playground leader in a community setting: does his role help shape staff expectations and norms?
- The role of "woman" in moving through a career in leisure services: does she experience a unique career cycle?

Examples of a *small group* as the case are:
- An informal group of adolescents who play pick-up basketball everyday after school: what are their motivations and benefits?
- The city Parks Board: what are their decision patterns when environmental issues are involved?

Examples of an *organization* as the case are:
- An inner-city high school engaged in a major redesign of its sports programming:

has its sports program made a difference in student self-esteem?

- A synagogue: does its youth religious training program contribute to social development?

Examples of a *community* as the case are:

- A small town's tourism development: how did the town successfully maintain control over strip development decisions?
- A neighborhood: how has the neighborhood's new park design affected communication patterns among the children?

Examples of an *event* as the case are:

- The annual Renaissance Faire: how have participants' entertainment interests changed?
- The staff meeting: what are the interaction patterns of the staff with each other and with the director?

Examples of a *time period* as the case are:

- A day at day camp: what was the day like?
- A week in the organization: what is the difference in problem-solving strategies used by the staff during a week in the summer versus a week in the winter?

So far the "case" has been presented as if it were a single entity. Yet, cases may also have subcases embedded within them (Yin, 1984). A case study of a tennis center, for example, might contain subcases of specific special events or teams of players operating within it. While a single case can be very useful in a qualitative evaluation study, multiple cases offer even more understanding of the processes and outcomes studied.

Of course, the question of just what case or cases to study arises. Miles and Huberman (1994, p. 27) offer this advice:

- *Start intuitively.* Think of the reason for doing the evaluation and build outward. Think of what you will *not* be studying as a way to firm up the boundary of what you *will* be studying. Admit that the boundary of what you are studying is never as rational and solid as you might hope it to be.
- *Define the case as early as you can.* Given that you have a starting conceptual framework and research questions, it pays to get a bit strict about what you are defining as a case. This will also help you clarify further both the framework and the questions.
- *Remember that sampling will define the case(s) even more.*
- *Do not spend all day at it.* If a starting conceptual framework and research questions are reasonably clear, a first cut at case definition usually takes no more than a few minutes.

Content analysis. Sometimes, instead of studying an individual, organization, or community case, a document is the case. This type of qualitative inquiry is known as *content* or *document analysis*. It is defined just as the name suggests: the analysis of the contents of a written, visual, or recorded document. Meeting minutes, long-range plans, mission statements, newspapers, magazines, speeches, advertisements, court reports, promotional videos, children's drawings—in fact, the contents of virtually any kind of written or visual communication can be studied for a recreation, park, sport, or tourism service evaluation. Documents are a useful and "ready-made source of data, easily accessible to the imaginative and resourceful investigator" (Merriam, 1988, p. 104).

An example of the use of documents can be cited from a study about college student out-of-class experiences (Kuh, et al., 1991). Here documents served as a way to learn about the college context for encouraging high-quality, free-time experiences of undergraduates at 14 colleges and universities. The documents that were found particularly helpful in understanding free-time suggestions made to students by the colleges included policies and procedures handbooks for faculty, students, and staff; promotional pamphlets, such as admissions viewbooks and student club recruitment brochures; college mission and goal statements; student newspapers; college histories; campus message boards; and table tents in the dining halls advertising events and activities. Even student clothing was studied as documents. For example, the researchers noticed almost no Wichita State University (WSU) students wearing WSU T-shirts, jackets, or hats. Could this mean a lack of school spirit? In following up on this query during interviews, students told the researchers, "We all have jobs, and you can't wear those clothes to work" (Whitt, 1992, p. 83).

Documents can be considered as two basic types: public records and personal documents (Whitt, 1992). *Public records* are materials created and kept for the purpose of officially accounting for an event. This might include park board meeting minutes, registration records for adult craft classes, organization and program budgets, playground and recreation center policy manuals, official correspondence of the organization director, etc. These documents are particularly useful in determining agency characteristics, priorities, and concerns. They also can help in identifying agency strengths and weaknesses, such as staff and financial resources or consistency of policies. Public records can also help the evaluator understand the organization's values (such as its commitment to diversity), and operating processes (such as in the hiring and evaluation of staff) (Whitt, 1992).

On the other hand, *personal documents* are first-person accounts of events and experiences (Merriam, 1988). People keep all sorts of personal documents—appointment calendars, letters, diaries, sketches, snapshots, scrapbooks, etc. As noted in the previous example, even people's T-shirts can be analyzed. Personal documents can help the evaluator understand how the person views his or her experiences. For example, a letter from a camper to a best friend, if available to the evaluator, may provide information about how the camp experience is perceived.

Content analysis is a qualitative, evaluative research design that enables you to discover information and meanings that, unlike other approaches, are unobtrusive. This advantage is discussed more in Chapter 10. For now, however, it is useful to appreciate the approach as relatively invisible to, and requiring minimal cooperation from, the persons or organizations being evaluated. This means the documents are usually also easily obtained.

The content analysis approach is typically used by evaluators in two ways. First, as we have already discussed, a document study can stand alone by serving as a *primary data* source about events, activities, and processes for an evaluation (Patten, 1990). Information from documents also might be used for *secondary purposes*. For example, the content analysis approach could help generate ideas for cases to use in a case study, questions to ask in a survey, or events to observe in an ethnographic study. Analysis of the fitness instructor's manual, for example, could raise questions about safety procedures. These questions could then become the focus of a case study of a fitness class.

To demonstrate how a content analysis is conducted, let's follow an illustration. Suppose an evaluator is interested in determining if there is gender bias in promoting sport programs in a YMCA. He wonders if the written or visual content of promotional brochures used to recruit participants to sport and fitness programs is biased in any way and, if it is, how. He decides to do a content analysis to obtain some answers to these questions. Thus, the evaluator must first plan how to select and order the "contents" that are available for analysis—in this case, the brochures. So, he decides to collect from the office files a copy of each brochure for each season from the past five years. Next, pertinent categories are developed that will allow him to identify what he thinks is important and then compare the presence of these categories among the various brochures he is analyzing.

Identifying pertinent categories is the critical task of content analysis. Care must be taken to define, as precisely as possible, those aspects of a document's contents that you want to investigate (Fraenkel & Wallen, 1993). These *categories* should be so explicit that another evaluator who uses them to analyze the same material would uncover approximately the same findings. In our illustration, suppose the evaluator selects the categories of "quantity" (are there equal numbers of sport and fitness programs for women and men?), and "action level" (what is the degree of energy required for women's versus men's sport and fitness programs?). These two categories become the basis for analyzing the brochures.

A coding sheet would then be prepared to tally the data, in each of these categories, as they are identified in each brochure. That is, every sport program in a brochure is counted according to which gender it is promoted for as well as the degree of physical exertion required. This counting process continues for each category and each brochure. Figure 7.4 offers an opportunity for you to try your hand at content analysis.

Figure 7.4: Try your hand at content analysis.

To learn more about conducting a content analysis, try this simple exercise.

1. Acquire from your local park, recreation, sport, or fitness organization a copy of the program offerings brochure. Sometimes these are in flyer or booklet form, and often they are distributed according to specific seasons, such as the winter program for a city parks and recreation department.

2. After a quick glance through the brochure, think of two to three categories, and their levels, that would be meaningful to your study. For example, the following categories and their measurement levels might be useful—use these ideas as starters for selecting your own.

Category	*Levels*
program location	indoor, outdoor
time of day	morning, afternoon, early evening, late evening
day of week	weekday, weekend, holiday
participant's gender	males, females, mixed
participant's age group	toddlers, children, teens, young adults, middle adults, adults, older adults
cost	free, $1.00 to $4.99, $5.00 to $9.99, $10.00 or more
program length	one day or less, one week, one month, two months, more than two months
required ability level	all ability levels, restricted to beginners, restricted to intermediates, restricted to advanced
program type	art, dance, music, sport, fitness, outdoor recreation

3. Set up a form that helps you tally the number of programs that fit in each category level. This could simply be a page with the categories and their levels listed across the top.

4. Fill in your form by counting the number of programs according to the category levels.

5. Sit back and study your completed form. What are the tendencies? In which category levels are there the largest number of programs? For example, does this agency tend to program mostly for youth, in team sports, on weekday afternoons?

6. Determine the implications of your findings. What program improvements would you recommend to the organization?

Historical study. Historical research is concerned with studying the past. While largely overlooked as a useful design in the evaluation of leisure services, certain forms of historical research can provide an important basis for making management decisions. Alternatively, an evaluative research project can include an historical component in order to round out what is learned through another research approach. Specifically, the historical design can be useful in these ways (Fraenkel & Wallen, 1993):

- To learn from past failures and successes.
- To determine if past strategies and solutions might be applicable to present-day problems.
- To assist in the prediction of future needs.
- To understand present-day policies and practices more fully.

The historical approach makes use of essentially two types of data: primary and secondary. *Primary data* are first hand accounts of what happened in the past and how people felt about it. For example, eyewitness accounts of how a recreation organization operated in the past might be studied from letters, diaries, charters, contracts and deeds, meeting minutes, and interviews with people who were involved with the organization at that time. *Secondary data* are second-hand accounts of what happened in the past and how people felt about it. The authors for this sort of information were not present in the organization at the time being studied, but offer their interpretation of what happened based on the primary sources they studied. Secondary sources for this kind of data might include meeting minutes summaries, other research reports, and newspaper articles.

Often it is necessary to examine historical information skeptically, or to appreciate how changing circumstances affect recorded facts (Kraus & Allen, 1997). For example, suppose an historical study of personal injury accidents of hikers using a state forest trail system is undertaken. One historical source of information would be the accident reports filed in the headquarters office. Suppose we notice in studying these files that 30 years ago there were 50% fewer accidents reported than there were this year. Does this mean that compared to the past more accidents occur now? Or, is it that the state forest managers are now more attentive to documenting the accidents?

Main Points

- Like in cooking, where there is no one "right" recipe for pie making, there is no one design that should universally be adopted for an evaluation study.

- Critical to choosing a design is knowing the use to which results will be put (that is, what are the information needs of decision makers). This information will tell you if you should be choosing a design that maximizes internal validity or external validity.

- Other things that should be considered in choosing a design are resource constraints and protection of human respondents.

- *Internal validity* focuses on determining whether or not a program works or is meeting its desired outcomes.

- *External validity* is the ability to generalize the study's findings to the "real" world or beyond the group sampled.

- The experimental research design, hypothetically, is considered the most scientific design. However, it is not prudent to adopt this design in leisure service settings.

- A number of quasi-experimental, pre-experimental and non-experimental designs exist for studies using a quantitative framework. Each of these designs has advantages and disadvantages.

- The most popular design in published leisure research to date is the *survey*. Surveys are used to address questions related to: prevalence, changes, and differences between groups of people related to attitudes, beliefs, preferences, and/or self-reported behaviors; and an *ex post facto* design examines (after the fact) causal relationships.

- When choosing a qualitative design, attention should be given to identifying a design that has *rigor*—or truthfulness, applicability, and consistency.

- Approaching an evaluation study from a qualitative perspective offers many possible designs. The most commonly used in recreation, park, sport, and fitness evaluations are ethnographic study, case study, and content analysis. Historical study is an underutilized qualitative design that also deserves further attention.

- An *ethnographic study* enables the evaluator to obtain a comprehensive understanding of regular, everyday experiences of a group or situation by intensely observing and interviewing over a sustained period of time.

- A *case study* is a special kind of ethnographic study in which a single individual, program, or organization is evaluated.

- *Content analysis* is an evaluation of a document, including public records and personal materials.

- *Historical study* seeks to determine how past occurrences affect contemporary management decisions.

Study Questions

1. What factors should be considered in choosing a research design?

2. What is *internal validity*?

3. What are some of the *threats to internal validity*?

4. What is *external validity*?

5. What are some of the *threats to external validity*?

6. What are the five elements of an *experimental design*? Are evaluators able to use this design often—why or why not?

7. Draw a *nonequivalent control group design*. When is this design used? How can matching or finding a suitable control group be approached?

8. When are *pre-experimental designs* used? What is the major criticism of such designs? Draw three such designs.

9. What are *non-experimental research designs*? Give an example of evaluation situations for which you can use a *survey* and *ex post facto* design, respectively.

10. What does *response rate* tell you? What is a decent response rate?

11. Explain how rigor of a qualitative design is affected by truthfulness, applicability, and consistency.

12. In what evaluation situations could you use an ethnographic study design? That is, what sorts of questions would you be able to answer using this design?

13. Give an example of an evaluation situation for which you could use a case study design.

14. Give an example of an evaluation situation for which you could use a content analysis design.

15. Give an example of an evaluation situation for which you could use an historical study design.

References

Andreas, R., Kuh, G.D., Lyons, J.W., & Whitt, E.J. (1989). *Final report: Wichita State University.* Bloomington, IN: College Experiences Study.

Babbie, E. (1998). *The practice of social research* (8th ed.). Belmont, CA: Wadsworth.

Baltes, P., Reese, H., & Nesselroade, J. (1986). *Life-span developmental psychology: Introduction to research methods.* Hillsdale, NJ: Erlbaum.

Bedini, L., & Wu, Y. (1994). A methodological review of research in *Therapeutic Recreation Journal* from 1986 to 1990. *Therapeutic Recreation Journal, 28,* 87-98.

Campbell, D., & Stanley, J. (1963). *Experimental and quasi-experimental designs for research.* Chicago: Rand McNally College Publishing.

Fraenkel, J.R. & Wallen, N.E. (1993). *How to design and evaluate research in education* (2nd ed.). New York: McGraw-Hill.

Green, L. (1976, April). *Research methods for evaluation of health education under adverse scientific conditions.* Paper presented at Extension Seminar in Health Education and Rural Health Care Research Forum, Phoenix, AZ.

Kiecolt, K., & Nathan, L. (1985). *Secondary analysis of survey data.* Thousand Oaks, CA: Sage Publications.

Kraus, R., & Allen, L.R. (1997). *Research & evaluation in recreation, parks & leisure studies.* Scottsdale, AZ: Gorsuch Scarisbrick.

Kuh, G.D., Schuh, J.H., Whitt, E.J., Andreas, R., Lyons, J., Strange, C.C., Krehbiel, L., & McKay, K. (1991). *Involving colleges: Successful approaches to encouraging student learning and personal development.* San Francisco: Jossey-Bass.

Lincoln, Y.S., Guba, E.G. (June 1986). But is it rigorous? Trustworthiness and authenticity in naturalistic evaluation. In D. Williams (Ed.), *Naturalistic evaluation: New directions for program evaluation, no. 50* (pp. 73-84). San Francisco: Jossey Bass.

Merriam, S.B. (1988). *Case study research in education: A qualitative approach.* San Francisco: Jossey-Bass.

Miles, M.B. & Huberman, A.M. (1994). *Qualitative data analysis.* Thousand Oaks, CA: Sage Publications.

Patten, M.Q. (1990). *Qualitative evaluation and research methods* (2nd ed.). Newbury Park, CA: Sage Publications.

Patten, M. (1997). *Understanding research methods: An overview of the essentials.* Los Angeles: Pyrczak Publishing.

Riddick, C. (1986). Leisure satisfaction precursors. *Journal of Leisure Research, 18,* 259-265.

Riddick, C., DeSchriver, M., & Weissinger, E. (1991, October). *A methodological review of research in Journal of Leisure Research from 1983 through 1987.* Paper presented at the National Recreation & Park Association's Leisure Research Symposium, Baltimore, MD.

Riddick, C., Spector, S., & Drogin, E. (1986). The effects of video game play on the emotional states and affiliative behavior of nursing home residents. *Activities, Adaptation & Aging, 8,* 95-108.

Rossi, P., & Freeman, H. (1993). *Evaluation: A systematic approach*. Newbury Park, CA: Sage Publications.

Stake, R. (1995). *The art of case study research*. Thousand Oaks, CA: Sage Publications.

Van Dalen, D. (1979). *Understanding educational research* (4th ed.). New York: McGraw–Hill.

Weisberg, H., Krosnick, J., & Bowen, B. (1996). *An introduction to survey research, polling, and data analysis* (3rd ed.). Thousand Oaks, CA: Sage Publications.

Weiss, C. (1972). *Evaluative research: Methods of assessing program effectiveness*. Englewood Cliffs, NJ: Prentice-Hall.

Whitt, E.J. (1992). Document analysis. In F.K. Stage (Ed.), *Diverse methods for research and assessment of college students* (pp. 79–90). Alexandria, VA: American College Personnel Association.

Yin, R.K. (1984). *Case study research: Design and methods*. (Applied Social Research Methods Series, Vol. 5). Beverly Hills, CA: Sage Publications.

CHAPTER 8

Sampling and Sample Size

What Will I Learn in This Chapter?
I'll be able to:

1. Define and give examples for sample, population, probability sampling, and nonprobability sampling.

2. List the advantages and disadvantages of probability and nonprobability sampling.

3. Explain how to implement a simple random sample.

4. Identify examples of stratified random sampling, systematic sampling, and cluster sampling.

5. Explain purposive sampling and cite examples of finding respondents who represent a heterogenous sample, a homogenous sample, an extreme case sample, an expert sample, and a time sample.

6. Recall a definition of quota sampling and cite a stratum example that could be used in carrying out a hypothetical study.

7. Discuss volunteer sampling and snowball sampling and give an example of each.

8. Explain what is meant by sampling error.

9. List factors that affect sample size.

10. Recall an approximate sample size for a quasi-experiment involving one experimental group.

11. Read an evaluation article based on either a quantitative or qualitative framework and be able to identify, by name, the type of sampling used in the study.

Selecting a sample entails answering two questions. First, what is the purpose of the study—what do you want to know? Second, whom do you want to know about? In evaluative research "the who" that is the focus for a study translates into designating the sample. A *sample* is a subset of a population. A *population* is the entire group we are interested in—it could be all the recreation professionals working in city *W,* in the entire county *X,* in the state *Y,* in the geographical region of *Z,* or the entire United States. If we study every member in the population we are conducting a *census.*

Conducting a census of a large-numbered population oftentimes is impractical. Instead, it is more efficient to study a sample or subgroup of the population. Two approaches are used in selecting a sample, or probability sampling and nonprobability sampling.

Studies that are based on a quantitative framework can employ either probability or nonprobability sampling. On the other hand, studies that pivot around a qualitative framework typically rely on nonprobability sampling. In a qualitative research approach a sample is selected according to who has the knowledge and experience needed for the study. Evaluators using qualitative approaches usually work with a small sample of people, nested in their context, and studied in-depth. Evaluators, using quantitative approaches, often strive for larger numbers of respondents who are selected at random and thus removed from their context (Miles & Huberman, 1994). People who are studied quantitatively are viewed as part of a social situation that has a logic and coherence of its own—and this is precisely what is useful to study.

Thus, in selecting a sample, it is critical to decide on the research framework in order to know how the sampling should be done. Figure 8.1 guides the following discussion according to the advantages and disadvantages of specific techniques in each of these two sampling approaches. It should be noted that some consider sample selection a highly technical task and one that should be guided by a professional statistician (Rossi & Freeman, 1993, p. 239).

The chapter is divided into four sections. The first two sections review probability and nonprobability sampling and some of the more common techniques used to obtain such samples. The third section addresses the issue of representativeness of the sample in terms of being aware of sampling errors. The fourth section presents factors that should be considered in determining the sample size for a study.

Probability Sampling

Probability sampling is based on chance. That is, every member of a population has the same chance of being chosen for the sample. Stated another way, in probability sampling every member of the population has the same chance of not being chosen for the sample. A sample that is drawn using *probability sampling* is described as a representative or unbiased sample. After drawing and studying a representative sample, generalizations or inferences to the population from which the sample was drawn can be made with a specifiable degree of error. Rather than take a census of an entire population, sampling saves in time and money. If done with care, sampling can yield very accurate information about the population under study.

A number of approaches to probability sampling exist. Among the more popular are simple random sampling, stratified random sampling, systematic sampling, and cluster sam-

Figure 8.1: Disadvantages and advantages of different types of samples.

Sampling Approach	Advantage	Disadvantage
Probability Sampling		
Simple random sample	Easy to use	Requires knowing all members of the population
	Sampling error can be approximated	Costly
Stratified sample	Representation of groups insured	Requires weighting (or drawing appropriate percentage in each subgroup)
Systematic sample	Easy to use	If care not taken, biased sample can be drawn
Cluster sample	Curtailed cost	Sampling error increases
Nonprobability Sampling		
Purposive sample	Easy to use Cheap	May not be representative of population
Quota Sample	Easy to use Cheap	May not be representative of population
Volunteer sample	Easy to use Cheap	May not be representative of population (requires weighting)
Snowball sample	Relatively easy to use	May not be representative of population

pling. Another approach that can be used by recreation organizations, especially at the local and county levels as well as by commercial enterprises, is multi-stage sampling.

Simple Random Sampling

One way to draw an unbiased sample is to use a *simple random sample*. A common way to execute this is to write down the name of each person in the population on a separate slip of paper, fold the slip, and put it into a container (for larger populations, the random selection is performed with a computer). Then, the slips of paper in the container are mixed and as many slips/names that are needed are drawn out of the container.

An alternative way to draw a simple random sample is to use a table of random numbers (see Figure 8.2). To use this table you must first give each unit or person in the population a unique number. If there are, for example, 99 or fewer persons in the population, choose any person and assign them the number 01, a second person 02, up to the 99th person the number 99. Depending on the table of random numbers (i.e., how many numbers are in each array) used, decide if you are going to use the first two numbers in the array, the second and third number in the array, etc. Referring to Figure 8.2 (which has three numbers in each array), it is decided the first and second number in the array will be used. The table of random numbers is consulted and without looking, a number array on the page is pointed to or selected. Suppose the first number chosen from the table of random numbers is 5 (found in row #8, column 16), and the number to the immediate right of 5 is 8 (found in row #8, column 17). Thus, the person renamed (by numbering) as 58 would be selected for the study. This selection process would continue until you have the number of subjects needed for the sample. One can decide to move away from the initially selected number array by moving through the table in a down, up, right, left or diagonal fashion. Continuing with the above example, it is decided to move in a downward fashion so the next person selected for the sample is 83 (found in row #9, columns 16 and 17).

Stratified Random Sampling

A *stratified random sample* is used when it is important that different subgroups or categories of persons are represented in the correct proportion when sampling. These subgroups or categories are known as *"stratum."* Examples of stratum that can be used are gender (thus, the population is divided into males and females), undergraduate matriculation level (or freshmen, sophomores, juniors, and seniors), or part of the town one lives in (or north side, south side, east side, or west side). Once the stratum has been identified and established, one needs to draw the same percentage of subjects (versus the same number) in each stratum found in the population.

Suppose, for instance, you were undertaking a study of the leisure interests and values of undergraduates at a university that has an underclass enrollment of about 10,000. Previ-

Figure 8.2: Table of random numbers.[1]

Row #	1	2	3	4	5	6	7	8	9	10	11	12	13	14	15	16	17	18
1	2	1	0	4	9	8	0	8	8	8	0	6	9	2	4	8	2	6
2	0	7	3	0	2	9	4	8	2	7	8	9	8	9	2	9	7	1
3	4	4	9	0	0	2	8	6	2	6	7	7	7	3	1	2	5	1
4	7	3	2	1	1	2	0	7	7	6	0	3	8	3	4	7	8	1
5	3	3	2	5	8	3	1	7	0	1	4	0	7	8	9	3	7	7
6	6	1	2	0	5	7	2	4	4	0	0	6	3	0	2	8	0	7
7	7	0	9	3	3	3	7	4	0	4	8	8	9	3	5	8	0	5
8	7	5	1	9	0	9	1	5	2	6	5	0	9	0	3	5	8	8
9	3	5	6	9	6	5	0	1	9	4	6	6	7	5	6	8	3	1
10	8	5	0	3	9	4	3	4	0	6	5	1	7	4	4	6	2	7
11	0	5	9	6	8	7	4	8	1	5	5	0	5	1	7	1	5	8
12	7	6	2	2	6	9	6	1	9	7	1	1	4	7	1	6	2	0
13	3	8	4	7	8	9	8	2	2	1	6	3	8	7	0	4	6	1
14	1	9	1	8	4	5	6	1	8	1	2	4	4	4	2	7	3	4
15	1	5	3	6	7	6	1	8	4	3	1	8	8	7	7	6	0	4
16	0	5	5	3	6	0	7	1	3	8	1	4	6	7	0	4	3	5
17	2	2	3	8	6	0	9	1	9	0	4	4	7	6	8	1	5	1
18	2	3	3	2	5	5	7	6	9	4	9	7	1	3	7	9	3	8
19	8	5	5	0	5	3	7	8	5	4	5	1	6	0	4	8	9	1
20	0	6	1	1	3	4	8	6	4	3	2	9	4	3	8	7	4	1
21	9	1	1	8	2	9	0	6	9	6	9	4	2	9	9	0	6	0
22	3	7	8	0	6	3	7	1	2	6	5	2	7	6	5	6	5	1
23	5	3	0	5	1	2	1	0	9	1	3	7	5	6	1	2	5	0
24	7	2	4	8	6	7	9	3	8	7	6	0	9	1	6	5	7	8
25	0	9	1	6	7	0	3	8	0	9	1	5	4	2	3	2	4	5
26	3	8	1	4	3	7	9	2	4	5	1	2	8	7	7	4	1	3

[1]From *Understanding Research Methods: An Overview of the Essentials* (p. 125), by M. Patten, (1997), Los Angeles: Pyrczak Publishing. Reprinted with permission of the publisher.

ous research reports that year in college has a profound effect on leisure. Your university's undergraduate population consists of 35% freshmen, 30% sophomores, 20% juniors, and 15% seniors. Thus, you ask the Registrar's office to print a random listing of undergraduates by rank. You know, by consulting a table of recommended sample size (see Figure 8.3), that you need at least a sample size of 370 (sample size will be discussed later in this chapter). Using the proportions found in the college population as a guide, you ask the Registrar to generate the 370 names in the following proportions:

Freshmen = 35% population or 129 names

Sophomores = 30% population or 111 names

Juniors = 20% population or 74 names

Seniors = 15% population or 56 names

One key, then, to using a stratified random sampling approach is to have some discernible and defensible reason for using the stratum you have chosen. A second key to using the stratified random sampling approach is to weigh or draw correctly the appropriate percentage in each strata.

Systematic Sampling

Systematic sampling is considered by some as an example of probability sampling and by others as nonprobability sampling. Where it belongs depends on how it is executed. In order to be considered an example of probability sampling, each person in the population must have an equal and independent chance of being selected.

The basic idea behind systematic sampling is that every *n*th person is selected. This nth could be set at every second person, every 10th person, or whatever. Once the number (or *n*th) has been determined, a list of the population members is consulted to choose the sample. The selection from this list is initiated by choosing a random starting point. For example, if the *n*th selected is 10, you consult a table of random numbers to choose one of the first 10 names as your starting point. After the initial person has been identified (using one of the techniques described for simple random sampling), then every 10th name appearing in the list is selected for the sample.

Traditionally, the list of population names is arranged alphabetically. Using such a list is not a problem as long as you go completely through the list to select the sample. For example, do not stop at the letter *m* since members of various ethnic origins tend to cluster at different points in the alphabet (Dorsten, 1996, p. 129).

Dorsten (1996, p. 129) points out that care must be taken so the arrangement of individuals in a population is not skewed in such a fashion as to result in an unintended biased sample being drawn. He recounts a story of how a study originally designed to use probability systematic sampling wound up using nonprobability systematic sampling instead. In this study, every other person entering a concert hall was surveyed. What the evaluator failed to consider was that people arrived primarily as couples—with women entering first. The resulting sample wound up being a biased one since mainly women were selected for the study.

An example of how systematic sampling has been used in leisure research is Havitz's (1995) study of the track and field competition held for masters athletes (or women age 35 and older and men aged 40 and older). Havitz noted (p. 4), "Questionnaires were handed out ... at the official championships registration table to each athlete whose name was on the systematic sample list. Starting from a random spot on the registration list, every fourth name was chosen."

Cluster Sampling

In *cluster sampling*, groups or cluster(s) are randomly selected, and then all the people within the group or cluster are surveyed or interviewed. For instance, suppose a researcher wanted to conduct a study of individuals attending four-year colleges or universities in the United States. A list of all these institutions could be made and broken down or stratified by geographical region or any other relevant variable, such as whether the school is public or private. From these lists, a sample of institutions could be drawn using random sampling. Lists of students at each selected institution could be obtained and then sampled. Cluster sampling is used to reduce expenses. It would be too expensive, for instance in the example cited above, to interview students at every college.

Nonprobability Sampling

If you do not identify all members of a population or you have not given everyone in the population a chance to be included (or excluded) in the sampling framework used in the study, you have introduced bias in the sampling. Such biases result in *non-probability* or biased *sampling* occurring.

Before turning to the various kinds of nonproability sampling techniques, a few words are needed regarding why such sampling is used, especially with studies using a qualitative framework. Often samples in qualitative studies evolve after the study is underway. This happens because initial contact with a respondent(s) suggests to you other persons who should be sampled. Miles and Huberman (1994) label this *conceptually-driven sampling*. That is, the inherent nature of the event studied points to the best people to interview or observe. Suppose a study is underway to understand how the structural characteristics of play apparatus instruct children's play behavior. Such "directions" as the apparatus height, materials (plastic versus wood), range of motion required, or any other things that can potentially influence children's play behaviors are observed. During these observations it might be noticed that adults who accompany the children augment these physical directions with their own behaviors and cues. Given adoption of the qualitative framework, observations of adults' behavior along with apparatus height, etc. would then be made.

In summary, it is up to the skill and judgement of the evaluators to set the boundaries and rationale for the sampling. When nonproability sampling is used, care should be taken to avoid unnecessary bias that can produce incorrect results. Four of the common approaches to nonprobability sampling are: purposive sampling, quota sampling, volunteer sampling, and snowball sampling.

Purposive Sampling

Often times a *purposive sample* is used by recreation organizations conducting evaluative research studies. Evaluators purposively seek out subjects they believe, based on the evaluator's judgement or intuition, will fulfill needs of the project. These individuals are simply considered as important sources of information. Some examples of purposive sampling are:

- In order to assess the resort's unique niche in the tourism market of the area, a general manager for a beach resort chooses guests who return to the resort annually for their vacation.
- As a way of determining student body satisfaction with the Friday night current political events lecture series sponsored by the college student union, a programmer chooses students who vary significantly from each other in their political views.
- To observe how a convention hall lobby is used, hour long observations are conducted in the lobby in the early morning, late morning, early afternoon, late afternoon, early evening, and late evening.

Purposive sampling draws samples according to a specific purpose. These purposes could be according to specific characteristics of people, recreational activity pursuits, park and recreation facilities, and even time periods.

One use for purposive sampling is to include in the study people, activities, or facilities who represent a wide and diverse range on a particular characteristic. These are called purposive sampling with a *heterogenous sample*. In the student union example cited above, the students were chosen for the evaluation of the weekly current events lecture series because they varied widely from each other on political views. The utility of a heterogenous sample is the process of deliberately selecting a diverse sample and observing commonalities in sample members' behaviors, attitudes, or characteristics. This strategy is most often necessary when exploring abstract concepts.

In contrast, when participants, activities, or facilities are chosen because they represent a narrow range on a particular characteristic, this is labeled purposive sampling with a *homogenous sample*. Here the purpose in the sampling is to focus and simplify what is studied.

An abstract idea is not the concern; instead, some specific information about a program or service is needed. For instance, suppose the board of directors of a soccer league wants to know how adult members feel about the league. Accordingly, as part of the spring pre-registration process, the first 20 persons signing up will be queried.

Another basis upon which to sample purposively is to form an *extreme case sample*. This is sampling that concentrates on the outermost or unusual values of a particular characteristic. An example of extreme case sampling is assessing those clients who responded the least favorably to an experimental activity therapy or technique. The beach resort manager, from the earlier example, who chose guests who return every year also employed extreme case sampling because these guests do not represent the "typical" guest at the resort—they are instead guests who enjoy the resort to an unusual extent. And still another example would be to choose to study the one park in the city's system that has the highest incidence of graffiti and litter.

Another way to sample with a specific purpose is to use purposive sampling with an *expert sample*. Suppose the family services director for a community church wants to understand the power hierarchy among the local youth population. He decides to interview those people he considers to possess the information he needs, or the high school principal, the high school custodian, the chief of police, and the teen center director. He has selected this sample because of their expertise in working with the town's youth.

Still another use of purposive sampling is to select a *time sample*. This usually means sampling across time or studying behavior of people at a specific time(s) of the day or week. The convention lobby observation example above uses a time sample. There may also be good reason to sample only a specific time. For instance, suppose the director of an older adult recreation center wants to find out what informal game activities (such as card playing) participants typically choose when they come to the center. Every day for two weeks she makes observations of the choices of every person who enters the center between 11 A.M. and noon. This time was chosen because it was the peak arrival time at the center—it was just before lunch was served!

Purposive samples are frequently used because they are relatively easy to obtain and inexpensive. Nevertheless, as Kerlinger (1986) note,s there is a much higher likelihood that random selection will provide a representative sample than one that is purposively selected.

Quota Sampling

Quota sampling is used to obtain representativeness on one or more characteristics by using a relative proportions approach. Quota sampling is the non-probability equivalent of stratified sampling. That is, the evaluator attempts, in a non-random, nonprobability fashion, to achieve a sample that equitably fills specific quotas. This means a population is divided into *stratum* or subgroups that are considered important, and the percentage of persons sought for these subgroups is set at what is believed to mirror the distribution in real life. Examples of quota sampling are:

- In order to find out how her coaching techniques are experienced by the runners, a track coach chooses the two runners with the fastest times and two runners with the slowest times in each running event.
- To measure users' reactions to swimming pool fees, the city aquatics director chooses to sample people from low-, middle-, and high-income groups, as well as people from each of the city's nine neighborhoods.
- A manager wants to know about the quality of visitors' park visits. Over an eight-hour period, the first male and first female seen after each 15-minute interval is in tercepted and asked to participate in the study.

In quota sampling, care must be taken to select the correct proportion in each subgroup. The number of persons sampled in the stratum should reflect the true proportions of sub-groups (or sub-populations) in the whole population. For instance, in the hiking trail example, perhaps in reality 75% of the trail users are male, thus the 50-50 percent quota of males and females will yield an under-representative sample of males and a over-representative sample of females.

Additionally, caution needs to be taken to select those subgroups that truly represent qualities important to the study. If socio-economic level is important to the evaluation question under examination, even if it is inconvenient or more costly, be careful not to leave out representatives from each socio-economic level. Robson illustrates the subtlety of socio-economic discrimination by pointing out,

> If home visits are involved, avoiding houses where there is a Rottweiler or other large dog, or sounds of a ghetto-blaster, or where there are not curtains, or the lift is out of order, etc. may be understandable behaviour on the part of the sensitive interviewer, but mitigates against representativeness in householders in the sense of all householders having an equal chance of appearing in the sample. (1993, pp. 140-141)

Volunteer Sampling

Volunteer sampling is also known as *convenience* or *accidental sampling*. A volunteer sample is a group that is conveniently available to be tapped for the evaluation. An example of a volunteer sample is deciding that, in order to assess a Girl Scout council's summer camp food service, the food operation in the camp closest to the council office will be examined.

Reliance on volunteer sampling can produce a biased sample. A case in point is when Ann Landers asked (Black, 1993, p. 50) readers to respond to the question, "If you had to do it over again, would you have children?" Over 10,000 persons responded, 70% saying "No!" In contrast, *Newsday* conducted a random sample of 1,373 parents and reported that

91% declared they would have children again. So can 10,000 persons be wrong? Maybe not, but certainly there is little guarantee that the 10,000 persons represented American parents. Indeed, relying on probability sampling laws, we should have greater confidence in the validity of the findings of *Newsday*—even though 1/10th the number of persons were involved in the sample relative to the numbers responding to Ann Landers' open forum!

It is important to remember that some people may volunteer to be involved in a survey because they have a "gripe" or complaint. Maybe those who respond to a newspaper survey, questionnaire, or agree to be interviewed as they leave a park are malcontents. For example, in reality, it may be that most of the park users are quite satisfied with their park experiences and that dissatisfied users will be disproportionately represented in the sample. Or maybe those who volunteer to participate in a study that might put them in a group to receive a novel activity are healthier or are different on some other important dimension when compared to those who do not agree to participate or step forward to participate. Permitting people to self-select themselves into a study results in not knowing how and what direction bias has been introduced and how, in turn, the results are affected. Are the participants better or worse off before they started our program? And how can and does that skew our results?

A second way volunteers can creep into our study is more subtle and just as problematic. Initially, we may have used some probability sampling technique to identify potential participants for a survey. For instance, a random sample of undergraduate students might have been drawn and asked to take part in a study dealing with leisure attitudes and activities. For any number of reasons, a large number of those initially identified and contacted to participate in the study elected to refuse to participate (they did not return the pre-paid postage survey form). Those who elected to participate in the study were volunteers. These cooperating individuals may be fundamentally different from non-volunteers or non-respondents. As a rule of thumb, response rates of $\geq$ 75% in a probability sample are considered to elicit responses similar to the population. Thus, if you read that a study initially set out to use a random sampling technique but got a response rate $\leq$ 75%, then in effect you should interpret results based on a volunteer (and hence biased) sample as being used to conduct the study (Rossi & Freeman, 1993, p. 239).

In sum, the obvious reason to choose volunteer sampling is that it is convenient. Convenience sampling saves time, money, and effort. Yet, just as obvious, the major disadvantage in this sampling method is it will quite likely produce biased and inaccurate information. For example, what if the Girl Scout camp closest to the council office just so happens to be the camp with the best (or worst) food? Is this a fair assessment of the food service across all the council's several camps? Thus, when possible, convenience sampling should be avoided for studies using a quantitative and qualitative framework. Nevertheless, it is recognized that sometimes a convenience sample is the only choice open to the evaluator. Perhaps costs, time limitations, or official restrictions prohibit full access to possible research participants. When this is the case, the study should be *replicated*, that is repeated with similar samples to help assure that the results were not just a one-time fluke (Fraenkel & Wallen, 1993).

In closing, there is, however, one sensible use of convenience sampling. This sampling method can be helpful in preliminary inquiries (or pilot studies, see Chapter 9) in order to gain an informal "sense" of a situation. Results from a convenience sample may help the evaluator design the full-fledged evaluative research study.

Snowball Sampling

In *snowball sampling* the evaluator identifies a small number of subjects with the required characteristics for the study, and these subjects in turn identify others who could be tapped for the study. This cycle of identifying potential recruits on the basis of recommendations by others who have been tapped for the sample repeats itself until the requisite numbers for the desired sample size are found—hence the analogy to creating a snowball. Snowball sampling is yet another form of non-probability sampling. This type of sampling is resorted to when subjects are "hard to find." Often snowball sampling is used in tandem with another sampling method. For instance, an evaluator initially uses purposive sampling in order to employ snowball sampling to identify individuals who match the specific characteristics sought. For example, the church family services director, in the earlier example, could ask the school principal and the police chief for recommendations of other people who have expertise in working with youth. Or suppose you want to identify elders who are non-users of a Congregate Meals Program, a program that serves weekday lunches as well as provides recreational activities. How will you find these non-users? First, you locate one non-user and convince that person to put you in contact with others he knows or thinks he knows do not use the program but are qualified to do so. Each of these non-users helps you contact others, who are also non-users.

Snowball is similar to the pyramid strategies associated with chain letters. A snowball sample must presumably be non-probability because it is unknown about how representative the sample is to the population that it hypothetically represents. Nevertheless, there are times that without using a snowball sample to identify a "special population" we would be unable to undertake a study.

Is the Sample Representative?

Regardless of sampling approach used (probability or non-probability) other sources of error exist. One such error has been classified as sampling error (Black, 1993, p. 52).

Samples drawn using probability techniques are subject to *"sampling error."* By this, it is meant that even though a sample may be initially selected or drawn using a probability selection technique, a non-random sample may occur. For example, quite by chance a so-called "random sample" might in fact contain a disproportionately larger number of males, dissatisfied users, and so on. Or if a survey of a community is conducted by using a random selection of numbers from a telephone book, sampling error results due to a number of causes (Black, 1993, p. 52). First, 7% of the households in the United States do not have telephones. Second, problems arise when computer-generated dialing of a random number is used. When no one answers, the computer system moves on to a new number, thus reaching those who are easiest to contact. Under these circumstances about 37% of the answered calls will be by males, even though males represent half of the population.

Determinants of Sample Size

Sample size is the number of persons needed for a study. How large a sample is needed is a very difficult question to answer and will depend on a number of things. Some of the factors that typically need to be considered in pondering sample size are nature of the study, variability within the population, and size of difference.

Factors Affecting Sample Size

The purpose of the study affects sample size. Studies that are focusing or assessing the impact of a program and use a quasi-experimental or experimental design will require a small sample size relative to a survey. In these situations, the focus is on internal validity. If the study is non-experimental (that is, a survey or *ex post facto* correlational design has been used), then the emphasis is on being able to generalize (or a focus on external validity, review Chapter 7). Again, when we talk about being able to *generalize* we chose a design and sample size that strives to maximize, to the extent possible under the circumstances at hand, the degree of certainty one has that the noted results apply to the population from whom the sample was drawn.

Another factor that affects sample size for surveys and *ex post facto* designs is variability within the population. If the population is very *homogenous* or has little variability in the dependent variable under study, you can use a smaller sample size in conducting the study. If the population, however, is very *heterogenous* or has a lot of variability, a larger sample size is needed.

Suppose, for instance, an organization wants to study leisure activity patterns among adults in New York City. There undoubtedly is great variability or heterogeneity in New Yorkers—ranging from inactive sedentary individuals to marathon runners. Thus, a large sample size would need to be drawn given the heterogeneity of New Yorkers.

Regardless of design used, if you are looking for a small difference, then a larger sample size is needed. For example, suppose a younger age cohort is slightly more active in high energy-requiring activities than an older age cohort. A small random sample might not divulge these subtle differences due to sampling error (again, errors created by random chance). Indeed, to the contrary, a small random sample might yield results that really are opposite to the truth—yielding the false impression that the older cohort, relative to the younger age cohort, is more active in higher energy-requiring activities.

Sample Size Guidelines

Figure 8.3 will be helpful in estimating sample size for studies using a survey or *ex post facto* correlational design. Using the sample size column (labeled the *n* column) that corresponds to the population size (*N*) will hold sampling error down to about ± 5%. That is, the true percentage in the whole or entire population should fall within ± 5% of the percentage obtained from the sample.

Let's take a moment to apply these guidelines to an example. Suppose you are the chair of a research committee for the state recreation society. A request has been made that you design a study to assess the burnout of therapeutic recreation (TR) professionals working in the state's acute psychiatric hospitals. The most recent number of persons reported working in this capacity is 200 (the population size). After consulting Figure 8.3, you know you need to choose randomly 132 TR professionals to survey. Reviewing the returned questionnaires (with a 90% response rate) you learn that 85% of the respondents reported the number-one issue for them is burnout. You can then say you are 95% confident, had you surveyed all 200 TR professionals, somewhere between 80% to 90% (or ± 5%) would have identified burnout as the number one issue confronting them.

A general rule of thumb is that increasing sample size increases precision as long as an unbiased sample has been drawn. There is, however, a point of diminishing returns. Examine Figure 8.3 and find out how many persons are needed in a sample if the population size is known to be 300? 600? (The correct answers are 169 and 234 persons, respectfully. Notice how the sample size did not increase that much, even though the population size was doubled—this illustrates the principle of diminishing returns!)

To make matters even more complicated in determining sample size needed when an *ex post facto* correlational design is used, statisticians typically advise that about 35 individuals are needed for each independent variable included in the study (Kerlinger & Pedhazar, 1973). Returning to the survey example of TR professionals working in acute psychiatric units, suppose another purpose of the study is to determine how five variables (such as number of years working in the profession, whether or not the individual had earned a master's degree, percentage of time spent in direct patient care, etc.) explain or predict burnout. In order to perform the statistics, sample size would then jump from a survey requirement of 132 to 175 (or five independent variables x 35 = 175 persons needed for the study).

For studies using a quasi-experimental model (reflecting an evaluation of the impact of an intervention program or service), experts tell us a minimum of 25-45 individuals are needed. Sample size in these kinds of studies becomes dependent on a number of things,

Figure 8.3: Recommended sample sizes (*n*) for finite size populations (*N*).[2]

N	n	N	n	N	n
10	10	220	140	1200	291
15	14	230	144	1300	297
20	19	240	148	1400	302
25	24	250	152	1500	306
30	28	260	155	1600	310
35	32	270	159	1700	313
40	36	280	162	1800	317
45	40	290	165	1900	320
50	44	300	169	2000	322
55	48	320	175	5500	327
60	52	340	181	2400	331
65	56	360	186	2600	335
70	59	380	191	2800	338
75	63	400	196	3000	341
80	66	420	201	3500	346
85	70	440	205	4000	351
90	73	460	210	4500	354
95	76	480	214	5000	357
100	80	200	217	6000	361
120	92	600	234	8000	367
130	97	650	242	9000	368
140	103	700	248	10,000	370
150	108	750	254	15.000	375
160	113	800	260	20,000	377
170	118	850	265	30.000	679
180	123	900	269	40.000	380
190	127	950	274	50,000	381
200	132	1000	278	75,000	382
210	136	1100	285	100,000	384

[2]From R. Krejcie and D. Morgan, (1970), "Determining Sample Size for Research Activities", *Educational and Psychological Measurement (30)*, p. 610, (p. 126). Reprinted with permission of Sage Publications.

most notably effect size, levels of power, and alpha level—technical considerations beyond the scope of this book but aptly described by Hedrick, Bickman, and Rog, (1993) as well as Henry (1990).

Main Points:

- In order to select a sample, one must first be able to answer two questions: (1) What is the purpose of the evaluation? and (2) About whom do you want to know?

- There are two approaches to sampling, or using probability or nonprobability sampling.

- Studies that are based on a quantitative framework can employ either probability or nonprobability sampling. Studies that center around a qualitative framework typically rely on nonprobability sampling.

- *Probability sampling* uses probability or chance so that every member of a population has an equal chance of being included in the sample. Four of the more common probability sampling techniques used in leisure research are simple random sampling, stratified random sampling, systematic sampling, and cluster sampling.

- *Simple random sampling* involves giving every person in the population the same chance of being selected.

- *Stratified random sampling* involves identifying a stratum and then using random selection techniques to draw a correct proportion for the identified stratum.

- *Systematic sampling* requires sampling every *n*th person in a population.

- *Nonprobability sampling* occurs when all members of a population have not been identified or when everyone in the population has not been given the same chance to be included in the sampling framework used for the study. Some of the more common nonprobability sampling strategies used in leisure research are purposive sampling, quota sampling, volunteer sampling, and snowball sampling.

- *Purposive sampling* involves seeking out subjects believed to fulfill the needs of the evaluation. Purposive sampling can be approached by trying to find respondents believed to represent a heterogenous sample, a homogenous sample, an extreme case sample, an expert sample, or a time sample.

- *Quota sampling* is used to obtain representativeness on one or more characteristics by using a relative proportions approach (or finding so many units that fulfill a quota specified for each subgroup).

- *Volunteer sampling* relies on using people, groups, etc. who are conveniently accessible to the evaluator. Such an approach is fraught with biases and thus should be avoided if at all possible.

- *Snowball sampling* identifies one individual with the required characteristic(s) for the study, and this person in turn identifies others who could be tapped for the study.

- All samples, regardless of whether probability or nonprobability sampling has been used, run the risk of having sampling error.

- *Sample size*, or the number of persons needed for a study, will depend on the nature or purpose of the study, variability in the population, and the size of differences being examined. For surveys and *ex post facto* correlation designs, a table for estimating sample size can be consulted in order to get an approximation of sample size. For studies using a quasi-experimental design, experts tell us a minimum of 25-45 individuals are needed.

Study Questions

1. What is a population? Sample?

2. What distinguishes probability and nonprobability sampling?

3. What is the difference between simple random sampling and stratified random sampling? Give an example of an evaluation situation you can use simple random sampling and stratified random sampling, respectively.

4. What is systematic sampling? Cluster sampling?

5. What is purposive sampling? What does it mean to use purposive sampling with a heterogenous ample? With a homogenous sample? With a time sample?

6. What is quota sampling? Volunteer sampling? Snowball sampling? Cite recreation—related examples of how each of these sampling approaches could be used.

7. How can sampling error occur when using probability sampling?

8. How large a sample do you need to conduct a study?

References

Black, T. (1993). *Evaluating social science research: An introduction.* Thousand Oaks, CA: Sage Publications.

Dortsen, L. (1996). *Interpreting social and behavioral research: A guide and workbook based on excerpts from journal articles.* Los Angeles: Pyrczak Publishing.

Fraenkel, J., & Wallen, N. (1993). *How to design and evaluate research in education* (2nd ed.). New York: McGraw-Hill.

Havitz, M. (1991). Measuring sector biases in recreation participants. *Journal of Park and Recreation Administration, 9*, 1-17.

Hedrick, T., Bickman, L., & Rog, D. (1993). *Applied research design: A practical guide.* Newbury Park, CA: Sage Publications.

Henry, G. (1990). *Practical sampling.* Newbury Park, CA: Sage Publications.

Kerlinger, F. (1986). *Foundations of behavioral research* (3rd ed.). New York: Holt, Rinehart & Winston.

Kerlinger, F., & Pedhazar, E. (1973). Multiple regression in behavioral research. New York: Holt, Rinehart, & Winston.

Krejcie, R. & Morgan, D. (1970). Determining sample size for research activities. *Educational and Psychological Measurement, 30*, 607–610.

Miles, M., & Huberman, A. (1994). *Qualitative data analysis.* Thousand Oaks, CA: Sage Publications.

Patten, M. (1997). *Understanding research methods: An overview of the essentials.* Los Angeles: Pyrczak Publishing.

Robson, C. (1993). *Real world research: A resource for social scientists and practitioner-researchers.* Oxford, UK: Blackwell.

Rossi, P., & Freeman, H. 1993). *Evaluation: a systematic approach.* Newbury Park, CA: Sage Publications.

Weisberg, H., Krosnick, J., & Bowen, B.(1996). *An introduction to survey research, polling, and data analysis* (3rd ed.). Thousand Oaks, CA: Sage Publications.

CHAPTER 9

Procedures

What Will I Learn in This Chapter?
I'll be able to:

1. List the steps to the "logic of measurement" and apply these steps to an example.

2. Define referent validity, judgmental validity, criterion related validity, construct validity, inter-observer reliability, test-retest reliability, parallel-forms reliability, and internal consistency.

3. Using a bulls-eye diagram, contrast unreliability and invalidity, reliability and invalidity, and reliability and validity.

4. Define non-reactive measure and name the two types of non-reactive measures that exist.

5. Locate an appropriate measuring instrument for a concept of interest to me.

6. Identify the tasks that can be accomplished by conducting a pilot study.

The first step in the implementation stage of evaluative research planning is to turn attention to the details related to concept measurement. In particular, a lot of time is spent on issues related to the logic of measurement and choosing from existing instruments. Another area that needs to be planned for is conducting a pilot study. Accordingly, this chapter will introduce you to the procedures necessary to execute an evaluative research study. Namely, issues surrounding measurement are discussed. Second, the need for pilot testing and ideas on how to implement pilot testing are reviewed.

Concept Measurement

There are basically two ways to operationalize, define, or measure concepts—either use an already existing instrument or create your own instrument. The focus of this chapter is on the former because there are so many existing measures at our disposal.

This concept measurement section has three subsections. First, the logic of measurement will be reviewed. Second, some things to consider when choosing an instrument will be reviewed. Third, resources that can assist you in finding existing instruments that probably will meet your needs will be identified.

Logic of Measurement

Each concept or construct identified in the research question, objective, or hypothesis must ultimately be measured. In other words, you must make a bridge between a concept to variable, from variable to measuring instrument, and from measuring instrument to units of measurement. Dixon, Bouma and Atkinson (1987) labeled this process as the *logic of measurement.* The logic of measurement consists of specifying 4 things (Figure 9.1) :

- First, recall *each concept/construct* under examination. Again, these concepts or constructs can be found in the research question, objective, or hypothesis.
- Second, select a *variable*(s) that reflects a working definition (technically known as the *nominal definition)* of each concept under inquiry.
- Third, select or devise a *measuring instrument* (technically known as the *operational definition*) for each variable.
- Fourth, specify *units of measurements* for each variable. In other words, a system for categorizing answers must be adopted or devised.

Some examples of how this logic of measurement can be applied appear in Figure 9.2.

The critical step in operationalizing a definition is selecting at least one *measuring instrument* or *indicator* for each concept under study. For instance, the concept "community reintegration" could be nominally defined by choosing an indicator for awareness of community leisure resources. And awareness of community leisure resources may in turn be measured by a test that measures knowledge of community leisure resources (Riley, 1991, p. 78). Operationalizing the concepts found in the research question, objective or hypothesis, means specifying measurements or indicators. The ideal is to have a high level or defendable "goodness-of-fit" (typically known as *referent validity*) between the operationlized indicator and the concept or construct (Grosof & Sardy, 1985, pp. 73-74). In other words, care should be taken so there is "good" referent validity. *Referent validity* means the selected instrument is an appropriate measure for the concept under examination.

Choosing Instruments

It is important to remember that when searching for a measure, the evaluator must be mindful of the nature or purpose of the study. If, for instance, a study's intent is to measure the impact of participating in an aerobics class on fitness, a decision will have to be made as to how fitness will be measured. Should the focus be on examining: Knowledge about physical fitness? Attitudes about physical fitness? Behavior(s) related to physical fitness? Physical

Figure 9.1: Moving from concept to measurement: Four questions to be decided.

1. What **concept**(s) is being studied?
2. How will each concept be nominally defined as a **variable**?
3. What operational definition or **measuring instrument** will be used for each selected variable?
4. What **units of measurement** will be used for each selected measuring instrument?

Figure 9.2: Examples of the logical order of steps to be decided in measurement.[1]

Concept	Variable	Measuring Instrument	Units Measurement
mental ability	intelligence	college grade point average	0 to 4 points
social support network	best friends	self reported count	0 to ???
body composition	body density	underwater (hydrostatic) weighting	lean-fat ratio
leisure	leisure time	self report amount of discretionary time/week	hours
good life[a]	quality of life[a]	time/day devoted to walking, hiking, playing outdoors, and engaging in sports[a]	minutes
		adult population taking annual vacation of ≥6 days/year[a]	% adult population
		time/day devoted to gardening and pets[a]	minutes

[1]From *The Joyless Economy* (p. 3), by T Scitovsky, 1976, NY: Oxford Press.

condition? If the program is speculated to have an affect on behavior, then the evaluator should make every effort to find a behavioral measure(s) rather than use an attitude measure. Choosing to measure attitudes, as an indirect measure of behavior, could be a compromise that would be subject to an incorrect understanding of the impact of the fitness program.

Another important point to remember when searching for a measure is to use multiple measures. In evaluating the success of a program, employee, physical plant, etc. it is advisable to consider multiple dependent variables and/or a couple of approaches to measuring the same concept. At best, each measure of the same concept can be viewed as only a partial glimpse of what is happening. Individually, each instrument captures a fraction of the larger concept. That is, each measure contributes a different perspective or facet of the concept—used collectively we should see a "truer" picture of program outcomes. It has been our experience that evaluators all too often sell themselves or whatever is being evaluated short by tunneling in and identifying only one variable for each concept.

For example, affect is a mental–health concept that can be reflected by any number of variables. Examples of variables that nominally define affect are anxiety, mood, and depression (see Figure 9.3).

As part of the background documentation on an instrument, normative data ideally exist. *Normative data* exists when studies have documented the way the instrument works (technically this whole process is known as *standardization*). That is, the instrument has been administered under controlled circumstances to a well defined group, and how this group performed on the instrument has been recorded and maintained. Such comparative

Figure 9.3: The effects of physical fitness training on pschological affect: Examples of variables (or nominal definitions) that can be used to examine affect.[2]

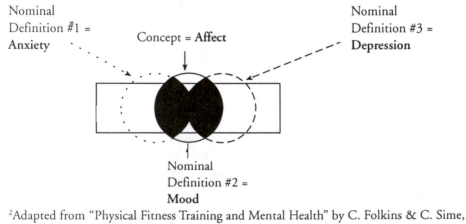

Nominal Definition #1 = Anxiety

Concept = **Affect**

Nominal Definition #3 = **Depression**

Nominal Definition #2 = **Mood**

[2]Adapted from "Physical Fitness Training and Mental Health" by C. Folkins & C. Sime, (1981), *American Psychologist* (p. 379).

data will pinpoint characteristics of the evaluation group that are similar or "unique" in terms of their divergence from other groups.

Using an instrument, for which normative data already exist, has the advantage of being able to make comparisons about the relative need for a program or the relative effectiveness of one program against another. It is unfortunate that few standardized instruments have yet to be developed to assist leisure service professionals. One exception, however, is Witt and Ellis' (1990) Leisure Diagnostic Battery (LDB). Normative data exist on the LDB for children and adults with a variety of backgrounds (persons with asthma, mental retardation, drug addiction, etc.) as well as therapeutic recreation and physical education majors.

A multitude of instruments, for a variety of concepts, have already been developed. When you start researching what has been developed, you are likely to encounter an experience akin to being in a grocery store warehouse. The shelves are packed with a variety of products. The trouble will be deciding which one is "best" for the evaluation at hand. Sorting or sifting through what is available one should be mindful of the: instrument's validity, instrument reactivity, and instrument's reliability.

Instrument's validity. An instrument is considered *valid* when it measures what it is supposed to measure and performs the functions that it claims to perform (Patten, 1997, p. 53). An instrument's validity is a matter of degree. At best, an instrument can measure only a sample of the social or psychological behavior, attitude, attribute, etc. underlying the construct. Some traits are inherently elusive. What, for example, is quality of life? Quality of recreational experiences?

There are basically several approaches for establishing the validity of an instrument (Carmines & Zeller, 1979). One approach uses judgmental or content validity. The second uses a criteria validity perspective. The third approach uses construct validity from an experimental perspective. And the fourth approach uses construct validity from a correlational approach.

In *judgmental validity*, judgments are made on the appropriateness of the instrument's contents. Judgmental validity can be established two ways. One way is that an individual decides on his own, the instrument has *face validity*. *Judgmental validity* can be determined by a panel of experts that reviews the instrument and decides it has *content validity*. Either approach to establishing judgmental validity entails deciding if the instrument contains items that indeed measure what they purportedly say they do. When evaluators are confronted with the task of devising an instrument, at the very least, they should use a panel of experts (e.g., staff of the agency) to establish the content validity of the measuring instrument.

In *criterion validity* comparisons are made to find out if a measure yields scores that relate to either a preselected criterion or standard. Criterion validity can be established one of two ways or by predictive validity or concurrent validity. *Predictive validity* documents the extent the test predicts what it is supposed to predict. Some preselected criteria is identified. For example, how well a newly developed test predicts success in a job, graduation from a master's program, etc. would be examples of efforts to establish predictive validity. *Concurrent validity* documents how well the results of a new test compare to the results of a known valid test. In other words, the known valid test becomes the standard by which to judge the new test. Both tests should basically yield the same results.

Construct validity uses a blend of subjective, logical judgments along with empirical data. One procedure for determining construct validity is experimental and involves documenting the degree to which certain traits or qualities underlie or account for performance. In other words, the investigator, relying on theory or judgment, speculates what characteristic(s) will distinguish high and low scorers on the test. For example, do well rested participants perform better on a ropes course exam than very tired participants? A reasonable prediction would be that fatigue level will affect ropes performance results. Thus, logically one would think that the data collected would confirm this judgment. If a study found that rest/fatigue level indeed was related to performance on the ropes course, then evidence for the construct validity of the measure exists.

Another approach to documenting construct validity is to correlate a test measure with other tests to determine if the measuring instruments are measuring the same or different constructs. For instance, we would expect a valid test of loneliness to correlate more highly with amount of time spent alone than with a leisure interests test.

In summary, there are five types of validity: judgmental validity, the simplest procedure, requires only a single concept and a single measure of the concept. Criterion validity with a predictive approach requires identifying a trait or characteristic that predicts an outcome. Criterion validity with a concurrent approach requires only one concept but two or more measures of that concept. Construct validity with an experimental approach requires identifying a trait or characteristic that is believed to be a criterion to diagnosing or predicting performance. Construct validity with a correlational approach requires two concepts, each having at least two measures. All four approaches to establishing validity are conceptually independent. This means ideally a measuring instrument should have documented validity in all four areas.

Instrument reactivity. Many measuring instruments are obvious to evaluation study respondents. That is, these measures "intrude as a foreign element into the situation they describe" (Russell, 1992, p. 30). When you ask people questions you make them aware that you are studying them, and sometimes this sets into motion atypical responses or the portrayal of attitudes that are socially acceptable yet not truly those of the respondent. This can invalidate the evaluation results—when people know their actions or words are being measured, they do not always respond normally or truthfully. Thus, interviews and questionnaires can create as well as measure responses. Such measuring instruments are, therefore, labeled *reactive measures* (Webb, Campbell, Schwartz, Sechrest, & Grove, 1981).

In order not to rely solely on such reactive measures in evaluation research, we frequently incorporate non-reactive measures in a study. *Non-reactive measures* examine naturally occurring information. This is not at all difficult to do; in fact we collect and make management decisions based on non-reactive information every day. The number of pre-registrations for a dance class tells us something of the effectiveness of our marketing strategy. The worn footpath across the grassy sections of the park indicate visitors' natural traffic patterns, which can be the basis of decisions about future trail construction or modification. The case load records at the campus counseling center help indicate the timing of stress for college students (such as during the final exam period), which in turn could help us better understand when to schedule recreational sport activities.

The point is that non-reactive measures can offer an additional source of information in an evaluation. Used simultaneously with the more typical measures, non-reactive measures can provide a triangulation of data for the project (Chapter 10 will discuss triangulation in depth). There are two basic types of non-reactive measures: physical traces and archival documents or records.

Physical tracing is finding and recording visible evidence of behavior. These are pieces of data, or traces, not specifically produced for the research project but nonetheless available and thus are exploited opportunistically. The debris from a party provides a trace about what went on; graffiti on the recreation center restroom walls offer a clue to the concerns of youth; food wastage in the camp dining hall adds to our knowledge of menu popularity. Physical traces are inconspicuous and anonymous; those who left them have no knowledge of their potential for use in an evaluation project.

Webb et al. (1981) distinguish between two broad classes of physical traces. On the one hand, there are *erosion physical traces*, where the degree of selective wear on some material produces the measure. Such measures can be an index to popularity—for example, the wear patterns on floor tiles in front of various museum exhibits. The degree of concern by substance abuse counseling center clients about AIDS could be measured by the rate at which informational brochures about the disease need to be replenished in the waiting room area. On the other hand, there are *accretion physical traces*. These involve the deposit or accumulation of material. For example, counting the number of alcohol containers left on the beach could yield a measure of the level of compliance with the city's "no containers" policy.

Although physical trace measures are easy (and sometimes even fun) to gather, there are limitations to their usefulness. First, certain accretion measures vary substantially in their survivability and their tendency to be deposited. Also, for erosion traces an extensive period of time needs to elapse before the data can be collected, such as the wear on new tile floors. A final limitation is the scant knowledge available about the persons producing the traces; their anonymity, the very non-reactivity of the measure, prohibits us from knowing anything else about them. What exactly did the visitors stare at as they stood in front of the display case? What were their reactions to the display?

Figure 9.4: Examples of archival data sources.

annual reports	photos
attendance rosters	professional organization records
budget/finance reports	public utility records
building permits	real estate records
calendars	sales records
census information	school records
chamber of commerce data	speeches
church records	tax assessments
city maps	traffic reports
health records	visitor and convention bureau reports
law enforcement records	
library records	voting records
meeting minutes	weather reports
newspaper and magazine articles	welfare records
notices	

The second type of non-reactive measure suggested by Webb et al. (1981) is *archival documents and records* (Figure 9.4). Two forms of archival data are continuous documents and episodic records. *Continuous documents* tend to be public, and include actuarial records (e.g., birth, death, marriage), political and judicial records (e.g., votes, court proceedings), other government records (e.g., city budgets), crime records, and mass media archives (e.g., newspapers). *Episodic records* are more discontinuous and private. Examples of episodic records include personal documents (e.g., entries in appointment calendars, diaries, letters, drawings), sales records, and certain kinds of institutional records (e.g., disciplinary action files).

To illustrate how continuous documents can be used to get a clue of the social conservatism of a community, book titles most frequently checked out at the local libraries might provide some insights. And, an indication of some of the issues youth are concerned about in their own lives might be revealed by examining the CDS requested for play at a teen dance.

As with physical traces, archival measures have limitations. There are usually problems of authenticity, representativeness, and accuracy (Goodwin & Goodwin, 1989). *Authenticity* concerns deal with whether the records are real. What is the history of the document? How was it obtained? *Representativeness* is about the record's ability to yield a true likeness of the issue. For example, how clear a picture do we get about the issues of concern to youth according to the music they choose for dancing? Finally, the *accuracy* of archival records is of particular importance. Who prepared the records, using what information sources, and for what purpose? The biases of the organization preparing the record could be something to be cautious about.

The case for including non-reactive measures in the evaluation of sport, fitness, recreation, and park services is strong. Remember, however, we are not advocating them as the sole data source. Rather, non-reactive measures should be incorporated, when possible for triangulation reasons—or as useful confirmatory tools in companion with reactive measuring instruments.

Instrument's reliability. An instrument is *reliable* to the extent, in a given situation, it yields the same or consistent results. The basic idea behind three of the four approaches used to document instrument reliability is to measure twice and then check to see if the two sets of measurements are consistent with each other (Patten, 1997, p. 69).

It is important to note that no instrument is perfectly reliable due to measurement error. There are many sources of unreliability. One source is that the wording or categories used in an instrument can be ambiguous. For example, if asked "How often do you experience recreation?" and response categories provided range from "very frequently" to "very infrequently," what ambiguous problems can you identify? (Answer: What is meant by "recreation?" "Frequent?" "Infrequent?") Other sources of unreliable or inconsistent results are the fatigue level and mood swings of subjects. Things that can trigger these problems include asking "a lot" of questions and/or the timing of the interview—is it done at the beginning or end of the day (after all, some people are "owls" others "larks!").

There are four approaches for documenting an instrument's reliability. These are inter-observer reliability, test-retest reliability, parallel-forms reliability, and internal consistency.

In *inter-observer reliability* two or more observers rate, at the same time but independently, some phenomena. These ratings are compared to determine the degree of agreement that exists. For instance, as part of a posttest two individual swimming experts can be asked to independently judge the 30 individuals in the class as to whether or not each is a "proficient" swimmer. Suppose for 25 individuals in the class the two judges are in complete agreement (i.e., their ratings for each of the 25 individuals are the same), and for the remaining five the two judges are not in unison. This means that the *inter-observer reliability correlation coefficient* is .83 (or 25 out of 30 is equal to 83% agreement). A correlation coefficient can range from 0.00 to 1.00. A 1.00 indicates perfect reliability—meaning the ratings by all observers are exactly the same. Experts tell us that an *inter-observer reliability coefficient* should be at least .60 (Patten, 1997, p. 69).

To measure *test-retest reliability* we measure the phenomena with the same instrument, at two different points in time and then compare these two sets of results. For instance, we want to know the reliability of a new test designed to assess leisure values. The test is administered with a group of adults on Monday and re-administered again one week later. Since leisure values normally do not change in a period of one week, we would expect consistent scores if the test is reliable. A correlational coefficient would be computed to indicate the test-retest reliability. The test-retest reliability coefficient of .80 and above suggests the instrument is stable over time (Fisher & Corcoran, 1994a).

Some instruments are developed in *parallel, equivalent,* or *"split-half" forms*. Each version is designed to be interchangeable with the other. The same content is supposedly covered in both forms even though the questions are different. *Parallel forms reliability* is established by administering one form (for example, the long adult version of the Leisure Diagnostic Battery) of the test to a group of persons and about one week later administering the second form (or the short adult version of the Leisure Diagnostic Battery) to the same group of individuals. Thus, each person will have two scores and these scores are used in a correlation coefficient to determine the parallel-forms reliability. Parallel forms reliability coefficients of above .80 are needed to consider the parallel forms as being consistent (Patten, 1997, p. 69).

Turning to *internal consistency reliability,* the focus is determining the extent each item used in the instrument is measuring the same concept. An instrument containing multiple items or questions is administered once. Intercorrelations between each conceivable pair of items are computed to determine how each item "fits" or correlates with every other item on the test. Cronbach alpha coefficient (the internal consistency reliability coefficient) should be $\geq$ .80 (Fisher & Corcoran, 1994a).

For example, suppose socioeconomic status (SES) is measured using the traditional approach of asking about the respondent's educational attainment, occupation, and income. Most likely the Cronbach alpha for this index would be higher than .80 since previous research has repeatedly indicated responses to these three questions are highly related— people with higher levels of educational attainment typically land more prestigious jobs and subsequently earn higher income. If for some reason we decided to try to measure SES by asking about a respondent's education, occupation and height, then the Cronbach alpha for this index would most assuredly be below .80. Such a value indicates that the various questions being used are not measuring or tapping the same unique concept. Indeed, common sense tells us it is ludicrous to envision height as having any bearing on SES—unless you are tall enough to play for the NBA!

In summary, an instrument can be reliable but invalid, unreliable and invalid, or valid and reliable. Do not assume that if an instrument has been documented as being reliable, then the instrument must automatically be valid (see Figure 9.5). Reliability alone is an insufficient criterion for selecting an instrument. For instance, an inaccurate scale might consistently report (perhaps to your delight) your weight as being 10 pounds lighter than your true body weight. This inaccurately calibrated scale could be described as consistently reliable but invalid. Remember, in order for an instrument to be useful, it must be both valid and reliable..

Figure 9.5: A bulls-eye analogy to validity and reliability.[3]

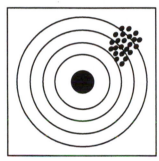 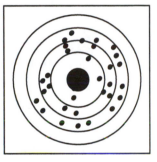 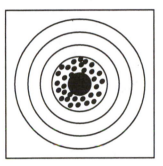

| Invalid but reliable | Invalid and unreliable | Valid *and* reliable |

[3]Adapted from *The Practice of Social Research* (p. 135), by E. Babbie, copyright © 1998, Belmont, CA: Wadsworth Publishing Co. Used with permission of the publisher.

Sources for Instruments. A variety of secondary sources exist for locating instruments useful for evaluation in recreation. These sources for measuring instruments are found in Figure 9.6. Additionally, research reviews and articles appearing in professional journals contain excellent sources for identifying potential measuring instruments for a study (see Figures 4.1 and 4.5).

As mentioned earlier, guidelines for creating your own measures are beyond the scope of this text. To be able to adeptly create an instrument, from scratch, requires years of formal education and training in *psychometrics* (a sub-speciality in the field of psychology that deals with test construction). As Grosof and Sardy (1985, pp. 162-163) point out, "Beginners seriously underestimate the difficulty of developing an instrument ... our advice to you if you are considering developing objective tests and rating scales is DON'T!"

It is, however, recognized that there will be times when you need to put together a questionnaire, especially to gather demographic-related background information on program participants. Some excellent references to guide you in these endeavors include those written by: Babbie (1995), Dillman (1978), Lankford and Mitra (1998), Payne (1980), Salant and Dillman (1994), Schuman and Presser (1996), and Weisberg, Krosnick, & Bowen (1996).

Figure 9.6: Sources of measuring instruments for leisure related evaluations.

Anastasi (1988)

Andrulis (1977)

Annand and Powers (1991)

Beere (1979)

Beere (1990)

Bellack and Hersen (1988)

Berryman, James, and Trader (1991)

Bolton (1987)

Bonjean, Hill, and McLemore (1967)

Brodsky and Smitherman (1983)

Burlingame and Blaschko (1997)

Chun, Cobb, and French (1978)

Ciarlo et al. (1985)

Comrey, Barkey, and Glaser (1973)

Conoley (1993)

Fisher and Corcoran (1994a)

Fisher and Corcoran (1994b)

Folkins and Sime (1981)

Freeman and Tyrer (1992)

Gallo, Reichel, and Anderson (1988)

George and Bearon (1980)

Goldman and Busch (1974)

Goldman and Sanders (1974)

Green and Lewis (1986)

Henerson, Morrison, and Fitz-Gibbon (1978)

Heresen and Bellack (1988)

Johnson (1976)

Johnson and Bommarito (1971)

Kane and Kane (1981)

Kestenbaum and Williams (1988)

Kirby (1991)

Lake, Miles, and Earle (1973)

Mangen and Peterson (1982)

McDowell and Newell (1987)

Miller (1977)

Moos (1975)

Murphy, Conoley, and Impara (1994)

National Recreation & Park Association (1993)

Ostrow (1990)

Riddick and Keller (1991)

Robinson and Shaver (1973)

Safrit and Wood (1989)

Scholl and Schnur (1976)

Shaw and Wright (1967)

Skalko, Van Andel, and DeSalvatore (1991)

Stumbo (1991)

Sweetland and Keyser (1997)

Thomas and Nelson (1996)

Pilot Testing

Most evaluative research studies (regardless of whether a quantitative or qualitative framework is used), require a pilot study. A *pilot study* is a dress-rehearsal, small-scale version, forerunner, walk through, or feasibility check to the full-scale study. Overall, the purpose of doing a pilot is to catch and solve unforeseen problems. A pilot study can accomplish any number of tasks. Some of the things that can be revealed by a pilot study are (adapted from Grosof & Sardy, 1985, p. 127):

- **To suggest or refine a research question(s).** Observing children's behavior on a playground may reveal, for instance, the importance of recording how both physical equipment and accompanying adults direct play patterns.
- **The need to revise a research hypothesis.** Hypotheses may be changed, dropped, or newly developed as a result of the pilot study.
- **Identify defects in questions.** For example, you might find that the survey question "What do you do for a living?" evokes an unexpected yet common response, "I work!"
- **Try out a number of measures to find out which one or two are best for adoption in the full-fledged study.** For instance, a pilot of how participation in a music therapy program affects nursing home residents may reveal that self esteem should be dropped as a dependent variable. It could be found that the chosen instrument is not discriminating or precise enough. Furthermore, and upon reflection, it may become more apparent that a chosen dependent variable (in this example, self esteem) is unlikely to be dramatically influenced by participation in a 10-week music therapy program. Instead, the pilot may reinforce inclusion of other dependent variables. The pilot of the music therapy program, for example, may support, in a full–fledged study, examining how sensory functioning and music appreciation are affected as a result of participating in a music therapy program.
- **Identify ways to improve methods (sampling, data coding, etc.).**

To be meaningful, the pilot study should be comparable, in terms of the sample characteristics, procedures, data collection and analysis to what has been planned for the full-scale study. It is also a good idea that the sponsoring organization has an opportunity, beforehand, to review and approve plans for the pilot study. Based on pilot study findings, necessary corrections are made. Any of the elements making up the scope, approach, or implementation of the evaluative research process can be revised, fine tuned or modified. Thus, in entering into the full-fledged evaluation study, one expects a better quality end product to emerge. Results of a pilot study should help avoid errors, or at the very least reduce them to a manageable minimum level. Every once in a while, a pilot study can reveal in advance that a full-scale study will be fruitless—sometimes evaluation projects that appear promising turn out to be impossible to conduct or not worth doing. In short, a pilot study in the long run can save time and money, and reduce heartache.

Main Points

- The steps involved in the *logic of measurement* are: (a) identify concept under examination, (b) select a nominal definition of the concept (via identification of a variable); (c) select an operational definition by choosing an instrument; and, (d) specify units of measurement.

- There should be a "goodness of fit" between the operationalized indicator and the concept under examination.

- In evaluating the success of a program, employees, physical plant, etc. it is advisable to consider multiple dependent variables and/or a couple of approaches to measuring the same concept.

- One way to go about choosing an instrument is to learn about its validity. Background information or documentation on the ways the instrument's validity has been established should be reviewed to determine if a particular instrument should be used in a study.

- Similarly, background information or documentation on an instrument's reliability should be checked out to decide if adoption of the instrument is warranted.

- Thought also should be given to incorporating non-reactive measures into a study. The two types of non-reactive measures are physical tracing and archival documents.

- Without just about any exception, a pilot study should be done as a forerunner to a full-scale study. Information gleaned from the pilot can prove to be invaluable in averting or managing problems related to the execution of the full-fledged study.

Study Questions

1. What are the four steps associated with the logic of measurement? Cite a recreation/sport management example using these steps.

2. What is referent validity? Is it important to be concerned with this—why or why not?

3. What are some guidelines or advice to follow when choosing from existing instruments?

4. What is instrument validity? Instrument reliability?

5. What is meant when it is noted that normative data exist for an instrument? How could this help you?

6. What is a non-reactive measure?

7. What is pilot testing? What things can be revealed from pilot testing?

References

Anastasi, K. (1988).*Psychological testing* (7th ed.). NJ: Prentice Hall.

Andrulis, R. (1977).*Adult assessment: A sourcebook of tests and measures of human behavior.* Springfield, IL: Charles C. Thomas.

Annand, V., & Powers, P. (1991). The benefits of therapeutic recreation in pediatrics. In C. Coyle, W.B. Kinney, B. Riley, & J. Shank (Eds.), *Benefits of therapeutic recreation: A consensus view* (pp. 205-234). Ravensdale, WA: Idyll Arbor, Inc.

Babbie, E. (1998). *The practice of social research* (8th ed.). Belmont, CA: Wadsworth Publishing Co.

Bailey, K. (1978). *Methods of social research.* New York: The Free Press.

Beere, C. (1979). *Women and women's issues: A handbook of tests and measures.* San Francisco: Jossey-Bass.

Beere, C. (1990). *Gender roles: A handbook of tests and measures.* New York: Greenwood Press.

Berryman, D., James, A., & Trader, B. (1991). The benefits of therapeutic recreation in physical health. In C. Coyle, W.B. Kinney, B. Riley, & J. Shank (Eds.), *Benefits of therapeutic recreation: A consensus view* (pp. 235-287). Ravensdale, WA: Idyll Arbor, Inc.

Bolton, B. (1987). *Handbook of measurement and evaluation in rehabilitation* (2nd ed.). Baltimore, MD: Paul H. Brooks Publishing Company.

Bonjean, C. Hill, R., & McLemore, S. (1967). *Sociological measurement: An inventory of scales and measurement.* San Francisco: Chandler.

Brodsky, S., & Smitherman, H. (1983). *Handbook of scales for research in crime and delinquency.* New York: Plenum.

Burlingame, J., & Blaschko, T. (1997). *Assessment tools for recreational therapy: Red book #1* (2nd ed.). Ravensdale, WA: Idyll Arbor, Inc.

Carmines, E., & Zeller, R. (1979). *Reliability and validity assessment.* Beverly Hills, CA: Sage Publications.

Chun, K., Cobb, S., & French, J. (1978). *Measures for psychological assessment.* Ann Arbor, MI: University of Michigan, Institute for Social Science Research.

Ciralo, J., et al. (1985). *Assessing mental health treatment outcome measurement techniques.* Rockville, MD: National Institutes of Mental Health (DHHS Publication No. ADM 86-1301).

Comrey, A., Backer, T., & Glaser, E. (1973). *A source book for mental health measures.* Los Angeles: Human Interaction Research Institute.

Conoley, J. (1993). *The mental measurements yearbook on CD-Rom and master index to test information.* Lincoln, NE: Buros Institute of Mental Measurements.

Dillman, D. (1978). *Mail and telephone surveys: The total design method.* New York: John A. Wiley & Sons.

Dixon, B., Bouma, G., & Atkinson, G. (1987). *A handbook of social science research: A comprehensive and practical guide for students.* New York: Oxford University Press.

Fisher, J., & Corcoran, K. (1994a). *Measures for clinical practice, a sourcebook: Volume I couples, families and children* (2nd ed.). New York: Free Press.

Fisher, J., & Corcoran, K. (1994b). *Measures for clinical practice, a sourcebook: Volume II adults* (2nd ed.). New York: Free Press.

Folkins, C., & Sime, W. (1981). Physical fitness training and mental health. *American Psychologist, 36,* 373-389.

Freeman, C., & Tyrer, P. (1992). *Research methods in psychiatry; A beginner's guide* (2nd ed.). London: Gaskell.

Gall, M.D., Borg, W.R., & Gall, J.P. (1996). *Educational research: An introduction.* White Plains, New York: Longman.

Gallo, J., Reichel, W., & Anderson, L. (1988). *Handbook of geriatric assessment.* Rockville, MD: Aspen Publishing.

George, L., & Bearon, L. (1980). *Quality of life in older persons: Meaning and measurements.* New York: Human Sciences Press.

Goldman, B., & Busch, J. (1974). *Directory of unpublished experimental mental measures: Volume II.* Human Sciences Press.

Goldman, B., & Sanders, J. (1974). *Directory of unpublished experimental mental measures.* New York: Behavioral Publications.

Goodwin, W., & Goodwin, L. (1989). The use of nonreactive measures with preschoolers. *Early Child Development and Care, 41,* 173-194.

Green, L., & Lewis, F. (1986). *Measurement and evaluation in health education and health promotion.* Mountain View, CA: Mayfield.

Grosof, M., & Sardy, H. (1985). *A research primer for the social and behavioral sciences.* Orlando, FL: Academic Press, Inc.

Henerson, M., Morris, L., & Fitz-Gibbon, C. (1978). *How to measure attitudes.* Beverly Hills, CA: Sage Publications.

Hersen, M., & Bellack, A. (Eds.). (1988). *Dictionary of behavioral assessment techniques.* New York: Pergamon.

Johnson, O. (1976). *Tests and measurements in child development: Volume 2.* San Francisco: Jossey-Bass.

Johnson, O., & Bommarito, J. (1971). *Tests and measurements in child development: Volume I.* San Francisco: Jossey-Bass.

Kane, R., & Kane, R. (1981). *Assessing the elderly: A practical guide to measurement.* Lexington, MA: Lexington Books.

Kestenbaum, C., & Williams, D. (1988). *Handbook of clinical assessment of children and adolescents.* New York: New York University Press.

Kidder, L., & Judd, C. (1986). *Research methods in social relations.* New York: Holt Rinehart.

Kirby, R. (Ed.) (1991). *Kirby's guide to fitness and motor performance tests.* Cape Girardeaux, MO: Ben Oak Publishing Company.

Lake, D., Miles, M., & Earle, R. (1973). *Measuring human behavior: Tools for the assessment of social functioning.* New York: Teachers College Press.

Lankford, S., & Mitra, A. (1998). *Research methods in park, recreation, and leisure studies.* Champaign, IL: Sagamore Publishing.

Mangen, D., & Peterson, W. (Eds.) (1982). *Clinical and social psychology: Volume 1 research instruments in social gerontology.* Minneapolis: University of Minnesota Press.

McDowell, I., & Newell, C. (1987). *Measuring health: A guide to rating scales and questionnaires.* New York: Oxford University Press.

Miller, C (1977). *Handbook of research design and social measurement* (3rd ed.). New York: Longman.

Moos, R. (1975). *Evaluating correctional and community settings.* New York: John Wiley.

Murphy, L., Conoley, J., & Impara, J. (1994). *Tests in print.* Lincoln, NE: University of Nebraska Press.

National Therapeutic Recreation Society. (1993). *Best of the Therapeutic Recreation Journal: Assessment.* Alexandria, VA: National Recreation and Park Association.

Ostrow, A. (Ed.) (1990). *Directory of psychological tests in the sport and exercise* sciences. Morgantown, WV: Fitness Information Technology.

Patten, M. (1997). *Understanding research methods: An overview of essentials.* Los Angeles, Pyrczak Publishing.

Payne, S. (1980). *The art of asking questions.* Princeton, NJ: Princeton University Press.

Riddick, C., & Keller, J. (1991). The benefits of therapeutic recreation in gerontology. In C. Coyle, W.B. Kinney, B. Riley, & J. Shank (Eds.), *Benefits of therapeutic recreation: A consensus view* (pp. 151-204). Ravensdale, WA: Idyll Arbor, Inc.

Riley, B. (1991). Quality assessment: The use of outcome indicators. In B. Riley (Ed.), *Quality management: Applications for therapeutic recreation* (pp.53-68). State College, PA: Venture Publishing, Inc.

Robinson, J., & Shaver, P. (1973). *Measures of social psychological attitudes.* Ann Arbor, MI: Institute of Social Research, University of Michigan.

Safrit, M., & Wood, T. (Eds.) (1989). *Measurement concepts with physical education and exercise science.* Champaign, IL: Human Kinetics.

Salant, P., & Dillman, D. (1994). *How to conduct your own survey.*New York: John A. Wiley & Sons.

Schitovsky, T. (1976). *The joyless economy.* New York: Oxford Press.

Scholl, G., & Schnur, R. (1976). *Measures of psychological, vocational and educational functioning in the blind and visually handicapped.* New York: American Foundation for the Blind.

Schuman, H., & Presser, S. (1996). *Questions and answers in attitude surveys: Experiments on question form, wording, and context.* Thousand Oaks, CA: Sage Publications.

Shaw, M., & Wright, J. (1967). *Scales for the measurement of attitudes.* New York: McGraw-Hill.

Skalko, T., Van Andel, G., & DeSalvatore, G. (1991). The benefits of therapeutic recreation in psychiatry. In C. Coyle, W.B. Kinney, B. Riley, & J. Shank (Eds.), *Benefits of therapeutic recreation: A consensus view* (pp. 289-352). Ravensdale, WA: Idyll Arbor, Inc. pp. 289-352.

Stumbo, J. (1991). Selected assessment resources: A review of instruments and references. *Annual in Therapeutic Recreation, 2,* 8-24.

Sweetland, R., & Keyser, D. (1997). *Tests: A comprehensive reference* (4th ed.). Austin, TX: Pro-Ed.

Thomas, J., & Nelson, J. (1996). Chapter 11: Measuring research variables. In J. Thomas & J. Nelson, *Research methods in physical activity* (pp. 214-248). Champaign, IL: Human Kinetics.

Webb, E., Campbell, D., Schwartz, L., Sechrest, L., & Grove, J. (1981). *Nonreactive measures in social sciences.* Boston: Houghton Mifflin.

Weisberg, H., Krosnick, J., & Bowen, B. (1996). *An introduction to survey research, polling, and data analysis.* Thousand Oaks, CA: Sage Publications.

Witt, P., & Ellis, G. (1990). *Leisure diagnostic battery.* State College, PA: Venture Publishing.

CHAPTER 10

Data Collection

What Will I Learn in This Chapter?
I'll be able to:

1. Define triangulation and explain why triangulation of methods is a good idea to use planning an evaluation study.

2. Recall the kinds of data that can be collected as part of an evaluation study.

3. Identify methods of data collection associated with studies using quantitative and qualitative frameworks.

4. Provide tips for writing questions that will be used in an interview or questionnaire.

5. Name factors that can affect response to interviews or questionnaires.

6. Distinguish between a structured and unstructured interview.

7. Define focus groups.

8. Name the three roles an evaluator can assume in participant observation.

Every evaluator is confronted with the question of how to collect information needed to address the scope of the study. A multitude of methods exists by which to gather information related to the research question, objective, or hypothesis. Before turning to a review of these data-collection techniques, we feel compelled again (as mentioned in Chapter 5) to pitch you a value we hold near and dear to our hearts. Namely, triangulation and its role in gathering information will now be discussed.

Triangulation

As a starting point to deciding how to gather information, we advocate that strong consideration be given to using triangulation (a term borrowed from navigation and military strategy). In *triangulation*, verification and validation efforts are directed at supporting a finding by showing that an independent measure agrees with the noted finding or at least does not contradict it (Miles & Huberman, 1984, p. 234).

Triangulation, in particular, can focus on *triangulation of methods*, which is checking out the consistency of findings generated by different data collection methods (Patton, 1990, p. 464). For example, interviews and observations are utilized permitting a comparison of results from the two data-collection techniques. As another example, insights learned from a focus group could help shape observations used in a quasi-experiment.

One rationale for using triangulation is that any bias inherent in a particular data source or method will be neutralized when used in conjunction with another data source and method (Creswell, 1994, p. 174). The reasons for combining methods in a single study are that it (Greene, Caracelli, & Graham, 1989):

- **Facilitates convergence of results.** For many evaluators, this is the ideal—we hope that different data-collection methods yield or underscore the same results.
- **Is complimentary.** Overlapping and different facets of a phenomenon may emerge.
- **Is developmental.** The first method is used to help inform the second method.
- **Is initiative.** That is, contradictions and fresh perspectives emerge.
- **Is expansive.** In other words, can add scope and breadth to a study.

The remainder of the chapter is divided into three parts. In the first part, the kinds of data that can be collected are reviewed. The second and third parts deal with data collection tools associated with quantitative and qualitative techniques, respectively, with special attention devoted to reviewing guidelines for developing or using these tools.

Kinds of Data That Can Be Collected

The data that are collected should relate to the scope of the study. We cannot overemphasize the importance of knowing the *why* behind each piece of information that is collected. Data collecting should not be entered into with a "fishing expedition" mentality. You should know why each piece of information is being collected. You should also know beforehand how the data will be analyzed and presented (the topics of Chapters 11 and 12).

In short, if you cannot answer these questions—"Why is it important to collect this information?" and "What will be done with the gathered information in terms of analysis and presentation?"—then the evaluation has not been planned carefully enough. Ultimately, you run the high risk of wasting your time and that of the people who are to be studied!

If data collection is conducted from the perspective of what must be asked in order to measure the variables in the study (recall Figure 9.1), the construction of the schedule or protocol (terms that will be discussed in a moment) becomes fairly straightforward. Again, as acknowledged at the beginning of this chapter, it is quite plausible if not desirable to use more than one technique of data gathering to get information on the same variable. For example, to find out if participation in a music therapy program had any influence on the social interaction of nursing home residents, interviews could be conducted with the nursing home residents themselves. Another technique for examining the same question could be to ask nursing home staff to complete a questionnaire, reflecting their thoughts on the social activity patterns of the residents. A third approach would be to use structured observations for recording group interactions of the residents (Riddick & Dugan-Jendzejec, 1988).

Basically the kinds of data collected can be categorized in one of five categories: Again, the kind of data collected along with the data collection techniques used will evolve around the scope of the study. The data categories are:

• *Attributes* or characteristics of what people are, often referred to as *demographic* characteristics. Virtually all interview schedules ask for background information about the respondent such as age, education, gender, etc.

• *Facts* relating to behavioral experiences (past, present, and/or future). For example, individuals can be asked to recall favorite recreational activities at certain ages in their life. Be careful not to confuse a question of fact with a question related to beliefs. For example, do you want to know about the amount of time children spend watching television (a fact), or do you want to know how parents feel about the amount of television their child/children watch (a belief)?

• *Attitudes* or gauging likes and dislikes of individuals. For example, program participants may be asked about their reactions to a recreation program (for instance, "Did you like the program?," "Was the instructor prepared?"). Or, front-line staff may be asked to identify the characteristics they like and dislike about their immediate supervisor.

• *Preferences* or a comparison of attitudes. For example, a survey of leisure preferences could ask about whether the individual "Preferred to play checkers or take a walk?" Or staff may be asked if they prefer to work 40-hour weeks or opt for a flexible time schedule.

• *Beliefs* or opinions about the objective state of the world (what is thought to be true) or about the relative importance of various things. Water park users, for example, could be asked about the "quality" of various aspects of park operations. Or a program manager may be asked to do a relative performance ranking of employees under her supervision.

Data Collection Tools for Quantitative Studies

This section will review two points related to data collection tools used in quantitative studies. First, the two principal data collection tools used in quantitative studies will be discussed, namely structured interviews and questionnaires. Second, some things that should be considered when developing your own interview or questionnaire will be highlighted.

Structured Interviews and Questionnaires

Two popular ways of collecting data, especially for studies related to quantitative frameworks, are interviews and questionnaires. *Interviewing* is a technique to collect information from an individual. The interviewer reads questions from an interview schedule to the *interviewee* or respondent. The respondent is not directly given the *interview schedule*, or the paper that contains the questions, to complete; rather, the interviewer records responses given.

There are two ways to conduct an interview, a *face-to-face interview* or by *telephone interview*. A face-to-face interview can be conducted in a variety of places—in the home, office, or leisure service setting. Some excellent resources for detailed information on how to conduct interviews are Dillman (1978), Fink & Kosecoff (1985), and Slant and Dillman (1994).

Interviews can be combined with other data-collection methods, such as projective techniques. As Bailey (1978, p. 179) notes, *projective methods* of data collection are used whenever direct questioning is inappropriate or whenever the true purpose of the study cannot be revealed. For instance, Riddick, Ansello and Seefelft (1987) interviewed five- to seven-year-old children, asking them which man portrayed in artist drawings at four stages of the life cycle (young adult, middle aged, young-old, and old-old) was most likely to do a specified leisure activity a lot of the time. The drawings were used as a projective method for collecting data on children's feelings about age-appropriate leisure activities.

Another popular device for collecting data is the questionnaire. Though most people do not realize it, a *questionnaire* is a self-administered interview (Grosof & Sardy, 1985). Questionnaires can be distributed in person to individuals or groups (e.g, as people are leaving a recreational event or finishing a recreational activity) or mailed to selected individuals.

The exact questions used in an interview or questionnaire can be those found in existing measuring instruments (see Chapter 9) or can be developed specifically for the study at hand. Traditionally, interviews and questionnaires have been conducted with "paper and pencil," but with the advent of the computer age, computerized scanning sheets and laptop computers are increasingly being used to collect and enter data right at the data-collection site.

Essentially, two formats can be used for responding to questions posed in interviews and questionnaires. First, there are *closed, structured, or fixed-choice questions*, in which possible answers are limited, specific and prerecorded. That is, the respondent chooses his answer from one of the possible answers provided (e.g., "YES-NO," or where along a "STRONGLY AGREE-SOMEWHAT AGREE–UNDECIDED–SOMEWHAT DISAGREE–STRONGLY DISAGREE" Likert continuum his response falls). Interviews using close-ended questions are commonly employed in executing studies based in a quantitative framework.

Then there are *open-ended, unstructured questions*, where the respondent has unlimited options for response. Essentially, the respondents answer in their own words. Interviews that use open-ended questions and semi-structured questions (see below) are most often associated with qualitative frameworks.

Preparation Considerations

Even though we realize that our initial recommendation (declared in Chapter 9) was to advise you against developing your own instruments, there are times when such an under-taking must happen. Problems encountered in the data-collection phase typically can be linked to either the substance and/or the wording of the questions being posed. Thus, a quick review follows on how to avert common problems associated with designing your own interview or questionnaire schedule. That is, remember:

• **Questions should be related to the stated purpose of the study.** The relevance or importance of the study needs to be made in no uncertain terms to the potential respondent, and then questions (sometimes called *items*) must be selected that are relevant to the stated goal(s) of the study. Dillman (1978) suggests that potential study participants be briefed in a cover letter or introductory statement that identifies the person(s) or organization con-ducting the study, what the study is about and its social usefulness (in terms of what the individual can relate to), makes a promise of confidentiality (that includes an explanation of why an identification number appears on the questionnaire—or to track respondents who do not respond in order to send out follow-up reminders), mentions a token reward for participation, and tells the potential study participant what to do if questions arise (who to contact and how). Figure 10.1 shows an example of how this advice was applied in a leisure related study.

• **Questions should permit only one interpretation.** For example, what is meant by "a lot," "Frequently," "During the last year (calendar year or past 12 months)"? A pilot study should detect these problems.

• **Questions should not be leading or too personal.** An example of a leading question is, "Of course, everyone takes out time every week in their schedule for leisure, so now I want you to tell me about your routine." Questions that are an invasion of privacy occurs should also be avoided. An example of an insensitive question would be, "Now, I would like to turn to the topic of your dating preferences and habits..."

• **Questions should not ask for knowledge the respondent does not have, either be-cause what is being asked requires a too precise or demanding answer or because the wrong person is being asked.** Consider, for example, the specificity being called for by the question, "Tell me now, exactly how many times did you walk or take a jog during the last six months?" An example of directing the question to the wrong person is to ask a mother,

Figure 10.1: Example of a cover letter to recruit study participants.

GALLAUDET G UNIVERSITY

DEPARTMENT OF PHYSICAL EDUCATION AND RECREATION

KENDALL GREEN
800 FLORIDA AVE. NE
WASHINGTON, DC 20002-3695

9 April 1997

Dear Margaret Schweinhaut Center Member:

Montgomery County Recreation Department and Gallaudet University are conducting a study of the effects of video game play. Although little has been written on the subject, we believe that it may be a meaningful and enjoyable recreational activity for senior citizens.

Your name was suggested to us by the staff of the Forest Glen/Margaret Schweinhaut Center as a possible study participant. You are one of a small number of individuals who are being asked to participate in our study. Your help is, therefore, essential to the study's success.

The study will last approximately five weeks. Of those individuals agreeing to serve in the study, one-half will be selected (using a lottery drawing) to be exposed to video game play, and the remaining one-half will not (technically known as control group members). At the conclusion of the study, the videogames will be left at the Center for about a month and anyone can then play them, including individuals who were originally assigned to the control group and study participants' grandchildren.

The videogame play group will be asked to commit about two hours a week to video game play. Video game machines will be located at the Center and special tokens will be provided for play. Further, *all* study participants will be requested to complete two questionnaires (which will each take approximately 20 minutes) and two reaction-time tests. Please be assured information provided by you will remain confidential—your name will never be cited in any report!

Please let us know of your interest in this scientific study by completing the enclosed postage paid postcard. I would appreciate receiving this card *no later than 25 April 1997*.

I would be most happy to answer any questions you might have about our study. Please feel free to call me at 202-651-5591.

Thanking you advance for your help, I remain

Gratefully,

Carol Cutler Riddick, Ph.D.
Professor

"What needs are satisfied when your adolescent teen engages in creative play?" Instead, it would be more appropriate to pose the question to the adolescent herself.

• **Questions should not be loaded.** You want the person to answer honestly and accurately. Do not ask questions that will trigger a socially desirable response. "How many times in the past year have you stolen supplies from the recreation department? Arrived to work late? Called in sick to work when you were not?" etc. will typically not evoke honest responses.

• **Questions should use the level of wording appropriate to the educational and cultural background of the respondents.** Those conducting the interview should not have to interpret what a question or word means. An example of a question violating this advice is, "Now, can you succinctly tell me about what leisure or recreation means to you? And to your significant others?"

• **Questions should not use acronyms, or if they do, make sure they are spelled out the first time.** One of the authors of this text vividly remembers once being asked to provide background information about herself by completing a checklist that contained the item "SOB." Perplexed, she asked what was being asked and with a chuckle the physician declared, "Oh what I really want to know is if you have experienced shortness of breath."

Furthermore, responses to questionnaires can be affected by a number of factors. Among the things to consider (Bailey, 1978; Dillman, 1978) are the :

• **Questionnaire format.** One or two page questionnaires and booklets that have an attractive cover page and make use of front and back pages so that length is somewhat downplayed appear to work best.

• **Choice of paper color and weight.** Some studies have suggested an off-white (yellow or beige) paper color is good since it prevents the questionnaire from getting lost on one's desk and at the same time is not viewed as an obnoxious color. If printing is going to be done on both sides, use 16-pound paper so print does not "bleed" through.

• **Order of questions.** Use a descending order of perceived social usefulness, or place questions the respondent is most likely to see useful first and those least useful last. Keep questions similar in content together. And make "cognitive ties" or transitions between sections so the respondent understands the flow.

• **Token financial inducements to participate.** This can involve offering money or some other item. For instance, it could be stated "The enclosed dollar is a goodwill gesture," " To represent how important you are to our study ...", or a promise that "Completed and returned questionnaires will result in the person's name being entered into a lottery to win one month free membership in the fitness club...," or "A penny (which has been enclosed) for your thoughts...."

• **Type of mailing.** First class with personalized address label seem to fare better than bulk mailings with computer–generated mailing labels.

• **Inclusion of pre-addressed, postage-paid return envelope.** This is a must to bolster questionnaire returns.

• **Timing of the mailing.** The entire month of December should be avoided when sending out questionnaires. And questionnaires should be mailed on a Monday or Tuesday—in case the questionnaire has to be forwarded to a new address, it should then arrive the same week it was mailed.

Dillman (1978) also persuasively argues for using a total design strategy when doing mail questionnaires, or having up to three follow-up phases: a postcard reminder sent one week after the initial mailing, a replacement questionnaire mailed three weeks after the initial mailing, and a second replacement mailing by certified mail seven weeks after the initial mailing.

Another area often overlooked, related to interviews, is the profound influence interviewers can have on what is or is not learned. Whenever possible the interviewer should have characteristics similar to those or shared by the population being sampled. As Bailey (1978) pointed out, some interviewer-related characteristics that should match those being interviewed, are dress, gender, ethnicity, age, socioeconomic status (often revealed in mannerisms, speech and language patterns, etc.).

Data Collection Tools For Qualitative Studies

Essentially there are three tools for collecting data for qualitative studies. These three tools, unstructured interviews, focus groups, and participant observations, will now be reviewed.

Unstructured Interviews

Again, an interview is a personal, face-to-face meeting between the researcher and a study participant. The researcher, applying a qualitative framework, typically enters the meeting with an *unstructured interview schedule*, which identifies beforehand general topics that will be discussed during the meeting. Sometimes the researcher can rely on a blend of a structured and unstructured interview, using what is known as a semi-structured schedule . A *semi-structured schedule* is a prepared interview guide containing specific open-ended questions as well as providing the interviewer the option to explore "unanticipated" topics.

According to Cunningham (1993, pp. 97–105), there are four types of unstructured, open-ended interviews, each being unique in purpose. The choice of which kind of interview to use should once again be guided by the focus for the study. These kinds of interviews are the descriptive information interview, discovery interview, problem-solving interview, and helping interview. Three of the four types of interviews have various applications to evaluating leisure services. The helping interview, however, is used as a counseling tool; thus it will be dropped at this point from further discussion.

1. Descriptive information interview. A whole range of data can be collected in the descriptive information interview (see Figure 10.2). The interviewee (again, the person being interviewed) can be asked about attributes, facts related to behavioral experiences, and self-evaluative information (such as attitudes, preferences, beliefs, reactions to hypothetical situations, and brainstorming ideas). The descriptive information-gathering interview can be associated with the past, present, or some future issue (e.g., consumer feedback regarding future service delivery plans; brainstorming to identify organizational goals, solutions, or recommendations). The descriptive information interview can also be used to gain insights into experiences. In these situations, the *critical incidents technique* can be used. That is, the individual is asked to describe an incident that does not rely on opinion, but instead on observation. For example, the person could be asked the following questions in order to gather information about his leisure satisfaction: "Think about a time when you felt especially satisfied after completing an activity at the Senior Center. Describe the situation. Now, think about a time when you felt especially dissatisfied after finishing an activity at the Senior Center. Describe the situation—what, in particular, was it about this situation that you found dissatisfying?"

2. Discovery interview. The discovery interview emphasizes the identification of concerns, impressions, suggestions, and ideas. The discovery interview can be a valuable tool for understanding an organizational problem perceived by the individual interviewee. The interviewee is provided with the opportunity to explore feelings, perceptions, interpretations, ideas and thoughts in response to general and specific questions (see Figure 10.3). After the general questions are posed, the interviewer uses specific probes that seek to encourage a greater exploration of issues.

3. Problem–solving interview. The problem-solving interview responds to the mutual interests of the evaluator and interviewee, with a focus on individual problem solving or goal setting. The interviewer attempts to develop a climate where mutual interests in sharing ideas for problem solving occurs. The interview is initiated by the statement, "Let's resolve the problem." Problem-solving interviews are most commonly used in personnel situations, where personal growth and change are the objective of management. The objective of the problem-solving interview in these kinds of situations is to aid the employee or volunteer to identify ways to change and improve. The interview provides a context where the individual can work out a solution to a problem or issue and begin to take action to resolve the situation. Figure 10.4 presents examples of questions that can be used in a problem–solving interview.

Focus Groups

Another qualitative way to gather information is to use focus groups. *Focus groups* are carefully planned group interviews done in a meeting setting. In order to stimulate and manage the group discussion, the moderator acts more as a facilitator than as an interviewer. Focus groups have been widely used in market and political research for testing reactions to new products or political positions (Krueger, 1994).

Figure 10.2: Example of data that can be collected from a descriptive information interview.

TYPES OF INFORMATION	TYPES OF QUESTIONS
Attributes	What is the highest grade you completed? What current certifications do you have? What administrative experience have you had? What recognition have you received?
Facts Related to Behavioral Experiences	Think of a time when.... Describe a recent experience that exemplifies your abilities as a playground leader.
Self-Evaluative Information A. Likes and Dislikes (Attitudes)	What are the aspects you like most about this recreation center? What are the aspects you like least about this recreation center?
B. Preferences	Do you prefer a supervisor who micromanages or someone who is available to you when you need him/her?
C. Strengths and Weaknesses (Beliefs)	What are some of the positive things you can say about your supervisor? What are some areas your supervisor needs to improve in?
D. Statement of Goal/Philosophy (Beliefs)	What are your career goals? What is your vision of the future for this organization?
E. Hypothetical Statements	What would you do if ...
F. Solutions/Recommendations	What suggestions do you have ...

Figure 10.3: Example of data that can be collected from a discovery interview.

1. What are some of the problems you have experienced with the public bicycle-trail system in Montgomery County? For each problem you identified, tell me your ideas of how the problem could be solved or prevented?

2. What are some of the positive things can you say about the public bike-trail system in Montgomery County? Which one biking-trail system characteristic is most important to you and why?

3. What are some of the goals or outputs that might guide us in making a better bicycle trail system in the county? What things should the county try to improve within the upcoming year? The next five years?

Figure 10.4: Example of data that can be collected in a problem-solving interview.[1]

1. What effect does the failure to meet your time–card deadlines have on others?

2. If our roles were reversed (i.e., you were the superior and I am the employee), what would you expect of me in terms of punctuality?

3. How *can* the organization help you do a better job in meeting deadlines?

[1]Adapted from Action Research and Organizational Development (p.102), by J. Cunningham, (1993). Reproduced with permission of Greenwood Publishing Group, Inc., Westport, CT.

The key to using focus groups successfully in the evaluation of leisure services is assuring that their use is consistent with the purposes of the project. As Higgenbotham and Cox (1979) point out, focus groups serve a variety of purposes. For example, focus groups are often a useful starting point for the design of questionnaires because they provide a means of exploring the potential ways respondents talk about issues. This technique then helps the questionnaire designer choose the best words for communicating with potential questionnaire respondents (see Figure 10.5).

Figure 10.5: Focus group exercise.

Your task is to design a question that measures people's attitudes or beliefs about a particular issue. This exercise demonstrates how the focus group method can help you.

1. Think of a topic familiar to you that involves some degree of controversy. For example, the use of all-terrain vehicles in state parks, or selling beer in city recreation centers, or the use of student fees to fund campus recreational sport facilities might be appropriate topics.

2. Design several questions with specific closed-ended responses about the topic you've chosen.

3. Now convene a small group (perhaps just a few friends) and ask the questions WITHOUT offering the response options you've also developed. Pay attention to how well your response alternatives match the answers provided by the group.

4. Near the end of the session, share your answers with the group and ask them how well they capture their opinions.

5. What have you learned about the use of group interviews?

A focus group can also be used for other reasons. Among them are to:
• Obtain general background information about a topic;
• Generate research hypotheses to test using quantitative data-collection approaches;
• Stimulate new and creative ideas;
• Diagnose the potential a new program or service will have for handling a problem; and
• Confirm results collected by another data-collection method (again, known as triangulation of methods).

Focus groups generally involve seven to twelve individuals who discuss a particular topic under the direction of a moderator (Steward & Shamdasani, 1990). While focused, the discussion is also relaxed and group members are encouraged to respond to each others' ideas and comments. Experience has shown that groups smaller than about seven persons may be dominated by one or two members, while larger groups are more difficult to manage and often inhibit participation by all members of the group.

Focus groups can be conducted in a variety of sites ranging from homes to offices. Professional focus-group facilitators often provide rooms designed especially for this purpose, with one-way mirrors (where viewers, such as agency administrators, may observe the interview in progress) and/or outfitted with audio or video equipment (to record the group discussion). A typical focus group session lasts from one and a half to two hours.

The focus group moderator is the key to assuring that the group interview goes smoothly. Thus, this person should be well trained in group dynamics and interview skills. Depending on the purpose of the session, the moderator may be more directive in leading the discussion or nondirective—letting the discussion flow on its own as long as it remains on the topic.

One of the strengths of focus group research is that it may be adapted to provide the most desirable level of focus and structure (Stewart & Shamdasani, 1990). For example, if the evaluator is interested in how health club members view the services offered at the club, the moderator can ask very general and nonspecific questions about these services in order to determine the most salient concerns on the minds of the participants. On the other hand, if a purpose of the evaluation is to determine health club members' reactions to a proposed service, the moderator can provide specific information about the intended service and ask very pointed questions. Also, the moderator might gradually increase the amount of structure and direction over the course of the interview. That is, she might begin with a series of general questions about the club's services and then direct the discussion to more specific service issues as the group proceeds.

You must recognize, of course, that the amount of direction provided by the moderator will influence the types and quality of the information obtained from the group. The moderator's directiveness must be determined by the broader evaluation agenda—the types of information sought and the way the information will be used. Figure 10.6 offers some ideas for moderator questions.

Focus groups are only one of several research techniques that involve groups. Although it is beyond the scope of this book to delve into them, you should be aware that the nominal group technique, the Delphi technique, brainstorming, and leaderless discussion groups may also be useful in the evaluation of leisure services (Russell, 1982). The point is that focus groups as well as other group discussion techniques are an additional tool in your evaluation kit. While they are not appropriate for every inquiry situation, they are proficient in gathering certain types of information. Focus groups are designed to do exactly what the name implies—focus—while also capturing spontaneity and synergism.

Participant Observation

As people's actions are a central aspect in any inquiry, an obvious technique for collecting information is to watch what they do. For example, Hutchison (1987) conducted observations of black, hispanic and white groups in neighborhood and regional parks in Chicago

Figure 10.6: Examples of focus group questions.[2]

Type of Questions	Purpose
Main research question	Broadly focused on issue studied. "The topic today is how you feel about the services at the new bowling center."
Starter questions	Used to get the group talking & comfortable with everyone. "Please take the index card in front of you and write down the single idea that comes to mind about improving services at the bowling center."
Leading questions	To carry the discussion to deeper meanings. "Why do you say that?"
Testing questions	To find the limits of an issue, pose an extreme yet tentative version. "Are you saying that the food in the snack bar is unfit for human consumption?"
Steering questions	Used to nudge the group back onto the main research question. "Well, to return again to your overall reactions to the bowling center, can you tell us ..."
Obtuse questions	To help the group go into territory it may find uncomfortable, ask questions in an abstract form. "What do you think a first-time user of the bowling center would think about the conduct of the center's employees?"
Factual questions	Questions that require a factual answer that can be answered easily. "About how many times a month do you bowl at the center?"
Silence	Often the best question is no question. Simply wait and allow group members time to respond.

[2](Adapted from "Dimensions that make focus groups work" by K. Wheatley & W. Flexner, 1988, *Marketing News*, pp.16-17.

to determine ethnic and racial variations in recreation activity choices. Detailed information was collected on the number of persons and social composition of each recreation activity group observed in the parks, including their age, gender, race, and type of social group (such as couples, family group, or unrelated individuals). Over the summer Hutchison's staff completed 3,072 observations, providing detailed information on the recreation behavior of more than 18,000 activity groups.

Another example of using observation to study racially based behavior comes from a study by Tyson, Schlachter, and Cooper (1988). They observed the behaviors of racially mixed game teams. Since they found that both black and white players cooperated to a greater extent with a black co-player than a white co-player, they concluded that there was evidence that reverse discrimination can happen in team play.

The kind of observing done in these two studies cited is known as participant observation. *Participant observation* is watching the actions of people from the vantage point of involvement with them. This means the person doing the observing has dual roles—participating as well as observing. The participant observer simultaneously experiences being both an insider and outsider in the situation (Spradley, 1980). Consider people playing poker. If you conduct an inquiry into this activity using participant observation, as an insider you will shuffle cards, deal hands, make bids, bluff, and win and lose. At the same time, as an outsider, you will view the game and the players (including yourself) as subjects—as objects to study with detached interest.

There are multiple dimensions to participant observer. For one, the amount of participation ranges from being a complete participant to minimal or passive involvement in the action. In Figure 10.7 the continuum of participation has been summarized.

Figure 10.7: Examples of the participant observation continuum.

Complete Participant	Marginal Participant	Passive Participant
highest amount of participation —————————————————>		lowest amount of participation
Playing basketball with gang members at the recreation center	Sitting behind a vendor at the community farmer's market	Videotaping stair-climbing machine use at the gym

The *complete participant* role is that in which the observer acts as naturally as possible, seeking to become a full member of the group. A study by Glancy (1988) illustrates this role. Glancy was interested in understanding adult play in unstructured settings. To accomplish this she observed, as a complete participant, what transpires at personal-goods auctions. From her report (p. 139),

> On sale days, the researcher arrived at the site early, having learned that attenders observed this custom. There, she did what the other attenders did. She surveyed the goods again, conversed casually with others, built friendships with some who attended regularly, watched the auction, bid on items of interest, discussed goods or customs and interests with attenders, and learned how to engage in the auction event and to appreciate it the way those in attendance suggested.

The *marginal participant* is in an observation situation where there is a lower degree of participation than found in the complete participant role (Robson, 1993). This can be done by adopting the role of a peripheral, though completely "accepted" participant. Examples of a marginal participant observer are being a member of the audience at a concert or sports event, someone sitting in a hotel lobby, or a coffee drinker at a coffee shop. The marginal participant assumes the role of spectator in a situation where there is already an accepted role for spectators. Sometimes those being observed can become suspicious about the marginal participant observer. To prevent this from happening it helps if the marginal participant observer copies the dress and behavior of the other spectators.

An alternative to the complete participant and marginal participant observer roles is that of the *passive participant*. Here the observer is present at the scene of the action but does not participate or interact with other people to any great extent (Spradley, 1980). About all you need to do is find an "observation post" from which to observe and record what is happening. Observations done in public places typically rely on the passive participant role. When assuming a passive-participation observer role, props may be useful to the observer. For instance, if you are observing in a children's playground, you might consider bringing along a child to give you an air of legitimacy.

An example of assuming a passive participant role is to viedotape lifters' interactions with each other and the equipment. Another example is to observe the physical proximity of students on a campus' grassy commons areas. One study that reported using a passive participant role to collect data is Campbell, Kruskal, and Wallace's (1966) investigation of racial integration in classroom settings. They found that there is a tendency of white and black students to sit by themselves in racially homogeneous groups.

Another way participant observations differ is in terms of the duration of the observation. Observing the actions of others may take place in a single event over a brief time frame, or at the other extreme may be done over a very long term with repeat observations. The duration of the other extreme may be done over a very long term with repeat observations. The duration of the observations should be determined by the research question behind the study—more broadly focused questions will simply take longer to answer than narrowly focused ones.

A final way participant observations vary is in terms of the degree to which the observer's intentions are known to the people observed. This ranges from being completely unknown, or being covert, to full disclosure of the identity as observer, or being overt. If covert observation is used, particular attention to the ethical ramifications is needed. Being in a situation where some people know they are being observed and others do not is also a possibility.

Which is the best way to observe people? As with choosing any data-collection technique, the form the observation takes in amount of participation, time, and covertness depends on the purpose you would like it to achieve. Participant observation is commonly used in an exploratory phase of an evaluation project to find out generally what is going on. That is, participant observation is done as a precursor to a later testing of insights or hypotheses gained in the observation. Thus, in this situation, marginal or passive participation, a minimal time commitment, and covert form of observation may be appropriate.

Participation observation technique can also be used to collect data that may complement or set in perspective data obtained by other means (i.e., triangulation of methods). Suppose, for example, information has been gained through a series of interviews. Observation might then be used to corroborate the messages obtained in the interviews. Perhaps a moderately active and overt participation over a longer time is the observation form most suitable for this purpose.

Finally, participant observation can be used as the primary method of collecting information in a particular study, especially when the main intention is descriptive. This suggests the form of the observation should be extensive, with full and overt participation.

Participant observation, regardless of how it is used, places a considerable responsibility on the shoulders of the observer(s). The reason is that the primary data are the interpretations by the observer of what was observed. The observer is the data-collection tool. Therefore, great sensitivity and personal skills are needed for worthwhile data.

One of the areas of required skill for the observer is in recording what is observed. Even with the most unstructured and casual observation situation, it is important to have a system that allows you to capture information unambiguously and as faithfully and fully as possible. In Glancy's (1988) observations of auctions, for example, a few field notes were unobtrusively recorded during the auctions on the back of the bidding registry card and on small note cards, similar to those used by most auction attenders to record their purchases. So, where possible, a record is made of what is observed on the spot and during the action itself. Such "memory sparkers" should include notations in abbreviation about the physical scene, the people involved, various activities of the people, and time sequencing (Baker, 1988).

As soon as possible after the observation the field notes must, as a matter of routine, be reviewed to add detail and substance. Getting a full record of what was observed may take as long as the original observation. Filling in the details should include (Lofland & Lofland, 1984):

- **Running descriptions** = specific, concrete descriptions of events;
- **Recall of forgotten material** = things that come back to you later;
- **Interpretive ideas** = notes offering an analysis of the situation;
- **Personal impressions** = your subjective reactions;
- **Reminders to look for additional information** = what you will look for during the next observation session.

A computer can be used in keeping field notes, as specialized software is available to analyze the contents of the observation transcript [examples of such software are HyperRESEARCH, QCA, Orbis—see Miles & Huberman (1994) for more details]. A good basic rule is that you should prepare the detailed notes of each observation session within 24 hours, and certainly never embark on a new observation session until you have fully sorted out your notes from the previous observation session.

While participant observations are not always the easiest methods for collecting information in evaluation research, they can provide information that may not be available any other way. The major advantage of using participant observations is that they can help determine what is actually happening in a particular situation, service, or program.

Main Points

- Triangulation of methods is testing the consistency of findings generated by different data-collection techniques. This is appropriate for an evaluation study because triangulation verifies and validates by comparing the findings of one data-collection method against another data-collection method.

- Data can be collected in five categories: attributes, facts, attitudes, preferences, and beliefs. To know what kind of data should be collected in a study, recall the scope of the study and what will be done with the gathered information.

- Data collection methods used in studies based on a quantitative framework are structured interviews and questionnaires.

- Questions posed in interviews or questionnaires can be set up to be answered using one of two formats, or a closed-ended or open-ended response.

- Care needs to be taken in writing questions for interviews or questionnaires. Furthermore, a number of factors can affect response rate (e.g., interviewer characteristics, order of questions, availability of token financial inducements to participate, appearance of schedule).

- Data-collection methods used in studies based on a qualitative framework are unstructured interviews (of which three are used in leisure-related evaluation projects—the descriptive information interview, the discovery interview, and the problem-solving interview), focus groups, and participant observation (where one of three roles can be assumed: the complete participant, marginal participant, or passive participant role).

Study Questions

1. What is meant by triangulation of methods? Why is it used?

2. What are the five kinds of data that can be collected in an evaluation study? How do you decide what kind of data to collect?

3. What are popular ways data are collected for studies using a quantitative framework?

4. What are the two response formats (and give an example of each) used in interviews and questionnaires?

5. What advice would you give to someone who is writing questions that will be used in an interview or questionnaire?

6. Identify some factors that can affect questionnaire response.

7. What are the popular ways data are collected for studies using a qualitative framework?

8. What is an unstructured interview? What are the three kinds of unstructured interviews commonly used in evaluating leisure services? Give an example of a question that could be used for each of these types.

9. What are focus groups? Why are they used?

10. What is participant observation? What are the three kinds of participant observer roles? Cite an example of each of these roles.

References

Bailey, K. (1978). *Methods of social research*. New York: The Free Press.

Baker, T. (1988). *Doing social research*. New York: McGraw-Hill.

Campbell, D., Kruskal, W., & Wallace, W. (1966). Seating aggregation as an index of attitude. *Sociometry, 29*, 1-15.

Creswell, J. (1994). *Research design: Qualitative & quantitative approaches*. Thousand Oaks, CA: Sage Publications.

Cunningham, J. (1993). *Action research and organizational development*. Westport, CT: Praeger.

Dillman, D. (1978). *Mail and telephone surveys: The total design method*. New York Wiley.

Dorsten, L. (1996). *Interpreting social and behavioral research: A guide and workbook based on excerpts from journal articles*. Los Angeles: Pyrczak Publishing.

Fink, A., & Kosecoff, J. (1985). *How to conduct a survey: A step by step guide*. Newbury Park, CA: Sage Publications.

Glancy, M. (1988). The play-world setting of the auction. *Journal of Leisure Research, 20*(2),135-153.

Greene, J., Caracelli, V., & Graham, W. (1989). Toward a conceptual framework for mixed-method evaluation designs. *Educational Evaluation & Policy Analysis, 11*, 255-274.

Grosof, M., & Sardy, H. (1985). *A research primer for the social and behavioral sciences*. Orlando, FL: Academic Press, Inc.

Higgenbotham, J., & Cox, K. (Eds.). (1979). *Focus group interviews: A reader*. Chicago: American Marketing Association.

Hutchison, R. (1987). Ethnicity and urban recreation: Whites, blacks, and hispanics in Chicago's public parks. *Journal of Leisure Research, 19*(3), 205-222.

Krueger, R. (1994). *Focus groups: A practical guide for applied research*. Thousand Oaks, CA: Sage Publications.

Lofland, J. & Lofland, L. (1984). *Analyzing social settings: A guide to qualitative observation and analysis* (2nd ed.). Belmont, CA: Wadsworth.

Miles, M., & Huberman, A. (1994). *Qualitative data analysis: A source book for new methods*. Beverly Hills, CA: Sage Publications.

Patten, M. (1990). *Qualitative evaluation and research methods* (2nd edition). Newbury, CA: Sage Publications.

Riddick, C., Ansello, E., & Seefeldt, C. (1987, October). *Children's perceptions of the age appropriateness for participation in selected leisure activities*. Paper presented at the 1987 National Recreation & Park Association's Leisure Research Symposium, New Orleans.

Riddick, C., & Dugan-Jendzejec, M. (1988). Health-related impacts of a music program on nursing home residents. In F. Humphrey and J. Humphrey (Eds.), *Recreation: Current selected research* (pp. 155-166). New York: AMS Press.

Robson, C. (1993). *Real world research: A resource for social scientists and practitioner-researchers*. Oxford, UK: Blackwell.

Russell, R.V. (1982). *Planning programs in recreation*. St. Louis, MO: C.V. Mosby.

Slant, P., & Dillman, D. (1994). *How to conduct your own survey*. New York: Wiley.

Spradley, J. (1980). *Participant observation*. Fort Worth, TX: Holt, Rinehart and Winston.

Steward, D. & Shamdasani, P. (1990). *Focus groups: Theory and practice* (Applied Social Research Methods Series, Volume 20). Newbury Park, CA: Sage Publications.

Tyson, G., Schlachter, A., & Cooper, S. (1988). Game-playing strategy as an indicator of racial prejudice among South African students. *Journal of Social Psychology, 128*, 473-485.

Wheatley, K., & Flexner, W. (1988). Dimensions that make focus groups work. *Marketing News, 22*(10), 16-17.

CHAPTER 11

Making Sense of Quantitative Information

What Will I Learn in This Chapter?
I'll be able to:

1. Select and interpret appropriate statistical tools for describing numerical data.

2. Distinguish nominal, ordinal, interval, and ratio scales of measurement.

3. Obtain a broad overview about information through tabled and graphed frequency distributions.

4. Make such relative comparisons as ratios, proportions, and rates.

5. Determine the central tendency of data; that is, describe a frequency distribution's center or "middle" with a single indicator.

6. Summarize the spread of individual scores by determining a measure of variability.

The information we gather or measure in evaluative research is essentially numbers or words—the number of participants in an adult fitness program, the percentage of the Black Diamond ski trail users who prefer longer operating hours, the adjectives checked by aquatics supervisors on lifeguards' performance forms, the ideas for new services voiced by infrequent health club users on slips of paper placed in the lobby opinion box. This chapter and the next chapter are about how to make sense of such information.

When information is first gathered from completed questionnaires, case study notes, field observation records, rating form responses, etc., it is inevitably poorly organized. Ordering and then analyzing such information is necessary because, generally speaking, data in their "raw" form do not speak for themselves. Analysis of information, then, is not an empty ritual—a textbook-required step—carried out between gathering the information and interpreting it. Thinking about how the data analysis might be carried out is an integral part of the initial study design process. Otherwise you may end up with a mish-mash of information, which no analysis procedure can redeem (Robson, 1993).

The intention of this chapter is to introduce you to a range of common statistical tools that are used in dealing with information often collected in an evaluative research study. The point is, once you have collected the data, you need to know how to organize, analyze and present it intelligently. Data come in all shapes and sizes—audio tapes, video tapes, notations on performance appraisals, responses to questionnaires, diary entries, reports of meetings, documents, etc. Nonetheless, most data fall into two categories—words or numbers. So we have *qualitative analysis* for words and other data that come in a non-numerical form, and *quantitative analysis* for numbers and other data that can be transformed into numbers. Since most of the studies you will conduct will call for both qualitative and quantitative analyses, it is important that you are able to deal competently with both. In this chapter we introduce the analysis of data in quantitative form, postponing the analysis of qualitative data for Chapter 12.

A vast extended family of quantitative (or statistical) analysis tools exists, and it would be foolish to expect everyone carrying out evaluative research to have all of it at their finger-tips. Therefore, the solution attempted here is to set out basic guidelines for selecting appropriate statistical tools, and to discuss how the results obtained from these tools might be interpreted. These selections, however, must be made at the study design stage of your project, not after you have collected the data, because it has major ramifications for what and how you ask and observe.

But here we have only introduced a small portion of the statistical tools available to you. Thus, beyond this coverage we advise you to ask for help from a consultant or other person familiar with the wide range of approaches to statistics. The advice should also help you locate computer software that will do the actual calculation work of the analyses for you. (There are also some excellent statistics books, such as that by Gravetter and Wallnau, 1998.) Even if you are on your own in this task, this chapter will familiarize you with a range of tool possibilities and enable you to implement some of the more commonly used tools yourself.

Types of Numerical Information

Information that is numerical comes in one of four ways: nominal, ordinal, interval, and ratio. For example, nominal data are the occupational labels of an organization's volunteer staff. Ordinal data include records kept over the years on the place finishers in the marathon races. If from an inventory of the aquatic facilities we know the average water temperatures in the pools, we are working with interval data. And, data are in ratio form if we know the amount of money collected for membership fees in our health and fitness club. Let us go back over these four types of quantitative data again.

A *nominal* scale of measurement labels observations so that they fall into categories. The word nominal means "having to do with names." Information that is nominally scaled uses names or labels: the gender of respondents to a questionnaire (named male and female), ethnicity (named African American, Asian American, European American, etc.), residence type (named rural, suburban, or urban), positions on a football team (named quarterback, lineback, etc.), and occupations (named sales, professional, skilled trade, etc.). Since nominally scaled information consists of labeled and discrete distinctions rather than numerical distinctions, no arithmetic-based functions (such as addition and subtraction) can be applied. For example, it would be inappropriate to "value" females with a score of two and males a score of one.

In an *ordinal* scale of measurement, observations are ranked in terms of size or magnitude. As the word ordinal implies, data are arranged in rank order. For example, the supervisor of a playground program is asked to rank her playground leaders. The resulting data indicate who the supervisor considers the best worker, the second best, and so on. Or, the number of first place, second place, and third place finishes for the swim club in the past 10 city meet seasons is also an example of observations that are rank ordered. College class standing (freshmen, sophomores, juniors, seniors) is still another example of ordinal data.

Figure 11.1: An example from practice: Midnight Basketball.

Directions: Read the following excerpt from an actual evaluation report and determine what scale of measurement was used to report the sources of funding.

> The slogan "Overtime is Better than Sudden Death" stretches across the gym walls in five Kansas City, Missouri, Night Hoops locations. In a world where connecting with youth is increasingly difficult, sports—basketball in particular—have become tools for reaching them. In Kansas City, the Mayor's Night Hoops program is not a panacea for preventing crime, but is a successful effort to relate to youth in a positive manner. The program is designed to meet youth in high-risk environments where they reside, then expose them to new information and experiences. Through the program the lives of thousands of young people have been transformed through positive relationships with coaches, caring adults, and other members of their community. Approximately 160 young people participated in this wholesome, secure, night-time summer activity in its initial year. Since then the program has expanded to five sites, serving more than 1,500 youth each year. With success comes external support. As the program's reputation for results spread, community leaders began to notice and get involved. Now 80% of the Night Hoops program is funded by the Kansas City Parks and Recreation Department. The remaining is made up by private donations and grants from the state. (Wilkins, 1997)

Answer: Information about the sources of funding for Night Hoops is in the nominal scale. That is, the sources are named in three categories: (1) city tax funding, (2) private donations, and (3) state grants.

Notice, however, that these data do not reveal how large or small the distances are between the rank orders. The swim club may have one first place winner in 75 % of the last 10 swim meets, but were these wins close or run-aways? Ordinally scaled data tell us that something is better or worse, but not by how much. This is a limitation of information measured on an ordinal scale, which means that like the nominal scale, we cannot apply arithmetic calculations.

This limitation is overcome in interval and ratio scales of measurement. Interval and ratio scales have equal intervals between numbers reflecting equal differences in magnitude. Let's take these scales one at a time. First, *interval* data are defined as rank-ordered information with equal units of measurement. What do we mean by equal units of measurement? On a ruler, for example, a one-inch interval is the same size at every location on the ruler, and the distance between inches two and four marked on the ruler is equal to the distance between inches seven and nine. Typical examples of interval data are water temperature, intelligence scores, and attitude scores. An interval scale is a more highly refined measurement scale than nominal and ordinal scales, yet it too has a limitation. A ratio cannot be determined because the zero point on the scale is arbitrary. While equal intervals between numbers on the scale reflect equal differences in magnitude, the interval scale does not have an absolute zero point that indicates complete absence of the quality being measured. For example, zero degrees water temperature certainly does not mean you will feel an absence of temperature to the water when you jump in!

Overcoming this limitation in the interval scale is the *ratio* scale. A ratio scale is defined as a rank order with equal units of measurement and an absolute zero. A ratio scale not only has equal intervals that reflect equal differences in magnitude, but also a meaningful zero point. For example, scores on the Scholastic Aptitude Test most likely measure aptitude on an interval scale—there is no such thing as a complete absence of (or zero) aptitude. However, a measure of the attendance of children in a play program is a ratio scale—it is possible for a child to have zero absences. Ratio scales are interval scales with the added characteristic of an absolute zero point. Thus ratio scales do reflect ratios of magnitude. That is, we can say that Jerome, who has missed four play sessions, has missed twice as much as Jamie, who has missed two sessions.

Unlike nominal and ordinal scales, interval and ratio scales allow basic arithmetic operations that permit us to calculate differences between scores, to sum scores, and to calculate average scores. This means that interval and ratio scales are more meticulous measures of information. As we consider data scaled from nominal through to ratio forms, we move from most primitive to most precise, because of increased mathematical utility (see Figure 11.3).

Knowing the scale of measurement of our information is more than an exercise. It will help us to determine which statistical analysis tools should be used. That is, selecting the correct tool will depend on knowing the scale of measurement of the data to be analyzed.

Figure 11.2: An example from practice: State Parks.

Directions: Read the following excerpt from an actual evaluation report and determine what scales of measurement were used to report the renters' judgement on the importance of cabin attributes and the annual incomes of the cabin renters.

> The challenges facing state parks generally result from conflict between their dual mission to preserve and protect areas of unique or exceptional scenic, scientific, cultural, or historical significance, while at the same time providing outdoor recreation facilities for the citizens of the state and its visitors. Several states have looked to cabins as a potential solution. Contrasted with more intense park developments such as lodges, convention facilities, and golf courses, cabins may represent an agreeable middle point on the natural vs. developed spectrum.
>
> West Virginia state parks were studied to determine if this supposition is true. Questionnaires were mailed to a sample of park cabin renters from the previous year. Among the information collected by the questionnaire was renters' income. It was found that cabin visitors are generally affluent, with most earning annual incomes greater than $60,000. The questionnaire also measured cabin renters' judgment on the importance of specific cabin attributes. For example, respondents rated cabin cleanliness, an efficient reservation, and a secluded location as most important, and availability of a television and telephone as least important. (Hollenhorst, Olson, & Fortney, 1992)

Answers: The cabin renters' judgment on the importance of cabin attributes is measured on an ordinal scale. Even though the questionnaire may have asked them to circle a number that corresponded to their perception of importance, the number only represented a rank order from most important to least important. The income of the cabin renters is a ratio scale. There are equal intervals in the scale, that is the distance between $10,000 and $20,000 is the same as that between $40,000 and $50,000. Plus, income has an absolute zero; it is possible to have no annual income.

Figure 11.3: Which Scale Is It?

Suppose you are administering a questionnaire about lifestyle to a sample of members of the fitness program. Your research question is how healthy are the program clients, and one thing you want to know is the amount of summer vacation they had last year. You are trying to determine the best way to ask the question and thus have developed three different options:

1. How many days of vacation did you have this summer? _____

2. How much vacation time did you take this summer?

    _____ not much (0-5 days)

    _____ some (6-10 days)

    _____ lots (11 or more days)

3. Did you have a summer vacation this year?

    _____ yes   _____ no

Questions:

1. In what scale of measurement will the answers to each question be? Why?

2. Therefore, which question will give you the most useful information for purposes of analysis? Why?

Answers:

1. Question 1 is in a ratio scale. Question 2 is in an ordinal scale. Question 3 is in a nominal scale.

2. Choose question one, because the ratio scale is the most precise for analysis purposes.

Describing Numerical Information

When numerical data are needed to describe the main features of the organization or people that have been studied, *descriptive statistics* are used. For example, describing a sample of children attending a summer camp designed to serve campers with asthma, the following information might be available: average age; average length of time since their asthma was first diagnosed; proportion diagnosed as mild, moderate, or severe asthmatic; average peak flow capacity by weight and age categories; etc. These characterizations are descriptive statistics. As such they meet the following objectives:

- Obtain a broad overview of the sample data.
- Determine a summary of the average, or center of the sample data.
- Determine how the sample data are spread out across categories.

We now describe each of these objectives in greater detail.

Broad Overview: Frequency Distributions

Frequency distributions are used to provide a broad overview of information. When you complete the quantitative data collection phase of an evaluation project, you usually end up with pages of numbers. Your immediate analysis task is to organize these numbers into some understandable form so that any trends in the data can be seen easily. One of the most common ways for organizing numerical data is to place the responses in a *frequency distribution*. This is simply a list of the categories of the information and the number of responses that correspond to the categories. Furthermore, within each interval and/or ratio-scaled category, the scores are organized into an order from highest to lowest. This enables us to see "at a glance" the entire set of responses. A frequency distribution shows us whether the responses are generally high or low, concentrated or spread out. It also shows us the location of any individual response relative to all the other scores in the data set. Frequency distributions can be presented as either tables or graphs.

Frequency Distribution Tables

Example 11.1 presents a simple *frequency distribution table* for the number of lawsuits in a county park system for a 10-year period. The category in this example, *park*, is a nominal scaled variable, and the names of the parks are listed in the left column. Also notice the frequencies (or count) of lawsuits, represented by the symbol f, for each of the parks are arranged in the right column.

Example 11.1. Number of Lawsuits in County Parks between 1988 and 1998
(An example of a frequency distribution table)

Park	Number (f)
Kanawha	13
Pioneer	10
Crestmont	7
Shawnee	3

Example 11.2 presents a frequency distribution table for the ratio-scaled variable of *alcohol intake*. Here the amounts of alcohol intake are arranged in the left column from highest to lowest. Also notice that instead of listing each option for the number of drinks consumed, the numbers are collapsed, or grouped.

Example 11.2: Alcohol Intake Among Center Clients
(An example of grouped frequency distribution table)

Beverages a Day	Number of Men	Number of Women
10 or more	20	5
8-9	31	9
6-7	110	82
4-5	95	96
2-3	2	5
0-1	0	1

When a set of data covers a wide range of values, it is unreasonable to list all the individual scores. In the alcohol consumption example above, this would mean we would have to list in the left column over 10 individual scores, which would make the table too long. So, as in Example 11.2, a *grouped frequency distribution table* is constructed. We do this by dividing the range of scores into groups and listing these groups in the left column of the table. There are several rules that help guide you in the preparation of a grouped frequency distribution table.

Rule 1. There should be no fewer than four groups and no more than eight groups. If the table has many more than eight groups, it becomes cumbersome and defeats the purpose of the grouped table in the first place. If the table has fewer than four groups, it would not tell you much about how the responses are distributed. Example 11.2 has six groups.

Rule 2. The width of each group should be a relatively simple number, such as 2, 5, 10 or 20. This makes it easier to understand: we are quickly able to see what the groups represent. The width of the groups in Example 11.2 (except for the interval 10 or more) is two.

Rule 3. All groups should be the same width. In Example 11.2 each group has a width of two (except for the group 10 or more).

Rule 4. The bottom score in each group should be a multiple of a simple number, such as 2, 5, 10 or 20. Again, this makes it easier for someone to understand the table. In Example 11.2 the bottom score in each group is a multiple of two.

Rule 5. All possible scores should be covered in the groups with no gaps and no overlaps, so that any particular score belongs and in only one group. In Example 11.2 this is taken care of by the *or more* designation. Another way of expressing this rule is through the two principles of exclusiveness and inclusiveness. *Exclusiveness* means that no response can be placed into more than one group; that is, each response has an "exclusive" place in the distribution. *Inclusiveness* means that every response is classifiable into an interval; that is, all responses are "included." For instance, in Example 11.2, if we did not have the interval *10 or more* and we had one respondent who drinks 14 alcoholic beverages each day, we would have violated the principle of inclusiveness.

Frequency Distribution Graphs

Graphs also help us overview the data with a frequency distribution. A *frequency distribution graph* is basically a "picture" of the information shown in a frequency distribution table. Several types of graphs, including the pie chart, bar graph, histogram, and polygon are discussed here.

A *pie chart* is best suited for displaying percentages of categories because it apportions the 360 degrees of a circle. Pie charts are most typically used to graph nominally scaled data, but it is also possible to display ordinal, interval, and ratio scaled data this way. Suppose we know that 56% of our athletics club members live in the central city area, 20% live in suburban locations, and 24% live in the rural areas. These proportions can be depicted by dividing 360 degrees of circle space accordingly (56% of 360 degrees = 202 degrees of the circle) as shown in Example 11.3. There are two guidelines for constructing a pie chart.

Rule 1. There should be five or fewer categories.

Rule 2. Display the pie wedges in either ascending or descending order of magnitude.

Example 11.3. Where Our Members Live
(An example of a pie chart)

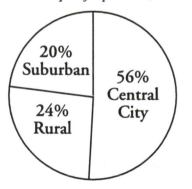

Next, we consider the bar graph and histogram. For both of these graph types, simply draw a bar above each score or category so that the height of the bar corresponds to the frequency of responses. The only difference between the bar graph and histogram is the scale of measurement of the data. When you are presenting the frequency distribution for data in a nominal or ordinal scale, the graph is constructed so that there is space between the bars. Here the separated bars depict that the scale consists of distinct categories. This is called a *bar graph*. When data are graphed from an interval or ratio scale, the bars are drawn so that they touch each other. The touching bars signal that the data are continuous, as with numerical scores. This is called a *histogram*. Examples 11.4 and 11.5 show the difference.

Example 11.4. Expenses for Convention Exhibitors
(An example of a bar graph)

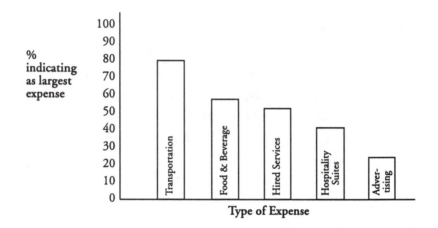

Example 11.5. Number of Correct Serves with Oversized Tennis Racket
(An example of a histogram)

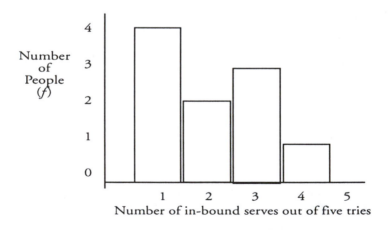

Rules for making a bar graph and a histogram are:

Rule 1. For both the histogram and the bar graph, the horizontal axis always depicts the variable category or score. In the above examples the horizontal axes are the type of expense and the number of in-bound serves.

216

Rule 2. Likewise for both graphs, the vertical axis always depicts the frequency, or count (such as percentage of respondents and number of people in the above examples).

Rule 3. For the histogram, the scores on the horizontal axis are listed in increasing value from left to right, and for both graphs the frequencies are listed on the vertical axis in increasing value from bottom to top.

Rule 4. The point where the two axes intersect should have a value of zero for both scores and frequencies.

Rule 5. The graph should be constructed so that its height is approximately three-quarters the length of its width. Violating this can result in graphs that distort the picture of the data.

A *polygon* is very similar to a histogram, except that a single dot is drawn above each score on the horizontal axis, instead of a bar, at a height that corresponds to the frequency on the vertical axis. A continuous line is then drawn connecting these dots. The line is anchored at the zero point at each end of the axes. As with a histogram, the frequency distribution polygon is for use with interval or ratio scales of measurement. Example 11.6 shows the same data as in Example 11.5 structured in a polygon rather than a histogram.

Example 11.6: Number of Correct Serves with Oversized Tennis Racket
(An example of a polygon)

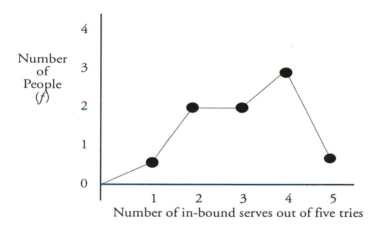

Proportions, Ratios, and Rates

A final way data can be broadly summarized is to calculate ratios, proportions, or rates. These are all forms of *relative comparisons*. For example, reporting that the graduation rate for college student-athletes is 6.6 gives us a comparison of the graduation success of student-athletes relative to all students at the college. What does 6.6 actually mean? We explore this statistic now. First, a caveat: data must be in either the interval or ratio scale of measurement for determining ratios, proportions, and rates.

A *ratio* is used to compare the frequency of one category or response with that of another. It is the simplest comparison. The ratio is expressed as so many cases of one response to one case of another response. This means:

Ratio of *A* to *B* = the elements in set *A* compared with the elements in set *B*

or,

Ratio of *A* to *B* = *A* divided by *B*

Suppose we want to compare the 23 participants in the outpatient activity therapy program who missed sessions last month because of "not being able to get off work," with the 10 participants in the same program who missed sessions because he or she "simply forgot." The ratio of the can't-get-off-work reason (A) to the forgetting reason (B) is:

A divided by B or 23 divided by 10 = 2.3

Thus, the ratio of the work reason to the forgetting reason is 2.3. This means that for every one patient who missed the sessions because he or she forgot, 2.3 patients missed because they could not get off from work.

A *proportion* is really a special kind of ratio—it is a ratio to the total. That is, proportions are used to compare the frequency of a category or response with the total frequency. This means:

Proportion = frequency of the category divided by total frequency

or,

A divided by the total (A plus B)

For example, suppose we wish to determine the proportion of playground injuries due to falls from the play equipment. Let us assume we know for our district that last year the number of playground injuries due to falls was 41, and the number of injuries due to other accidents was 27.

The proportion of injuries due to falls from the play apparatus =
41(A) divided by 68 ($A+B$ or 41+27) = .60

If we multiply this value by 100 we convert the proportion into a *percentage*: .60 x 100 = 60%. Thus sixty percent of playground injuries were caused by falls from the equipment. (This number is actually correct according to the US Consumer Product Safety Commission (Henderson, 1997)). Percentages are the most commonly reported form of proportions.

Still another method of comparison is the rate. *Rates* are defined as the frequency of occurrence of a particular outcome. They are calculated by dividing the actual number of occurrences by the number of possible occurrences. That is,

Rate = # of actual occurrences divided by # of possible occurrences

To demonstrate, let's suppose that for a college, the number of graduating student-athletes equaled 64. This number, 64, represents the number of *actual occurrences*. Further, let's suppose that the total number of student-athletes who started college four years ago was 97. This is the number of *possible occurrences*. Therefore, to calculate the graduation rate for student-athletes,

Rate = 64 divided by 97 = .66

This means that .66th of a person graduated. Since it is hard to visualize this, we usually multiply this answer by a base. For example, suppose we choose the base of 10,

.66 multiplied times 10 = 6.6

This means that the graduation rate of student-athletes is 6.6 per 10 student-athletes.

Measures of Central Tendency

The objective in determining central tendency is to describe a frequency distribution's center or "middle" with a single indicator. This indicator (a category or number) should be that value that is most representative of all the scores in the distribution. The common language for this is the *average*; however, we must be more specific than this because there are many kinds of averages. Let us discuss the three most common averages: mean, median, and mode.

The *mean* (specifically the arithmetic average) is only appropriate for interval and ratio scaled data. It is computed by adding all the scores in the distribution and dividing by the number of scores. Suppose the number of miles jogged per week for four participants in our personal training program are:

3 7 4 6

The mean for this information is the sum of the miles jogged divided by the number of joggers, or:

$$\overline{X} = \frac{\text{the sum of } X}{N}$$

where $\overline{X}$ is the symbol for the mean, X designates the scores, and N is the symbol for the number of scores. So, 3 plus 7 plus 4 plus 6 divided by 4 equals 5. The mean is five miles jogged per week.

Although the procedure of adding the scores and dividing by the number provides a functional definition of the mean, there is an another definition that may give you a better understanding. This is to think of the mean as the number of miles participants in our personal training program would jog per week if the miles were distributed equally among everyone in the program. If all persons in the program were participating equally, they'd each jog five miles.

The *median* is another tool for determining the centrality of information. It is defined as the middle value; half of the sample values will be larger than the median value and half will be smaller. The median, in other words, is the score that divides a distribution exactly in half. To determine the median we:

Step 1. Arrange the raw data into ascending order.

Step 2. Identify the middle value.

For example, suppose we know the scores given by the manager in our organization for the quarterly review of staff performance. The rating scale was based on 0 to 25, with 25 representing perfect performance. We arrange these staff performance scores in ascending order:

$$5 \quad 7 \quad 8 \quad 8 \quad 8 \quad 9 \quad 12 \quad 15 \quad 17 \quad 19 \quad 23$$

We see that the median performance score for the 11 staff members is 9. This is the middle score; it leaves the same number of values (five) to the left of it as to the right. So if we want a summary measure of average that identifies the center staff performance value, we would choose the median value of 9. (Not such good staff performance!)

In this example there is an odd number of scores, so finding the middle position in the distribution is straightforward. We can actually visually determine it. If there is an even number of values, the median is the mean of the two middle values. For example, suppose there are 10 staff in our sample:

$$5 \quad 7 \quad 8 \quad 8 \quad 8 \quad 9 \quad 12 \quad 15 \quad 17 \quad 19$$

The two middle performance scores are eight and nine. We locate the median by finding the point halfway between the middle two scores. Thus, the median is the mean of these two values:

8 plus 9 divided by 2 equals 8.5

The median staff performance is now 8.5.

The median is appropriate for ordinal, interval, and ratio scaled data. It is not appropriate for nominal data, because nominal data cannot be arranged in rank order, from lowest to highest.

A tool for summarizing centrality in information that is appropriate for all scales of measurement is the mode. The *mode* is defined as the most common response in a distribution of responses. It is the most popular category, or most frequently occurring score. The mode is the score or category that has the greatest frequency. It is used to describe what is typical for any scale of measurement. Suppose, for example, the Chamber of Commerce asks a sample of 100 adults to name their favorite restaurant in town. These data might look like the results shown in Example 11.7. First, in which scale of measurement are these data?

The answer is nominal data because the scale of measurement involves categories of responses (restaurants). Now, what is the modal response? Nick's English Hut is the mode because it is the restaurant most frequently named as the favorite.

Example 11.7. Favorite Restaurants
(An example of the mode)

Restaurant	# Who Prefer (frequency)
Southside Cafe	6
Fisherman's Dock	17
Nick's English Hut	35
Flora's	20
Uptown Cafe	30
Mustard's	15

The mode, therefore, is an appropriate measure of centrality for nominally scaled information. It is also appropriate for ordinal, interval, and ratio data. But, be careful! The mode is always a score or category, not a frequency. For example, in the data presented in Example 11.7 the mode is Nick's English Hut, not the frequency of 35.

It is possible for a distribution to have more than one mode. To illustrate, let's consider an example using ratio data. Suppose we have information on the ages of participants in our midnight basketball program. They are presented in Example 11.8.

Example 11.8. Ages for Midnight Basketball Participants

12	14	18	9	10	18	19
13	18	21	14	14	10	23

To determine the mode for this ratio-scaled information we:

Step 1. Arrange the raw data in ascending order.
Step 2. Count the number of times each value occurs.

This is shown in Example 11.9.

Example 11.9. Ages for Midnight Basketball Participants
(An example of the bimode distribution)

9	10	10	12	13	14	14	14	18	18	18	19	21	23

Now we see that the mode is both 14 and 18 years of age. Each occurs three times in the data set. Thus, these two ages are the most typical for the sample of midnight basketball players. And, since there are two ages that are most typical, we say that the distribution is *bimodal*. When a distribution has more than two modes, it is called *multimodal*.

Measures of Variability

The final objective of descriptive statistics is to summarize the spread of the individual scores. These descriptive statistics are known as *measures of variability*. They provide a measure of the degree to which scores in a distribution are spread out or clustered together.

To illustrate, suppose we are determining the effectiveness of an after-school math tutoring program at the Girls Club. At the end of the fall semester of tutoring, math test scores are recorded. For the five girls in the tutoring program, their fall math exam scores were: 91, 84, 78, 65, 60. The tutoring program is continued the next semester and for the five girls in the program, their spring math exam grades were: 96, 91, 86, 84, 82. In which semester is the spread of math grades the greatest? In which semester are the grades clustered together? This spread of grades across the distribution is its variability, and we can see that the variability is larger in the fall semester. There are ways of describing the variability of scores in a distribution with a single number. The two measures we will discuss are the range and the standard deviation.

The *range* is the distance between the largest score and the smallest score in the distribution. So, simply,

$$\text{Range} = X(\text{max}) - X(\text{min})$$

Thus for the fall semester math scores the Range = 91 - 60 = 31; and for the spring semester math scores the Range = 96 - 82 = 14. These single numbers (31 and 14) tell us what we could also determine by just looking at the distribution: the math scores had more spread from each other in the fall and were more homogeneous in the spring (31 is a higher number than 14). While this may seem obvious and unnecessary with a sample of only five scores, for larger distributions where eye-balling is harder, the range is more useful.

Yet the range can be problematic. The reason is that it is completely determined by the two extreme values in the distribution and ignores the scores in between. To illustrate, let us go back to the math tutoring program at the Girls Club. Suppose the following year, with five different girls, the fall math scores are 90, 86, 80, 75, 70, and the spring math scores for these same girls are 90, 89, 88, 88, 70. In calculating the range for each distribution, we compare the two extreme scores (Range = 90 - 70) and we get the same result; the range for each distribution = 20. But as we can see by studying all the numbers in the two distributions, the scores in between the two extremes are spread quite differently from each other. Four of the math scores in the spring semester are more closely clustered together. This is the problem with the range. Because the range does not consider all the scores in the distribu-tion, it often does not give as accurate a description of the variability.

To correct this problem, the *standard deviation* is often a more important measure of variability. The standard deviation uses the mean of the distribution as a reference point and measures variability by accounting for the distance between each score and the mean; it is, in other words, the average distance from the mean. When the standard deviation (notated as SD) is equal to 0, there is absolutely no spread of the scores. And as the size of the standard deviation increases, the spread of the scores around the mean increases. While most calcula-tors have a function for determining the standard deviation, following along with the hand calculation of a standard deviation shows us exactly how it works.

Step 1. Calculate the mean.

Step 2. Subtract this mean value from each score. This is called the deviation score.

Step 3. Square each of these deviation scores.

Step 4. Add these squared deviation scores together.

Step 5. Divide this sum by N - 1 (where *N* represents the number of responses).

Step 6. Take the square-root of this answer. The result is the standard deviation.

Let's illustrate these steps with the spring math scores from the second year of the math tutoring program. First we calculate the mean: 90 + 89 + 88 + 88 + 70 divided by 5 = 85. Now we can calculate the standard deviation (Example 11.10) by first determining how far each score is from this mean. This is the deviation score.

Example 11.10. Calculation of the Standard Deviation for Spring Math Scores in the Second Year.

Girl	Math Score	Deviation Score	Squared Deviation Score
Josie	90	5	25
Jamie	89	4	16
Judy	88	3	9
Jill	88	3	9
Joleen	70	-15	225
$\overline{X} = 85$			Total= 284

Now, we sum all the squared deviation scores: 25 + 16 + 9 + 9 + 225 = 284. We divide this sum by N - 1, that is 5 - 1, so that: 284÷4=71. And take the square root of this answer:

square root of 71 = 8.43. Thus 8.43 is the standard deviation of the second year's spring math scores.

What does 8.43 mean? Think of it as describing the typical distance of math scores from the mean. That is, the average difference between individual and average math scores is 8.43 points. To compare this conceptually, the standard deviation for the fall math scores from the second year is 8.07. As this answer designates, the average distance of math scores from the mean in the fall distribution is a little smaller than for the spring.

Selecting the Best Descriptive Statistic

Now that you understand a variety of ways of describing numerical data, how do you decide which measure to use? The first answer is that it depends on your objective for describing the information. Do you want to address the distribution's center or spread? Or the proportion, rate, or ratio of the information? There are other answers to the question "which measure is best" as well. For example, for measures of central tendency, the mean is most often preferred. Because the mean uses every score in the distribution, it usually is a good representative value. Yet, because it uses every score, the mean is affected by extreme scores and thus is less useful in this situation. Similarly, the most commonly used measure of variability is standard deviation, which is also affected by extreme scores. Also, the sample size will

Figure 11.4: Descriptive statistics according to scale of measurement.

Scale of Measurement	Frequency Table	Frequency Graph	Central Tendency	Variability	Other
ratio/interval	simple, grouped	histogram, polygon	mean, median, mode	standard deviation, range	percentage, rates, ratios
ordinal	by categories	pie, bar graph	median, mode	range	
nominal	by categories	pie, bar graph	mode	none	

affect the usefulness of a particular descriptive statistical tool, and open-ended distributions will make some measures indeterminable. Beyond these issues and problems, there are three prime considerations to help you determine the worth of any statistical tool. The statistic should:

1. Provide a stable and reliable description of the responses. Specifically, it should not be greatly affected by such "irregularities" as extreme scores in the data set.
2. Have a consistent and predictable relationship with other statistical measures (not covered in this chapter).
3. Be appropriate to the scale of measurement.

Figure 11.4 offers a quick comparison of descriptive statistical tools according to the scale of measurement.

The statistical tools we have covered in this chapter are called descriptive statistics because they characterize numerical information. There are many more descriptive statistics available that we did not discuss, plus there are many more statistical tools available that go beyond description. To suggest where you might go next in learning about statistics, we offer several options.

For example, there are *measures of relationship* (such as correlation and chi-square) that tell us how closely associated two sets of data are with each other. For example, a swim club coach may want to know the relationship between diving performance and muscular strength, or a youth sports director at an Army base might find it useful to know if the girls are more likely to be interested in team sports than the boys. In addition to measures of association there are also *inferential statistical tools* that tell us differences among data sets. For example, we might want to know if retirement home location makes a difference in retirement satisfaction, or if weather conditions make a difference in the violent behavior of children on the playground. Such inferential statistical tools as the *t* test and analysis of variance provide the answers to questions such as these.

A Footnote on Computer Statistical Software

Many of the examples in this chapter had very simple data sets that could be rather easily statistically analyzed by using a basic calculator. However, as the size of the data set increases, hand calculations become more tedious and difficult. That is why reference was frequently made in the chapter to using computers to do the statistical calculations.

Many leisure service organizations, and all colleges and universities, have statistical software packages available for personal-use computers such as Macintosh and IBM. Some of these smaller computers have large enough memories to even run the more sophisticated statistical packages like SPSS and SAS, formerly used only on the larger mainframe computers. More likely, however, your organization will have purchased a smaller statistical package to run the quantitative analyses needed in evaluation projects. Some of these programs, such as Minitab, SYSTAT, Excel, and MYSTAT, are relatively inexpensive, come with good documentation, and are easy to learn.

Although using the computer for statistical analyses is important, a word of caution is needed. Despite the marvelous efficiency of computer statistical packages, they will not do the thinking for you (at least not yet). If you expect to get meaningful answers to your evaluation questions, you will need to know what information and which instructions to give to the computer. Thus, it is still necessary that you understand the statistical procedures that are being performed by the computer. You will still have to select the appropriate analysis for your specific application. Therefore, our best advice is to travel beyond the instruction in descriptive statistics given in this chapter. If you are a student, enroll in a statistics course at your school, or if you are a practicing professional, numerous universities offer correspondence and television courses in statistics.

Main Point

- The purpose of descriptive statistics is to simplify and organize numerical information. These data may be organized in a table or graph, or they may be summarized by computing single values that describe their center and the spread. A decision map follows:

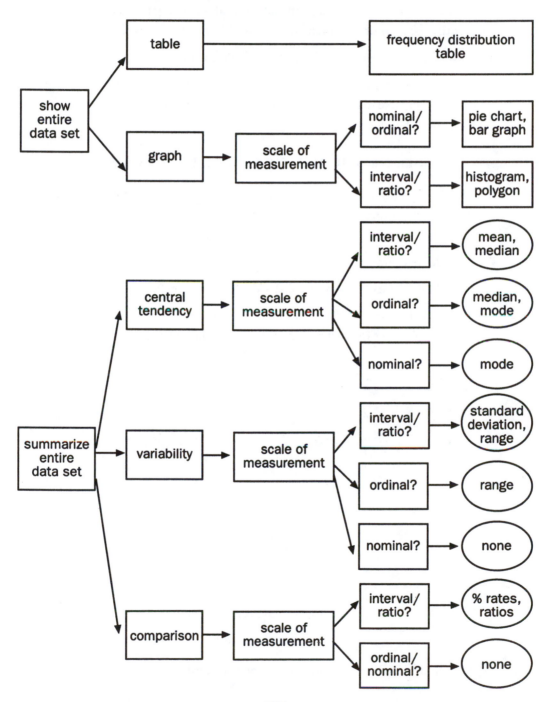

Study Questions

1. What is quantitative analysis and how is it different from qualitative analysis?

2. List and define the four scales of measurement. Why is it important to know the scale of measurement of information for analysis purposes?

3. A questionnaire asks respondents to report age, gender, marital status, annual income, favorite pastimes, and attitude toward increasing park entrance fees. Identify the scale of measurement that would probably be used for each.

4. How does a frequency distribution describe information?

5. Place the following ages of children attending the summer camp in a frequency distribution table that shows the proportion and the percentage as well as the frequency of each age:

    10, 11, 13, 9, 8, 9, 10, 10, 7, 6, 8, 9, 10, 14, 13, 12, 13, 9, 8, 16

6. Which graph would be appropriate to show the number of gold medals, silver medals, and bronze medals won by the United States during the Winter Olympics? Why?

7. How do percentages, rates, and ratios describe information?

8. How do measures of central tendency describe information?

9. Compute the mean, median, and mode for the number of summer vacation days shown in the following frequency distribution table:

# of days	f
9	2
8	3
7	6
6	3
5	1
4	1
3	0
2	0
1	1

Which measure best describes the center of this information? Why?

10. How do measures of variability describe information?

11. Why is the standard deviation defined as the standard distance from the mean?

12. Determine the range and standard deviation for the number of summer vacation days reported in question nine above. Which measure best describes the variability of this information? Why?

References

Gravetter, F.J., & Wallnau, L.B. (1998). *Statistics for the behavioral sciences: A first course for students of psychology and education* (5th ed.). New York: West Publishing.

Henderson, W. (April 1997). Catching kids when they fall: Guidelines to choosing a playground surface. *Parks and Recreation, 32*(4), 84-92.

Hollenhorst, S., Olson, D., & Fortney, R. (1992). Use of importance-performance analysis to evaluate state park cabins: The case of the West Virginia State Park System. *Journal of Park and Recreation Administration, 10*(1), 1-11.

Robson, C. (1993). *Real world research: A resource for social scientists and practitioner-researchers*. Oxford, UK: Blackwell.

Wilkins, N.O.(1997, March). Overtime is better than sudden death. *Parks and Recreation, 32*(3), 54-61.

CHAPTER 12

Making Sense of Qualitative Information

What Will I Learn in This Chapter?
I'll be able to:

1. Understand the importance of inductive thinking to the analysis of qualitative data.

2. Begin the analysis of qualitative data by preparing field notes.

3. Proceed with the analysis by focusing the data from the prepared field notes.

4. Use data displays of the focused data to derive themes for the findings.

5. Draw and verify conclusions based on the analysis.

Suppose you have completed a series of observations of weight lifters using the conditioning room at the fitness center. You have also interviewed personal trainers who work with the lifters. Your observation and interview notes are written in your own hand in several spiral notebooks. They total 157 pages. What do you do now? How do you make sense of all these words? How do you organize it so you can locate the important findings? Since you have collected the information using qualitative methods, you will need qualitative analysis tools. Whereas the previous chapter focused on statistical tools for quantitative data, this chapter discusses the tools needed for analyzing qualitative data.

Qualitative data analysis is primarily an inductive thinking process, unlike quantitative procedures that rely more on deductive thinking. With an inductive process, patterns and relationships emerge from the data after they have been collected, rather than having been superimposed as hypotheses onto the data prior to their collection. This technique involves the process of developing topics or categories through comparison of data parts. Techniques for doing this are the basis of qualitative data analysis. But let us first set the stage by reviewing inductive thinking (Chapter 5).

Inductive thinking means that understanding emerges from the information. Categories and patterns come from the data set itself. The results are specific to these data. The process entails several cyclical phases:

- Analyzing continuously throughout the study
- Selecting, focusing, and simplifying the information written up in notes
- Categorizing and ordering the focused data
- Drawing and verifying conclusions

These cycles are depicted in Figure 12.1. The process moves back and forth between collecting and analyzing raw data and recasting tentative analyses. Gradually, more advanced levels of synthesis are achieved after each cycle. Let us overview each phase of the cyclical model before moving to more of the details in the remainder of the chapter.

Analysis begins as soon as the first bits of information are gathered. It continues in a parallel way throughout the collection of the rest of the data, because the analysis informs and drives what is collected next. That is, because you see a particular pattern emerging in the data, you set forth in your observations, interviews, or document analysis to find additional support for that pattern. The analysis proceeds by initially segmenting, or dividing,

Figure 12.1: Model for inductive data analysis.

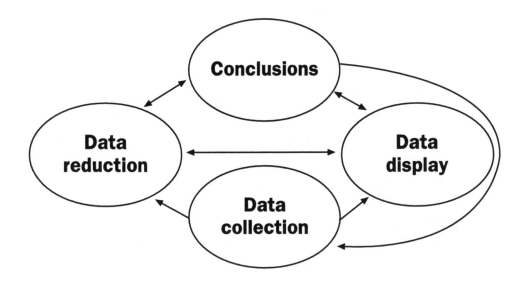

(Adapted from Miles & Huberman, 1994, p. 12)

232

the information into relevant parts, or units of meaning. This process usually begins with reading all of the data to gain a sense of the whole. These pieces of meaning are categorized according to an organizing system, with all material ultimately belonging to a category. The organizing system emerges from the data. That is, the categories are informed by the information. Initially these categories are preliminary and tentative, and remain as flexible working tools, rather than rigid rules. The main intellectual activity throughout the analysis is comparison—comparing and contrasting every part of the data and assigning it to a category. Eventually the tentative patterns are "checked" and if they pass muster, they become the conclusions of the study. Sound logical? Creative? That is the whole point of inductive thinking. Be patient. The rest of this chapter gets quite specific on how the above overview is accomplished.

Overall, analyzing qualitative data is an eclectic activity—there is no one "right" result. The reason is that there is no single prescription or fixed formula for how to proceed. Each analyst must find his or her own "style of intellectual craftsmanship" (McMillan & Schumacher, 1993, p. 484). However, although there are no fixed analysis procedures, the evaluator is not allowed to be limitlessly creative. "Qualitative analysis can and should be done artfully, even playfully, but it also requires a great amount of methodological knowledge and intellectual competence" (Tesch, 1990, p. 97). Teaching you this knowledge is the task of the rest of this chapter. We draw heavily for this discussion on Miles and Huberman's book, *Qualitative Data Analysis* (1994), and recommend this as a resource for further information on making sense of qualitative information.

Notes Preparation

Notes you take during observations, interviews, and focus groups usually represent a condensed version of what actually occurred. It is just not possible to write down everything that goes on or everything respondents say. This problem is corrected, of course, if you are permitted to audiotape or video record what you see and hear, which is more likely to be possible with interviews and focus groups. Otherwise you begin qualitative data analysis with a *condensed account*—often phrases, single words, and unconnected sentences (Spradley, 1980). Even if it seems inconvenient, a condensed set of notes will be of enormous value because they were recorded on the spot. Once you have returned from the observation or interview, you will expand your notes into an *expanded account* (Spradley, 1980). That is, you fill in details, recalling things that were not written down in the condensed account.

Now, as the amount of expanded accounts begins to grow, some early decisions about *note management* will be necessary (Miles & Huberman, 1994). You will need to develop a system for keeping your notes tidy—for example, putting them into a loose-leaf notebook, in file folders, or on file cards. You will also need a way to cross-reference. Information in one file will need to indicate where linked information is in another file. For example, a file on a specific personal trainer would also need to indicate the files containing information on the weight lifters who work with that trainer. Finally, in managing the expanded accounts, you will need a system of labeling the files. For example, AG PTJ 7198 O1 could mean the Allied Gardens Gym, personal trainer James, July 1, 1998, observation number one.

Focusing the Collected Data

After an interview or an observation, and the development of an expanded account, there is often a need to pause and consider: What are the main themes I have learned so far? What do I understand at this point? This is a matter of focusing the data, as you proceed with collecting it, and there are three ways this can be done: the focused summary, coding, and memoing.

Focused Summary

To begin, write a series of interim summaries on a card or piece of paper. This *focused summary* contains two or three "chunks" of main theme information and a short list of questions based on the notes. You should also reference the summary according to where in your notes the full account can be found. Figure 12.2 provides an illustration.

Figure 12.2: Example of a focused summary.

Observation #1 of James, Personal Trainer
7/1/97
Allied Gardens Gym

Main Themes that Struck Me from this Observation:

Highly rigid interaction between James and weight-lifter clients—
almost militaristic.

Workout routines are completely prescriptive, much like a required curriculum.

J's thoroughness is big role in seeing that routine is completed fully according to "prescription."

New Target Questions for Next Observation:

How do the weight lifters react to rigid approach of trainer? Is there a gender distinction in reaction? Does length of time involved in training affect ones reaction to a rigid training aproach?

Are there consequences if lifter does not complete routine correctly or fully?

How are workout routines developed? Does lifter have a role?–Need to address this question in interviews.

These focused summaries are useful in several ways. First, as you can tell from the questions posed in the example, they become a guide for planning the next observation or interview. They might also be useful in reorienting you to the situation when returning to the expanded account later. In fact, it is helpful to attach a copy of each summary to the top page of the expanded account of the observation so that it remains with the data it summarizes. Finally, the focused summaries set up for the next step in data analysis (Miles & Huberman, 1994).

Coding

A second activity required in focusing the information is *coding*. In the early stages of a qualitative study, most all of the information you gather looks important and promising. Coding helps keep the mounting quantity of data reasonable so that the truly meaningful patterns are able to emerge. Codes are tags or labels for assigning meaning to the information compiled. Codes are usually attached to phrases, sentences, or whole paragraphs in your expanded account of the notes. Yet, it is not the words themselves but their meaning that matters (Miles & Huberman, 1994). For example, following are some observation notes for an evaluation of how a hotel lobby is used. The codes run along the left column beside the notes.

TOUR   Man and woman couple approach the end of the couch. They are dressed as tourists though conservatively. Woman sits down; man stands and studies tourist brochure/map. Woman rises after about 20 seconds to look at map too. Hotel staff member (in yellow bellman-type jacket) approaches and exchanges some words (I can't hear). Both tourists sit down on the couch and

10MIN   resume study of brochure. After 10 minutes young man approaches (not in hotel uniform) and inquires "Mr. and Mrs. .....?", fingering folded sheet of

MEET   paper. Couple affirms and they get up and follow man out front door.

(Russell, 1991)

To code these notes you need to determine the essential meaning to either the entire sequence or to its parts. To demonstrate, three codes have been developed. Each captures a unique aspect of what was observed: who used the lobby, for how long, and for what use. "TOUR" indicates that the lobby users were probably tourists; "10MIN" codes the length of time spent in the lobby by these tourists; and "MEET" shows that the lobby's primary purpose in this case was as a place to meet (although the reason for the meeting is unknown). As shown, the codes should be entered in the margin of the expanded account notes.

To keep track of your codes so that a consistent coding scheme is used, prepare a *code book*. For qualitative data, this is simply an alphabetized list of the codes and their translation. For the example above the code book, with codes added for illustration, might look like this:

Types of Lobby Users:
   TOUR = tourists
   BUS = local business people
   REC = local people using the lobby as part of another recreational activity

Amount of Time:
   #MIN = number of minutes

Lobby Use:
   MEET = for meeting with others for another purpose
   CHECKIN = for processing hotel check-in procedures
   REST = to relax or rest in between activities

As you code subsequent notes, this directory list will remind you of what the earlier codes mean, and will help you begin to see patterns in the data. You may also wish to rename some codes as new information is added, or further differentiate by establishing additional codes. The code book allows you to keep track of all this. The coding should begin to stabilize about two-thirds of the way through the data collection process.

Memoing

There is another strategy for focusing the data: memoing. Glaser's (1978, pp. 83-84) definition of *memoing* is: "the theorizing write-up of ideas about codes and their relationships as they strike the analyst while coding. . . . It can be a sentence, a paragraph or a few pages. . . . It exhausts the analyst's momentary ideation based on data with perhaps a little conceptual elaboration." You write memos to yourself; they are little descriptions of how you would tie together different pieces of data into some kind of general understanding. Thus, a memo is a sense-making tool. As Miles and Huberman (1994, p. 74) see it: "[memo writing] often provides sharp, sunlit moments of clarity or insight—little conceptual epiphanies."

We suggest that you continuously give priority to memoing. When an idea pops into your mind, stop at that very moment and write it down. Remember memos are about ideas, not a recounting of the data; recounting data is the purpose of the focused summary previously discussed. Memoing should start as soon as the first of the data starts coming in and usually continues right up to the writing of the final report. Like coding, memoing should begin to stabilize about two-thirds of the way through the data collection process.

Memos should always be dated, entitled by the key concepts contained in them, and linked to specific places in your notes (Miles & Huberman, 1994). For example, a memo from the hotel lobby utilization study example might look like this:

Memo: Lobby Use Mid-day (19 Dec. 1991)

At this time of day, the lobby appears mostly used to wait for and meet business associates for lunch in one of the hotel restaurants, although not by all. Others appear to be settled in—using the lobby to do some work or recreational reading—like they were in a comfortable living room. (O10 12.19.92 P8)

(Russell, 1991)

In this memo example, the heading provides the date and key concept. At the end of the memo is the identification of the location of the insight in the notes.

Memos are kept separate from data files and notes. As the evaluation process continues, memos will accumulate and can themselves be sorted to build more comprehensive understanding. The point of memos is that it helps you move more easily from raw data to a conceptual level—building toward a more integrated understanding of events and interactions.

Data Displays

So far in this chapter we have discussed a series of tools for the initial analysis of qualitative data. These efforts continue throughout data collection. As the process proceeds, you will begin to see and hear things that will leap out at you as "the answers" to your evaluation research questions. Yet the analysis you have been doing to this point is not enough. Thus, you will have to resist the temptation to feel "finished." In fact, one of the important reasons you have begun data analysis while still collecting data is to improve data collection itself. Falling into the trap of premature closure can be a mistake, as you will cease to think about unanswered aspects and needs for additional information.

At this point, therefore, the analysis of the data advances by developing a data display. Such a display helps in developing and verifying descriptive conclusions about the phenomena we are evaluating. *Data displays* supply the basic material for plausible reasons for why things are happening as they are (Miles & Huberman, 1994).

A display is a visual chart that presents information systematically. The display is a narrowed view of the information that enables you to view the full data set in a single format. While there are various types of display formats, the two more popular, and thus the focus of our discussion here are the matrix and network. Matrices are constructed with rows and columns, and networks entail a series of "nodes" with links between them (Miles & Huberman, 1994). Which one you use depends on what you are trying to understand.

Matrices

A *matrix display* is helpful for understanding the connections among information—it offers an "exploratory eyeballing," a "thumbnail sketch" (Miles & Huberman, 1994, p. 93). A matrix is essentially the pulling together of two lists: one list is the column and the other list is the row. Continuing to draw upon the hotel lobby observation example, a matrix display is presented in Figure 12.3.

What are the two lists in a matrix? To answer this question, let's think of television programs. Almost all of us watch TV everyday, but let's assume we are trying to understand this cultural phenomenon for the first time. As part of the "study" of our culture it comes time for us to develop a matrix display. We determine that TV programs have at least these categories:

1. News
2. Comedy
3. Talk
4. Sports
5. Drama

This is our first list—we call it a list of TV program "types" or the *domain* studied.

While the items, or categories, on this list are similar in that they are types of TV programs, they are also unique in that they have different attributes. In fact, that which distinguishes the types of TV programs is their attributes. An *attribute* is any element of information regularly associated with a category (Spradley, 1980). What are the attributes of sports programs? In what ways are these different from the attributes of comedy programs? One attribute that distinguishes is perhaps "length of program"; sports programs tend to last several hours while the most common time duration of a comedy program is one-half hour. Another attribute that enables us to contrast TV programs is the "degree of prior scripting." Whereas a comedy program is completely prescripted, a sporting event on TV is completely non-prescripted—we never know ahead of time which team will win! The attributes become the second list.

So, we are now able to construct a matrix data display. Here is the result for just the two categories of sports and comedy programs.

Domain: Type of TV Program	Attributes:	
	Length of Program	Prior Scripting
Sports	Lengthy–several hours	None
Comedy	Brief–1/2 hour	Fully

As you can conclude from this simplistic illustration, the process of building a matrix data display is easy. To review, here are the steps (Spradley, 1980):

Figure 12.3: Example of a matrix display—kinds of hotel lobby waiters.

Types	Attributes			
Solos	**Waiting Behavior Intensity**	**Posture**	**Emotion**	**Object of Waiting**
Watchers	most intense/ focused on the action of waiting/can be distracted/increases with time	often inert/ lots of micro-flow/pacing/ narrow range of motion	anticipation/ can be impatient	other persons/ transportation
Workers	usually focus is not on waiting, but on work/rarely distractred		patient/ studious/ contemplative	other persons/ a meeting/ transportation
Players	focus not on waiting, but on play/occasion-ally distracted	relaxed	usually patient/ preoccupied	other persons/a meeting/ transportation
Shifters		posture shifts are 1st clue kind of waiting		
Groups				
Socials	Varies	often seated opposite or at right angles	lighthearted/ recreational spirit/often animated	other persons/ transportation/ a meal/ social
Ad Hoc Committees	more casual/ less intense work than a lobby–held working meeting		highly animated	other persons/ transportation/ a meal/the "business"

(Russell, 1991)

Step 1: Select a domain for analysis. In Figure 11.3, the domain was type of hotel lobby "waiters"; in the example above the domain was type of TV program. You will find that a domain with less than 10 items, or categories, makes the process more manageable. However, the actual number does not matter all that much; select any domain for which you have collected information that contrasts the items. The domain and its categories become the column list.

Step 2: Inventory your data for all attributes of the chosen domain. For example, in the hotel lobby study, the researcher's memos contained the idea about types of waiting observed in the lobby. The study did not begin with the purpose of studying waiting behavior; the beginning research question was simply to assess how the lobby was used. It was in the memoing that "waiting" was formulated as the most common use. In inventorying the observation notes, the contrasts are flushed out. These *contrasts*, or attributes, should be clearly distinguishable. That is, for the attributes of TV programs, we have observed that sports programs are long and comedy programs are short. Thus, programs are clearly distinguishable along a time contrast. The attributes become the row list in the matrix.

Step 3: Prepare a matrix worksheet and fill it in. As already illustrated, this provides the working surface for the matrix. It contains the list of types of the domain in a column on the left, and the list of contrasts in a row across the top. Now, fill it in according to the data in your field notes, focused summaries, and memos. Leave enough room in the matrix worksheet to write in up to a short phrase of information. Again, check the example in Figure 12.3.

Step 4: Prepare a list of contrast questions for missing attributes and conduct additional data collection. One of the best benefits of a matrix is that it will quickly reveal the kinds of information you next need to collect (Spradley, 1980). Every blank space or question mark in the worksheet suggests the sort of observations or interviews you need to do. Of course, there is nothing wrong with leaving some blanks or questions in the matrix; you will have to be the judge in terms of the amount of time and interest you have.

Step 5: Prepare a completed matrix. The final matrix will become an approximate outline for the final report. But it may not be the only such outline. Some evaluators using qualitative methods prepare a data display matrix for as many domains as possible, while others limit their study to one or just a few central domains. Our suggestion is that you examine at least two domains, and thus prepare at least two separate matrices.

Networks

A data display with a *network* format is useful when you want to focus on order and more than a few domains at the same time. In Figure 12.4 a simple network display has been designed to show the "life cycle" of the relationship between a weight lifter using the weight room in the gym and the personal trainer. By using the network framework, we are able to simultaneously

Figure 12.4: Example of a network data display: Life cycle of the relationship of a weight lifter and personal trainer.

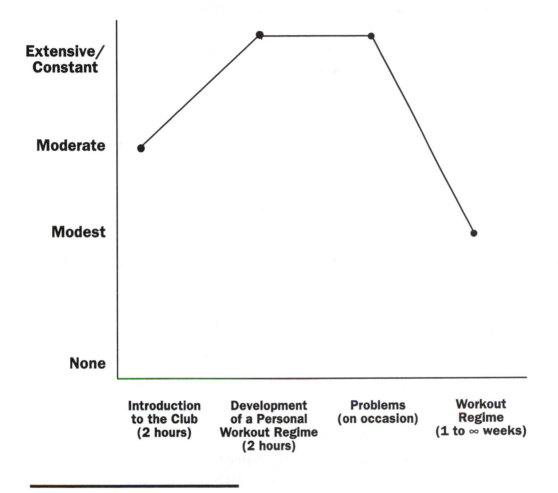

display the domains of workout series (with attributes frequency, duration, intensity) and sources of workout goals (with lifter and trainer as attributes), as well as the order in which they take place.

In the network the points are events, and the links have the implicit meaning "is followed by" or "is related to" or "is a part of" (Miles & Huberman, 1994). The network is ordered; each point is labeled. You can see patterns readily: for example, that the personal trainer's involvement with the lifter is an inverted "U." That is, it rises to a peak in the beginning of a lifting program.

The steps to preparing a network are similar to those for creating a matrix. The only difference is that instead of preparing two lists of categories (domains and attributes), for a network you identify events and relationships. Essentially, in both a matrix and a network, you are making choices on how to partition the data. Yet, a matrix and a network are not the same thing. There are differences:

- **Descriptive versus explanatory intent.** Are you trying to lay out data to see what is there (matrix), or do you want to generate some explanations about why things happen as they do (network)?
- **Partially ordered versus completely ordered.** Are you placing data in rows and columns that represent descriptive categories (matrix), or are you ordering the categories in some specific way, such as by time, influence, intensity, roles, procedure (network)?
- **Two domains versus more than two.** Are you comparing and contrasting two domains (matrix) or three or more (network)? A network gives you the means for moving to more complexity if the data require it.

To summarize this section of the chapter, some remaining questions will be answered. Where does the evaluator get the ideas for a matrix or network? Through inductive thinking the ideas are a "translation" of the coded notes, the focused summaries, and the memos. When should a matrix or a network be developed? By displaying data in these ways during the last phases of data collection, focus is gained on what you know and what you do not know. Can both forms of data display be used? Certainly–for any given evaluation question you can develop many different displays using the same set of domains as well as different domains. Each has advantages and each has trade-offs, so by preparing several you are better able to understand the totality of what you are studying. Can data displays be modified? Again, certainly! In fact, this is part of the point. The matrices and the networks you create will almost always evolve. The later ones will be more data-sensitive than the earlier ones, as things become clearer to you (Miles & Huberman, 1994).

Formatting data into displays is a decision-making tool. It determines which understandings will be analyzed and in which ways. If a variable is not in the display, it will not get compared and contrasted to another variable. So be careful not to let the display itself bully the data into shortcuts.

Drawing Conclusions

Now comes what, to many evaluators, is the hardest part. The procedures in qualitative data analysis that we have described so far are tools to finding meaning in the information gathered. There comes a time when these tools must finally produce the conclusion. Yet this actually isn't so difficult because people are natural meaning-finders. We are constantly trying to make sense of things. At this point in the analysis, the evaluator needs to commit to a final sense or meaning of what has been learned in the evaluation. Here's how (Miles and Huberman, 1994):

Tactics for Building Conclusions

There are many ways to build conclusions. The following are suggestions, and you can pick and choose from the list according to the ones that match your natural way of thinking.

• **Clustering.** The data display tools enable us to "clump" information into patterns or themes. Typically patterns of similarities or differences emerge. The patterns identified in the data displays provide hunches for further pattern seeking; thus, in drawing conclusions, the clustering process continues as we move to higher levels of abstraction. It is impossible to tell you exactly how to do clustering; with inductive thinking the more complex patterns will just jump out at you—they will simply happen. For example, try the exercise in Figure 12.5.

Figure 12.5: Exercise in noting patterns, themes.

Think about the matrix in Figure 12.3 to see what themes "jump out." Make a list of these themes. When you have finished compare your list to that below. The themes noted below actually "happened" for the researcher in the study.

Conclusions Drawn from Matrix of Waiting in a Hotel Lobby

1. Lobby waiting intensity varies greatly, but for the longer times, waiting can be quite focused.

2. The lobby often serves as a "staging area" for events elsewhere—both in and out of the hotel.

3. Use of the lobby by "locals" is very evident; their usage may be even greater than that of hotel guests.

4. Lobby activity wraps around meal times. That is, it occurs both before and after dining in the hotel restaurant as well as in restaurants outside the hotel.

How did you do? What exactly did you do to accomplish the exercise? Some suggestions for clustering might be useful to you, but these are not at all prescriptive for getting it done. One way might be to construct an *integrative diagram* (McMillan & Schumacker, 1993). This exercise involves combining the matrices and/or networks you have already constructed. How well do these data displays overlap onto each other? An integrative diagram often helps you move to a more abstract analysis by allowing you to ask different questions about the data. Another strategy for clustering might be to do a *cross-analysis* (McMillan & Schumacher, 1993). Usually presented in matrix format, categories are crossed with one another to generate new insights. These cross-categories sometimes show contradictions in the already analyzed data and suggest areas in which more general patterns might be logically uncovered.

• **Seeing plausibility.** Conclusions also are derived from the act of determining what makes good sense, or what fits. This is the plausibility basis for conclusions, or "it just feels right." While we do not recommend this as the sole tactic for drawing a conclusion, there is no denying that many scientific discoveries at least initially appeared to their inventors in this way. Plausibility, if used carefully and in union with other more systematic approaches, is certainly a valid means to drawing conclusions.

• **Making metaphors.** Metaphors are often useful in drawing conclusions. As a literary device, metaphors involve comparing two things via their similarities, while ignoring their differences. For example, the idea of the "empty nest" phase of a parent's life is a common metaphor for concluding the experience of children growing up and leaving home. A metaphor from the hotel lobby example might be, "the lobby is the stage for a series of one-act plays, complete with entrances and exits. . . . with the drama or comedy varying in terms of plot and performances" (Russell, 1991).

• **Counting.** Even though this chapter focuses on analyzing qualitative rather than quantitative data, counting is still useful in drawing conclusions. After all, when a theme or a pattern has been identified, it essentially is being noted that something happens a number of times. When we say a theme is important, we have come to that conclusion, in part at least, by making counts of its occurrence. Suppose in an evaluation study, 62% of the interviewees mentioned lack of child care as their reason for irregular participation in a fitness program. By counting the number of respondents mentioning this reason, a theme emerges in the interview notes. Counting enables us to see rapidly what is contained in a large batch of data.

• **Subsuming particulars into the general.** Whereas clustering involves clumping things that go together and giving them a common label, there is a related approach that entails determining whether things are a part of a more general category. According to Glaser (1978), this is a matter of looking for "basic social processes" that are more general in description than the specific things being analyzed. For example, suppose the behaviors you have observed in an after-school program are bickering, arguing, refusing, offering, and soothing. In subsuming these particulars into the general, these behaviors could be viewed as part of a more general category such as negotiation (Miles & Huberman, 1994).

Subsuming is the process of drawing a conclusion by moving up a step on the abstraction ladder. It is accomplished by shuttling back and forth in your thinking between the notes and conceptual categories. This continues until new data do not add to the meaning of the general category.

Making Conceptual Coherence

The various tactics that have been discussed—clustering, making metaphors, subsuming particulars—make discrete bits of information come together into a more conceptual whole. How is this actually accomplished? When you are trying to determine what an action or statement means, the mental activity involves "connecting a discrete fact with other discrete facts, and then grouping these into lawful, comprehensible and more abstract patterns" (Miles & Huberman, 1994, p. 261). In doing this we are no longer just dealing with "knowables," but also with "unknowables," and are connecting the two with successive layers of inductive paste.

So, at this juncture, we are ready for the next and final step in drawing conclusions. We now move from the metaphors and clusters to *constructs*. The findings of the study must be tied to the overarching explanations for the "how" and "why" of what has been studied. Constructs are broader applications of the patterns or concepts that have been noticed in the data. At last you have to ask yourself "Do any broader constructs put these patterns together the way I am putting them together?" Your greatest ally in this step will be your understanding of the research literature. Here again is where thoroughness in conducting the review of related literature pays off. Are there any constructs from theories or models from the work of other researchers that your patterns fit? In addition, you will find it useful to look back to the literature for constructs that conflict with your findings (Eisenhardt, 1989).

For example, do your patterns seem to support the construct of "leisure-job" from Neulinger's (1981) paradigm? Or, is Mannell's (1984) self-as-entertainment more explanatory? These are constructs from the leisure research literature. Perhaps, on the other hand, your findings are more appropriately linked with such social psychological constructs as cognitive dissonance or group conformity. Whatever, the idea is to make conceptual additions to your findings to make them applicable more broadly.

Verifying Conclusions

The data analysis is not quite finished. The last step (Figure 12.1) is to confront the issue of validity. "Qualitative analyses [like quantitative analyses] can be evocative, illuminating, masterful—and wrong" (Miles & Huberman, 1994, p. 262). Therefore, conclusions must be double checked. This will enable others, such as our governing board or supervisor, to have more faith in the evaluation. While there are many ways of verifying conclusions, those that will be featured are checking for data quality and testing explanations.

Checking for Data Quality

Essentially, it must be determined if the data on which conclusions have been based are "good" data. First, we check for *representativeness*. That is, is the information typical? To consider this more carefully it is useful to explore how our data might not be typical.

If atypical respondents or events have been sampled, then we run the risk of relying on data that may not be representative of the situation we have studied. For example, if only those people who can be easily contacted are interviewed, conclusions are likely to be based on nonrepresentative information. Here is some advice for checking for representativeness:

- Sample a few more cases and see if the findings from these match the conclusions.
- Look for contrasting cases in the data and determine whether they indeed are extreme in their difference from the conclusions.
- Select, at random, two or three people from the situation studied and ask them to "check" for typicality in the conclusions.

Another way to check the quality of your data is to determine if there are *evaluator effects*. As an evaluator you can naturally influence what you study. Unless completely nonreactive data-collection methods are used, your presence will alter the usual status quo—you will create behaviors in others that would not have occurred ordinarily (Miles & Huberman, 1994). Also, the behaviors studied can affect the researcher. They can lead you to form biased conclusions—to "swallow the agreed-upon or taken-for-granted version of local events" (Miles & Huberman, 1994, p. 265).

So we have two possible sources of bias here: (a) the effects of the evaluator on the data, and (b) the effects of the data on the evaluator. How can we check for evaluator effects? Here are some suggestions:

- Stay as long on site as possible.
- Use nonreactive measures where you can.
- Do some of your interviewing off site.
- Triangulate with other data collection methods; do not overly depend on qualitative methods (see Chapter 10).
- Keep your research questions firmly in mind; keep thinking conceptually and not sentimentally.

Testing Explanations

At last, it is time to test explanations. There are two ways we might do this: replication of findings and checking rival explanations.

Basically, findings are more dependable when other research confirms them. This is called *replication of findings*. You can accomplish replication in several ways. At the most basic level, you are replicating as you collect new information from new respondents or from new events (Miles & Huberman, 1994). New data qualify old data collected in your study by testing their generality. At a more rigorous level, you can also test your explanations via replication by studying different cases or situations, and then tracking through all of the cases to see whether the conclusions are repeated. For example, suppose we have studied local authority over tourism development for a rural tourist site. To check our conclusions about one town, we replicate the study in another town, and look for matching patterns. Of course, the most demanding form of replication of findings is when other studies have been done independently with different measurement tools.

One last way to help you confirm your conclusions is *checking out rival explanations* (Miles & Huberman, 1994). During data collection, it is quite easy to get busy making sense of each bit of information. Later on, it is even easier to commit yourself to a particular explanation. During the last stages of data analysis, it can become too late to consider any other explanation than the one arrived at early on. The capable evaluator using qualitative methods, however, looks for the most plausible, "well-grounded-in-the-data" explanation. This often means holding on to several possible (and even rival) explanations until one of them gets increasingly more compelling as a result of more, stronger, and varied sources of evidence. This means you give each rival explanation a "fair" chance. Foreclosing too early on one explanation is a danger sign of bias (Miles & Huberman, 1994, pp. 274-275).

Main Points

- Qualitative data analysis is primarily an inductive thinking process. Contrastingly, quantitative data analysis relies on deductive thinking.

- Data analysis of qualitative data begins with well organized and thorough field notes.

- Next, the collected data needs "focusing." This can be accomplished by preparing focused summaries, coding, and memoing.

- Data displays—either matrix or network—help to develop and verify descriptive conclusions.

- Drawing conclusions requires the use of such tactics as clustering, seeing plausibility, making metaphors, counting, and subsuming particulars into the general.

- Conceptual coherence in the conclusions is then found by developing constructs of understanding.

- Verifying conclusions means checking the data quality and testing explanations.

Study Questions

1. Explain the difference between inductive and deductive thinking. Which one is associated with qualitative data analysis? Why?

2. Why are focused summaries, coding, and memoing needed for focusing the qualitative data?

3. What do data matrices and networks accomplish in qualitative data analysis? Under what situations is each most appropriate?

4. Choose two of the tactics discussed for drawing conclusions and illustrate with an example you have developed or found in a research journal.

5. What is the difference between a "concept" and a "construct?" How is a construct used in qualitative data analysis?

6. To finish the analysis we must check for data quality. How do we accomplish this?

References

Eisenhardt, K.M. (1989). Building theories from case study research. *Academy of Management Review, 14*(4), 532-550.

Glaser, B.G. (1978). *Theoretical sensitivity: Advances in methodology of grounded theory.* Mill Valley, CA: Sociology Press.

Mannel, R.C. (1984). Personality in leisure theory: The self as entertainment. *Society and Leisure, 7*, 229-242.

McMillan, J.H,. & Schumacher, S. (1993). *Research in education: A conceptual introduction.* New York: Harper Collins.

Miles, M.B., & Huberman, A.M. (1994). *Qualitative data analysis: An expanded source book.* Thousand Oaks, CA: Sage.

Neulinger, J. (1981). *To leisure: An introduction.* Boston: Allyn and Bacon.

Russell, R.V. (1991). Observation of a hotel lobby. [Field notes].

Spradley, J.P. (1980). *Participant observation.* Chicago: Holt, Rinehart and Winston.

Tesch, R. (1990). *Qualitative research: Analysis types and software tools.* New York: Falmer.

CHAPTER 13

Writing and Presenting Reports

What Will I Learn in This Chapter?
I'll be able to:

1. Organize the content of the evaluation report.

2. Master some important rules for the style, format, and readability of the written report.

3. Develop strategies for actually getting the final report written.

4. Appreciate the importance of advance preparation and practice for the orally delivered report.

No evaluative research project is finished without a report. Unless a report is made, the only beneficiary of the effort is you the evaluator. The evaluation report—both written and delivered orally—is straightforward. It communicates what has been done to answer the evaluation problem and the resulting recommendations. It is factual and logical. Though it makes no pretense at being a literary production, the evaluation report still should communicate clearly.

Preparing a good report is hard work, and after the excitement of collecting and analyzing the information is completed, report writing can seem tedious. Yet, you will find there is no better way, than through report writing, to share your results and recommendations with those in positions to use them. As well, there is another, perhaps unexpected, benefit to preparing a report. When you begin the report preparation process you will find it a useful way to clarify and organize your own understandings on what the evaluation results mean and how they might lead to recommendations.

We begin this chapter by presenting the objectives for organizing the content of an evaluation report. Then suggestions are given for both written and orally delivered reports.

Organization of the Content

While the specific nature of the report is determined by the nature of the project itself and the audience to whom it is addressed, it generally has a fundamental format. Basically, the report should achieve three objectives. It should:

1. **Render a clear orientation to what has been evaluated.** The purpose behind the evaluation study should be easily understood from the report.

2. **Present the information found and used in the study.** This includes explanation of how the information was acquired and a presentation of data analysis.

3. **Propose a logical link between the analyzed information and policy and practice decisions.** Interpretations, conclusions and recommendations contained in the report should be substantiated by the information.

We now discuss each of these objectives and amplify them into the six sections of the evaluation report (Figure 13.1).

Figure 13.1: Organization of an evaluative research report.

Objective 1: Orientation to what was evaluated

Section I.   Research problem, purpose, questions (or objective)
- purpose
- justification/significance
- definitions
- delimitations

Section II. Background including rationale, relevant literature or previous studies
- review of related literature
- historical context
- overview of the organization

Objective 2: Information that answers questions evaluated

Section III. Methods
- data collection plan
- measurement tools
- information sources
- analyses performed

Section IV. Results: according to research questions

Objective 3: Interpretations of answers that instruct recommendations

Section V.   Conclusions
- summarization
- interpretation

Section VI. Recommendations for practice
- derived from the findings
- practical

Orientation to the Evaluation Problem

The first objective is to set forth the purpose of the evaluation. At the beginning of the report we need to create a "meeting of the minds" between the writer/speaker of the report and the reader/listener of the report (Leedy, 1980). Readers and listeners should be able to understand through the merits of the report alone the evaluation problem and its importance. Many reports are of poor quality because the preparer did not approach it from the standpoint of identifying the problem, setting it forth clearly, and providing a rationale for its importance. Orientation consists of laying out the:

1. Problem, purpose, research question or objective for the evaluation. After a few introductory remarks, the first section of the report should set forth the scope of the evaluation project. (Review Chapter 6 for a full explanation.) To convince the reader/listener of the report that the study was necessary, this first section must be accomplished thoroughly and clearly. Compare the following statements according to their thoroughness in providing a clear focus and justification for the study:

- This study was important because it produced new ideas for planning and managing next year's Summer Camp Jobs Fair.
- The purpose of this evaluation was to increase student attendance in the Summer Camp Jobs Fair by identifying reasons for low participation. Attendance records kept by the campus Placement Center indicate a five-year decline in both the number of students who enter the jobs fair room and the number of students actually employed by camps as a result of the fair. The inference drawn was that publicity about the fair was at fault, however casual comments made last year by several students suggested student interests and needs also warranted investigation. Thus, his project appraised the fair's publicity methods, as well as student summer job seeking behaviors and interests.

While both statements report the same thing, the latter does so more thoroughly and clearly. It assumes the reader of the statement has no experience with the jobs fair, and explains not only the *purpose* of the evaluation, but also its *justification* or significance. The purpose for the study, and its problem statement are set forth. Also, an argument is presented for the worth of the study. Without it, as in the first example, the reader is left to wonder, "why bother?"

In this first section of the report, any ambiguous or specialized terms should be defined, as well. For a meeting of the minds, the reader and the evaluator must be concerned with the same orientations to the problem, the same concepts, the same ideas. This is accomplished by a careful *definition of any terms* that may be open to varied interpretation. In the above example, the idea of a "jobs fair" should be defined, as well as "publicity" and "student summer behavior."

Any *delimitations* should also be set forth in the first section. All those who read or listen to the report should know precisely how far the evaluation effort extended and where the limits were set. What aspects of the problem have not been studied? For the above example, we would need to know that only undergraduate users of the fair were surveyed, thus focusing the evaluation on why students participate in the fair (rather than focusing on why they do not).

2. Background. The second section of the report provides a description of the evaluation setting. Depending on the nature of the evaluation, this may include a *review of related literature* (see Chapter 4). Such a summary of previous work may be useful to orienting the report consumer because it further demonstrates the need for the evaluation, and compares this particular evaluation endeavor against the broad background of efforts by others in the field. In the jobs fair evaluation example, this section of the report would summarize the conclusions of other studies on college student summer job seeking patterns. Often the major weakness of many literature reviews is that they cite references without indicating their relevance or implications for the evaluation study addressed in the report.

Other sorts of background information may be necessary in the second section as well. For example, a case study evaluation of an agency may require an *overview of the agency itself* : its physical location, goals, services delivered, staffing, physical properties, budget and financing, etc. Setting an *historical context* may also be appropriate.

Acquired and Analyzed Information

The second objective of the evaluation report is to succinctly present the gathered and analyzed information. This objective has two sections: methods and findings. After explaining why the research was done, what led up to it, and what other work was found to be relevant, the next sections describe what was actually done and what was found.

3. Methods. In the methods section of the report the procedures you used to study the evaluation problem are described in enough detail to enable others to understand how the findings were obtained. Berg and Latin (1994) refer to this as the "cookbook" section of the report because it provides precise details on how the research was conducted. The information presented in this section will enable others to determine whether the findings can be trusted as reliable and valid.

The methods section for most evaluation reports includes (1) the overall plan for collection of the information, (2) the measurement tools used to collect the information, (3) the sources of the information, and (4) the analyses performed on the information. Often these four aspects of the section are described in the report in the order listed here.

The methods section should, then, begin with a description of the *overall design* (Chapter 7) of the study, putting the approach used into its proper context. For example, here we explain that we used a survey approach in our jobs fair evaluation. The *sampling and operational procedures* (Chapters 8 and 9) and *data collection methods* (Chapter 10) used in the study should also be described in turn, noting how they were developed or modified to meet specific needs. For the jobs fair example this may mean we state that we stopped every fifth student who entered the jobs fair room and asked them to complete a questionnaire we developed. Further, we describe the variables the questionnaire measured. We might also indicate that we pilot tested the questionnaire on a convenience sample of students beforehand, and had a total of 230 students complete the revised version.

Take care when preparing this section that the methods described are directly linked to the evaluation problem presented in the first section. Any limitations experienced with the methods should be mentioned and discussed as these may have implications for the results, and are certainly of interest to anyone wishing to use the methods for a similar purpose.

There should also be a description of *how the information gathered was analyzed* (Chapters 11 and 12). For example, we discuss in the jobs fair evaluation report that we analyzed the quantitative data from the questionnaire with percentages, means, and standard deviations. Depending on the audience for the report, it may be worthwhile to include copies of any rating forms, questionnaires, or interview schedules that were used during the course of the project. These are usually included as appendices to the main report.

4. **Results.** The fourth section of the report presents the results. Often labeled *the findings*, they are the results and analyses of gathered information. The findings may include the results of either qualitative or quantitative analyses, or both. Regardless, it is best to present the findings in terms of the evaluation problem or question(s). You have gathered a mass of information, which you have analyzed according to a specific problem or question studied. There is, then, in this section of the report a one-to-one correspondence: certain results relate to certain evaluation questions. For example, the reasons students participate in the jobs fair would be discussed together as they answer the question about participation, and the actual jobs students receive as a result of the fair are grouped together to answer a separate question about the fair's benefits.

The findings should be reported completely. They may, of course, be summarized into tables, charts, graphs, descriptive summaries, lists of responses, illustrative quotations, and so on (see Chapters 11 and 12), but it is important that the findings be exhibited as evidence for the recommendations that follow later in the report. Generally each finding is presented by beginning with a brief introduction followed by a fuller commentary. When the findings are extensive, it is customary to present them in summary form in the body of the report, and then provide more complete detail in an appendix.

Practice and Policy

The final objective of the evaluation report is to interpret the findings into recommendations for professional practice and policy. This links the evaluative research project to its justification: gathering information that can be used to make practice and policy decisions. In a good report conclusions and recommendations flow smoothly from the results.

5. Conclusions. A discussion of the evaluation conclusions forms the fifth section of the report. Conclusions include both *summarization* and *interpretation* of the findings. Whereas the previous section reported the findings, your purpose here is to inform the report audience about the meanings and importance of the findings. For example, in this section of the report you provide the conclusion that the fair is generally accomplishing its purpose, but more students would likely participate if planners were more thorough with the implementation details.

Conclusions can be presented as a simple list but it is better to place them in narrative form. Conclusions should be written concisely, and should cover only that which is relevant to the evaluation's purpose. There should be a summary and interpretation for each of the evaluation questions. While the conclusions must be based directly on the findings, it is often appropriate to incorporate into the discussion the relationship between your findings and conclusions, and those in other relevant studies in the literature. When these other conclusions are available, identifying similarities and differences with your results is a necessary step in a comprehensive understanding of the evaluation.

Achieving a meaningful conclusions section is difficult. The balance between describing findings obtained and identifying conclusions drawn requires some degree of "stepping back" from the study and determining what is at the core of what is now known. Yet, in order to be useful the evaluator must bridge the gap between the findings and their significance for answering evaluation questions that have been posed. A common shortcoming in this section is believing that the report has fulfilled its responsibility by simply listing the findings, and making no attempt at meaningful interpretation. On the other hand it is also problematic when the report draws conclusions based on interpretations that cannot be defended with findings from the study.

Frequently evaluators fail to develop the findings fully. We cannot turn over the information too often; look at it from too many angles; chart, graph, and arrange it in too many ways; inspect it from too many vantage points. Do not be satisfied with your first impressions about the meaning of your findings. Ask naive questions about the findings. "Doodle" with them. Sometimes very simple questions will yield startling insights (Leedy, 1980). Every question and vantage point may not be useful, but that is beside the point. What is important is that we leave no results unnoticed. To practice the ability to interpret findings and draw conclusions, try the exercise in Figure 13.2.

6. Recommendations. Finally, the sixth section of the evaluation report offers recommendations for professional practice and organization policy. This part of the report is very important; it is the link to action. For example, based on your findings and conclusions, you may recommend that marketing of the jobs fair begin two weeks earlier. Or, you may recommend that exit interviews be conducted with students as they leave the fair in order to provide more thorough feedback to the camp directors. Recommendations may suggest a new

Figure 13.2: Practice exercise in drafting conclusions and making recommentations.

1. Select a journal article (or other research report) that is in an area of interest to you. Let it be on a subject that you have done considerable reading, and/ or have some experience. Also, select a study that has a fairly simple design.

2. Tape a piece of paper over the report's "discussion" section—that part where interpretations and conclusions are drawn.

3. Read the article carefully up to the covered discussion section.

4. Now, write your own discussion of the results. Interpret the results in terms of the problem/questions of the study, the literature reviewed, and the results reported in the findings sections.

5. Write about what the results might mean for professional practice and/or policy.

6. Remove the paper from the article, and compare your discussion with that of the original report author. Did you hit the main points? Do not be so concerned at this time with the polish of your writing or differences in writing style.

7. If you are using this book as part of a class assignment, it might be informative to share your conclusions with those of your classmates.

(Adapted from, Drew, 1980, p. 311)

direction for a program, a change in personnel policies, a shift in resource allocation, an extension of services, a new organization philosophy, or leaving things as they are. Whatever, recommendations provide managers and governing boards suggestions for improving the operations of the leisure services organization. Most importantly, recommendations should be clearly *derived from the findings*, and be *practical* (Robson, 1993)—they are data-based suggested courses of action that are capable of implementation.

The recommendations section also addresses the strengths and weaknesses of the research procedures and recommends better ways of conducting the evaluation the next time. As a result of doing a study, particularly after attempting to interpret the meaning of the findings, you know what information is still needed. In the evaluation of the Summer Camp Jobs Fair, the respondents to the questionnaire were identified, let us suppose, by their rank in school, gender, and hometown geographical location. But information about the students' majors was not collected. As a result of interpreting the findings, we recognize that another possible explanation for student lack of interest in summer jobs in camps may be related to attendees' majors. So, in this section of the report we acknowledge this shortfall and recommend that later evaluations include retrieving these data.

The Written Report

Evaluative research projects are typically reported in written form. Even if it was a very small enterprise, there ought to be a written record of it. Without this written trail, the lessons learned from the study could be lost or worse, not incorporated into program, personnel, and management decisions. Even though style and format considerations have been touched upon in this chapter, additional suggestions for the written version of the evaluation report are presented here.

Style

The classic criteria of "clarity, force, and ease" apply to all writing (Miles & Huberman, 1994, p. 301). Accordingly, the final report must be written accurately and in a convincing manner. Accomplishing this requires attention to writing style.

Matters of writing style are connected with choice of *voice*. You have choices about the voice of your evaluation reports, and the following discussion is intended to help you make these choices. As based on van Maanen, 1988, there are two possible voices:

Realist: a direct, matter-of-fact style of reporting with an invisible writer

Chronicalist: written narratively from the evaluator's viewpoint, with personalized authority.

The differences among these two voices lie along a continuum from less to more routine. The examples in Figures 13.3 and 13.4 demonstrate this. Figure 13.3 shows the realist voice, often associated with studies using quantitative approaches, while the voice in Figure 13.4 is a chronicle style and frequently associated with qualitative studies. Both voice options are correct and useful; their choice depends on the requirements of your particular report audience and purpose.

Since the information is the central "character," in order to let the "facts speak," most reports have traditionally been written in the more impersonal third person and passive tone of the realist. For some time, the "I" was outlawed in scholarly writing, for it was considered to be a sign that the writer was intruding, possibly giving subjective opinions where objective facts were supposed to speak for themselves. This led to the substitution of contorted third-person constructions (i.e., "The author has come to the conclusion ...") or of the passive verb style (i.e., "The following conclusion has been derived ...") in places where it was inevitable to refer to things the writer did. Today it is generally agreed that it is pointless to pretend that a report wrote itself. Therefore, the use of "I" even in the realist voice is again perfectly acceptable where it is natural and necessary (i.e., "I concluded that ...").

Figure 13.3: Example of realist voice.

The problem of this study was to evaluate the effectiveness of the New York State Municipal Day Camp Safety Regulations passed in 1985. The study examined not only the safety effects of the law, but also other factors affected by legislation.

The subjects of the study were municipal summer recreation programs. The programs were divided into those that became registered with the New York State Health Department as day camps and those with organized summer recreation programs that were not registered. Seventy-two nonregistered and sixty registered programs responded to a mail questionnaire. In-depth interviews were also conducted. The questionnaire data were analyzed using Chi-square test of association, t-tests, and other statistical measures.

Before the legislation, programs that became registered with the New York State Health Department as day camps were statistically different in the following areas: the budget was higher, the ratio of camper to counselor was lower, and a greater number of activities were offered. They also had a recreation director with a degree in recreation or related field, and had a greater likelihood of being located in the Southern Region of New York State than programs that did not register with the state. After registration there were no significant changes in the differences between groups. The programs were not significantly different in municipality characteristics, director's characteristics, or in accident rates. The legislation did not lower accident rates. The in-depth interviews indicated there were large differences in the way the law was enforced.

In conclusion, the legislation helped guide some municipalities about what made a good program. Many felt they had better programs after registering. It is recommended that the law needs to be more specific in some of the wording and it needs to be less strict so that more programs can afford to comply.

(adapted from Moiseichik, 1989, thesis abstract).

Figure 13.4: Example of the chronicalist voice.

To begin to understand leisure's meaning in cultures other than developed Western societies, we report the results of fieldwork conducted recently with women in an African refugee camp. We had anticipated our refugee camp visit before we left

Figure 13.4: Cont.

the United States by interviewing Sudanese expatriots and by gathering printed materials. Our first contacts in Kenya provided additional information, as we met in Nairobi with African and non-African employees of nongovernmental organizations (NGOs) working to provide nutritional and health aid to Sudanese in both southern Sudan and Kenya. We learned details of the political situation and about efforts related to provision for the basic needs of the southern Sudanese still in Sudan as well as the Sudanese refugees.

During our day in the Kakuma refugee camp we made direct observations, conducted individual interviews with three male and two female southern Sudanese refugees, and held four focus group meetings. We had difficulty determining an appropriate place to begin interviews with people living in the starkest of circumstances. For numerous moments we simply listened to what our interviewees and focus group members wanted to tell us. We asked them how they spend their time and about their feelings. We did not ask directly about the role of leisure. In fact, it was not until we began to search for patterns in our field notes that we realized a leisure meaning in their daily life experiences.

In focusing our analysis on the lives of refugee women three themes emerged that could be associated with leisure: abundance of time, changing roles, and assistance dependency.

(Adapted from Russell & Stage, 1996, pp. 109-111)

There are other guideposts to report writing. First, is *verb tense*. The evaluation report tells what happened. It is the evaluator reporting what was done to answer questions about excellence of services already performed. This means that the evaluation effort is history. Thus, since you are reporting on what has already happened, the report should be written in the past tense.

Other advice about style is also worthwhile. For example, incorrect *grammar* and careless *construction of sentences* introduce ambiguity and generally impede communication. The examples in Figure 13.5 represent typical grammar problems. For help on problems not addressed in the figure and for more comprehensive discussions of grammar and usage in general, consult one of the manuals on English text listed in Figure 13.6. Computer software (such as Grammatik or Correct Grammar) can also be an aid, but do not replace your knowledge of grammar and sentence structure.

Figure 13.5: Frequent grammatical errors.

1. Gender and number in pronouns:

To avoid gender discrimination in pronouns, instead of using the plural (they, them, their), use the singular (he/him/his or she/her) in general statements. Also, common practice now is to alternate gender in the pronoun. The pronoun and the noun must agree: both must be either in singular or plural form.

Correct: Regardless of the attitudes of program participants, they willingly agreed to be interviewed.

Correct: Regardless of a program participant's attitude, she agreed to be interviewed.

Wrong: Regardless of a program participant's attitude, they agreed to be interviewed.

2. Dangling participles:

In using participial or gerund phrases, make sure that the subject of the main clause agrees with the implied subject of the participial or gerund clause.

Correct: When arriving at the recreation center, the senior citizens felt a sense of excitement.

Correct: Arriving at the recreation center, the senior citizens felt the excitement of the party.

Wrong: Arriving at the recreation center, the party appeared to them very exciting.

3. Agreement of subject and verb:

A verb must agree in number (singular or plural) with its subject despite intervening phrases that begin with such words as including, plus, and as well as.

Correct: The percentage of positive responses to the questionnaire as well as the return rate of the questionnaires increases with the age of the program participant.

Wrong: The percentage of positive responses to the questionnaire as well as the return rate of the questionnaires increase with the age of the program participant.

4. Who and whom:

Use who as the subject of a verb and whom as the object of a verb or a preposition. Quick check: if you can substitute he or she, who is correct; if you can substitute him or her, whom is the correct pronoun.

Correct: Name the participant who you found scored above the median.

Wrong: Name the participant whom you found scored above the median.

Figure 13.5: Cont.

Wrong: Name the participant that you found scored above the median.

Correct: The participant whom I identified as the youngest dropped out.

Wrong: The participant who I identified as the youngest dropped out.

Wrong: The participant that I identified as the youngest dropped out.

5. That versus which:

That clauses are essential to the meaning of the sentence; *which* clauses can merely add further information.

Correct: The information that was given out at the meeting was used in the analysis.

Correct: The information from the meeting, which was quite thorough, provided a useful insight to the analysis.

Wrong: The information from the meeting, that was quite thorough, provided a useful insight to the analysis.

(Adapted from the *Publication manual of the American Psychological Association*, 1994, pp. 32-41)

Figure 13.6: Recommended writing style and grammar manuals.

American Psychological Association. (1994). *Publication manual of the American Psychological Association* (4th ed.). Washington, DC: Author.
   The editorial style used in many park, recreation, and sport journals and books.

Bates, J.D. (1980). *Writing with precision: How to write so that you cannot possibly be misunderstood* (3rd ed.). Washington, DC: Acropolis Books.
   Discusses the principles of clear, effective writing with special focus on letters, memoranda, and reports.

Day, R.A (1979). *How to write and publish a scientific paper.* Philadelphia, PA: ISI Press.
   Provides instructions for the writing, preparation, and submission of manuscripts for publication.

Fowler, H.W. (1965). *A dictionary of modern English usage* (2nd ed.). New York: Oxford University Press.
   A classic dictionary of grammar, spelling, punctuation.

Figure 13.6: Cont.

Sabin, W.A. (1992). *The Gregg reference manual* (7th ed.). Lake Forest, IL: Glencoe
A general guide on punctuation, grammar, spelling and other basics; includes tips on proofreading.

Skillin, M.E., & Gay, R. M. (1995). *Words into type* (4th ed.). Englewood Cliffs, NJ: Prentice-Hall
Detailed guide to the preparation of manuscripts, including grammar and word usage.

Strunk, W., Jr., & White, E.B. (1979). *The elements of style* (3rd ed.). New York: Macmillan.
A classic that offers concise, clear advice on writing well.

University of Chicago Press. (1993). *The Chicago manual of style* (14th ed.). Chicago: Author.
Editorial guidelines used in some park, recreation and sport journals and books.

Zinsser, W. (1990). *On writing well: An informal guide to writing nonfiction* (4th ed.). NewYork: HarperCollins.
Informal discussion of principles for uncluttered writing.

Redundancy is another caution for clear writing. We often become redundant in an effort to be emphatic. Use no more words than are necessary to convey your meaning. In Figure 13.7 the italicized words are redundant and should be omitted. Redundancy belongs to another writing style problem: *wordiness*. Wordiness is caused by embellishment and flowery writing, which are inappropriate for evaluation reports. For example, change "based on the fact that" to "because,"and "there were several participants who completed" to "several participants completed."

Other advice includes avoiding *empty words* and *colloquialisms*. Saying that "the leaders of the program did a great job," "the cold hard facts," or "recently" does not communicate any real meaning about what the leaders actually did, why the facts are so basic, and how near is recent. Likewise avoid such vacant words as "unique." Everything is, strictly speaking, unique in that it is unlike everything else. Instead, write more specifically about what makes something so unique. Further, in constructing sentences, keep related words and phrases together and take care not to overwhelm a reader by loading a sentence with too many concepts. To simplify a complex sentence with numerous points, break it down into a list, or bullet, format.

Figure 13.7: Redundancy examples.

The italicized bold words are redundant and should be omitted:

They were ***both*** alike

a total of 68 participants

Four ***different*** groups were contacted

absolutely essential

in ***close*** proximity

completely unanimous

summarize ***briefly***

the reason is ***because***

has been ***previously*** found

(from American Psychological Association, 1994, p. 27)

Another writing tip is to give *examples*. Most of us write very abstract sentences. We know what we mean, but others may have to select among various meanings based on their own experiences. Examples clarify our meaning. This is also the function of using tables and figures. To help ensure clarity, it is good practice to prepare each table and figure so that it is easily understood even if taken out of the context of the report. Further, be sure you have a clear purpose for each table.

A final consideration is which style *format* to adopt. Essentially, you should follow the accepted style guidelines prescribed by your situation. For example, if you are conducting an evaluation as part of a college assignment (e.g., thesis, capstone course project) be sure to check the prescribed rules of your academic program. Likewise, your agency may have a standard set of guidelines that all written reports must follow. If not, you will find it useful to acquire a basic style manual (see Figure 13.6). Regardless of the specific style formula you adopt, for appearance sake the report should be consistent in such things as line spacing, font, margins, heading format, paper size, and footnote set-up.

Elements

In addition to the organizational sections for an evaluation report previously discussed (see Figure 13.1), written reports usually have these additional elements: the cover, executive summary, table of contents, and appendices.

The *cover* is more important than perhaps you assumed. It establishes the first impression. In order to establish a good first impression, the cover should be professional and informative. Usually this means it includes the title of the evaluation project, the aspect of the organization or service evaluated, the names of the evaluators, and dates (of the evaluation study and for the report). If appropriate, a cover letter placed behind the cover might be included to transmit the report from the evaluator to the organization director or board.

The *executive summary* is simply an abridged or abstract version of the report. Usually quite brief (a page or less), the most important points of the project are presented. This summary must be able to stand alone, reporting the purpose of the study, how it was conducted, and the major conclusions and recommendations. It is written to be accessible to a wide audience, as sometimes it will be distributed to people not directly involved in the organization (such as news media), who may not have access to the full report. Ironically, the executive summary is usually located before the main report, even though it is a good idea to write it after the rest of the report is prepared.

Lengthier evaluation reports should include a *table of contents* that shows the outline and location of headings and subheadings. If there are numerous tables and figures, a *tables/figures list* with page numbers should follow the table of contents. *Appendices* come after the report and include any material that is too detailed or secondary to be included in the main report. Such items as questionnaires, interview schedules, lists of interviewees or dates of observations, correspondence, and raw data are appropriately placed in the appendix. Always refer to the contents of the appendices at appropriate places in the main body of the report.

Readability

The report must ultimately communicate clearly and thoroughly. And of course there is nothing wrong with it being interesting as well! In large part, meeting these mandates requires paying attention to the audience for the report. Reports are supposed to be written for specific audiences, to achieve specific effects. Thus, reasonable clarity about audiences helps. Understanding the *audience* for your report dictates what is emphasized in the report, and the level of complexity needed to convey essential facts.

Generally speaking, you need to make choices among reader types. For example (Miles & Huberman, 1994):

Local respondents: the people who provided the information for the evaluation

Program operators: people running and/or deciding about the program/service evaluated

Professionals: people engaged in the same sort of work as that studied, but in different settings

Policy makers: governing boards, organization officials, legislators

Other researchers: colleagues in an academic setting

General readers: purchasers of trade books

Mass readers: purchasers of magazines and newspapers

All of these types of readers are potential audiences for an evaluation report in a park, sport, recreation situation. You will, however, most likely write for program operators, policy makers, and other professionals.

What do you hope will occur when a particular type of reader reads your report? Although that cannot be really predicted or controlled, getting your intentions clear can make a profound difference in the report's readability. Any evaluative research report may be written from certain general *stances* (Miles & Huberman, 1994):

Scientific: add to existing information on a topic, deepen understanding, expand or revise existing concepts, convince the reader of the report's worth and value

Activist: enable improved decisions, provide guidance for action, show connections between findings and local problems, mobilize for specific action

Aesthetic: entertain, amuse, arouse feeling, enable vicarious experiencing

Moral: clarify and sharpen moral issues, raise consciousness, emancipate

What a menu of options! The important question is which effects you desire for which types of reader. If your audiences are policy makers and program operators, then writing the report from the activist stance is likely to be central. On the other hand, if your audience is other researchers, then the effects of theoretical advancement, or more likely convincing the readers of the report's credibility, is more important. Our advice is to make a matrix for your study of reader types by intended effect types. You may find that more than one report is needed: a brief newspaper column that raises consciousness about the worth of the program, the major document that focuses on showing connections between findings and problems for program operators, and a scientific article for a professional magazine.

Getting the Report Written

An evaluator's life between the completion of the data analysis and the report writing is sometimes burdensome. We feel we have finished the evaluation study; after all, *we* know the answers to our research questions and *we* know what should be done about these answers to change a program or service. Thus the following hints for really finishing the evaluation study—that is, completing the written report—are offered.

1. Begin to write the report while you are still working on the plan for the evaluation study itself. The problem, background, and procedures sections could be prepared before you collect the data. If you wait until after all data are collected to begin writing the report, it may take extra time to gather, reorganize, and remember the steps you carried out and the rationale for each. In some research situations, a study proposal including these three sections is prepared and approved before data collection anyway, and this is definitely required when seeking human subjects clearance.

2. Outline each section of the report before writing. Writing from an outline helps preserve the orderly presentation of information. An outline identifies main ideas, defines subordinate ideas, and helps you discipline your writing. It also helps you notice missing material. After writing a first draft from the outline, set it aside. When you write something, you know precisely what you meant, so at the moment your writing seems all right. After three or four days of other activities and other writing, return to the earlier pages. You will have a fresh perspective and be able to more clearly read what you have actually written. The sentences that are unclear or awkward can be revised, and explanatory material that is missing can be added. Also, reading the paper aloud enables you to detect problems not noticed before.

3. Most of us have to work very hard to write reports that others can read with understanding, and so revision is an important writing ally. When you have corrected the report based on your re-readings, give a copy to a colleague for a critical review. Listen to your colleague's advice particularly regarding ambiguity, quantum leaps of logic, etc.

All of these tips for writing the report require time, which means you need to invest more time in writing the report than you may have anticipated. Successive drafts are usually needed. The results, however, will be greater accuracy and thoroughness and clearer communication.

Orally Delivering the Report

Often an oral presentation is needed to report on an evaluation study. You may be asked to provide an overview at a governing or advisory board meeting, or at a staff meeting. As well, you may have occasion to present a report at a professional convention, symposium or workshop. The orally delivered version of a report can be a critical element in the worth of the evaluation. Many people will not take time to read a large report document, but will listen to an oral presentation if it is well done. Material delivered verbally should differ from written material in its level of detail, organization, and presentation. Therefore, you need to prepare and deliver an oral presentation differently from the way you would prepare a written document.

Preparation

Giving an oral report does not simply mean that you talk your way through the written report. Oral presentations that really communicate require a different sort of planning. Granted, as with the written report, the audience wants to know what you studied and why, how you went about the research, what you discovered, and implications of study results (American Psychological Association, 1994). Beyond this, however, the presentation should seek to persuade. You are presenting information carefully and honestly, yet you are also trying to "sell" the conclusions you derived. In part, the ability to implement the recommendations outlined in the study will depend on convincing the audience of the soundness of what you did, how you did it, and the logical connection between the results and the recommendations.

Thus, the most important advice for an oral presentation is to keep it simple, concentrating on only one or two main points. Then keep reminding the audience about these central points by relating each major section of the presentation to them. The traditional speaker's advice is still valid: "Tell the audience what you are going to say, say it, and then tell them what you have said." For most evaluation reports the central point will be the question or questions answered by the study. Provide only a sketch of the details of the data collection procedures (or provide a handout), because a listener cannot follow the same level of detail as a reader. A verbal presentation should create awareness about a topic and stimulate interest in it; colleagues or staff members can later retrieve the details from the written report, copies of which you may want to have available.

Other aspects of an oral presentation to prepare include the introduction, visual aids, and the fielding of questions. The *introduction* sets the tone and expectations. Most audiences will listen carefully at the beginning of a talk and then decide whether further listening is warranted. This means you must not only get their attention from the start, but also give them reasons to continue paying attention. While the task of planning how to secure the audience's initial attention tempts us to the dramatic, keeping the introduction appropriate to the evaluation situation is important if we are to be taken seriously by the audience.

This caution does not mean that we forgo a creative, lively introduction. For example, to introduce an evaluation report on the impact of recreation center programs for the neighborhood's at-risk youth, a few minutes of audio-taped testimonies from several of the youth interviewed for the study could be played. Or, the introduction to an evaluation report on the utilization of recently purchased cardiovascular work-out machinery in the fitness club could incorporate shocking national adult health problem statistics.

Every presentation benefits from the use of *visual aids*. A chart, graph, or other pictorial depiction of the overall pattern of the results convey an at-a-glance structural concept often more effectively than can words alone. But these too must be carefully planned. The use of slides, a flip chart, overhead transparencies, handouts and props run the risk of further confusing or irritating the audience instead of clarifying and illustrating as you have intended. In essence visual aids need to be big, simple and clear. Use large print or illustrations, keep the amount of information communicated by the aid limited, and spend the extra time needed to make them of high quality. (See Figure 13.8 for guidelines for visual materials.)

Keep in mind that when people are looking at the visual aid, they are not listening. This means do not use too many. A handout that complements the oral presentation can be helpful as well. Yet merely repeating in the handout what is being said in the presentation is not always effective. This is why care must be taken to distribute the handout at a choice moment. For example, for a handout that does repeat the presentation, consider distributing it to the audience at the end of the presentation to avoid distracting them from what is being said.

Figure 13.8: Guidelines for visuals.

Good visuals:

- Augment rather than duplicate the report

- Convey only essential information

- Omit visually distracting detail

- Are easy to read

- Portray a readily apparent purpose

- Are carefully planned and prepared

(American Psychological Association, 1994, p. 142)

Providing an opportunity for the audience to *ask questions* is usually included in a presentation. Prepare for this by planning for the time allotment and anticipating the questions—even the unexpected ones! Also prepare by reminding yourself to handle questions with a positive, respectful attitude. Do not feel that you have been personally threatened if you receive difficult questions, and do not enter into an argument or other antagonism with the one member of the audience whose question challenges your work. In this case it might be useful to respond with "That is an interesting point you are making, what do you think?"

Practicing

Guaranteeing that the audience listens to your presentation is not as unpredictable as it may appear. Once the presentation has been well prepared, practicing it significantly adds to your ability to be effective. This advice is not just for inexperienced speakers, but is a continuing source of success for those with years of public speaking experience.

Rehearse your presentation until you can speak comfortably and look at your notes only occasionally. Practicing out loud in front of a mirror or even in front of someone else will help you resist reading your presentation. Reading a paper usually induces boredom and can make even the best study sound second-rate (American Psychological Association, 1994). Instead, talk with your audience just as you would in conversation. Having written notes in front of you while speaking will help you keep your focus. To help you resist temptation to begin reading from these notes, however, use an outline of topic sentences rather than a complete script.

The best practice is under conditions similar to the actual presentation. You are prepared when you can succinctly tell your audience, eye-to-eye, what you want them to know (American Psychological Association, 1994). Equally important is that you can do this in the time you have been allotted. Timing also takes planning and practice. The main culprit to exceeding the time frame, even with practice of the speech, is visual aids. If your presentation includes slides or other visuals, practice their timing and placement in your talk. "PowerPoint" presentations enhance your ability to stay on time, but can also produce a pacing that is too rapid. Also practice emphasizing major material on the screen, rehearse saying nothing while the audience first studies the handout you have passed out, and make sure you, or whomever is helping you, knows how to operate the projection equipment.

Main Points

- The objectives of an evaluative research report are to:

  - orient to the problem(s) or question(s) evaluated,

  - explain how the information gathered and analyzed answers the question(s) evaluated,

  - interpret the answers toward making recommendations for improvements

- To be professionally prepared, the written report is carefully planned and developed according to appropriateness of writing style and format, clarity and conciseness, and readability.

- Orally delivered reports require a matched attention to preparation. This should include advance rehearsal and visual aids.

Study Questions

1. What is the purpose of the evaluative research report? Why is it a critically important step in the evaluative research process?

2. List the six sections of the report and a key purpose for each.

3. How are the purposes of a written and orally delivered report different?

4. Which voices for writing style are most appropriate for each of the reader or audience types?

5. Assess your own ability in following the advice for getting the report written. What do you need to improve?

References

American Psychological Association. (1994). *Publication manual of the American Psychological Association* (4th ed.). Washington, DC: Author.

Berg, K.E., & Latin, R.W. (1994). *Essentials of modern research methods in health, physical education, and recreation.* Englewood Cliffs, NJ: Prentice Hall.

Drew, C.J. (1980). *Introduction to designing and conducting research.* St. Louis: The C.V. Mosby Company.

Leedy, P.D. (1980). *Practical research.* New York: Macmillan Publishing.

Miles, M.B., & Huberman, A.M. (1994). *An expanded sourcebook: Qualitative data analysis.* Thousand Oaks, CA: Sage.

Moiseichik, M.L.J. (1989). Differences between registered and nonregistered programs under the 1985 New York Day Camp Safety legislation. Dissertation. Bloomington, IN: Indiana University.

Patton, M.Q. (1982). *Practical evaluation.* Newbury Park: Sage Publications.

Robson, C. (1993). *Real world research: A resource for social scientists and practitioner-researchers.* Oxford, UK: Blackwell.

Russell, R.V., & Stage, F.K. (1996). Leisure as burden: Sudanese refugee women. *Journal of Leisure Research, 28*(2), 108-121.

Van Maanen, J. (1988). *Tales of the field: On writing ethnography.* Chicago: University of Chicago Press.

CHAPTER 14

From Results to Policy and Practice

What Will I Learn in This Chapter?
I'll be able to:

1. Develop logical recommendations, providing useful information, and incorporating tactics that increase the acceptance of recommendations.

2. Identify, depending on the target audience, ways of disseminating recommendations according to target audiences.

3. Choose recommendations for implementation according to their practicality, importance, compatibility and time requirements.

After reporting on the findings and conclusions for an evaluative research study we must decide how to put them to use. What do the findings mean in terms of program objectives? How can the findings be utilized to bring about changes in the organization's services? What next steps are necessary? As the evaluator we interpret the findings from the study to the decision makers by answering questions such as these. We develop recommendations for policy and practice decisions. The best evaluative research results will be useless unless the recommendations stemming from them are used to improve services.

The point of this chapter, and perhaps the most important point of this book, is how to develop and use the recommendations from a study. We have organized this point into two parts: ideas for developing recommendations from study findings and advice on putting recommendations to work for service improvement.

Making Recommendations

Care is required in developing recommendations based on evaluation results. Both art and science play a role in the shaping of programmatic and policy recommendations that are actually implemented. Although we devoted some discussion in Chapter 13 to writing recommendations in reports, it is important to revisit the topic here because of the vital link between making recommendations and using them. If the results of the research are the basis for transforming programs, procedures, and policies, the recommendations must be doable.

The likelihood that evaluation results will yield useful decisions for your organization is increased by three factors: making a sound and reasoned transition between research findings and suggested actions, the ability of the study to provide information actually needed, and the acceptance of the recommendations by persons responsible for their implementation.

Logical Recommendations

Recommendations that work transform evaluative research findings into answers to pressing questions. An organization needs to know how to solve service delivery problems, reach new target markets, operate more equitably, increase fiscal resources, etc. To address such needs the organization relies on research for answers. There are times, unfortunately, when recommendations from an evaluation study in actuality are not based on the study. That is, sometimes recommendations stretch beyond the actual facts derived from the research. For example, suppose a study found that 32% of the state park campsites troubled by noise and vandalism are occupied by parties where all campers are younger than 22 years of age. What recommendations for operational change at the park might be suggested from this finding? Should the park initiate a promotion campaign to attract more older campers, or institute higher minimum age requirements for renting a campsite? In order to substantiate these recommendations, data would need to have been collected that demonstrate young people "cause" noise or vandalism in the campground. If we do not have actual information on their behaviors while using the campsites, such recommendations are inappropriate. To help you practice making recommendations that logically follow a study's findings, review Figure 14.1 and then attempt to complete the exercise in Figure 14.2.

Providing Useful Information

Another reason a study may not produce usable results is that the information obtained does not match the information needs of the organization. Providing recommendations that will be followed, then, also depends on providing answers to questions of importance. How to accomplish this was the subject of earlier chapters, but it is worthwhile to reemphasize the importance of designing and carrying out good evaluative research again. For example, knowing what the participants in an after-school program think about the program's leaders will not help the agency identify alternative means of financing the program. In evaluative research we have a responsibility to provide the best possible information that is available about that specific aspect of service delivery that the organization needs to know about.

In spite of well designed and carried out research, occasionally, the outcome of the study still may note little more than that the objectives of a particular service are not being met. The reasons why the objectives are not being met may not be identified in the final

Figure 14.1: Example of making recommendations.

The Study

The purpose of a study conducted by Backman and Veldkamp (1995) was to examine the relationship between the quality of an agency's services and recreation activity program loyalty. One hundred adult participants in two aquatic programs at a small YMCA completed a survey.

Findings

a. Older participants exhibited more activity loyalty (propensity to participate in a particular recreation program at the agency).

b. Reliability of services was the most important service quality, regardless of participants' activity loyalty.

c. Attention paid to individual needs was the least important service quality, regardless of participants' activity loyalty.

d. Those participants with low activity loyalty perceived the agency's service assurance (employees' enthusiasm, trustworthiness, competence, credibility, and politeness) as ineffective.

e. Low-loyalty users also reported agency responsiveness (willingness to help users and provide prompt services) as ineffective.

Conclusion

There is a link between high service quality rating and long-term customer loyalty. Agencies dedicated to delivering excellent services will be more effective in retaining participants, or by developing loyalty.

Recommendations

1. For policy: Participants' service quality perceptions should be continually assessed so to build loyalty.

2. For practice:
   a) This agency must begin to provide training opportunities for existing staff to develop enthusiasm, trustworthiness, competence, credibility and politeness skills.
   b) The agency must develop a system to answer user questions promptly. Clear, precise answers related to when the program will begin and the optimal skill level to participate in the program are necessary.

3. For additional research:
   a) Since previous research points out that participants have a zone or range of service performance that they consider to be satisfactory, future research needs to examine the notion of participant tolerance.
   b) An evaluation should be conducted to determine the cost effectiveness of implementing the proposed changes.

Figure 14.2: Now you try making recommendations.

Another study (Turco & Lee, 1996) reported on the "not in my back yard" (or NIMBY) syndrome as related to the development of rail-trails. Read the following description of this study and practice drawing your own set of recommendations for policy, practice and additional research. Discuss your recommendations with others by focusing on findings-based reasons for your ideas.

The Study

Despite increasing demand for trail systems, recreation and park planners sometimes face opposition to trail development from homeowners with property adjacent to future trails. This opposition is often referred to as the NIMBY Syndrome, and has prevented the development of numerous projects. The purposes of this study were to determine whether or not residents' attitudes toward an adjacent rail-trail had changed since its construction; the nature and direction of the attitude changes; and, the social costs and benefits experienced by these residents. Questionnaire results from 156 homeowners living adjacent to the Constitution Trail in Bloomington, Illinois were analyzed.

The Findings

a. The majority of homeowners had favorable attitudes about the adjacent rail-trail.
b. The social benefits recognized by the homeowners included convenience for exercise, socialization, and flower/garden planting.
c. The social costs reported included trespassing, litter, invasion of privacy, theft, and vandalism.
d. Those homeowners who experienced vandalism and invasion of privacy were slightly more likely to express negative attitudes toward living next to the trail than those who experienced other social costs.

Conclusion: For some residents, NIMBY Syndrome associated with adjacent rail-trail development can be remedied over time.

Recommendations

1. For policy:

2. For practice:

3. For future research:

(For possible answers, refer to the noted article.)

report, perhaps because it was beyond the scope of the evaluation, or "answers" could not be identified with the study procedures used.

Recommendations may also not be used because the evaluator may be afraid to go out on a limb and offer unpopular suggestions. Yet, this is also the task of evaluative research. Sometimes "harsh" judgments about what needs to be done must be addressed, otherwise decision makers in the organization may not have the full advantage of the potential of research for improving services.

Political realities can also help explain evaluation results that do not produce usable recommendations. Recommendations that do not correspond to the political situation faced by organization are not likely to be implemented. For example, if a new mayor has recently been elected on the campaign promise to reduce city taxes, it is doubtful that a recommendation to finance a new public golf course through increased taxes will be implemented. Even though this recommendation may be absolutely accurate and logical based on the findings from a study, the political reality will probably render the recommendation null and void.

The political circumstances may lead, then, to compromise between the actual and the ideal in carrying out evaluation recommendations. At times this can even be desirable; the utility of the recommendations may be enhanced by such compromise. For example, perhaps more innovative sources of funds, other than taxes, can be found to finance the new golf course. The parks department decision makers might not have thought of these alternative solutions without the political realities of the situation.

Acceptance of Recommendations

A primary instinct of organizations is self-preservation. Although most recreation and park professionals recognize the need to assess how well they are doing, the process of being assessed is often threatening. Also, some staff members have inadequate skills to make necessary changes. For these and other reasons, studies that suggest policy or programmatic change are often met with at least some reluctance.

As already discussed in Chapter 1, to overcome potential resistance to change, during the design and implementation of a study, staff and service participants should be involved. The utilization of findings can further be enhanced from discussions held with staff and participants prior to making the recommendations formal. The greater their involvement in the interpretation of results and the framing of recommendations, the greater the likelihood that the recommendations will be accepted and implemented (Theobald, 1979). A common error is to suggest policy or operational changes without first discussing them with those staff members and participants most affected.

For example, the campus recreational sports providers at Indiana University evaluated the holiday usage by students and faculty of the two indoor fitness and sport facilities and determined that the greatly reduced use during this time period warranted closing one of the facilities. While the administrators of the facilities did confer with other campus officials prior to instituting this holiday operations change, they did not discuss it with the "regular" participants of the facility to be closed. The outcry from a small but very vocal angry group of patrons ultimately meant extra work for the director and new public relations problems to solve. The lesson learned in this case was that prior consultation with staff and participants can lessen resistance to change, and the change itself may be appropriately modified based on pertinent information gained from these conversations.

In summary, we offer the following advice for enhancing the acceptance of evaluative research based recommendations:

- Do not automatically assume that your version of what the solution should be is the one that could or should be implemented. This should be negotiated with others who are also involved.
- Accepting recommendations requires a certain amount of faith and ability to deal with ambiguity and uncertainty. Therefore, do not skimp on efforts to explain and clarify.
- Effective change takes time. Approach it developmentally and gradually.
- Do not expect all, or even most, people or groups to accept the recommendations. Work through the process incrementally.

(adapted from Fullan, 1982, p. 91)

Using Recommendations

The purpose of all evaluative research in leisure services is to inform action. If a study is to be done as more than simply an exercise in research methods, its recommendations need to be used. In some organizations dissemination of recommendations is the responsibility of the researcher, while in others management level people are in charge of dissemination. It is important to be clear about this responsibility because dissemination cannot be ignored.

Dissemination of Recommendations

Once the report is completed, the recommendations require dissemination. Dissemination is the process of communicating information about evaluation results to those persons and organizations that could use the information. In doing this it may be helpful to consider the typical audiences for recommendations according to three types: fully invested people, interested people, and slightly interested people.

Most obvious are those *persons who have the most invested* in the organization or service and who are thus actively awaiting the conclusion of the evaluation project (Moore, 1987). This coud be such stakeholders as the program's director, the organization's administrator, the advisory board, the stockholders, the city council, or others who will want to read or hear not only the complete final report, but will need to consider in some detail the results, conclusions, and recommendations. It is not difficult to disseminate to this audience, as it will not be necessary to "sell" the evaluation results to them. Nevertheless, it is important that the report is organized so it can best communicate with them.

This "most invested" audience has very likely already been involved in the design of the evaluation project, and contributed to a preliminary draft of the final report. As discussed above this usually results in a very authoritative report which helps ensure a high degree of commitment by those involved. However, there are additional strategies for disseminating evaluation recommendations for this audience. These include:

• **Provide copies of the written report.** Select those persons and/or groups with the most interest in the study report and provide them with full copies. You should choose the level of reproduction and distribution according to a balance between high quality and cost. More expensive publication of the report is justifiable when it will be widely distributed. In addition to the distribution of personal copies to members of this audience category, it is also worth making copies available at libraries, government offices, and in your agency's main office.

• **Call a staff meeting to discuss the recommendations.** Having given the report to those who want or need it, it is often worth providing an opportunity for them to get together to discuss the matter. Most likely this will involve agency staff. Meeting one-on-one with certain staff members to discuss the implications of the recommendations prior to the meeting of the entire agency staff may also be appropriate.

• **Meet with the agency's policy makers.** The board of directors, the recreation commissioners, or other decision makers for the organization may need to reevaluate service or program goals to determine if they are realistic in comparison to the recommendations. Since this may require difficult discussions or concentrated thinking, a retreat or workshop format might work best. In any case, before meeting with either staff or policy makers, it is advisable to schedule time beforehand for these stakeholders to read and digest the report.

• **Develop a "program" of recommendations.** Once all the recommendations are available and communicated, the organization's decision makers should establish a list of priorities, with a time line for accomplishing them. It may not be possible for all recommendations to be implemented immediately or simultaneously; matters such as available resources may force the development of the plan. Sometimes evaluators help the organization determine a progression of action beginning, perhaps, with simpler and easier changes and gradually, over time, adding the more complex or major changes. This is covered in more detail later in this chapter.

• **Build a positive agency climate.** Beyond the need to implement a specific set of recommendations from a particular evaluative research project, it is important to develop positive attitudes about the process of evaluation in general among staff and participants. Evaluators need to help people see the connections between findings and what is going on in an organization. That is, efforts should be directed at fostering an ethic about how research can improve the delivery of leisure services. Refer back to Chapter 1 for ideas on this point.

• **Plan carefully for dealing with negative or controversial recommendations.** It is wise to honestly examine the accuracy, as well as the limitations, of the results in light of how they are to be used. Before making a recommendation to terminate a service, program, or staff member you must be confident with the results. If the results from a study are unclear, it may be prudent to recommend instead further evaluation using different data collection or analysis methods.

Another audience for evaluation recommendations is *those who will find something of interest* or value in the study, but who would not automatically seek a copy of the final report (Moore, 1987). It will be necessary to stimulate an interest in this group by "selling" the report to them and encouraging them to consider the conclusions more carefully. Exactly who this audience is will be unique to the organization's particular situation, but may include such examples as potential program financial sponsors and professional colleagues in other organizations. Program participants might also be included in this audience for your organization. Even though this group's interest in the evaluation is originally latent, once they know the importance of the report, they may want a fair amount of detail.

For those with latent interest in the report, the following ideas are suggested:

• **Conduct an "in response" campaign.** If the latent audience is program participants, a useful public relations strategy might be to develop simple and quick ways to give feedback to them on the study results. For example, some organizations distribute "the survey says" flyers at facility front desks that highlight the study's conclusions and the changes the organization is making accordingly. Also, bulletin boards that overview the improved services as a result of the evaluation study could be prepared. Efforts such as these also provide a convenient way to thank program participants for filling out the questionnaires or agreeing to be interviewed, thus also paving the way for their future participation in another study.

• **Write and submit a journal article.** If the audience is professional colleagues, the aim is to provide a summary of the research in a way that links it to organizations beyond the one evaluated. An often effective way to do this is a journal article. The benefit of publishing an article about the project is that it offers useful knowledge to other colleagues. To accomplish this it is important to select the journal most likely to be read by the desired target audience. (See Chapter 4 for a list of many of the research journals in parks, recreation, sport, and tourism.) Each of these journals is read by a somewhat unique audience, and each has specific guidelines for preparing and submitting articles. Once you have prepared your article, and before mailing it, ask a few colleagues to read it and give feedback as a prospective reader of the journal. Also, if the guidelines (usually printed inside the journal itself) are unclear about the procedures for reviews, revisions, resubmissions, etc. ask the journal editor to review these with you.

• **Prepare a popularized version of the report.** The latent audience also may be interested in acquiring or purchasing a popularized version of the full report. This is often the case when the research is relevant to a group of organizations that are similar, such as universities in a state or government departments in a city. This version of the report is usually written in more summary style and may be briefer. Sometimes these are made available in pamphlet, brochure or booklet form. There does, however, need to be some certainty that it will be read or will sell to justify the expense involved in rewriting and publishing. This can, however, be a useful way of not only communicating the results, but garnering positive public relations for the organization.

• **Give a presentation at a professional conference.** Conferences are good places for stimulating interest in evaluative research projects. There are a growing number of conferences in parks, recreation, sport and tourism that issue a general call for papers. Announcements of these are usually found in the newsletters and journals of professional organizations. Often the instructions stipulate sending an outline or abstract of the presentation to the conference organizers. Some conferences are attended by thousands of people, such as the National Recreation and Park Association's annual Leisure Research Symposium. Other conferences where evaluation results about park, recreation, and sport organizations are presented include those sponsored by the American Camping Association; the American Association for Health, Physical Education, Recreation and Dance; and the American Therapeutic Recreation Association. These meetings provide a means of announcing the existence of the research and may result in favorable publicity for the leisure service agency.

Some conferences also provide poster sessions. A poster or one-dimensional display is prepared that conveys the essence of the research. At a scheduled time during the conference interested people go to the room containing the posters to discuss the work in detail with the researcher. This opportunity for personal discussion and informal sharing can be very valuable.

The third audience type for evaluation results and recommendations is those who want to know something of the major findings and recommendations but, beyond this, *have little interest*. Perhaps this audience is the local newspaper, or other community service organizations or agencies. Dissemination strategies for this audience include:

• **Issue a press release.** A press release can be developed and sent to local newspapers and professional magazines. This release should begin with a lively eyecatching sentence that will both encourage editors to include the item and readers to read it. The whole release should be no longer than one page, and written so that an editor can cut it after the first paragraph without losing any of the sense of the main points. Work with your agency's public relations director on this.

• **Insert research results into other organization documents.** Many recreation organizations publish a seasonal flyer of the program schedule as well as an annual report. Insert into these very brief (such as one paragraph in a box) extracts of the evaluation's findings. These can be peppered throughout the brochure if the study evaluated the agency in general, or matched with the studied program's listing.

In summary, the aims of dissemination according to these three types of audiences should be to give the first group the full results, conclusions and recommendations and to provide them with an opportunity to discuss them. For the second group, an engaging summary and a way of obtaining fuller information should be provided. For the third group, a signal to the existence of the research should be made available.

The art of good dissemination of evaluative research lies in selecting the strategies that best suit both the study and the potential decision makers. As a reminder, dissemination actually begins at the outset of the research when information about the existence of the project is communicated to those who make up the potential audience for the results. During the entire evaluation process there should be a continuous flow of information about the project. Plan to provide periodic updates about the progress of the project to advisory boards and funding sources. Additionally, provide status reports for the community at large. For example, prepare a series of press releases for the local newspaper and organization newsletter to inform the public as well as service users about the project. Brief the staff on preliminary data collected and ask for their ideas on ways to analyze them. All of this helps create an informed environment into which the final results, conclusions and recommendations will be released.

Choosing Recommendations for Implementation

Once the recommendations have been proposed and disseminated, the board, staff or others must sometimes decide which ones, or how many, of the recommendations to implement. Deciding this priority is usually based on the factors of importance, practicality, compatibility, and time (Theobald, 1979).

Importance, or the relative priority of different recommendations, is vital in determining next steps. Recommendation priorities must be judged against the organization's mission. Even if the powers to be are convinced that all recommendations are ultimately needed, some recommendations will obviously be more central to the goals of the organization than others and thus need to be implemented more quickly.

Concerning *practicality*, budgetary constraints or the availability of specifically qualified staff will influence the organization's choice of which recommendations to implement initially. If the recommendation is not practical within the organization's currently available resources, it may have to be postponed until more immediate changes are made that pave the way.

Also, recommendations that are *compatible* with each other may be more likely selected for immediate implementation. For example, suppose the following recommendations have been made:

1. Prior to departure from the home port, cruise passengers should be given a half hour orientation to the ship's activities program.
2. Cruise staff should return to the ship and be ready for work three hours before departure rather than the one hour currently stipulated in the employee's manual.

The implementation of the first recommendation is made more likely because of the second recommendation. In other words, the two recommendations are compatible.

A final consideration in the choice of recommendations for implementation is considering *time* requirements. Some recommendations may be accomplished immediately, while others may take a weeks, months, or even years. Most organization administrators will typically be more interested in supporting recommendations that can be executed in the immediate future. Recommendations that entail years to implement, on the other hand, may languish on paper on an administrator's desk rather than be implemented. As with most of us, people prefer immediate answers to immediate questions and problems. This suggests it is important to develop recommendations as a progression across time—to propose a series of intermediate steps toward the accomplishment of long-range recommendations.

Applying Findings to Other Situations

Sometimes other organizations and/or programs with similar traits as those studied originally find the results applicable to them. For example, the finding that juvenile criminal activity dropped 24% in Cincinnati, Ohio during the first 13 weeks of their late night basketball program (NRPA, 1996), suggests that this program may be useful for other similarly sized Midwestern cities. Further, reading in the professional literature that summer late night weekend recreation activities in Phoenix, Arizona reduced juvenile crime by 52% (NRPA, 1996), suggest that recreation activity can act as a deterrent to crime and thus might add credence to another agency's budget request for night programming for youth.

Such utility of evaluation findings across organizations is called *external validity* (as we discussed in Chapter 7). External validity deals with the potential for broader application of the results of a study, or its *generalizability*. Such generalizability is justified to the degree that the people and conditions involved in the replicated program are similar to the people and conditions of the original study.

Actually, "good" evaluative research has a broader application of results. Yet, care must be taken when generalizing findings to other situations. Results may be generalized only when there are strong similarities between the organization/program evaluated and the organization/program that seeks to apply the evaluation results (Berg & Latin, 1994). Let's illustrate this caution.

The National Recreation and Park Association (1996) reported on one adult softball tournament that generated $50,000 when 50 teams from outside the city participated. It was further estimated that the capital costs of building a one million-dollar softball complex could be repaid after only 20 tournaments, and that every tournament after that is profit that could be reinvested into other community needs. Suppose we want to determine whether our city should expect the same return and thus make the decision to build a tournament size softball complex. To do this we must first be informed about the similarities of our city with the city in the report. How large is the city? Where is the city located, and what is the population base in the surrounding locale? Is it in a climate conducive to a longer softball playing season? Had the agency previously sponsored regional softball tournaments and thus could rely on already established experience and reputation? Did the city in the report have an existing staff already available to manage the new complex? The answers to questions such as these help determine whether our city might expect similar financial success from building a softball complex.

Unfortunately, there is no specific criterion available to help determine when results of a study can be applied in another situation. One must simply use good judgment in determining their similarity. Also, such research procedural issues as respondent selection bias, instrument validity and reliability, evaluator expertise, etc. must be taken into account when determining the generalizability of findings. Finally, it is important to remember that some evaluative research is based on observations of a single sample. Until the study is replicated one or more times and similar results found, it will be difficult to convince others that the program or service being considered is generalizable.

Main Points

- The likelihood for evaluation results to yield information that enables organizations to make intelligent and rational decisions is increased by three factors: making a sound and reasoned transition between research findings and suggested actions, the ability of the study to provide information actually needed, and the acceptance of the recommendations by persons responsible for their implementation.

- Once the evaluation study is completed and reported, its recommendations require dissemination. Dissemination is communicating information about evaluation results to those persons and organizations that could use the information. These audiences are of three types: those with full interest, those with latent interest, and those with some interest in the project.

- Once the recommendations have been proposed and disseminated, the organization's staff must sometimes decide which ones or how many of the recommendations to implement. Deciding this is usually based on the factors of practicality, importance, compatibility, and time

- Technically, the only fully justified application of the results of a single evaluation study is to the organization or participants studied in that particular study. However, other organizations and/or programs with similar traits as those studied originally may sometimes deem the results applicable to them.

Study Questions

1. Upon what does the likelihood for results to yield useful decisions for the agency depend?

2. What are the types of audiences for research recommendations? Identify one dissemination strategy for each type.

3. How does an organization choose which research recommendations to implement?

References

Backman, S.J., & Veldkamp, C. 1995. Examination of the relationship between service quality and user loyalty. *Journal of Park and Recreation Administration, 13*(2), 29-41.

Berg, K.E., & Latin, R.W. 1994. *Essentials of modern research methods in health, physical, education, and recreation.* Englewood Cliffs, NJ: Prentice Hall.

Fullan, M. (1982). *The meaning of educational change.* New York: Columbia University Press.

Moore, N. 1987. *How to do research,* (2nd ed). London: The Library Association.

National Recreation and Park Association. 1996. *The benefits of parks and recreation, putting the pieces together: Resource guide.* Arlington, VA: Author.

Robson, C. (1993). *Real world research: A resource for social scientists and practitioner-researchers.* Oxford, UK: Blackwell.

Theobald, W.F. 1979. *Evaluation of recreation and park programs.* New York: John Wiley & Sons.

Turco, D.M., & Lee, K.L. 1996. NIMBY Syndrome among homeowners adjacent to rail-trails. *Abstracts of Presentations, 1996 Leisure Research Symposium, National Recreation and Park Association.* Kansas City, MO.

PART III: EVALUATIVE PLANNING MODEL

Chapter 15: Program Evaluation

Chapter 16: Assessment

Chapter 17: Personnel Performance Appraisal

Chapter 18: Evaluation of Physical Plant

Chapter 19: Evaluation of Marketing

Evaluation can be used to monitor and manage multiple facets of an organization's operations. Part III, then, presents real-life applications of how evaluation is used by recreation, park, tourism, and sport organizations. It is an application of the evaluative research model presented in Part II. Even though every aspect of an organization's operation has the potential for being evaluated, we feature the evaluation of programs, participant needs, personnel, the physical plant, and marketing.

Chapter 15 addresses program evaluation within the context of program goals, objectives, and outcomes; as well as the role of input and intervening variables in program evaluation. Chapter 16 discusses how assessment can be used to plan programs that affect people directly in terms of their leisure attributes, functional abilities, and/or specific skills. In Chapter 17, personnel evaluation or performance appraisal is explored. Chapter 18 collects together multiple applications of evaluative research in leisure service organizations for determining the adequacy of open space, facilities, equipment, operating procedures, concessions, and risk management. Finally, Chapter 19 outlines ideas for evaluating an organization's marketing.

CHAPTER 15

Program Evaluation

What Will I Learn in This Chapter?
I'll be able to:

1. Recall the phases involved in program planning and evaluation.

2. Differentiate between a goal and an objective.

3. Recall the characteristics of a "good" objective.

4. Identify the kinds of populations that can be identified in an objective.

5. List the categories of recreation program outcome measures; and be able to cite an example of each.

6. Discuss why science can neither "prove" nor "disprove."

7. Define and provide examples of input and intervening variables.

8. Read an evaluation research report and be able to identify the independent, intervening, and dependent variables used for the study.

9. Recall criteria for selecting input and intervening variables.

In the real world, recreation organizations have a working knowledge of their mission. Having this general or overall sense of direction is true regardless of whether the organization is a public or entrepreneurial enterprise. Organizational mission statements may include: offering instruction in any number of recreation activities (swimming, dance, gymnastics, etc.), facilitating play experiences in any number of activities (such as softball, basketball, tennis, etc.), and providing facilities (for example, an open gym, parks, a golf course). These mission statements or directives become the nuclei for planning specific recreational programs that are offered.

Program evaluation is inextricably linked to program planning (Figure 15.1). An organization's mission(s) influences program planning. Program goals that reflect an organization's mission are identified. These program goals can, in turn, precipitate the need for pre-program assessment. Program objectives are then identified and ultimately serve as the outcomes examined in program evaluation. In other words, a post-program evaluation or assessment is undertaken in order to ascertain the extent specified objectives have been attained. Many times program evaluation becomes expansive so as to include examination of how factors, other than program participation (such as input and intervening variables—ideas that will be discussed later on in this chapter), are tied to the attainment of program objectives.

Figure 15.1: Program planning and evaluation process.

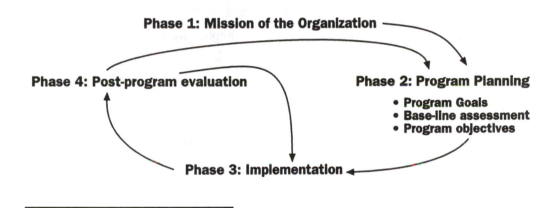

This chapter is divided into four major sections. These sections address goals, objectives, program outcome measures, and the role of input and intervening variables in program evaluation.

Crafting Goals

The cornerstones of program evaluation are goals and objectives. Program *goals* are abstract, idealized statements of desired outcomes. Operationalized statements of goals are known as *objectives* (see Figure 15.2). Patten (1987, p.38) notes that, "The real challenge of program evaluation is to ... turn on the lights, and take a close look at what's going on in comparison to what we think should be going on." In other words, program evaluation compares what is happening to what you hope will happen.

Rossi and Freeman (1993, p. 106) point out, "... evaluators often are more like detectives than social researchers, trying to unearth and make sense out of the original reasons for the program." Thus, it is not uncommon for evaluators to assist by defining or redefining program goals for new, not-so-new and old programs.

Figure 15.2: Examples of program goals and objectives for an aerobics class.

Program Goals for Aerobics Class	Corresponding Program Objective
Participants will experience improved:	At the end of a two-week aerobics class, participants will:
1. Physical health	1. Experience a 5% decrease in their one-minute resting heart rate.
2. Mental health	2. Report a higher positive body image (relative to self-reported body image at the beginning of the aerobics program).
3. Social health	3. Report that at least one person, outside of class, has commented on some aspect related to their improved physical fitness (e.g., weight loss, decreased look of "flabbiness," improved muscle tone, etc.).

If one or more goals are being put forth for a program, how do you decide on which goals to hone in or accept? Weiss (1972, pp. 30-34) reviews a number of considerations in choosing goals. Two of the more important points, in our opinion, in selecting and crafting goals that deal with practicality, relative importance, and incompatibilities.

1. Relative Importance. Deciding relative importance of competing goals will require making value judgements. Staff will need to decide what is critical or vital to their mission and what is secondary. Initially, identification of program goals can be challenging. Program designers often have intuitive reasons for offering a program. Thus, staff may be working at cross-purposes. Mary, for instance, thinks the program is aspiring to improve physical health; whereas, Joe thinks it is set up to improve social well-being. These discrepancies in program goals must be worked out before an evaluation can be undertaken. Policy makers and program managers need to collaborate until agreement can be reached.

2. Incompatibilities. Typically, a program has more than one goal. The reason for this is that most programs are multifaceted. Given the nature of leisure services, programs are typically set up to satisfy a number of needs. Choosing one goal is short sighted—what happens if that goal is not realized? Focusing on one goal can provide ammunition for program critics to condemn, or even worse yet, close the program down. Nevertheless, there can be incompatibilities among the stated goals. A model program, for example, seeks to optimize the physical abilities or health of participants. The same program also has an articulated goal to be cost effective. Clearly, these two goals are in conflict—health can be improved, but such an endeavor can be costly.

Objectives

Program objectives should reflect specific intended consequences of the program. In other words, what the program is trying to accomplish should be made explicit. Program objectives reflect assessment results. For instance, suppose you are the manager of a private health and fitness club. Popular demand necessitates programming a lot of different level aerobic classes during each week. Program goals have been set for these classes (Figure 15.2). Individual participants enrolling in any of these classes will be encouraged to undergo pre-program (or baseline) and post-program assessment. This assessment is done to determine participants resting heart rate and self-perceived body image. These assessment results will ultimately permit determining whether program objectives set for the aerobic classes have been met or satisfied.

Identifying and writing objectives that are clear, specific, and measurable is a difficult task [for excellent references on the topic, see Gronlund (1995) and Mager, (1984)]. In order for a good program evaluation to be conducted, a good program objective should have four characteristics. That is, a good objective should be characterized by: specificity, measurability, criteria, and identification of a delineated population.

1. Specificity. Program objectives must be *specific*. An action verb behavior must be identified in the written objective that can be observed or self-reported. An objective that states, "Participants will improve their knowledge about how to dance," is not precise because it is left open to differing interpretations—is the emphasis on making a high grade on a written exam that covers dance steps? Demonstrating certain dance steps? Or something else? Vague words that are open to interpretation, and therefore should not be used as part of an objective statement, are *learn, know, understand,* and *appreciate.* In contrast, words that can be used with clarity in developing program objectives include *list, identify, demonstrate,* and *perform.*

2. Measurable. Program objectives also must be identified that can be measured. The specific action verb behavior identified in the objective must be able to be operationalized. That is, the identified behavior must be a characteristic or trait that permits measurement or testing. Luckily, a battalion of measurement tools exist to measure any number of variables (see Chapter 9). The challenge becomes identifying and agreeing upon indicators or proxy measures of selected constructs.

3. Criteria. Objectives must also contain *criteria* or yardsticks that will indicate how much progress towards an objective marks success. Suppose an Activities for Daily Living program for individuals with mental retardation enrolls 50 persons, graduates 30, places 10 in jobs, of whom 7 are working six months later. Is this success? A tiny change may be better than none! No change is better than regression. Program promoters and detractors can interpret the same criteria differently. "Fully 50% of the students..." boasts the program advocates; whereas, the program detractor sighs "Only 50%...." Whether you are an optimist or pessimist will determine if you "see" the glass half full or half empty. Regardless, articulated criteria must be part of program objectives

4. Which Population? Before a program is offered, the objectives for the program should delineate the population to be served by the program. On the surface, the population being served should be straightforward. It is important to remember, however, the notion of population can be conceptualized three different ways: target population, population-at-risk, and population-in-need.

A *target population* is defined as a group of individuals, usually described according to some social or demographic characteristic (such as age) or location (such as, adult residents of Montgomery County, Maryland). Targets may also be designated as direct or indirect—depending on whether the program is delivered to the targets immediately (the *direct target audience*) or eventually (the *indirect target audience*). Most programs or services are set up for a direct target audience. Sometimes program planners design services to affect a target population indirectly by first making the program's direct target population a group that will eventually have an impact on the indirect population. Suppose a program has been planned, using the "Train the Trainers" approach, to teach soccer to volunteer coaches. As envisioned, the direct population, or first wave of volunteer coaches trained, will then fan out into the community and offer soccer workshops to other parent recruits (the indirect target population), who have volunteered to become assistant coaches.

A target population in turn can be drawn from a population-at-risk or a population-in-need. A *population-at-risk* is those individuals with a high probability of having or acquiring a problematic physical (such as cardiovascular accident), psychological (such as drug addiction), or social condition (such as belonging to a gang). A *population-in-need* is a group of individuals who currently manifest (or have) the problematic condition. Suppose a recreation department has decided to offer a summer program for "troubled youth." The target population could be children-at risk—or those identified by the school system as having behavioral problems. Then again, the recreation program could serve children-in-need—or those who have been adjudicated through the legal system and deemed youthful offenders.

Program Outcome Measures

Again, in conducting a program evaluation, it is paramount that goals and objectives for the program have been determined. Objectives identify outcomes anticipated as a result of participation in the provided service or program. In other words, program evaluation is tailored along the lines of determining accountability in terms of outcome measures. There are three kinds of outcome measures or those that relate to measuring impact on people, organizations, and/or efficiency.

Measuring Effects on People: Impressions Regarding Service Delivery

One approach to program evaluation is to examine impressions users have about varying aspects of service delivery—such as program satisfaction, personnel, physical plant and facility operations, and marketing. Any variety of mechanisms (survey, focus groups, etc.—see Chapter 10) can be used to collect attitudinal information from the perspectives of sampled (see Chapter 7) clients/participants, staff and other persons. In therapeutic recreation settings or special recreation programs, this *others* category could include recording the impressions of family members.

1. **Program Satisfaction.** Participants can be asked about their *overall satisfaction* with a program. That is, a specific leisure activity can be identified as the referent and then respondents can be asked to self-report overall satisfaction derived from participation in the activity; as well as be queried regarding how participation in the activity satisfied specifically such needs as educational, social, physiological, psychological, relaxation, and aesthetic (Beard & Ragheb, 1980). Another approach for gauging satisfaction is to collect information on how expectations affect satisfaction. As Orlander (1977) points out, satisfaction is a relative concept because people's expectations influence their overall satisfaction. One way to understand and explain satisfaction is the discrepancy theory (Connolly, 1984). The *discrepancy theory* suggests that satisfaction is a function of perceived benefits relative to the expectations the individual has for the experience. Using this framework, one could predict activity or program satisfaction along the lines depicted in Figure 15.3. In other words, individuals would be considered satisfied if either their high expectations were met (Cell 1) or if benefits exceeded expectations (Cell 2). Contrastingly, individuals would be considered dissatisfied if their expectations were unfulfilled (Cell 3). And finally, individuals whose low level expectations were realized could be characterized as being either satisfied or dissatisfied (Cell 4). That is, some persons may be content (or satisfied) when their low expectations are met, whereas other persons may not relish a self-fulfilling prophecy of minimal benefits (and hence a dissatisfied state occurs).

Still another aspect of program satisfaction relates to inquiring about *accessibility characteristics* of a program. By this, we mean gathering opinions regarding the cost of the program ("Is it affordable?"), and the target population's beliefs regarding convenience-related factors (for instance, hours of operation and location of service).

2. **Personnel.** Consumers of leisure services, as well as supervisors, can be queried regarding their beliefs or feedback on the practicing qualities of leisure service providers (e.g., friendliness or courteousness, knowledge of subject matter, teaching abilities; Chapter 17 will delve into personnel appraisal in more detail).

3. **Physical Plant and Facility Operations.** Leisure program participants (coupled with staff observations) can also be asked for their impressions regarding aspects of physical plant operations (Chapter 18 will cover this in greater detail). That is, were the following elements found to be satisfactory or:

• **Concessionaire/merchandise offerings.** For instance, are the range and quality of food, souvenirs, and the like satisfactory?

• **Crowd management.** Is the waiting period in line (to register, purchase tickets, retrieve a towel, order food, etc.) acceptable? Is the parking lot safe?

• **Housekeeping.** Are specific areas in the facility (such as bathrooms, showers, changing rooms, gym area, pool deck, concessionaire area) sufficiently clean?

4. **Marketing.** Evaluating the impact marketing has on consumers has many guises. The foci can be on: examining awareness of an offered service or program, identifying the marketing source(s) that promoted service awareness, and determining reasons for use and non-use of an offered service that in turn can be addressed in advertising (Chapter 18 presents additional information on this topic).

Figure 15.3: Schematic illustrating discrepancy theory for explaining participant's satisfaction with a program (expectation versus outcome).[1]

| | | **Benefits** | |
		High	Low
Expectations	High	Satisfied (Cell 1)	Dissatisfied (Cell 3)
	Low	Satisfied (Cell 2)	(Dis)satisfied (Cell 4)

[1]From "Evaluative Research of Leisure Services: Application of Discrepancy Theory to a Day Camp for Nursing Home Residents," by C. Riddick and M. DeSchriver, 1986, *Journal of Park & Recreation Administration*, p. 59. Copyright 1986 by American Academy for Park and Recreation and Park Administration. Reprinted with permission.

Measuring Effects on People: End-Result

End-result program evaluation is aimed at measuring the effects a program has directly on the individual. Scriven (1967) has labeled this kind of outcome evaluation as *summative* in nature. For instance, suppose you are implementing a program to provide recreational activity to nursing home residents, with the ultimate goal of bringing about a better quality of life (as measured by self-concept and satisfaction with leisure). Ascertaining whether or not recreational activity participation in the end resulted in improved self-concept and increased leisure satisfaction would be the foci of an end-result program evaluation.

One way to measure end results is within the context of how well program objectives have been met. More specifically, program objectives have been written with an emphasis on desired effects individuals will experience from program participation. Program objectives can be cast in one of three categories (leisure attributes, functional abilities, or skill level) and/or one of six domains (how the individual participant is impacted in affective, cognitive, emotional, physiological, psychological and/or social areas (see Chapter 16). Program evaluation then focuses on examining the extent participation in the program has affected one or more of these categories and/or domains.

What becomes critical when undertaking an end-result evaluation is choice of research design to execute the evaluation. Again, the research design that is adopted will have profound implications on the conclusions that can be reached concerning how the program truly impacts on the individual (see Chapter 7).

Measuring Effects on Organizations

Sometimes goals for a program are aimed at changing institutions. In this situation, indicators of program outcome will be measures of institutional characteristics. Institutional characteristics can be aggregated from data about individuals in the organization.

One way to evaluate effects of a program on an organization is to look at *effort-evaluation* or the percentage of staff who are involved in direct provision of services. Many times, the number of staff or staff hours worked is reported in the nomenclature of *Full-Time-Equivalents* (FTE). For instance, it might be reported that it takes six FTE to operate a recreational swim program on a weekly basis. In other words, the equivalent of six FTE (the sum of part-time and/or full-time workers) to run the swim program is 240 hours per week (or six persons times 40-hour work week equals 240, though these hours do not necessarily need to be worked by six persons—full and part-time help could be configured to work the needed hours).

If agency effect is measured by using some measure related to effort-evaluation, it is important that the tradeoffs of this approach are recognized. On the one hand, this sort of effort evaluation is the easiest type of evaluation to perform. Thus, it is done quite frequently. Nevertheless, it is important to understand the primary assumption being made in effort evaluation. That is, the assumption is that the effort made has a positive effect. Amount of effort, then, is equated with quality. For instance, if in an annual report the number of FTE used in a hospital therapeutic recreation is cited, then the assertion being made (directly, or in so many words) is that the existence of the quantifiable resources of staff results in improvements in the health of the patients. This may or may not be the case! Rather than perform such leaps in logic, it would be better to undertake an end-result evaluation.

Another approach for evaluating effects on an organization is to look at coverage. The term *coverage* refers to the extent to which participation by the target population achieves the levels specified by program planners (Rossi & Freeman, 1993, p. 176). Most programs are set up with the notion that it is desirable to serve a large proportion of the intended audience.

The formula for measuring coverage (or coverage efficiency) is:

$$100 \text{ X} \quad \frac{\text{Number in need served}}{\text{Total number in need}} \quad \frac{\text{Number not in need served}}{\text{Total number served}}$$

The formula can yield positive and negative values between $\pm$ 100. A positive value of 100 occurs when the actual number served equals the designated target population in need and no inappropriate targets are served. A negative value occurs if inappropriate targets are served. For example, in a particular geographical area, 1,000 elders are identified in need of a Congregate Meals Program. Of those 1,000, 700 are served that are in need. The coverage value obtained by the formula would be +40 [or 100 X (700/1,000)-(300/1,000) = 100 X 40/1,000 = +40], meaning 40% of the desired target population was reached. Another example is suppose 1,000 individuals have been identified as targets for a program. As it turns out, of the 1,000 program participants, only 100 are appropriate targets The coverage efficiency value would be -80 [or 100 X (100/1,000)-(900/100) =100 X -800/1,000 = 100 X -.8 = -80]. This -80 value indicates that 80% of the program participants were inappropriate targets for the program.

According to Rossi and Freeman (1993, p. 178) the most common coverage problem in social service programs is the failure to achieve full target audience participation either because of bias in the way participants are recruited or because potential participants reject the service or program being offered. *Bias* means the degree to which subgroups of a population participate differentially. Bias can arise out of self-selection. Some subgroups may voluntarily participate more frequently than others. For example, a fitness center may attract the more fit. Bias can also happen when potential participants reject a program due to the negative attitudes of personnel affiliated with the program. Program personnel may react favorably to some clients while rejecting others. For instance, fitness center staff may be "turned off" by an individual who has experienced an amputation or stroke, thus an Amputee Club or Stroke Club may not retain participants due to the subtle (or not so subtle) messages resonated by staff.

Measuring Efforts Relative to Effects (Efficiency Assessment)

Knowing the degree that an implemented program has met its desired outcome, in terms of effects on people, is important. In a lot of situations, however, it is equally crucial to be informed about program outcomes compared to their costs. Rossi & Freeman (1993) view efficiency analyses as an extension of, rather than an alternative to, impact or outcome evaluation. Decision makers are increasingly confronted with the task of choosing how to allocate scarce resources in order to put them to optimal use. While political factors can affect the decisions that are made, the relationship between costs and outcomes in each program is another piece in the mosaic from which decisions emerge.

A systematic approach to resource allocation analysis is better known as an efficiency assessment (Rossi & Freeman, 1993, p. 364). Simply stated, an *efficiency assessment* is a comparative perspective that provides a frame of reference for relating costs to program results. Efficiency assessment is a tool by which the efficiency of programs can be judged by conducting either a cost-benefit analysis and/or a cost effectiveness analysis.

The terms cost-effectiveness and cost-benefit are commonly used interchangeably. Although there is not total agreement on the definitions of these two terms, they do have distinct meanings. As will be elaborated on, the difference between the two types of analyses is the way in which the effects of a program are expressed. Regardless, in order to conduct an efficiency assessment, a program must have known and estimable impacts. It is senseless to do an efficiency analyses on ineffective programs!

1. **Cost-benefit** analysis, with few exceptions, measures in monetary terms both the costs (direct and indirect) and benefits (tangible and intangible) of the program or equipment under consideration. Cost-benefit studies can be used to compare programs or equipment that have differing objectives because a common denominator—money—exists. The problem with cost-benefit analysis is that there is great difficulty measuring, in dollar terms, the benefits of a program.

Nevertheless, most cost-benefit results are reported in terms of subtracting costs from benefits. For instance, a program that costs $150,000 and has benefits calculated at $300,000, would result in a net benefit of $150,000 (or $300,00-150,000). Sometimes cost-benefit results are reported as the ratio of benefits to cost. In the last example this ratio would be 2:1.

2. **Cost-effectiveness** measures the cost of achieving whatever the service or equipment achieved (or the magnitude of substantive outcome). In other words, cost-effectiveness examines the amount of service output divided by the amount of service input (effort, calculated in dollars) required to produce it. The output, however, is not specified in terms of money. In cost-effectiveness analysis, programs with similar goals are evaluated and their costs compared.

An example of a cost-effectiveness study is one reported on how different approaches improved the math and reading performance of elementary children (Levin, Glass, $ Meister, 1987). The cost-effectiveness ratio of peer tutoring, adult tutoring, combined peer and adult tutoring, and computer-assisted instruction was .34, .07, /.22, and .15, respectively. Results indicate, perhaps surprisingly, that peer tutoring was more cost-effective than the computer-assisted program.

Another example of how cost-effectiveness can be applied is to imagine evaluating the cost effectiveness of a library-on-wheels for rural primary aged schoolchildren. Costs and effects could be expressed that for each $100 project dollars spent, how much reading scores increase by grade level unit.

A number of controversies do, however, surround the implementation of efficiency analyses. While a detailed discussion of these controversies is beyond the scope of the book, the gist of the arguments for not using efficiency analyses is highlighted below:

- Technical requirements and expertise may be beyond the resources of the evaluation project. The limited knowledge of evaluative research staff may not permit the execution of the study. Or the data necessary to do this sort of analyses simply may not be available.
- Deciding upon the "correct" procedures to use in the cost-benefit and cost-effectiveness analyses. There is not always agreement regarding the conversion of inputs and outputs (what, for instance, is the value of human life?) into monetary values, inflation rate used, opportunity costs, secondary or "spillover" effects, discount rate (or how much, in monetary terms, to reduce costs and benefits that are dispersed through time), etc.

Role of Input & Intervening Variables in Program Evaluation

Program evaluation can be straightforward. Then again, it can become more complex. That is, program evaluation can entail examining how independent variables, other than program participation, result in changes in the dependent/outcome variable(s). After a quick review of "cause-effect" logic, these other independent variables—namely input and intervening variables—are discussed. This chapter ends with ideas on how to go about selecting relevant independent variables for inclusion in a program evaluation.

Cause and Effect

Before discussing input and intervening variables it is first necessary to review the concepts of controlling variables and cause and effect (the latter was briefly discussed in Chapter 7). The interest in this is predicated on the need to ensure the effect observed by participating in an intervention/activity/program is due to the limited number of variables that control is being maintained over rather than some other factors. Establishing a program's impact translates into linking the program as the "cause" of some specified effect. Essentially, what is transpiring is establishing causality (though admittedly, according to scientific principle, one can never truly establish causality!).

In social sciences, *causal relationships* are typically stated in terms of probabilities. If we say, "A is a cause of B" what we really should say (for the sake of accuracy) is "If we introduce A, B is *more likely* to result than if we do not introduce A." The latter clarification does not imply that B *always* results if A is introduced, nor does it mean that B occurs only after A has been introduced.

Statements often appear in reports along the lines "there was a significant difference between the scores of two groups," and this finding is subsequently used to justify the existence of a "cause and effect relationship" between the two variables. Babbie (1995, p. 4) states that, "... it is seldom the case that one variable absolutely and completely causes another." In truth, many events have multiple causes that may not be at all obvious.

Let us consider an example. If you measure how fast 50-year-olds and 30-year-olds swim 50 yards freestyle in a Masters swim tournament, within each group the times will not be the same. While 30-year-olds will tend to be faster than 50-year-olds, not all the adults in the older group will be slower than all those in the younger group. Age is not related to a certain finish time or speed. Even if a representative group of all adults having the same birth date were chosen, their speed would vary. If a graph were plotted of the various swimming times of a large number of people sampled, the results would show that swimming speed varies normally around a mean for an age group. Also, the mean swimming time of 30-year-olds would probably be lower than that of 50-year-olds, and a statistical test would reveal that the two age groups did not belong to the same population.

But these data alone do not unveil the "cause" of the differences in swimming times, either within the groups or between the two age groups. All that can accurately be said is that there is a *tendency* for younger adults to be faster swimmers than older adults. It would be wrong to conclude that age alone "causes" a person to be a faster or slower swimmer. Indeed, the actual "causes" of swimming speed may be underlying biological processes (percent body fat, muscle tone, lung capacity, etc.) and previous social psychological histories (previous swim instruction, frequency and amount of training, etc.).

Thus, when a statistically significant difference is reported, it is probably easier to tell what the finding does not mean rather than tell what it does mean. Statistical significance does not tell us the "cause" of swimming speed. There is the real chance that there is no individual "cause." Consumers of evaluation reports are challenged to decide how well the evaluator controlled or accounted for all the possible "causes" as well as how well the evaluator justified the identification of the cause of the observed effect. Thus, a conscientious evaluator must identify limitations of their study by identifying potential sources of alternate explanations (i.e., point out other possible "causes" to any noted effect).

Definitions of Input, Intervening, Program Operation and Bridging Variables

Input variables deal with aspects of the program context. These variables are thought to be relevant to explaining program success (Babbie, 1995, p. 343). These input considerations or ingredients then become part of the study. Input variables assume the role of independent variables. Figure 15.4 portrays the interrelationship among the kinds of variables commonly used in evaluation research.

Figure 15.4: Types of variables involved in evaluation of leisure services.

Independent Variable(s)	Intervening Variable(s)	Dependent Variable(s)
• Intervention/Program Participation	Mediators	• Outcome, Output, Response, or "Effect"
• Inputs	• Program Operations • Bridging Factors	

Most evaluations require the definition and quantification of input variables. While many variables can be studied, the reality is that limited resources (in particular, a limited time frame to complete the study) necessitate focusing on a few 'relevant" variables; rather than examining an array (the so-call "smorgasbord" approach) of variables. *It is important to note that depending on the circumstances, a variable(s) could be considered either an input or an intervening variable.*

Examples of input variables include noting variations in:

1. Principles, methods, and/or formats used. For instance, what leadership principles and programming techniques were used? And what format was used to offer the activity (e.g., group size).

2. Resources used. This includes curricular materials as well as any resource used in the delivery of the program (whether these resources were constructed, purchased, or rented).

3. The activities engaged in by the individuals under study. When possible, it is best to separate the various aspects of a multi-faceted program into specific activities. Suppose, for example, a residential camp for adolescents includes horse back riding, swimming, canoeing, arts and crafts and so on. Thus, for monitoring purposes, it may be advisable to separate these activities into separate sets of service. Indeed, Baker and Witt (1996, p. 76) reflect that their evaluation of after-school programs was hampered by not examining how the "different mix of activities" offered in the schools affected noted outcomes.

4. Length of service. This includes the duration (or how often the program is offered—once a week? Twice a week? Etc.) and/or the intensity of the program (or the length of each program or class—1 hour? 2 hours? Etc.).

Furthermore, there may also be *intervening variables*, or factors that mediate between inputs and outcomes for which measures need to be identified (refer to Figure 15.4 for a schematic representation of this idea). These factors are envisioned as tempering the association or relationship between input or intervention variables. There are two kinds of intervening variables. One kind has to do with program operation variables. The second kind are so-called "bridging variables."

Program operation variables or *extraneous variables* are variables that deal with the implementation of the program or some aspect of how the program operates. Variations in the program itself can affect evaluation results. Examples of program operation variables include:

1. Staff/volunteer numbers, characteristics, and/or continuity. A ratio dealing with number of staff and/or volunteers to number of persons served may be useful. Patten (1987, pp. 20-21) suggests that it may be appropriate to monitor the degree of reliance on professional versus volunteer staff. Scott, Witt, and Foss (1996) as well as Patten (1987) point out any number of program operation elements may be important to examine. Examples of such variables are "quality" characteristics of staff (in terms of nurturing and caring characteristics, confidence, credibility) as well as the extent participants experienced continuity of leaders versus having multiple leaders (due to staff attrition, scheduling, etc.).

2. Attendance, number served, and/or size of the program. Attendance may have a dramatic effect on what and how much is learned. For instance, Baker and Witt (1996) found after-school programs impacted academic performance and self-esteem for those elementary-aged students most involved in the program (i.e., participated in a lot of activities). Likewise, the number served or size (single site versus multiple sites) of the program operation can impinge on program outcomes.

Bridging variables are mediating variables that influence or temper the effects of a program intervention. Learning and behavior change theories, for instance, provide us with the identification of bridging variables by asserting that learning is affected by any number of things including attitude mind set, previous learning, etc.

Suppose the effects of a leisure education program (offered in two formats or 1:1 or a small group setting) on leisure behaviors (such as kinds of activities participated in, frequency of participation) is being evaluated (Figure 15.5). One variable considered critical in explaining positive changes in leisure behaviors is attendance (a program operational variable). Some bridging variables for tracing how participation in a leisure education program effects leisure behaviors (the measured outcome or dependent variable) might be participants": interest in the subject matter and decision making skill mastery. Mastery, for instance, can be envisioned as a bridging or linking variable that relates or acknowledges the interplay between learning and skill mastery to a behaviorally-related outcome variable. In summary, what might have been originally envisioned as simply studying how participation in leisure education program affects leisure behaviors, now has expanded to include variables (identified by theory) that permit controlling for the possible influence of other potential independent variables.

Figure 15.5: Understanding how participation in a leisure education program can affect leisure behaviors: Schematic example of the interrelationships among independent, intervening, and dependent variables.

INDEPENDENT VARIABLES	INTERVENING/INDENDENT VARIABLES	DEPENDENT VARIABLE
Intervention = Participation in leisure education program	Program operations variable = Attendance	
Input variable = Participation in 1:1 or small group setting	Bridging variable = Interest in subject matter	Leisure Behaviors
	Bridging variable = Decision making skill mastery	

Deciding on Input and Intervening Variables

Recreational services are action programs that by their very nature are complex undertakings. These services incorporate a range of components and procedures. In some cases, a program may be expressed in terms that appear clear and reproducible—for example, a tennis instruction program or a craft class. In other instances, it may become difficult to describe what the program really is in terms of content and/or operations. A program can have internal variations in operation from day-to-day and from staff member to staff member. Insights about what actually is occurring might be gleaned from observations, discussion with program staff, review of records, etc.

Becoming familiar with the content of the program enables one to have insights on what to attribute program success. Evaluators need to have fundamental understanding of how and why a program or service worked. Weiss (1972, p. 74) challenges us to "...discover the reality of the program rather than its illusion." Remember, that the purpose behind program evaluation is to assist decision making. Decision makers often times need to know what it was that worked or did not work, what it is that should be adopted or modified, etc. In other words, program implementation needs to be monitored. When it is known which aspects of the program are associated with success, then there is a basis for recommendations about future modifications and/or replications. Thus, the focus of a program evaluation may be to identify the nature or component of the program that is responsible for the noted change. This enables one to learn about the relative effectiveness of different strategies or components. We get a clue as to why the program is working.

Another way to go about identifying input and intervening variables is to evaluate variable significance. One way to weigh variable significance [adapting Black's (1993, p. 66) thoughts] is to:

• Avoid variables that have a narrow perspective and limited programmatic significance. Be careful not to be so narrow in outlook and to focus on too few variables as to make the results not applicable to real life. Situations can be trivialized in order to collect data but the study really has little if any social or program significance. (Remember Senator Proxmire's Golden Fleece Award lists? In particular, the federally funded study examined why dogs bark?)

• Select variables that are significant and can be measured. Professional literature can provide one with insights in this regard. For instance, theories in education, sociology, psychology, etc. may reveal input and intervening variables for inclusion. Likewise, practical experience may shed some light. For example, if it has been noticed that people with certain characteristics are more likely to show up for every program session and others attend erratically or not at all, then it may be worthwhile to include these characteristics as independent variables. Variables chosen should be unambiguous and well defined.

• Avoid potential confusion by selecting a small number of variables. The inclusion of too many variables can result in a large data base that yields no new understanding of interrelationships among the variables. This state of affairs typically emerges when evaluators have no clear question or hypotheses to guide the data collection process. It is better to stick with a fewer number of variables for which there is greater understanding and logic for their inclusion.

Main Points

• The foundation for program evaluation is the organization's mission. In turn, the organization's mission should be reflected in the goals set for a program. Program goals can in turn precipitate the need for pre-program assessment. Objectives are then identified, and serve as the outcomes examined in post-program evaluation or assessment.

• Program goals should be chosen that anticipate consequences, have relative importance, and are compatibile.

• Program objectives should reflect intended consequences of the program. A good program objective should have four characteristics: specificity, measurability, criteria, and identification of identifiable population (a target population, population-at-risk or a population-in-need).

• Program outcome measures can investigate impact on people in terms of their impressions regarding a program.

- Program outcome measures can also relate to measuring impact on people in terms of end-result. End-result evaluation measures the effects a program has directly on the individual. Impact on the individual can be approached by determining how program participation has affected one or more of three categories (leisure attributes, functional abilities, or skill level) and/or one or more domains of the individual (affective, cognitive, emotional, physical, psychomotor, or social).

- Yet another way program outcome measures can be approached is to measure effects on organizations. Examples of such measures are those that relate to organization effort and coverage.

- Another angle to gauging program outcome is to measure efforts relative to effects, or efficiency assessment. Efficiency assessment is conducted either a cost-benefit analysis or a cost-effectiveness analysis. Cost-benefit measures in monetary terms both the costs and benefits of the program. Cost-effectiveness measures the cost of achieving whatever the program achieved—programs with similar goals are evaluated and their costs compared.

- Program evaluation usually entails examining the likelihood that independent variables, other than program participation, results in changes in the dependent outcome variable.

- Guidance for selecting independent variables (input and intervening variables) can come from understanding the content of the program, practicality, and/or weighing variable significance.

Study Questions

1. What are the phases involved in program planning and evaluation?

2. Give an example of a program goal and a related program objective.

3. Identify the three kinds of populations that can be addressed in an objective.

4. Identify some of the impressions that can be solicited from program users regarding thoughts about service delivery.

5. What is meant by end-result program evaluation?

6. How can program effects on a recreation organization be evaluated?

7. What is meant by cost-benefit analysis? Cost effectiveness analysis? Under what circumstances are these sorts of analyses done?

8. What is an input variable? Program operation variable? Bridging variable? Why might such variables be examined in a program evaluation?

References

Babbie, E. (1995). *The practice of social research* (7th ed.). Belmont, CA: Wadsworth.

Baker, D., & Witt, P. (1996). Evaluation of the impact of two after-school programs. *Journal of Park and Recreation Administration, 14,* 60-81.

Beard, J., & Ragheb, M. (1980). Measuring leisure satisfaction. *Journal of Leisure Research, 12,* 20-33.

Black, T. (1993). *Evaluating social science research: An introduction.* Thousand Oaks, CA: Sage Publications.

Connolly, P. (1984). Program evaluation. In C. Peterson & S. Gunn (Eds.), *Therapeutic recreation program design: Principles and procedures* (pp. 136-179). Englewood Cliffs, NJ: Prentice-Hall.

Gronlund, N. (1995). *How to write and use instructional objectives* (5th ed.). Englewood Cliffs, NJ: Prentice-Hall.

Levin, H., Glass, G., & Meister, G. (1987). Cost-effectiveness of computer-assisted instruction. *Evaluation Review, 11,* 50-72.

Mager, R. (1984). *Preparing instructional objectives* (2nd ed.). Belmont, CA: Lake Publishing Company.

Orlander, F. (1977). *Consumer satisfaction: A skeptic's view.* Aarthus, Denmark: Institut for Markedsokonomi.

Patten, M. (1987). *Creative evaluation* (2nd ed.). Newbury Park, CA: Sage Publications.

Riddick, C., & DeSchriver, M. (1984). Evaluative research of leisure services: Application of the discrepancy theory to a day camp for nursing home residents. *Journal of Park and Recreation Administration, 4,* 53-60.

Rossi, P., & Freeman, H. (1993). *Evaluation: A systematic approach.* Newbury Park, CA: Sage Publications.

Scott, D., Witt, P., & Foss, M. (1996). Evaluation of the impact of the Dougherty Arts Center's creativity club on children-at-risk. *Journal of Park & Recreation Administration, 14,* 41-59.

Scriven, M. (1967). The methodology of evaluation. In R. Tyler, R. Gagne, & M. Scriven (Eds.), *Perspectives in curriculum evaluation* (pp. 139-183). AERA Monograph Series on curriculum Evaluation, No. 1. Chicago: Rand McNally & Co.

Weiss, C. (1972). *Evaluation research: Methods of assessing program effectiveness.* Englewood Cliffs, NJ: Prentice-Hall.

CHAPTER 16

Assessment

What Will I Learn in This Chapter?
I'll be able to:

1. List the steps to the assessment process.

2. Identify criteria for choosing an assessment instrument.

3. Recall the categories and domains of assessment tools.

Have you ever taken a swimming test? If so, whether you realized it or not, you were assessed. Indeed, you most likely were assessed twice—at the beginning of summer to determine or confirm class placement and then again at the conclusion of summer to determine if you mastered swimming to the point where you earned a certificate or badge of accomplishment.

Assessment is an ingredient to the planning of recreational services or programs designed to have effects on the individual participant (see Chapter 15). Howell (1984, p. 235) sums up how assessment data are used by observing such data are "a guide in either the provision, development, or facilitation of leisure experiences for the client based upon the changes, clarification, improvement, or reinforcement needed."

Assessment is inextricably linked to program evaluation (recall Figure 15.1). As highlighted in Chapter 15, a program can be evaluated in terms of its effects on people. This essentially means program participants can be assessed twice during their affiliation with a program. That is, assessment results can identify pre– and post–program entry levels related to participants' leisure attributes, general functioning abilities, and/or specific recreation skills. Scriven (1991, p. 60) points out assessment is frequently used as a synonym for evaluation. Assessment identifies and confirms attainment of program purpose(s). In other words, assessment is used to monitor client change and thus assists with program evaluation. While there are several ideas in this chapter that are discussed in other chapters in different contexts, we think assessment is important enough to feature separately here.

The remainder of this chapter is divided into two parts. The first section will discuss the assessment process. The second part presents categories of assessment tools.

Assessment Process

The selection and use of assessment instruments involves a seven-step process (a modification of Dunn, 1984) that includes:

1. Ascertaining the purposes of the recreation service.
2. Specifying the content or areas that the assessment should cover. The content area(s) specified should logically be related to the purpose(s) of the service (or Step 1 above).
3. Identifying criteria for instrument selection.
4. Searching and reviewing available assessment instruments.
5. Comparing available assessment instruments to identified selection criteria.
6. Selecting an assessment instrument(s).
7. Using the selected instrument(s) to collect information systematically.

In order to conduct an assessment successfully, you first must be clear about the focus for the assessment. The focus for the assessment should hinge on the purpose(s) behind why the particular recreation service is being offered. burlingame and Blaschko (1997) suggest a classification system for assessment foci by examining either leisure attributes, functional abilities, and/or skill level. Again, choosing which one (or more) of these areas to concentrate on will depend on the purpose envisioned for the leisure program. For example, the most likely assessment focus for an aquatics program would be to record and monitor swimmer skill level.

In addition to identifying the assessment focus, selecting an assessment instrument requires considering a number of things and making trade-offs. One of the factors that can affect assessment instrumentation selection are the characteristics of program clientele—for example, age and developmental and/or functional level. Other important considerations that should influence assessment instrument choice are the instrument's documented validity and reliability (Chapter 9), resource demands (or personnel requirements needed to administer or interpret an instrument), and cost of acquiring copies or use of a copyrighted test. Regarding the latter, burlingame and Blaschko (1997) vividly remind us of the importance of obtaining permission to use copyrighted material or run the risk of incurring a $50,000 fine for each copyright infringement!

Before reviewing categories of assessment tools, one thing needs to be pointed out. That is, there is a pervasive feeling that recreation, and in particular therapeutic recreation, sorely lacks quality assessment instruments (Howell, 1984, p. 255; Stumbo, 1994, p. 233). The crux of the problem appears to stem from the fact that many of the assessment instruments used lack validity and reliability. Again, as reviewed in Chapter 9, consideration should be given in particular to these qualities of an assessment instrument before selecting it for use. The instruments that are cited in Figures 16.2–16.4 have been extracted primarily from the writings of burlingame and Blaschko (1997) and Stumbo (1991). These were selected on the basis of having documented validity and reliability. It is, however, important to remember that a multitude of sources exist for identifying instruments—the evaluator is urged to consult the measurement resources cited in Chapter 9.

Assessment Tools

A conceptual road map for selecting assessment tools is to juxtapose the three–category classification system of burlingame and Blaschko (1997) with an adaptation of the educational domain typology of Krathwohl, Bloom, and Masia (1964) (see Figure 16.1). That is, the educational domain classification system can be selectively imposed across three categories (leisure attributes, functional abilities, and skill level) so that the foci of assessment also becomes a matter of deciding on, within these three categories, whether to examine affective, cognitive, emotional, physiological, psychomotor, or social domains. An explanation of this matrix will now follow.

Figure 16.1: An assessment classification schema.

Focus of Assessment	Within Category Focus/Domain					
	Affective	Cognitive	Emotional	Physiological	Psychomotor	Social
Leisure Attributes	X					
Functional Appraisal		X	X	X	X	X
Skills	X	X			X	

Assessment Tools Dealing with Leisure Attributes

Leisure attributes can be subdivided into two subcategories. The first subcategory is leisure interests and activity pursuits, and the second subcategory examines affect.

One approach for understanding the attributes of interests and pursuits is to rely on economics. That is, economists would define interests as *felt need*, and would point out that *felt need* can be examined from any three points in time—the past, present or future. *Felt need* inquires about what an individual would have liked to do. An example of a question that assesses felt need from the past–time perspective is to ask, "Looking back this past year, what recreational activity did you not participate in but wished you had?" And an example of a question that assesses felt need, from a present–time perspective is to ask, "What recreational activity do you wish you were presently involved in but are not?" For whatever reason(s) the individual may not have undertaken an activity or used a provided service—even though she has an interest or desire in doing so. Measuring felt need can be difficult because need perceptions are relative to person, time, and place.

Activity pursuits, in economic nomenclature, are labeled *expressed demand. Expressed demand* (sometimes called *marked demand*), in contrast, is determining what a person has actually done. One issue related to measuring expressed deman, is deciding on a time frame for reporting leisure activity choices. For instance, assessing expressed demand could be done by asking, "What recreational activity did you do most of this past year? Past five years?"

Moreover, within an examination of felt need or expressed demand, leisure interests and behaviors can be assessed two ways. One way is to inquire about specific activities (swimming, bicycling, hiking, etc.). The other approach is to ask about categories or clusters of interests or activity pursuits. For example, individuals may be asked about their leisure interests and behaviors in such categories as mental activities, social activities, outdoor activities, arts and crafts, high– and low–risk activities, group and individual activities, and active and passive activities. Generally, a checklist approach is used to assess leisure interests or activity pursuits. Examples of such instruments are the Leisure Activities Blank, behavioral subscale of Leisure Attitude Measurement, Leisure Preferences Inventory Scale G to the Leisure Diagnostic Battery, Leisure Interest Measurement, Leisurescope Plus, Ohio Functional Assessment Battery, and the State Technical Institute's Leisure Assessment Process (STILAP) (see Figure 16.2).

Additionally, within a focus on leisure attributes, one can also examine affect dimensions of the participant. *Affect or affective domain* emphasizes "a feeling, emotion, or a degree of acceptance or rejection" (Krathwohl, Bloom, & Masia, 1964, p. 7). Thus, within the confines of a recreation context, one can assess feelings, emotion, or degree of acceptance or rejection related to a leisure construct. Examples of such instruments that assess affect as related to leisure attributes are Leisure Attitude Measure (in particular, the affective subscale), Leisure Motivation Scale, Leisure Satisfaction Scale (which examines both overall satisfaction as well as educational, social, physiological, psychological, relaxation, and aesthetic satisfaction derived from one's leisure), Leisurescope Plus (examines motivation feelings and satisfaction towards clusters of activities), and Self–Perception for Children.

Assessment Tools for Functional Abilities

Functional abilities appraisal can be undertaken in any one of five domains (see Figure 16.3). That is, individuals can be assessed regarding their cognitive, emotional, physical, psychomotor, and social functioning.

Figure 16.2: Selected assessment tools measuring leisure attributes.

I. Leisure Interests & Activity Pursuits	Felt Need		Expressed Demand		For More Information Contact:
	Individual Activity	Activity Cluster	Individual Activity	Activity Cluster	
Leisure Activities Blank (McKechnie, 1975)	X	X	X	X	Consulting Psychologists 380 3rd Ebayshore Road Palo Alto, CA 94300 (650)969-8901
Leisure Attitude Measurement (Ragheb & Beard, 1991a		X		X	Idlyll Arbor, Inc. PO Box 720 Ravensdale, WA 98051-0720 (425)432-3231
Leisure Diagnostic Battery (Witt & Ellis, 1982)		X			Venture Publishing 1990 Cato Avenue State College, PA 16801 (814)234-4561
Leisure Interest Measurement (Ragheb & Beard, 1991b)		X			Idlyll Arbor, Inc. (see above)
Leisurescope Plus (Schenk, 1998)		X	X		Idlyll Arbor, Inc. 25119 S.E. 262 Street PO Box 720 Ravensdale, WA 98051-0720 (425)432-3231
Ohio Functional Assessment Battery (Olsson, 1994)		X	X	X	Psychological Corporation 555 Academic Court San Antonio, TX 78204-2498 (800)228-0752
State Technical Institute Assessment Process (STILAP) (Navar, 1990)	X	X	X	X	Idyll Arbor, Inc. (see above)

Figure 16.2: Cont.

II. Affect	For More Information Contact:
Leisure Attitude Measurement (Ragheb & Beard, 1991a)	Idlyll Arbor, Inc. (see previous page)
Leisure Motivation Scale (Beard & Ragheb, 1990)	Idlyll Arbor, Inc. (see previous page)
Leisure Satisfaction Scale (Ragheb & Beard, 1991c)	Idlyll Arbor, Inc. (see previous page)
Leisurescope Plus Schenk, 1998)	Idyll Arbor, Inc (see previous page)
Self Perception for Children (Harter, 1982)	Susan Harter Department of Psychology University of Denver 2155 Race Street Denver, CO 80208-0201 303-556-8565

Figure 16.3: Selected assessment tools dealing with functional appraisal.

Domain	Assessment Tool	For More Information Contact:
Cognitive	Comprehensive in Evaluation Therapy (CERT)-Physical Disabilities (Parker, Ellison, Kirby, & Short, 1988)	Idyll Arbor, Inc. PO Box 720 Ravensdale, WA 98051-0720
	Comprehensive in Evaluation Therapy (CERT)-Psych Revised (Parker, 1996)	Idyll Arbor, Inc. (see above)
	General Recreation Screening Tool (burlingame & Blaschko, 1988)	Idyll Arbor, Inc. (see above)
	Ohio Functional Assessment Battery (Olsson, 1994)	Psychological Corporation 555 Academic Court San Antonio, TX 28204-2498 (800) 228-0752
Emotional	CERT-Physical Disabilities	Idyll Arbor, Inc. (see above)
	CERT-Psych Revised	Idyll Arbor, Inc. (see above)
	General Recreation Screening Tool	Idyll Arbor, Inc. (see above)
	Leisure Diagnostic Battery (Witt & Ellis, 1990)	Venture Publishing, Inc.. 1990 Cato Avenue State College, PA 16801 (814) 234-4561
Physical	CERT-Physical Disabilities	Idyll Arbor, Inc. (see above)
	Ohio Functional Assessment Battery	Idyll Arbor, Inc. (see above)
	Health/Fitness Testing (American College of Sports Medicine, 1997)	Human Kinetics Books PO Box 5076 Champaign, IL 61825-5076 (800) 747-4457

Figure 16.3: Cont.

Domain	Assessment Tool	For More Information Contact:
Psychomotor	CERT-Physical Disabilities	Idyll Arbor, Inc. (see above)
	General Recreation Screening Tool	Idyll Arbor, Inc. (see above)
Social	CERT-Psych Revised	Idyll Arbor, Inc. (see above)
	Ohio Functional Assessment Battery	Idyll Arbor, Inc. (see above)

The *cognitive domain* emphasizes thinking and deals with what people know, understand, comprehend, or express (Krathwohl, Bloom, & Masia, 1964, p. 6). The emphasis can be on assessing short– or long–term memory. For example, the individual may be asked to remember or reproduce something that has presumably been learned or experienced. Cognitive functioning can also encompass assessing orientation to reality, expressive language skills, receptive language skills, attending and concentration skills, literacy level (reading and/or writing abilities), and learning ability. At a more complex level, the individual may be asked to solve some intellectual task (for instance, a math or logic problem) for which the individual has to determine the essential problem and then reorder given material or combine it with ideas, method, or procedures previously learned. Another complex level of cognitive functioning that can be assessed deals with decision–making ability.

The Comprehensive Evaluation in Recreational Therapy (CERT)-Physical Disabilities assessment tool (see Figure 16.3) includes measures of cognition (judgment/decision–making ability, attention span, memory, orientation, feedback utilization, problem solving, directionality, right-left discrimination, form perception, and figure-ground discrimination), communication (verbal and written expressive and receptive skills), and adjustment to disability. The Comprehensive Evaluation in Recreational Therapy (CERT)-Psych Revised instrument also contains assessment of attention span and memory. The General Recreation Screening Tool assesses language use, language comprehension, numbers, object use and understanding, following directions, problem solving, and attending behavior. And the Ohio Functional Assessment tool assesses learning, retention, memory, attention span, and some communication and decision making skills.

Emotional domain encompasses a number of things, including coping style used to deal with conflict or argument situations, emotional response or expression, adoption of frustration–related behaviors, response to authority, freedom in leisure, and perceived leisure control. The CERT-Physical Disabilities assessment (see Figure 16.3) measures emotional behavior (by highlighting frustration tolerance level and display of emotions). The CERT-Psych Revised instrument also includes expression of hostility assessment. Perceived freedom in leisure is measured in the Leisure Diagnostic Battery (by summing scores on the Perceived Leisure Competence Scale, the Perceived Leisure Control Scale, the Leisure Needs Scale, the Depth of Involvement in Leisure Scale, and the Playfulness Scale). Finally, the General Recreation Screening Tool contains a section that measures emotional control.

The *physiological domain* includes an assessment of functioning in a multitude of areas related to physical health. Categories that can be assessed include: sight or vision, hearing, bowel and bladder control, upper extremity manipulation (arms, hand, and grasp), ambulation (or ability to walk), coordination and balance, hand–eye coordination, strength, endurance, and body weight. The CERT-Physical Disabilities, for example, assesses sensory abilities (including visual acuity, ocular pursuit, depth perception, extremity–tactile sensation, auditory acuity, and auditory discrimination). Another example of an instrument that assesses physical functioning is the Ohio Functional Assessment Battery (see Figure 16.3). In particular, this test assesses motor performance skills. Lastly, the American College of Sports Medicine (1997) has issued standards and guidelines for assessing health/physical fitness.

The *psychomotor domain* emphasizes physical movement and focuses on how people control or move their bodies (Krathwohl, Bloom, & Masia, 1964, p. 7). A simple psychomotor task that could be assessed is determining some muscular or gross motor skill, such as ability to throw a basketball. A more complex psychomotor skill that could be assessed would be determining ability to manipulate some material or object, such as drawing. Finally, a high–level psychomotor task ear–marked for assessment would be neuromuscular coordination, such as serving a tennis ball. The CERT-Physical Disabilities test measures gross and fine motor movement, locomotion (or movement of the body from one place to another), and motor skills (including coordination, balance, reaction time, and movement planning ability). The General Recreation Screening Tool (see Figure 16.3) includes sections that deal with assessing a variety of psychomotor functioning abilities (such as gross motor, fine motor, hand–eye coordination).

The *social domain* focuses on social interaction. Areas that can be assessed include social skills (ability to initiate and respond to conversation, eye contact, etc.) and engagement in cooperative and competitive group behaviors. Examples of functional assessments in the social domain are found in the CERT-Psych Revised test (which assesses ability to form social relationships, leadership ability, group conflict behavior, and competition in a group setting) and the Ohio Functional Assessment Battery (which assesses self–esteem and cooperation).

Assessment Tools for Specific Skills

As indicated in Figure 16.1, assessment tools dealing with specific recreation skills can fall into three areas: affect related to a specific skill, cognition related to a specific skill, and psychomotor abilities related to a specific skill.

Assessments related to affect can be modified to include a referent to a specific recreational skill. That is, an individual could be queried about his attitude or motivation derived from engagement in a specified recreational skill activity. For example, during the first swim class, participants can be asked about their feelings related to swimming (such as attitude about the value of swimming or motivation for learning swimming).

Assessments have also evolved to measure knowledge about and/or proficiency in specific skills directly related to leisure pursuits (Figure 16.4). Perhaps the most popular proficiency skill assessments are the swimming competency tests of the American Red Cross, YMCA, and YWCA. These assessments can measure both cognitive (paper and pencil tests) and psychomotor (e.g., in water rescue) abilities. Additionally, the Coast Guard and American Red Cross have developed tests to assess boat (canoes, sailboats, motorboats, etc.) skill competency; whereas three organizations [Professional Association of Diver Instruction (PADI), Scuba Schools of Instruction (SSI), and the National Association of Underwater Instruction (NAUI)] have developed assessments for scuba diving.

At least three instruments exist that provide competency assessment of activity clusters. Again, an activity cluster is a grouping of activities that share some similar characteristic or denominator. For example, the Leisure Diagnostic Battery's Perceived Leisure Competency Scale A inquires about leisure competency in four areas of activities, or cognitive, physical, social, and in general (see Figure 16.4). The Perceived Competence Scale for Children examines competence in athletic and cognitive activities, and the STILAP also investigates an individual's competencies in physical, mental, and leadership and interpersonal skill activities.

Lastly, another approach to skill assessment has been to focus on daily living skills that can affect recreational participation. The Bus Utilization Skills Assessment, for example, measures functional skills and maladaptive behaviors that can be associated with using public transportation (see Figure 16.4). The Community Integration Program protocol measures a variety of skills (knowing how to travel, shop, use a bank, etc.).Likewise, the Ohio Functional Assessment Battery assesses money management skills.

Figure 16.4: Selected assessment tools measuring skills in individual activities, activity clusters, and supporting daily living activities.

I. **Skills in Individual Activities**	**For More Information Contact:**
Boating	Coast Guard
	Consult Yellow Pages or Phone
	(800)368-5647
Scuba	Professional Association of
	Diver Instruction (PADI)
	Consult Yellow Pages
	Scuba Schools Instruction (SSI)
	Consult Yellow Pages
	National Association of
	Underwater Instruction (NAUI)
	Consult Yellow Pages
Swimming	American Red Cross
	Consult Yellow Pages
II. **Skills in Activity Clusters**	
Leisure Diagnostic Battery	Venture Publishing, Inc.
(Witt & Ellis, 1990)	1999 Cato Ave
	State College, PA 16801
	(814)234-4561
Perceived Competence Scale	Susan Harter
(Harter, 1982)	Department of Psychology
	University of Denver
	2155 Race Street
	Denver, CO 80208-0204
State Technical Institute	Idyll Arbor, Inc.
Assessment Process (STILAP)	P.O. Box 720
(Navar, 1990)	Ravensdale, WA 98051-0720
	(425)432-3231

Figure 16.4: Cont.

III. Supporting Daily Living Activities

Bus Utilization Skills Assessment (burlingame & Peterson, 1997)	Idyll Arbor, Inc. (see above)
Community Integration Program Protocols (Armstrong & Lauzen, 1994)	Idyll Arbor, Inc. (see above)
Ohio Functional Assessment Battery (Olsson, 1994)	Psychological Corporation (see above)

Main Points

- Assessment is inextricably linked to program evaluation. Many programs are evaluated in terms of their effects on program participants. This typically means participants are individually assessed twice during their affiliation with a program.

- The assessment process consists of seven steps: (a) ascertaining program purpose(s), (b) specifying content area(s) for the assessment, (c) identifying instrument selection criteria, (d) reviewing available assessment instruments; (e) comparing available instruments with selection criteria, (f) selecting an assessment instrument, and (g) using the selected instrument to collect information.

- Assessment tools generally fall into one of three categories, or those that measure leisure attributes, functional appraisal, and specific skills. An educational domain classification system can be interwoven across these three categories so that the foci of assessment also become a matter of deciding on whether to examine affective, cognitive, emotional, physiological, psychomotor, or social domains.

Study Questions

1. Explain how assessment is related to program evaluation.

2. List the seven steps related to the assessment process.

3. Identify criteria that can be used in choosing an instrument for assessment.

4. What are the two ways assessment tools can be classified?

References

American College of Sports Medicine. (1997). Health/fitness facility standards and guidelines. Champaign, IL: Human Kinetics Books.

Armstrong, M., & Lauzen, S. (1994). *Community integration program*. Ravensdale, WA: Idyll Arbor, Inc.

Beard, J., & Ragheb, M. (1990). Measuring leisure motivation. Journal of Leisure Research, 15, 219-228.

burlingame, j. (1988). *General recretion screening tool*. Ravensdale, WA: Idyll Arbor, Inc.

burlingame, j., & Blaschko, T. (1997). *Assessment tools for recreational therapy* (2nd ed.). Ravensdale, WA: Idyll Arbor, Inc.

burlingame, j., & Peterson, J. (1997). Bus utilization skills assessment. In j. burlingame & T. Blaschko, *Assessment tools for recreational therapy* (2nd ed). (pp. 223-230). Ravensdale, WA: Idyll Arbor, Inc.

Dunn, D. (1984). Assessment. In C. Peterson & S. Gunn, *Therapeutic recreation program design: Principles and procedures* (2nd ed.) (pp. 267-320). Englewood Cliffs, NJ: Prentice Hall, Inc.

Harter, S. (1982). The perceived competence scale for children. *Child Development, 53*, 87-97.

Howe, C. (1984). Leisure assessment and counseling. In E.T. Dowd, *Leisure counseling: Concepts and applications* (pp.234-253). Springfield, IL: Charles C. Thomas Publishers.

Krathwohl,, D., Bloom, B., & Masia, B. (1964). *Taxonomy of educational objectives, handbook II: Affective domain*. New York: David McKay.

McKechnie, G. (1975). *Manual for leisure activities blank*. Palo Alto, CA: Consulting Psychologists Press.

Navar, N. (1990). *State technical institute leisure activities project*. Ravensdale, WA: Idyll Arbor, Inc..

Olsson, R. (1994). *Ohio functional assessment battery*. Tucson, AZ: Therapy Skill Builders.

Parker, R. (1988). *Comprehensive in evaluation therapy (CERT): Physical disabilities*. Ravensdale, WA: Idyll Arbor, Inc.

Parker, R. (1996). *Comprehensive in evaluation therapy (CERT): Psych revised*. Ravensdale, WA: Idyll Arbor, Inc.

Ragheb, M., & Beard, J. (1991a). *Leisure attitude measurement*. Ravensdale, WA: Idyll Arbor, Inc.

Ragheb, M., & Beard, J. (1991b). *Leisure interest measure*. Ravensdale, WA: Idyll Arbor, Inc.

Ragheb, M., & Beard, J. (1991c). *Leisure satisfaction measure*. Ravensdale, WA: Idyll Arbor, Inc.

Schenk, C. (1998). *Leisurescope plus*. Tallahassee, FL: Leisure Dynamics.

Scriven, M. (1991). *Evaluation thesaurus* (4th ed.). Newbury Park, CA: Sage Publications.

Stumbo, N. (1992). *Leisure education II: More activities and resources*. State College, PA: Venture Publishing.

Witt, P., & Ellis, G. (1990). *Leisure diagnostic battery*. State College, PA: Venture Publishing.

CHAPTER 17

Personnel Performance Appraisal

What Will I Learn in This Chapter?
I'll be able to:

1. Define personnel performance appraisal.

2. Identify reasons for evaluating personnel.

3. Define the management by objectives (MBO) approach to performance appraisal.

4. Describe the techniques that can be used in applying standards to assessing performance.

5. Recall the major problem associated with using a comparison between individuals as the approach to conducting a performance appraisal.

6. List guidelines for minimizing the chance that disputes will emerge from the performance appraisal system adopted by an organization.

7. Explain the kinds of errors (halo error, leniency error, severity error, and central tendency error) that can be made in performance appraisals.

Park, recreation, and sports management organizations consist of people. Though various kinds of people work in the organization—professionals, staff, volunteers—the backbone of operations are all personnel. When these human resources become the foci of evaluation, this is technically known as performance appraisal.

In order to address the topic of performance appraisal, this chapter has been divided into six sections. That is, the remainder of this chapter addresses: What is performance appraisal and why do it; What to assess; How to measure performance; Who should do the appraisal and when; How to communicate performance appraisal results and employee development plan; and Examination of the organization's performance appraisal system.

What is Performance Appraisal and Why Do It

Performance appraisal is measuring the extent that an employee or volunteer is able to perform his/her work. Performance information can serve three general purposes. The first purpose is to provide feedback about the worker's strengths and weaknesses. The second reason for doing performance appraisals is to support a worker reward system. That is, performance appraisal results are used as a means for allocating rewards (e.g., merit increases) to workers who perform their work well. A third reason is to document reasons for certain personnel actions, such as promotion or firing.

While most organizations understand the value of performance appraisal, there are a few critics. One pundit described it as one of the seven deadly diseases afflicting American management practice (Milkovich & Boudreau, 1997, p. 100)! Despite the costs and conflicts associated with conducting performance appraisals, most managers believe performance appraisal is a valuable endeavor.

Differences in individual performance can have a huge impact on the organization's ability to achieve its purpose. The skills, abilities, traits, and behaviors the worker brings or does not bring to the job can have profound effects on the quantity, quality, and efficiency of services delivered (Chapter 15). Hunter, Schmidt, and Judiesch (1990), for example, estimated the difference between high performers and average performers in an array of jobs. The results were astonishing. High performers outperformed average performers for: Routine blue-collar work, by 15% (represented in the parks and recreation field, for example, by maintenance workers who are not supervisors); Crafts work, by 25%; Routine clerical work, by 17%; Clerical decision making, by 28%; and Professionals, by 46%. This study suggests then that "high" performing recreation professionals accomplish about 50% more work than their "average" counterparts.

What Performance to Assess

As true with conducting program evaluation, many things could be measured in a performance review. For instance, the state of New Mexico's performance appraisal system evolves around assessing competencies (or how the employee does the job) and job assignments (or tasks performed in the position). When it comes down to it several things can be appraised regarding the worker or their skills, abilities, traits, behaviors, and/or results (Figure 17.1). Human resource experts suggest that multiple performance measures be used (Milkovich & Boudreau 1997).

A profile of how performance is appraised in leisure service organizations on a national level is unknown. At least one study exists, however, that reveals criteria typically used to measure performance of managerial or supervisory workers (figure 17.2).

Figure 17.1: Examples of performance criteria.[1]

Skills/Abilities/Traits	Behaviors	Results
Adaptability	Attendance	Accident rate
Certification	Customer service orientation	Customers served
Communication abilities	Drug abstinence	Customer satisfaction
Conceptual thinking	Follows rules/adherence to	Production levels
Creativity	policy	Production quality
Customer service	Maintains equipment	Sales
Dependability	Maintains records	
Desire to achieve	Obeys instructions	
Eye-hand coordination	Performs tasks	
Honesty	Productivity	
Initiative	Reports problems	
Interpersonal Skills	Submits suggestions	
Job knowledge	Theft	
Judgement		
Leadership		
Licenses		
Loyalty		
Orientation		
Problem-solving ability		
Quality		
Reliability		
Self control/stress resistance		
Teamwork		

[1]Adapted from *Human Resource Management* (p. 104), by G. Milkovich & J. Boudreau, 1997, Chicago: Irwin; and *Performance Appraisal and Development: User's Manual* (pp. 17-19), by New Mexico State Personnel Board, undated, Albuquerque, NM: New Mexico State Personnel Board.

Figure 17.2: Performance areas commonly appraised of managers/supervisors.[2]

Criteria	% of Firms That Used Criteria
Quality of work	93%
Quantity of work	90%
Initiative	87%
Cooperation	87%
Dependability	86%
Job knowledge	85%
Attendance	79%
Need for supervision	67%

[2]From "Performance Appraisal Programs," by the Bureau of Natural Affairs (1983, February), *Personnel Policies Forum.*

Related to criteria that can be used for an employee performance appraisal are behaviors that relate to organization citizenship. *Organization citizenship* are those helpful and cooperative behaviors that are considered "extra" in the sense they go beyond the specific tasks associated with a job. Examples of such behaviors include: helping others, sharing or creating new ideas, and defending and promoting the organization's goals.

Regardless of what performance criteria are selected, the measures that are chosen as the basis for the performance appraisal should have four characteristics. These characteristics—being goal related, observable, understandable, and controllable—are described below.

1. Goal related. The performance measure selected for a worker should relate to deciding the goal or purpose behind the appraisal. The key question that must be answered is "Who will be using the appraisal information and what do they do with it?" If the appraisal is used to assign workers to training, then focusing on individual characteristics (such as knowledge) may be the most appropriate criteria to select. If appraisal information will be used to allocate rewards, then the most valuable performance measures might focus on results (see Figure 17.1). And if the information gleaned from an appraisal is going to be used to support a termination, then the most valuable performance measures might be counterproductive behaviors, avoidable accidents, or injuries due to the worker's (in)actions, drug use, or theft.

2. Observable. Employment laws as well as common sense dictate that selected performance criteria be those that are objective, observable, and measurable. Again, current human resource management advice is not to examine just traits, but also to emphasize behaviors and outcomes or results. If one desired to emulate corporate America, then personnel performance in leisure service settings would be approached from the perspective of "What did the employee actually do this year to make a big difference in our organization?" rather than deciding on whether the worker was a nice person!

3. Understandable. The person(s) doing the performance appraisal as well as the employee need to understand what exactly is being evaluated. Exactly what is being assessed and how it is being assessed must be clear to all parties concerned. As Milkovich and Boudreau (1997, p. 105) report, the more employees feel they understand the appraisal system, the more likely they are to agree with their supervisor's ratings.

4. Controllable. Performance measures that the employee can control should be selected. For instance, using a customer satisfaction survey as the sole performance indicator for the park district's head maintenance engineer does not make a lot of sense. This kind of approach is more appropriate to use for recreation center staff who come into direct contact with park users. If measures are chosen that the worker has little control over, the receptivity of the worker to the performance appraisal is going to be diminished.

Figure 17.3: Performance assessment comparisons.[3]

Comparison to Agreed Objectives	Comparison to Job Standards	Comparison Between Individuals
Management by objectives (MBO)	Physical observation Checklists Rating scales Critical incidents Behaviorally-anchored rating scale (BARS) Essays/diaries 360-degree appraisal	Ranking Forced distribution

[3]From *Human Resource Management* (p. 107), by G. Milkovich & J. Boudreau, 1997, Chicago: Irwin.

How to Measure Performance

There are two major decisions that must be made when conducting a performance appraisal. The first, already addressed above, is what to measure. The second major question is deciding how. Basically there are three ways to do the appraisal or to compare the worker's performance to: mutually agreed-upon objectives, standards, or other individuals (Figure 17.3).

Management by Objectives (MBO)

In MBO, the rater and the person being appraised set objectives to achieve by a certain date. Whatever is agreed upon is then cast into a written contract.

Figure 17.4 presents how an MBO approach is used by the Boulder Parks and Recreation Department. In this organization, objectives are tied to key responsibilities contained in the employee's job description. After six months, the employee is evaluated in terms of where she is relative to attainment of her job-related objectives. At this six-month juncture, the employee is asked to perform a self-appraisal and identify ways to improve herself, objectives are restated or modified, and a development plan is drafted for attaining the stated objectives (Figure 17.5). Then annually, the employee is again re-evaluated and provided an opportunity to conduct their own self appraisal (Figure 17.6).

As mentioned in Chapter 15, objectives should identify behaviors that are observable and measurable. A mnemonic device that managers are using to assist them are to remember to write SMART objectives (Milkovich & Boudreau, 1997, p. 106):

> Specific results are obtained.
>
> Measurable in quantity, quality, and/or impact.
>
> Attainable, challenging yet within view.
>
> Relevant to the work unit, organization, and career.
>
> Time specific, with deadlines to expect a result.

Comparison of Performance to Standards

Another way to approach a performance appraisal is to compare the worker to standards that describe desirable (or undesirable) performance. Five techniques are popular for doing this or the use of: checklists, rating scales, critical incidents, behaviorally-anchored rating scales, and essays/diaries.

1. Checklists. A checklist contains a series or set of adjectives, descriptive statements, or behaviors (Figure 17.7). The rater reviews each item and decides if the statement describes the worker's performance (if so, the rater checks the item); and if not, the rater leaves it blank. Each statement is scored to reflect its positive or negative impact on job performance. Sometimes a final performance rating is calculated by summing the scores for the items checked.

Figure 17.4: An example of management by objectives approach to performance appraisal.[4]

Employee:

Position/Job Title:

Evaluation Period Beginning/Ending:

Employee's Supervisor:

Key Responsibilities (from job description)	Relative Importance (% of time or effort required)
Total (must equal 100%)	

Key Performance Factors:

(For accomplishing key responsibilities, objectives are decided upon by the supervisor and employee at the initial evaluation planning meeting.)

-
-

[4]From "Performance Evaluation Plan," January, 1997, *City of Boulder Supervisor's Reference Manual*, p. 33, Boulder, CO. Adapted with permission from Boulder City Manager.

Figure 17.5: Semiannual employee self-appraisal and planning worksheet.[5]

Employee:
Position/Job Title:
Evaluation Period Beginning/Ending:
Employee's Supervisor:

Employee Planning and Appraisal Comments

This worksheet is to be completed in preparation for your semiannual performance evaluation and review. It will provide a basis for discussion in regard to your past work performance, current job expectations, goals, and future assignments. Please complete the worksheet and return it to your supervisor prior to your semiannual evaluation.

What have you learned since your last appraisal?

What aspects of your work and overall performance are the strongest?

What difficulties have you encountered in performing your job duties?

What do you want to learn during the next six months?

How can your supervisor assist you in meeting these goals?

List any ideas you have for improving the effectiveness of your position or your department?

What have you done since your last appraisal to improve yourself/you skills?

Describe ways you have reflected the SPIRIT of Boulder.

[5]Adapted from "Performance Evaluation Plan," January, 1997, *City of Boulder Supervisor's Reference Manual*, p. 63, Boulder, CO: Boulder City. Adapted with permission from Boulder City Manager.

Figure 17.6: Annual employee self-appraisal and planning worksheet.[6]

Employee:
Position/Job Title:
Evaluation Period Beginning/Ending:
Employee's Supervisor:

1. What were your major accomplishments during the past 12 months?

2. What was your biggest learning experience and how has it impacted you, or changed the way you approach your work?

3. What area of professional development are you concentrating on at this time?

4. What assistance do you need, and from whom (me, as your supervisor, co-workers, etc.), in order to continue working on this professional development area?

5. What are the major goals for the next six months and the next 12 months?

6. What are the most significant issues that must be addressed in order to accomplish these goals?

7. How do these goals address the "challenges" previously identified by me, your supervisor? Please list below.

8. What do you want my role, as your supervisor, to be in helping you achieve those goals?

9. How would you like your work to be acknowledged or appreciated by me, your supervisor? Your co-workers? Other members of the organization?

[6]From City of Boulder Parks and Recreation Department files, undated, Boulder, CO: City of Boulder. Adapted with permission from Boulder City Manager.

Figure 17.7: Example of a checklist.[7]

Work Performance Skills

Place Check in Column if
Statement Describes Employee

1. Prompt in meeting deadlines for newsletters, monthly reports, trip sign-up sheets, etc. _____

2. Keeps Cluster Director informed of what is going on, problems, etc. _____

3. Able to interpret and communicate Senior Adult Program policies, directions, and instructions to seniors _____

4. Shows initiative in using and carrying out program-planning skills _____

5. Demonstrates knowledge and use of existing resources _____

6. Demonstrates constructive use of time _____

7. Possesses rapport with the public, Recreation Department staff, and other agencies _____

8. Responsive to questions and needs of seniors _____

9. Able to be flexible _____

10. Able to improvise and remain calm as problems arise _____

11. Uses good judgement _____

Supervisor's Comments (if any):

Employee's Comments (if any):

Supervisor's Signature _____ Date _____

Employee's Signature _____ Date _____

[7]Adapted from "Montgomery County Department of Recreation Senior Adult Programs Club/Center Coordinator" form, undated, Rockville, MD: Montgomery County Recreation Department.

Figure 17.8: Example of a graphic rating scale.[8]

1. DOES NOT MEET EXPECTATIONS
Performance is considerably less than quality/quantity of work expected of this position. Needs extensive improvement in one or more aspects. Requires a great degree of supervision. Performance is unsatisfactory.

2. MEETS EXPECTATIONS
Performance meets or occasionally exceeds the quality and/or quantity of work expected of this position. Performs job duties under general supervision. Understand and follows direction when direct supervision is needed. Responds positively to feedback and utilizes it to improve performance.

3. EXCEEDS EXPECTATIONS
Performance is consistently exceptional. Performs all tasks in an outstanding manner with minimal supervision.

1. CUSTOMER/PUBLIC RELATIONS
This factor concerns all employees' general day-to-day relations with the public served by the City of Boulder. It involves greeting the public, dealing with their problems/concerns, telephone procedures, personal presentation and appearance, peer relations, and maintenance of composure in difficult situations.

_____ Does not meet expectations   _____ Meets expectations   _____ Exceeds expectations.

COMMENTS:

2. DIRECTLY SUPERVISING EMPLOYEES
This factor involves the direct supervision of co-workers, seasonals, volunteers and interns. When acting in a supervisory capacity, understands and organizes information needed by subordinates, communicates this information clearly. Effectively plans and coordinates activity of others on a day-to-day basis, even in difficult situations. Accurately evaluates the performance of others and effectively assists/guides others to perform to their highest standard and meet the expectations of the department.

_____ Does not meet expectations   _____ Meets expectations   _____ Exceeds expectations.

COMMENTS:

Figure 17.8: Cont.[8]

3. COMMUNICATION SKILLS

When communicating judgments, information, and decisions, is able to influence the actions of other. Can exercise good judgement and implements decisions by accepting and utilizing feedback. Is flexible and adjusts position based on feedback. Consistently acknowledges through performance the importance of being an attentive listener. Continually strives to improve the team concept through good communications efforts.

_____ Does not meet expectations   _____ Meets expectations   _____ Exceeds expectations

COMMENTS:

4. PROFESSIONAL ORIENTATION

Can work under pressure with minimal supervision. Recognizes and responds to relationships between own job and overall organizational objective. Utilizes available resources and researched current job-related information. Consistently represents the City and our natural resource policies and programs with a high standard of professionalism.

_____ Does not meet expectations   _____ Meets expectations   _____ Exceeds expectations.

COMMENTS:

5. RESPONSIBILITY FOR SAFETY OF SELF AND OTHERS

When performing routine job duties, effectively evaluates situations and takes appropriate safety precautions. Anticipates unsafe situations and acts accordingly. Assumes responsibility for safety of self and others. Consistently communicates issues of safety with co-workers.

_____ Does not meet expectations   _____ Meets expectations   _____ Exceeds expectations.

COMMENTS:

6. EXCHANGING COMPLEX, NON-ROUTINE INFORMATION

If required by Administration, Council or Boards, can communicate complex information to diverse groups or individuals; can modify the presentation of this information to ensure the effectiveness of the information exchanges. Can effectively communicate to outside agencies/resources, complex, non-routine information during critical incidents.

_____ Does not meet expectations   _____ Meets expectations   _____ Exceeds expectations.

COMMENTS:

7. ADDITIONAL FACTOR(S)

(write here)

_____ Does not meet expectations   _____ Meets expectations   _____ Exceeds expectations

COMMENTS:

Job knowledge, skills, and behavior
Areas of strength:

Recommended improvement areas:

Plan for improvement:

Overall evaluation (please write "needs improvement", " meets expectations", or "exceeds expectations"):

Employee comments:

My signature indicates that I have reviewed this evaluation and discussed it with my supervisor.

_____   _____
Employee   Date

_____   _____   _____
Supervisor Conducting Interview   Date   Next level management

[8]From "Mountain Parks Performance and Appraisal Plan," January, 1997, *City of Boulder Supervisor's Reference Manual*, p. 59. Boulder, CO: City of Boulder. Adapted with permission from Boulder City Manager.

2. Rating scales. Rating scales have been around a long time and are widely used. The idea behind the rating scale is to identify job performance criteria and for each the evaluator rates (usually using a continuum either ranging from "Unsatisfactory" to "Outstanding" or "Does Not Meet Expectations" to "Exceeds Expectations") the individual. Each criterion identified can have equal weighting or be weighted more heavily or lightly. When the rating scale appears as a graph, line, or series of boxes along which performance levels are marked, this is known as a *graphic rating scale* (see Figure 17.8).

3. Critical incidents. *Critical incidents* are statements describing effective as well as very ineffective behaviors deemed critical to performance. Critical incidents can be combined with most of the other performance appraisal techniques, the most common being behaviorally-anchored rating scales (which will be reviewed next).

4. Behaviorally-anchored rating scales (BARS). *BARS* use a rating scale along with critical incidents that act as anchors for different points in the scale. The anchors that are used are supposed to be job specific and relate to a performance dimension. The evaluator reads each critical statement and rates the worker accordingly (Figure 17.9).

5. Essays/diaries. Evaluators can describe strong and weak aspects of the worker's behavior over time by composing an essay(s). In writing the essay the evaluator can consult a diary that has been maintained to record observed critical incidents of either a positive or negative nature. Essays also can be used in tandem with rating scales or BARS in order to document and elaborate upon the performance rating.

Comparison of Performance Among Individuals

Organizations turn to this kind of performance appraisal when decisions must be made regarding allocation of rewards. Who, for example, from a pool of 10 has earned the right to attend a professional conference in a warm location in the middle of a frigid winter?

Typically alternation ranking is used to make this comparison. With *alternation ranking,* the evaluator first determines who is the highest performer then who is the lowest performer; then who is the second-highest and the second-lowest, and so on and so forth.

With small numbers, ranking can be fast and easy to understand. With large numbers of people to rank it becomes complicated. Perhaps the biggest criticism comparing the performances among individuals is that it fosters rivalry and discourages teamwork (Milkovich & Boudreau, 1997, p. 111).

Which Technique to Use

Which approach is best to use is situational (Figure 17.10). Factors to consider include characteristics of the environment the worker is expected to perform in (is it a stable situation or an unstable and stressful environment?), purpose(s) behind the appraisal (e.g., feedback, allocating rewards), costs related to development and implementation of the appraisal, margin of

Figure 17.9: Behaviorally-anchored rating scale (BARS) for a teen club leader.

Performance Dimension:

Concern for individual group members: attempts to get to know individual and responds to their individual needs with genuine interest.

This teen club leader (fill in name) _____ :

Rating Scale: Circle description that best describes employee.

Good (1)	(2)	(3)	(4)	Poor (5)
Recognizes when a member appears upset and asks if person has a problem (s)he wants to discuss.	Offer educational materials/ information/skills training regarding constructive use of leisure time.	Sees a person and recognizes him/her as a group member and says "Hi."	Fails to follow up with teen members.	Criticizes a teen club member for not being able to solve his/her own problems.

Figure 17.10: Evaluations of performance assessment techniques.[9]

Technique	Providing Feedback and Counseling	Allocating Rewards and Opportunities	Minimizing Costs	Avoiding Rating Errors
Management by objectives (MBO)	*Excellent:* Specific problems, deficiencies, and plans are identified.	*Poor:* Nonstandard objectives across employees and units make comparisons difficult.	*Poor:* Expensive to develop. Time consuming to use.	*Good:* Tied to observations, reflects job content, low errors.
Checklist	*Average:* General problems identified, but little specific guidance for improvement.	*Good-Average:* Comparative scores available, and dimensions can be weighed.	*Average:* Expensive development, but inexpensive to use.	*Good:* Techniques available to increase job-relatedness and reduce errors.
Graphic rating scale	*Average:* Identifies problem areas, and some information on behaviors/outcomes needing improvement.	*Average:* Comparative scores available but not easily documented and defended.	*Good:* Inexpensive to develop and use.	*Average:* Substantial opportunity for errors, though they can be linked to specific dimensions.
Behaviorally-anchored rating scales (BARS)	*Good:* Identifies specific behaviors leading to problems.	*Good:* Scores available, documented, and behavior-based.	*Average:* Expensive development, but inexpensive to use.	*Good:* Based on job behaviors, can reduce errors.
Essay	*Unknown:* Depends on essay topics chosen by evaluators.	*Poor:* No overall score available, not comparable across employees.	*Average:* Inexpensive development, but expensive to use.	*Unknown:* Good observation can reduce errors, but lack of structure poses danger.
Comparing individuals (ranking, forced distribution)	*Poor:* Based on general factors, with few specifics.	*Poor-Average:* Overall score available, but difficult to defend.	*Good:* Inexpensive to develop and to use.	*Average:* Usually consistent, but subject to halo error and artificiality.
360-degree appraisal	*Average:* General problems identified, but little specific guidance for improvement.	*Poor:* Non-standard objectives across employees and units make comparisons difficult.	*Poor:* Expensive to develop. Time-consuming to use.	*Good:* Tied to observations, reflects job content, low errors.

[9]From *Human Resource Management* (p. 120), by G. Milkovich & J. Boudreau, 1997, Chicago: Irwin.

rating error the organization adopts, etc. Generally speaking, a mix of different methods will assist the organization in getting a more complete picture of the worker under scrutiny.

Who Should Do the Appraisal and When

Other issues that should be considered with performance appraisal are who should judge performance and when. Generally one person, usually the worker's immediate supervisor, judges performance. Counter to common practice, human resource management experts point out that subordinates and peers can provide more information than supervisors because they have regular opportunities to observe different behaviors in their colleagues relative to what a supervisor sees (Milkovich & Boudreau, 1997, p. 106). Related, when it comes to evaluating supervisors, more progressive organizations rely on subordinates' evaluation of their boss (Milkovich & Boudreau, 1997, p. 114). The boss summarizes the anonymous reports and then meets with subordinates to discuss how (s)he plans to improve.

Figure 17.11: 360-degree performance feedback.[10]

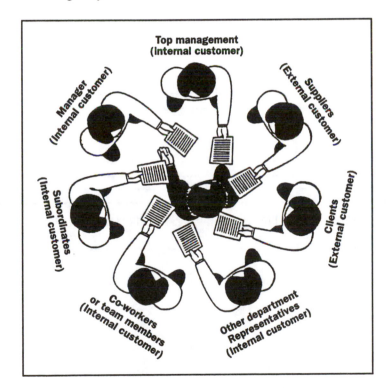

[10]From "Companies Evaluate Employees from All Perspectives" by J. Millman, R. Zawacki, C. Norman, L. Powell, & J. Kirksey, (1994, November), used with permission of ACC Communications, Inc./*Personnel Journal*, (now known as *Work Force*), Costa Mesa, CA., p. 100. All rights reserved.

Figure 17.12: Example of how competency can be evaluated using a 360-degree appraisal.[11]

Weighting percentage   Supervisor: 70%   Employee: 20%   Peer: 5%   Customer: 5%

Competency #1: Customer Service
Examples/Definition _____
_____
_____

Competency #2: Team Work
Examples/Definition _____
_____
_____

Competency #3: Specify_____
Examples/Definition _____
_____
_____

Competency #4: Specify_____
Examples/Definition _____
_____
_____

Competency #5: Specify_____
Examples/Definition _____
_____
_____

Competency #6: Specify_____
Examples/Definition _____
_____
_____

PEER IDENTIFICATION	CUSTOMER IDENTIFICATION
_____	_____
_____	_____
THE ABOVE METHODS AND POSITIONS/INDIVIDUALS HAVE BEEN IDENTIFIED FOR THE PEER(S) PORTION OF THIS APPRAISAL.	THE ABOVE METHODS AND POSITIONS/INDIVIDUALS HAVE BEEN IDENTIFIED FOR THE PEER(S) PORTION OF THIS APPRAISAL.
EMPLOYEE SIGNATURE	EMPLOYEE SIGNATURE
SUPERVISOR SIGNATURE	SUPERVISOR SIGNATURE

[11]Adapted from *Performance Appraisal and Development: User's Manual* (p. 53), by New Mexico State Personnel Board, undated, Albuquerque, NM: New Mexico State Personnel Board.

A relatively new approach to identifying the persons who should be involved in appraisal has been dubbed the "360-Degree Appraisal (Milkovich & Boudreau, 1997, p. 112)." The *360- degree appraisal* requires that a number of persons, representing different perspectives (e.g., management, co-workers, subordinates, clients) fill out anonymous questionnaires dealing with an appraisal of the worker (Figure 17.11). The worker also completes a questionnaire evaluating him/herself. Results are shared with the worker by their supervisor or a member of the human resources department of the organization. The 360-degree appraisal can be implemented in such a way that the employee's performance is compared to some pre-designated standard. Employees of the state of New Mexico's Department of Energy, Minerals, and Natural Resources can elect, in their first year of employment, to have results from 360-degree assessment recorded in their formal appraisal (Figure 17.12).

Regarding the question of when to assess performance, common practice is that quarterly appraisals are done over a year's period for probationary employees and for an employee promoted to a new position. Then employees are appraised once a year (usually on the anniversary date the individual began working, began working in the new position, or at the same time for a group of individuals with the same job title). Nevertheless, human resource management experts are now suggesting that the best timing for performance appraisals is at the end of an important task or project or when key tasks are supposed to have been completed (Milkovich & Boudreau, 1997, p. 116).

How to Communicate Performance Appraisal Results and Employee Development Plan

A study by Yukl and Tracey (1992, p. 526) revealed that the strategies used by managers to communicate performance appraisal results are a decisive factor in motivating individuals to change their performance (Figure 17.13). The employee's group affiliation (subordinate, peer, or superior) determines which strategies are effective and which are ineffective. Lessons that have been learned are:

- Subordinates were more likely to increase their commitment to a task if inspirational appeal, rational persuasion,and consultation were used, whereas pressure had a negative effect;
- Peers were more likely to increase task commitment if inspirational appeal, consultation, rational persuasion and exchange were used; while coalition and legitimating had negative effects;
- Superiors' increased task commitment was more likely to happen when rational persuasion and inspirational appeal were used.

Tied to sharing performance appraisal results is identifying an employee development plan. An in-depth development plan should especially be written for any employee receiving a "Needs Improvement" or "Unsatisfactory-Unacceptable" rating on a performance appraisal.

Figure 17.13: Strategies to influence employees to improve their performance.[12]

Tactic	Definition
Rational persuasion	Using logical arguments and factual evidence to persuade the person that a proposal is likely to attain task objectives.
Inspirational appeal	Making a request that arouses enthusiasm by appealing to the person's values, ideas, and aspirations or by increasing the person's self-confidence.
Consultation	Seeking the person's participation in planning a strategy, activity, or change; or offering to modify a proposal to deal with that person's concerns and suggestions.
Ingratiation	Trying to get the person in a good mood or to think favorably of the influencer before asking to do something.
Exchange	Offering an exchanged of favors, indicating willingness to reciprocate at a later time, or promising to share the benefits if the person helps accomplish a task.
Personal appeal	Appealing to feelings of loyalty and friendship before asking the person to do something.
Coalition	Seeking the aid of others to persuade the person to do something or using the support of others as a reason for the person to agree or comply with the request.
Legitimacy	Claiming the authority or right to make a request because it is consistent with organization policies, rules, practices, or traditions.
Pressure	Using demand, threats, or persistent reminders to get a person to do something.

[12]From "Consequences of Influence Tactics Used With Subordinates, Peers, and the Boss" by G. Yukl & J. Tracey, 1992, *Journal of Applied Psychology*, p. 526. Copyright © 1992 by the American Psychological Association. Adapted with permission.

The *development plan* addresses the steps the employee needs to take to achieve a satisfactory rating or evaluation and/or meet goals set for him/herself. A development plan benefits all employees as well as the organization itself. If the employee fails to comply with the development plan and continues to receive unacceptable evaluations, the record of non- compliance can become the basis for disciplinary action or firing.

The city of Boulder (Figures 17.5-17.6) and the state of New Mexico (Figure 17.14) have developed excellent development plan forms. New Mexico's emphasis is on short-term goals (focusing on the job the employee is currently being paid to perform) and long-term goals (focusing on new skills needed for promotions). New Mexico's process continues by identifying: what knowledge, skills, and abilities are necessary for the attainment of each goal; what resources are available for the employee to obtain the desired knowledge, skills, and/or abilities; and actions the supervisor and employee can take to support attainment of articulated goals.

Examining the Organization's Performance Appraisal System

Maximizing Success

The performance appraisal system in place for an organization can be examined from a number of vantage points. A few of these areas will be discussed below: maximizing success, guidelines for averting disagreements, evaluator training, and organizational decisions.

Milkovich and Boudreau (1997, p. 115) state that the success of an organization's performance assessment system will hinge on three factors:

•**Employees accept the performance appraisal system.** This acceptance will avert disagreements from popping up. Acceptance is more likely when explicit expectations are in place. The worker needs to know precisely what (s)he are being evaluated on and how, and (s)he is agreeable to the performance appraisal plan. Furthermore, acceptance is more likely to occur when the worker has participated in the process (for example, collaborated on the development of MBO).

•**Employees have a sense of being treated fairly.** This encompasses adopting fair performance criteria and assuring the evaluator will do the appraisal without error or bias. There must be a trust between raters and those being rated.

•**A formal system is in place to arbitrate the process and/or findings.** Hopefully, good criteria and a fair evaluator(s) are used. In the event they are not and questionable results ensue, then a process for disputing the results must be in place.

Figure 17.14: Employee development plan.[13]

JOB TITLE:
EMPLOYEE'S SHORT-TERM GOALS:
EMPLOYEE'S LONG-TERM GOALS:
KNOWLEDGE, SKILLS, AND ABILITIES NECESSARY FOR SHORT-TERM GOALS Knowledge: Skills: Ability:
KNOWLEDGE, SKILLS, AND ABILITIES NECESSARY FOR LONG-TERM GOALS Knowledge: Skills: Ability:
SOURCES FOR TRAINING AND EDUCATION: CLASSROOM: ON-THE-JOB TRAINING: NEW/TEMPORARY JOB ASSIGNMENTS:
ACTIONS TO BE TAKEN BY SUPERVISOR IN SUPPORT OF EMPLOYEE DEVELOPMENT:
ACTIONS TO BE TAKEN BY THE EMPLOYEE IN SUPPORT OF EMPLOYEE'S DEVELOPMENT

[13]From *Performance Appraisal and Development: User's Manual* (p. 48), by New Mexico State Personnel Board, undated, Albuquerque, NM: New Mexico State Personnel Board.

Guidelines for Averting Disagreements

Guidelines for averting performance appraisal-related disagreements, based on a review of court cases (adapted from Milkovich & Boudreau 1997, p. 122), are:

1. Performance appraisals should be based on a job analysis [see Teague (1980) for some advice on how to write dynamic job descriptions].
2. Provide evaluators and employees with written performance standards or objectives that have been based on the job analysis.
3. Train the performance appraisal evaluators to use the rating instrument(s) properly.
4. Document instances of poor performance.
5. Ratings should be reviewed by upper-level management personnel.
6. Provide counseling and guidance to assist poor performers to improve.
7. Provide a formal appeal mechanism.

Regarding the last point, not all organizations have a formal process for handling disagreements. While it is unknown what percentage of leisure service organizations have a formal appeals process, perhaps what has been noted for large American companies is illustrative of the state of affairs in our profession. That is, three-fourths of large American companies report no formal appeals process or mechanism in place to handle disagreements centering around performance appraisals (Milkovich & Boudreau, 1997, p. 121).

Disagreements are averted when people feel that the performance appraisal process has treated them fairly and their civil rights have not been violated. What organizations must remember is that the worker must perceive a fair or "due process" performance appraisal system has been put in place. In particular, from the worker's perspective, three general features that should be present in the organization's appraisal system deal with adequate notice, fair hearing, and judgement based on evidence (Taylor et al., 1995).

Evaluator Training

A fair performance appraisal system hinges on the training of the evaluators. Naturally errors can be made in performance appraisal. These various errors have been labeled as *halo error* (when a general impression causes similar ratings on different dimensions—such as rating someone high on knowledge of the job because they have strong social skills), *leniency error* (recording overly favorable ratings to an entire group), *severity error* (recording overly unfavorable ratings to an entire group), and *central tendency error* (or despite large differences among the group of individuals being rated, rates everyone near the middle of the scale). In the final analysis, training evaluators about errors in performance appraising appear to help them avoid making mistakes.

Organizational Decisions to be Made Regarding Performance Appraisal

In summary, leisure service organizations engaged in performance appraisals need to periodically examine a number of issues. These issues include reviewing: why do appraisals, how to do appraisals (what performances to assess and how), who is involved in the appraisal, the timing of the appraisal, how performance appraisal results are communicated, establishment of an employee development plan, and the training needs of evaluators. Ultimately, organizations must decide how much time and effort are worthwhile to put into performance appraisal relative to payoff. At a minimum, recreation organizations should review the performance-related evaluation standards required for public agency accreditation (Commission for Accreditation of Park and Recreation Agencies, 1996).

Main Points

- Performance appraisal is measuring the extent an employee or volunteer is effective or adequate in his/her work.

- The results of a performance appraisal can serve one of three purposes: provide feedback to the worker about his/her strengths and weakness, support a performance reward system, and/or provide a paper trail or documentation to sustain personnel actions.

- A worker can be assessed regarding his skills, abilities, traits, behaviors, or results. Performance appraisal should focus on more than one of these areas.

- Regardless of performance criteria selected, performance measures should be: goal related, observable, understandable, and controllable.

- There are three bases for comparison in measuring performance: Management by Objectives (characterized by the manager and worker identifying SMART objectives), standards (which can be assessed by checklists, rating scales, critical incidents, behaviorally-anchored rating scales, and essays/diaries); and, compared to other individuals.

- Common practice is to do quarterly appraisals over a year's period for probationary employees and for any employee promoted to a new position.

- Human resource management experts are also now suggesting that the best timing for performance appraisals is at the end of an important task or project, or when key results are supposed to have been completed.

- Strategies used to communicate performance appraisal results are a decisive factor in motivating individuals to change their performance. Among these strategies are rational persuasion, inspirational appeal, consultation, ingratiation, exchange, personal appeal, coalition, legitimating, and pressure. Research indicates that the affiliation of the individual the performance appraisal evaluator is trying to change—subordinate, peer, or supervisor—affects which strategy should be used.

- An employee development plan should be written for all employees.

- An organization's performance assessment system success will depend on if the employees being rated: accept the system and have a sense of being treated fairly, and believe the performance results are fair. Additionally, organizations must have a formal system in place to handle disputes.

- A key way to avoid disagreements is to provide adequate training for performance appraisal evaluators. This training should include focusing on how to avert committing leniency, severity, and central tendency errors in the performance appraisal.

Study Questions

1. What is performance appraisal? And why is it done?

2. What areas can be assessed in a performance appraisal? Should one area be focused on when a recreation/parks/sports management worker is being appraised—why or why not?

3. What four characteristics should be present in any performance criteria that are chosen?

4. Briefly define the Management by Objectives approach to measuring performance.

5. What are the five techniques used to compare performance to standards.

6. Under what circumstances might using a comparison between individuals be a useful to conducting a performance assessment? When is it not such a good idea to use this approach?

7. Who do you think should do a performance appraisal of a recreation/parks/sports management intern? Justify your answer.

8. What is typically the timing of performance appraisals—that is, when do many organizations do them?

9. Does it make a difference how performance appraisal results are communicated in terms of motivating individuals to change their ways? How?

10. What is an employee development plan? When is it done?

11. What three things are related to the success of an organizations performance appraisal system?

12. What are some guidelines for averting performance appraisal related disagreements?

13. Briefly define the three kinds of errors that can be made in performance appraisals.

References

Boulder Parks and Recreation Department. (1997, January). *City of Boulder Supervisor's Manual.* Boulder, CO: City of Boulder.

Bureau of National Affairs. (1983, February). Performance appraisal programs. *Personnel Policies Forum,* Survey No. *135.*

Commission for Accreditation of Park and Recreation Agencies. (1996). *Self-assessment manual for quality operation of park and recreation agencies: A guide to standards for national accreditation with commentary and suggested evidence of compliance.* Asburn, VA: National Recreation and Park Association American Academy for Park and Recreation Administration.

Hunter, J., Schmidt, F., & Judiesch, M. (1990). Individual differences in output variability as a function of job complexity. *Journal of Applied Psychology, 75,* 28-42.

Milkovich, G., & Boudreau, J. (1997). *Human resource management* (8th ed.). Chicago: Irwin.

Millman, J., Zawacki, C., Powell, L., & Kirksey, J. (1994). Companies evaluate employees from all perspectives. *Personnel Journal, 11,* 99-103.

State of New Mexico Personnel Board. (Undated). *Performance appraisal and development: User's manual.* Albuquerque, NM: State of New Mexico.

Taylor, M., Tracey, K., Renard, M., Harrison, J., & Carroll, S. (1995). Due process in performance appraisal: A quasi-experiment in procedural justice. *Administrative Science Quarterly, 40,* 495-523.

Teague, M. (1980). Performance appraisal: A bold plan. *Therapeutic Recreation Journal, 1,* 4-12.

Yukl, G., & Tracey, B. (1992). Consequences of influence tactics used with subordinates, peers, and the boss. *Journal of Applied Psychology, 77,* 525-535.

CHAPTER 18

Evaluation of the Physical Plant

What Will I Learn in This Chapter?
I'll be able to:

1. Consider how evaluation can be used in making decisions about the organization's physical plant.

2. Explain how an open-space survey or a standards approach can be used in evaluating open space.

3. Outline a system of evaluation for facilities and equipment that assesses routine maintenance, preventive maintenance, and design aesthetics.

4. Suggest ways of evaluating the operating procedures of areas and facilities.

5. Identify how an evaluation should be conducted in assessing concessions and contract provisions.

6. Evaluate the adequacy of an organization's risk management plan.

Ecological land usage, public site beautification, community development, historic preservation, facility renovation, equipment upkeep, multiple use of public and private spaces, and other efforts are common aspects of a recreation, park, sport, and tourism organization's total service delivery. Today's manager must use sophisticated methods in order to balance demands for citizen participation in the planning and design process, environmental and social impact assessment, and cost-effectiveness of public and private investments. In this chapter we overview evaluation for open space, facilities and equipment, and operating procedures. Special treatment is given to the allied consideration of the evaluation of an organization's risk management plan, and concessions and subcontracts.

Open Space
Open space is multi-purpose and open-function, offering opportunities for conservation, aesthetics, and recreation. Greenbelts are a typical example. Usually in areas designated

as open space, the level of construction and development is minimal with the natural landscape of the space providing the main feature.

Site Inventory

Evaluating open space can take two different approaches. One is conducting an open-space survey. For this, constituent input (using, for example, focus groups) on the use of the space is coupled with a site inventory. A site inventory records the characteristics of the space, such as the prevailing wind, soils, drainage, geological formations, slope, types of vegetation and location, and wildlife areas. Such data collection tools as aerial photographs, topographical maps, and soils maps are used. The purpose is to determine the suitability of the undeveloped land for recreational uses. To help you organize a site inventory of an open-space area, a checklist can provide a way to make sure all aspects are evaluated. Figure 18.1 illustrates.

One important site element to evaluate is the visual factor. This is the overall personality of the area. For example, after walking or driving through a community, you soon become aware that different neighborhoods have different visual characteristics. These result from different architectural, historical, or geographic features. In terms of open space, the visual personality of the area typically derives from the characteristics of the trees. Trees have different forms, colors, and texture (Arnold, 1980) that contribute to the visual presence of the site. Assessing noise types and levels adjacent to the open space, as well as pedestrian, automobile, or commercial traffic proximity, is also part of the personality of a site. Further, enhancement of wildlife habitat helps to make an area interesting and more pleasant to be in. Wildlife are only able to live in places that meet their needs for food, water, protective cover, space, and movement. In inventorying a site for wildlife, check the shape and size of the area, as well as the heterogeneity of plant materials.

Another element about a site that is important to inventory is biological. Are the plants ecologically adapted to the site? Are there conditions that limit plant growth? Plants are important to the ability of open spaces to serve recreational uses, therefore plant growth and development should be evaluated. Appraising the biological adequacy of an open space area usually involves, therefore, an evaluation of the soil. This is especially critical for open spaces in urban areas. Unlike undisturbed, natural soils, urban soils have been drastically impacted, altering their ability to support plant growth. It is important to assess soils for such characteristics as bare soil surfaces, soil compaction, the presence of man-made materials and contaminants, drought or soggy conditions, and nutrients (Craul, 1988). Inventorying the biology of an open space also entails evaluating air quality, climatic conditions, and lighting.

Standards

An all together different approach to evaluating open space is reliance on standards. Standards are usually expressed as the ratio of undeveloped acreage to the total population,

Figure 18.1: Site inventory checklist.

Check off each of the following elements that exist in each site. If 75% or more are present, the site can be considered of high quality for recreational uses.

Visual Factors

____ Tree forms harmonize with the adjacent architecture and landforms. Round, oval, columnar, or broad-base pyramidal tree forms are most compatible with urban landscapes.

____ Seasonal tree colors complement or contrast the surrounding architecture and land forms. Color effects are best achieved by the use of a mass of the same seasonal colors. Single speciment trees are usually ineffective.

____ Tree textures relate to the surrounding architecture and landscape. Beware of random mixing of textures.

____ There is adequate noise-control planting. Plantings for noise control should be located as close to the source of noise as possible.

____ There is adequate traffic-control planting. Plantings can help control pedestrian traffic through the open space, and trees can be used to delineate major automobile routes with minimal disruption of the natural site.

____ Planned wildlife habitat areas are as large as possible.

____ Wildlife areas are curvilinear and irregular (rather than linear), with undulating, irregular edges.

____ Wildlife area plants include a variety of species, sizes, and ages.

Biological Factors

____ Water drains into the soil quickly.

____ Soil is not compacted and does not exhibit crusting.

____ Soil pH is not excessively low nor high for the geographical location.

____ Saline and sodium levels in the soil do not exceed those appropriate for the geographical location.

____ Soil is fertile—natural litter from trees and plants provide for nutrient recycling.

____ The soil is free from construction and industrial debris and contaminants.

____ There is no airborne sulfur dioxide injury to plants and trees (yellow or tan areas between the leaf veins).

____ There is no fluorine damage to plants and trees (ship-like turning up of the leaf blade and dried-up needle points on conifers).

____ Plants are adapted to the regional extremes of temperature, precipitation, and wind.

____ The amount of light available meets the light needs of the plants and trees.

(adapted from Bernatzky, 1978; Craul, 1988; and Kays, 1982)

with the most common figure cited as 10 acres of space per 1000 community (Kraus & Curtis, 1990). As you already probably suspect, there are limitations to the standards approach. Communities differ widely in residential housing patterns, fiscal capability, and recreation interests; therefore, no single standard can apply equally well to all locales. Nonetheless, evaluation of the provision and adequacy of open space for people remains an important function. This is why government agencies in all locales maintain their own standards for the amount and condition of the open space, often incorporating these standards into zoning approvals for residential and/or commercial development.

Facilities and Equipment

The structures of your organization's physical plant—the buildings, courts, fields, equipment, furnishings, and other items that make up the constructed aspects of space—are important indicators of service quality. Regardless of agency size or purpose, high quality facilities and equipment require continual evaluation of these key components: routine maintenance, preventive maintenance, and design aesthetics.

Routine Maintenance

Routine, or general, maintenance is an important determinant in the full and effective utilization of a facility. The basic function of maintenance is to keep indoor and outdoor facilities and equipment working. A program of good routine maintenance will encourage use of the facility. Additionally, it will lengthen the longevity of the facility.

Most organizations develop written maintenance plans for managing routine maintenance operations (see Figure 18.2). These plans typically include:

- **Maintenance standards.** The minimal acceptable level of maintenance is specified. Sources of these standards are those published by professional organizations. For example, the American College of Sports Medicine (1997) has health/fitness facility standards that include the maintenance of a wide range of facilities including gymnasia, court sports areas, locker rooms, and spa areas. It might also be useful to consult The National Playground Institute for safety specifications on playground equipment.
- **Routine maintenance tasks.** Specific tasks, such as lubricating, painting, repairing, planting, watering, weeding, and mowing, are listed.
- **Procedures for maintenance.** Concise descriptions are noted on how to carry out maintenance.
- **Frequency.** Guidelines for when tasks are done—daily, weekly, monthly, seasonally, biannually, or annually—are specified.

- **Materials, supplies, and tools.** Details about the materials and supplies needed to perform the tasks are specified.
- **Personnel.** Minimum number of people and the skills required to carry out the tasks are addressed.

The extent to which a written maintenance plan has been implemented can be revealed through evaluation. A regular system of evaluating the adequacy of an organization's facility and equipment maintenance operation will ultimately enable the provision of an attractive

Figure 18.2: Example of a written routine maintenance plan.

Facility: Baseball Field

Maintenance Standard	Routine Maintenance Tasks	Procedures for Maintenance	Frequency Needed	Materials Needed	Personnel
Fields, outfields, dugouts, and spectator areas free of debris and trash.	Remove debris and trash.	Systematically walk the area. Empty all trash containers.	Daily	Trash bags, 1 stick puncher, gloves	1 grounds crew member
Eliminate holes on infield surface.	Fill holes.	Add extra soil, rake, and tamp firm.	Daily, before games.	Extra soil, tractor with box trailer, shovel, rake, tamper.	1 grounds crew member
Wet infield to minimize dust and loss of soil due to wind.	Hose down infield.	Dampen infield surface with hose spray or broadcast calcium chloride.	Daily, before games.	Hose with nozzle, broadcast spreader, calcium chloride.	1 grounds crew member

(adapted from Sternloff & Warren, 1984, pp. 29-31)

and safe recreational experience for participants, as well as long-term cost savings by minimizing deterioration of facilities. For equipment still under warranty, it is important that corrections be done quickly and correctly by the manufacturer to minimize risk to participants. Eventually the evaluation will provide a rational basis for deciding when and how to renovate, replace, or rejuvenate facilities. In order to make sound decisions about the renovation of existing facilities and the construction of new ones, maintenance evaluation findings can substantiate the need for necessary funding by demonstrating that the improvements are indeed required in spite of an adequate maintenance regime. The evaluation of facility and equipment maintenance is also an appraisal of staff effectiveness, as problems with maintenance often stem from problems with the training and supervision of staff.

One useful way to evaluate maintenance staff effectiveness is a workload/cost tracking system (Siderelis, 1979). According to the state of Pennsylvania's *Park Maintenance Management Manual* (1979), this process requires six steps.

> **Step 1:** Inventory and categorize the various types of maintenance work functions (carpentry, field preparation, leaf collection, mowing, plumbing, etc.) and facilities (baseball fields, gymnasiums, ice skating rinks, etc.) you are maintaining.
>
> **Step 2:** Determine your information needs, such as what documentation you need for maintenance budget requests and what you need to know (such as how long tasks take) in order to make proper maintenance decisions.
>
> **Step 3:** Develop a data-collection form with your staff that provides space to record the information decided in the second step above.
>
> **Step 4:** Train your key supervisory staff first in the data-collection procedures and then have them provide training for the remaining staff.
>
> **Step 5:** Pilot test your workload/cost tracking system for a minimum of one month; then make changes for full implementation.
>
> **Step 6:** Evaluate reported data each month.

The evaluation of facility and equipment cleanliness is another important element in routine maintenance. Exceptional cleanliness means that every aspect of the operation, including walls, carpets, court surfaces, equipment and uniforms, is impeccably clean. Evaluating your organization's facility cleanliness will mean not only a safer, more pleasant environment for participants, but also ultimately the cost savings of reduced wear and tear of the facility itself. For some recreation, park, and sport organizations, maintaining a clean environment seems an almost insurmountable goal because of a high volume of usage and/or problems with vandalism and carelessness by users. For example, in Metro Dade County, Florida, keeping public beaches clean of the cans, paper, cigarette butts, plastic bags and bottles, and other refuse left behind by 40,000 visitors a day is certainly a major accomplishment (Kraus & Curtis, 1990). Cleanliness can be addressed as part of a written routine maintenance plan (discussed above).

Preventive Maintenance

A system of preventive maintenance to minimize unscheduled operations shutdowns and major breakdowns should be a continuing concern of every leisure services organization that operates with a physical plant (Sternloff & Warren, 1984). Preventive maintenance is nothing more than the adage, a stitch in time saves nine. The stitch in time may be such simple things as ensuring that there is adequate wood chips under the picnic tables, or that a regular system of insect control is applied to trees and shrubs. In some organizations, preventive maintenance work is included in the routine maintenance plan. Regardless, the essential requirement is a systematic inspection procedure to identify small, but accelerating, problems and promptly doing the needed maintenance work (Sternloff & Warren, 1984).

A systematic inspection procedure simply means regularly identifying potential breakdowns. Areas typically included in the inspection are:

door closers	door hinges	drains
exhaust fans	fan belts	faucets
filters	light bulbs	light fixtures
motors	pumps	toilets

In order to evaluate the preventive maintenance system, the maintenance supervisor should maintain concise daily records of all work completed for each piece of equipment (Sternloff & Warren, 1984). Major repair jobs should also be noted by placing a dated and descriptive tag on the equipment repaired. These records, if properly kept, provide a work history for all facilities and equipment that is useful in making new purchase decisions in case of breakdowns.

Design

Ideally, all elements of a facility work together to create a positive impact. Creative and high quality materials and design concepts are used to provide a style, or special feeling. The building works well together with its use, providing a visual cue to a well-run organization.

Park, recreation, sport, fitness, and tourism facilities are designed to meet often widely different objectives. There are, however, several general design objectives applicable to all situations. These are:

- **Economy of operation.** It is important that facilities be designed to minimize their operating costs. Specifically, a good design can reduce personnel and energy costs.

- **Flexibility.** Facilities should be designed to be flexible so that they can respond to changes in user tastes and interests.
- **Safety and security.** Government legislation and professional ethics require that facility designs protect users and staff from undue safety and security risks. Sometimes the need for safety and security compromises aesthetics. For example, a parking lot with no landscaping can help prevent car theft and muggings, but is also unattractive.
- **User-friendliness.** Designing a facility that is user-friendly means looking at every aspect of the usage from the journey to the facility through to the return home. Standing in line to use the restroom at a football stadium is an example of an unfriendly design.
- **Welcoming to users with special needs.** For participants in the program who use wheelchairs, have hearing or vision impairments, and also for parents with babies, it is essential that the facility be accessible.
- **Aesthetic appeal.** The size, form, color, and materials of the facility are pleasing to see for both users inside and passers-by outside.
- **Environmentally friendly.** Leisure service facilities need to minimize waste, be energy efficient, and use non-toxic materials.

To evaluate facility design, the preconstruction aspects are examined first. Planning for the development of facilities requires paying attention to numerous sources of information. In addition to the data-collection methods already discussed (questionnaires, interviews, focus groups, non-reactive measures, etc.), there are ready-made information sources that are particularly appropriate to assessing initial facility development decisions, such as commercial and government documents. Foremost are census data, which contain statistics on gender, age, marital status, ethnic origin, race, employment, educational level, family income, and years of residence down to the block or census-tract level. This information is available from the U.S. Department of Commerce Census of Population. Also, special census data for selected cities contain statistics on transportation modes, populations with disabilities, and housing conditions.

As part of pre-construction or renovation decisions, evaluation can take the form of a survey or checklist. A focused survey conducted by either experienced members of the staff and/or in consultation with outside experts and constituents can yield baseline information on the existing qualities of the facility against the desired (or mandated by law or professional practice) qualities. For example, older recreation facilities often do not usually comply with the facility accessibility requirements of the Americans with Disabilities Act. (See Bullock & Mahon, 1997, for a detailed discussion.) A survey of the current facility that focuses on what changes will be needed in order to bring the facility into compliance with this law will be necessary prior to planning a renovation project. The plans are then drawn up to incorporate the results from the survey.

Another approach to evaluating the design adequacy of facilities is comparison with standards. Over several decades, professionally developed and agreed-upon standards have served as a means of evaluating the adequacy of recreation facilities. These have typically been presented as the ratio of specific facility types to the total population of the community. For example, there should be a baseball diamond for every 6,000 residents, a tennis court for every 2,000, and an artificial skating rink for every 30,000 (Kraus & Curtis, 1990). Standards provide a way of measuring the adequacy of facilities not as optimal goals, but rather as minimal levels. Such standards provide a way to measure how closely the organization's physical resources match quality-related criteria.

As we mentioned before, however, there are limitations to the standards approach to facility evaluation. Because communities differ widely, no single design standard for baseball diamonds, tennis courts, and skating rinks can capably apply to all communities. To overcome this problem, recent standards have focused on a reasonable guideline approach. An example of the reasonable guideline approach is the accreditation program for public park and recreation agencies. Sponsored by the American Academy for Park and Recreation Administration and the National Recreation and Park Association, adherence to the set of 152 standards produces a national "accredited" seal of approval for the organization. Recall from our discussion in Chapter 2 that the standards in this program are not written as a ratio; instead, they are specific statements of recommended practices in facility design.

Comprehensive Equipment and Facility Evaluation

The accreditation program for public park and recreation organizations mentioned above is based on the ideal that periodically a comprehensive assessment of all equipment and facilities is undertaken. This simply means considering together all the data resulting from the separate routine and preventive maintenance, and design inquiries and judging how well the organization is doing overall. A basic rating form for accomplishing this is demonstrated in Figure 18.3.

Operating Procedures

All facility use is based on a system of operations management. Operations management is the day-to-day management of the site, usually accomplished through a set of operating procedures. These procedures dictate the operation of every location including the front desk, food handling areas, and supply cabinets. Procedures for everything from opening and closing hours, to keeping track of equipment, to ticketing and reservations, to security and crowd control should be written down and consistently included in staff training. And, of course, a regular system of review of all procedures should be conducted. To highlight evaluation of operations management, crowd control and keeping track of the equipment inventory are singled out as examples.

Figure 18.3: Example of comprehensive equipment/facilities rating form: Aerobics studio.

Rating Form Instructions: Using the following scale, fill in each blank according to how well each aspect of the aerobics studio is managed in terms of routine maintenance and preventive maintenance. Also rate the design elements. After all ratings are completed, column and row totals will indicate the overall level of equipment and facility quality.

3 = exceptional

2 = standard

1 = poor

	Routine Maintenance	Preventive Maintenance	Design	Totals
Floors	____	____	____	____
Lighting	____	____	____	____
Music System	____	____	____	____
Leader Platform	____	____	____	____
Mirrors	____	____	____	____
Temperature Controls	____	____	____	____
First Aid Equipment	____	____	____	____
Ventilation System	____	____	____	____
Schedule Posting	____	____	____	____
Waiting Area	____	____	____	____
Storage Space	____	____	____	____
Ceiling	____	____	____	____

(adapted from IRSA, 1987)

Operating procedures should include what to do in case of a crisis. Although rare, such crises as a fire in the restroom, a fall from an amusement ride, an animal attack at the zoo, an outbreak of food poisoning from the food service, and other problems must be anticipated by establishing operating procedures. In most of these cases the response procedures are planned prior to the incident, and then the staff waits for the crisis to occur before applying them. To some extent, however, operating procedures put into place on a regular, here-and-now basis can help prevent the crisis. Our example is crowd control.

Figure 18.4: A crowd management case.

It's a Friday night in Houston. Fifteen armed and uniformed police officers patrol the grounds. Four of the officers watch the crowd in the main area, while others watch over the trouble zones behind. At the entrance, four officers look on as people walk through the metal detectors that line each gate, while two others patrol the parking lot in their police car.

A prison yard? A gathering of a notorious motorcycle gang? A Woodstock-style concert? No, just a football game at Alief Hastings High School, the largest high school in Texas. Security for the 4,800 students is provided by the school district's own police department. Their assignment is to ward off problems before they occur. At Alief Hastings they call this "proactive policing."

At James W. Robinson High School, a suburban school with 2,500 students in Fairfax, Virginia, police officers cover the football games too. "On a typical night we have eight officers on patrol. But if a large crowd is expected or if there have been problems in the past because of a rivalry between the schools, we may increase the number of officers to 10 or even 16—and that would be in addition to our school security officers and administrative staff," explains Paul Jansen, director of student activities.

(from Rochman, 1997, pp. 15-16)

In the case presented in Figure 18.4 the presence of uniformed police officers is a component of Alief Hastings High School's operating procedures for the football stadium. At Robinson High, the security plan relies on the collaborative efforts of school administrators, security staff, and the local police. What is not presented about the operating procedures in the case is that Robinson High officials also take into account the type of sport, the expected crowd size, and the relationship between Robinson High and its football game opponent. In addition, for each type of event, the crowd management plan notes what type of lighting will be necessary and communications systems (such as walkie-talkies and cellular phones) that should be used (Rochman, 1997). How was this plan developed? It was based on an evaluation of what worked and didn't work with previous crowd management strategies.

The New Jersey State Interscholastic Athletic Association distributes a booklet on crowd control to every high school in the state (Rochman, 1997). Using an evaluation approach that brought a panel of experts together with school athletics directors and students, the resulting booklet is focused on preventing existing problems from escalating and new problems from developing. The crowd control procedures in the booklet include contacting the visiting school as early as possible to discuss the game and any prior or existing problems; sending a map and directions to the visiting school; creating separate, opposing-side-spectator entrance and departure gates, concession stands, and restrooms; not admitting elementary or junior high school students unless they are accompanied by adults; and scheduling the game in the afternoon rather than at night.

In short, evaluation of operating procedures usually relies on input from both facility users and staff. Development of crowd control procedures, as illustrated in the case situation in Figure 18.4, could be based on such evaluation tools as participant observations of events and facilities, focus groups of event/facility participants, and interviews of staff members and community stakeholders.

By its very label, equipment inventory tracking suggests another important example of where evaluation can be applied to operating procedures. Keeping track of sport, craft, camping and other sorts of recreational equipment requires constant use of an inventorying research instrument. Figure 18.5 provides sample inventory cards—one for tracking equipment purchases, another for equipment lending, and a third for equipment loss.

These inventory cards are based on paper and pencil technology. Recently, computer technology is coming into widespread use for keeping track of equipment. Knowing not just the number, but the type, size, color, condition and current location of thousands of helmets, gloves, racquets, tents, first-aid kits, and ceramics sponges is "what separates those who issue equipment and those who manage it" (Cohen, 1997, p. 43).

As part of the evolution of computer technology, commercial companies have developed bar-coding technology. Unfortunately, using bar-coding to keep track of equipment requires at least one computer, a software package, and bar-code scanners—beyond the financial capability of many leisure service organizations. Furthermore, proper implementation of such a system is time-consuming as it requires a complete and accurate inventory, the development of bar-codes and matching identification system, and a great deal of data entry (Cohen, 1997). Yet enthusiasts of this inventorying tool claim the benefits outweigh the effort and expense. In the long run, equipment managers seem to benefit through time and money savings, reduction in lost equipment, and decrease in liability risks. Regarding the latter, for example, efforts at preventing injuries can be shown if a manager named in a lawsuit can document how a specific piece of equipment has been maintained and repaired. Of course this can backfire in a lawsuit as well; where procedures of equipment care are not followed, the inventory will document this too.

Figure 18.5: Equipment inventory log cards.

Equipment Purchase Log

Item	Quantity	Unit Cost	On Hand	Disposal

Equipment Lending Log

Quantity	Item Issued	Date Out/Date In	Manager

Lost Equipment Log

Reporting Name	Item Lost	Date Lost	Amount Owed	Amount Paid	Date Paid

Concessions and Contracting

Some leisure service organizations do not manage particular aspects of the physical plant themselves. Instead, certain functions that occur in the organization are sub-contracted to an outside vendor or management company. For example, arrangements are made between the park, recreation, or sport organization and private individuals or businesses to sell merchandise or services in parks, stadiums, golf courses, etc. Provision of recreation program services can also be sub-contracted out. Subcontracting of maintenance and security to private companies is becoming more widespread. Concessions in such areas as boat rentals, food service and retail shops are most common (Kraus & Curtis, 1990).

Concessions and sub-contracts permit a recreation organization to provide services it might otherwise not be able to offer because of limitations in staff expertise or bureaucratic regulations. The advantage of consessions and contracts is increased efficiency. For governmental leisure service organizations in particular, commercial consessionaires and contractors can often carry out certain functions more economically and without political influences (Kraus & Curtis, 1990). When the arrangement is well made, the leisure service organization also saves on capital investment in equipment and supplies, has well-trained specialists, and no in-house personnel problems. The disadvantages, however, include loss of control as to when and how well jobs are completed, and if care in establishing the contract is not taken, the cost may actually be higher (Sternloff & Warren, 1984). Usually, concessionaires pay a percentage of their gross revenue to the organization and may also pay an annual fee for the concession privilege (Kraus & Curtis, 1990).

Since the major reason for using concessions and subcontracts is to provide a service more effectively and efficiently, evaluation should ask these same questions. What have been the cost savings? Has the subcontract met or exceeded productivity or quality expectations set forth by the organization?

When using subcontracts and concessions, an important part of their evaluation is an initial and precise definition of the work to be done through the contract, including clear specification of the quantity, quality, and price of the work. From here, evaluation proceeds to determine if these definitions and specifications were achieved. The more specific expectations have been detailed in the contract, the easier will be the evaluation.

For example, an evaluation should assess the level of accomplishment of the following (Sternloff & Warren, 1984):

1. **Was a reputable firm selected?** Recognizing that a low bid does not necessarily represent the best sub-contractor, is the firm you've chosen able to justify in terms of quality and quantity its cost to you and your constituents? Are your constituents satisfied?

2. **Have you established detailed and complete contract specifications?** Assess the accuracy of the terms of the contract. These should be reviewed annually and revised when appropriate.

3. **Have you inspected the concession's or sub-contractor's work?** Usually staff inside your organization inspect the work of outside vendors/sub-contractors to determine specification compliance.

A common evaluation approach with concessions and contracts is cost-benefit analysis, which we've already discussed in Chapter 16. This technique evaluates the outcomes of the concession or contract by relating its benefits to its cost. Another typical approach is the use of standards. An example of this is the Concessions Operational Performance Program of the National Park Service (U.S. Department of the Interior, National Park Service, 1986).

In essence this approach establishes operational standards for facilities and services offered in the national parks by outside concessions, provides a systematic method for determining their performance level on these standards on a periodic and annual basis, and through comprehensive evaluations of each facility and service, permits concessioners the opportunity to correct deficiencies without being unfairly penalized (U.S. Department of the Interior, National Park Service, 1986, Chapter 20, p. 1).

The standards established for each type of facility or service are composed of distinct elements that are pertinent to satisfactory performance. Based on the degree of their importance to visitor and/or employee's well being and enjoyment, these elements are classified as "major-first priority," "second priority," and "minor-third priority" (U.S. Department of the Interior, National Park Service, 1986, Chapter 20, p. 1). Conformance to the standards is measured periodically through a comprehensive evaluation on each individual concession facility and service operating in the national parks. At the end of the year the periodic measurements for each operation are summarized and an average periodic rating for the year is computed. Such average ratings are then transferred to the Concession Operational Performance Report Form 10-629 (Figure 18.6) and an annual average rating for all like facilities or operations calculated. Finally, the superintendent reviews the ratings and assigns an overall verbal rating of "satisfactory," "marginal," or "unsatisfactory."

Risk Management

Undoubtedly, evaluation of the organization's physical plant leads to an evaluation of the risk management plan. While a solid evaluation plan for open space, facility and equipment maintenance, and operation procedures certainly contributes to the management of risk in the organization, periodic and direct review of the risk management plan itself should be undertaken.

Risk management encompasses anticipating what might go wrong, planning ways to avoid something going wrong, and outlining ways to respond appropriately when something does go wrong. In managing a recreation, park, tourism, and sport organization the entire endeavor of risk management may be viewed as evaluative research. The reason is that the crux of risk management is the systematic analysis of facilities and programs in an effort to identify and avoid potential risk situations.

Having a risk management plan means your organization is taking a proactive approach to managing risk (Peterson, 1987). It is a planned strategy for protecting against undue risk to participants. In situations where legal action has been taken against your organization, a thorough and followed risk management plan is evidence of intent to act professionally. While there are several ways to develop a risk management plan, a 13-step approach modified from the advice of Peterson (1987) is worth reviewing because it illustrates how a risk management plan can evolve, as well as demonstrates the role of evaluation in creating the plan.

1. **Develop philosophical and policy statements** about your organization's belief in developing a risk-management, loss-prevention, and control program. A preliminary review

Figure 18.6: Concession operational performance report, National Park Service.

CONCESSIONS
NPS-48
Concessioner Review Program-Operational Performance

SAMPLE - CONCESSIONS OPERATIONAL PERFORMANCE REPORT -·FORM 10-629

EXHIBIT 3
Chapter 20
Page 1

FORM 10-629
(6/82)

UNITED STATES DEPARTMENT OF THE INTERIOR
NATIONAL PARK SERVICE

CONCESSION OPERATIONAL PERFORMANCE REPORT

CONCESSIONER: U.S. Concessions Co.　　　REGION RMRO

DATE: Oct. 1982　　　PARK Anywhere Nat't Park

INDIVIDUAL FACILITY ANNUAL SUMMARY RATING

Instructions: List below the annual rating that has been assigned to each facility/service as set forth on the Summary of Periodic Operational Ratings form. Round off all rating scores to the nearest tenth. (For Food Service Sanitation, see Summary of Periodic Food Service Sanitation Rating Scores, Standard No. I.)

Location - List each facility/ service by name and/or location.	PHS I	FOOD III	BEV & IV	BOAT ACCOM. V	MDSE. VI	AUTO VII	TRANSP. VIII	MARINA IX	H—MHORSE X	SKI XI	INTERP. XII	EMP. HOU. XIII	SHOWERS XIV	LAUNDRY S/T XV	TLR L/T XVI	BATH XVII	RIVER RUNNERS XVIII	BOAT XIX	RHUSTIC XX	GOLF XXI	SWIM
Blue Sky Inn	*87*	*3.7*		40															40		
Park Village	95	3.5	3.0	4.0																	
Lake View	88	4.0	4.0				5.0											4.3			
Total Score (Add down)	*270*	*11.2	7.0	8.0			5.0											4.3	4.0		
Divide No. of Fac. Ratings	3	3	2	2			1											1	1		
ANNUAL AVG. RATING SCORE	*90*	*3.7	3.5	4.0			5.0											4.3	4.0		

SAFETY Std. No. II   This area is rated once annually as Satisfactory, Marginal or Unsatisfactory. The Safety Rating is not arrived at numerically and therefore is not included above. For the OPERATIONAL PERFORMANCE RATING to be considered Satisfactory, both Safety and Sanitation must have a rating of Satisfactory, unless a full explanation is provided on FORM 10-631.

PHS RATING SATISFACTORY
Satisfactory, Marginal, Unsatisfactory

SAFETY RATING SATISFACTORY
Satisfactory, Marginal, Unsatisfactory

OPERATIONAL PERFORMANCE RATING: SATISFACTORY
Satisfactory, Marginal, Unsatisfactory

The Concessioner's Operational Performance Evaluation for 19___ is recorded above. This rating is based on the Superintendent's review of the following factors as presented in the park's evaluation documents:

1. The average annual ratings as set forth above.
2. A review of the individual facility and service ratings and/or the degree to which they fluctuated.
3. A & B Deficiencies uncorrected at the time of follow-up evaluations.
4. "C" Deficiencies not corrected in a timely manner.
5. Any specific action(s) being taken to eliminate Unsatisfactory conditions.
6. Consideration of both positive and negative visitor comments.

Superintendent's Signature　　10-12-82　Date

Concessioner's Signature
(To signify receipt of rating)　　10-20-82　Date

**NARRATIVE CONCERNING STATUS OF THE CONCESSIONER'S OPERATIONAL PERFORMANCE MUST BE PROVIDED ON FORM 10-631.

of existing statements found in ordinances, charters, master plans, and administrative handbooks will help get you started. Have your governing authority formally adopt these philosophical and policy statements.

2. Develop a set of goals and objectives that give direction and establish time frames for completing specific risk management tasks.

3. In the planning, construction, and modification of open space sites and indoor and outdoor facilities, work closely with architects, engineers, program specialists, landscape architects, and builders to assure that there is elimination of all potential site and building hazards, and that there is conformance to building codes, and other national, state, and local laws and regulations.

4. Provide participants with programs that have been developed by professionals, as well as supervised by professionals. This means that activities are well planned and led by an adequate number of qualified personnel who use appropriate techniques according to participants' skill and experience levels. Develop a plan of supervision encompassing the best and most reasonable standard of care for each site, facility, and program.

5. Assemble all the safety rules and regulations pertaining to your organization's services and the procedures used to enforce them. Establish reporting and record-keeping systems to monitor these rules and regulations.

6. Develop a routine, systematic method for safety inspections and investigations. Establish a regular pattern of inspections and demand that it be kept. A series of checklists could be useful; be sure the safety inspections reflect manufacturer's recommendations plus all national, state, and local laws and standards. For example, playground equipment manufacturers typically provide inspection checklists for their product.

7. Keep accident reports on all injuries. These should state the facts in an objective and unbiased manner and in sufficient detail to allow for later analysis. You will also want to record how often and where accidents occur, the severity of the accidents, time of day, and other specifics about the situation. These records provide both a documentation of what happened in case of legal question, as well as a source of data to be analyzed when reviewing the organization's risk management plan. Figure 18.7 provides a checklist that might assist you in conducting an accident/incident reporting assessment.

8. Develop a single procedure for handling emergencies and adapt it to all settings. Procedures for giving first aid and CPR, emergency telephone calls, evacuation plans for facilities, etc. should consistently be a part of employee training as well.

9. Analyze your current practices regarding releases, waivers, and agreements to participate according to contemporary legal advice. Is the wording of the waiver reviewed regularly with legal counsel? Are parental consent releases obtained for minors? Are the medical waivers readily accessible in the event of an emergency? Revise practices based on this analysis.

10. **Identify the ways available to you for insuring against risk.** Consult your organization's legal and insurance advisors. Keep competent legal and insurance advisors on call in case you need them.

Figure 18.7: Checklist for assessing accident/incident reporting and investigation procedures.

Reports   YES   NO

A. Are paper routes for reporting and investigating accidents
    and injuries established and functioning?   ____ ____

B. Are designated persons trained in proper accident reporting
    procedures and investigative techniques?   ____ ____

C. Are the accident reports reviewed by the director of the organization?   ____ ____

D. Do reports include corrective action taken?   ____ ____

E. Are pictures and other visual aids used in identification
    and documention of accidents?   ____ ____

F. Are witness statements documented?   ____ ____

Follow-up Actions

G. Is there a process for developing recommendations and for
    implementing corrective actions?   ____ ____

H. Is there a procedure for the organization director's follow-up
    with an injured person to ensure that adequate care and response
    were delivered?   ____ ____

I. Are periodic reviews of accident reports conducted to determine
    trends, patterns, or prominent problem areas?   ____ ____

J. Are medical emergency policies and procedures with all
    staff periodically reviewed?   ____ ____

K. Is there an accident/incident review meeting with staff on a
    regular basis?   ____ ____

(Adapted from United Educators Insurance Risk Retention Group, Inc., n.d.)

---

11. Develop a comprehensive program of in-service training for the entire staff, including members of the governing board and volunteers. Assess this training in terms of whether staff are prepared in safety techniques, emergency procedures, hazard recognition, transportation policies, policies on alcohol and drug use, use of emergency equipment, and accident reporting and investigation.

12. Your risk management plan, when adopted, provides a practical and philosophical base for building a solid public relations strategy. While there is no substitute for showing genuine concern of an injured person after an accident, a good public relations program can often help reduce unhappy feelings that may later lead to a lawsuit.

13. Regularly review all aspects of your risk management plan. Establish periodic review procedures. As an example, Figure 18.8 contains the last page of the risk management plan for the Division of Recreational Sports at Indiana University.

Figure 18.8: Last page of risk management plan for the Division of Recreational Sports, Indiana University.

XII. Review

The Division of Recreational Sports Risk Management plan shall be reviewed on an annual basis by the director, associate director and the program director for Facility Support. The review shall include the modification of work practice controls, the process of inspections, and risk reduction procedures for any new programs that are implemented. Consultation, in regard to annual updates, should take place in cooperation with the Program Services and Facilites coordinator of the HPER building, as well as with the Risk Management Office.

A. Annual Review Documentation

Date of Review   *Names of Reviewers*

Main Points

- Evaluating open space can take two different approaches: open-space survey and reliance on open-space standards.

- Regardless of agency size or purpose, high-quality facilities and equipment require continual evaluation of these key elements: maintenance, cleanliness, operating procedures, and design aesthetics.

- Most organizations develop written maintenance and cleanliness plans for managing routine maintenance and cleaning operations. Evaluation of this plan is required.

- Evaluation of facility operating procedures usually relies on input from both facility users and staff. Inventorying is often a useful research tool in this area as well.

- To evaluate aesthetics and design, we begin with pre-construction aspects. Commercial and government documents, professional standards, as well as the survey form can be useful tools.

- The evaluation of concessions and contracts essentially means assessing whether these arrangements provide a service more effectively and efficiently.

- Conducting a risk management survey enables a critical look at risk management practices.

Study Questions

1. There are many reasons for evaluating the recreation organization's physical plant. What are three reasons mentioned in this chapter? Can you think of others that weren't discussed here?

2. What are the two ways for approaching an open-space evaluation? What is the difference between these two approaches?

3. What elements of facility and equipment operations must be evaluated?

4. What are standards? Describe at least two physical plant evaluation situations in which standards are typically used.

5. What is an inventory? Describe at least two physical plant evaluation situations in which inventories are typically used.

6. How does evaluative research assist with the development of sound risk management practices?

References

American College of Sports Medicine. (1997). *Health/fitness facility standards and guidelines*. Champaign, IL: Human Kinetics Books.

Arnold, H.R. (1980). *Trees in urban design*. New York: Van Nostrand Reinhold.

Bernatzky, A. (1978). *Tree ecology and preservation*. Amsterdam, the Netherlands: Elsevier Scientific Publishing.

Bullock, C., & Mahon, M. (1997). *Introduction to recreation services for people with disabilities: A person-centered approach*. Champaign, IL: Sagamore Publishing.

Cohen, A. (1997, August). Keeping track...of everything. *Athletic Business*. 43-47.

Craul, P.J. (1988). Assessing soil for urban tree survival. *Grounds Maintenance. 23*(9), 28, 30, 84, 85-89.

International Recreational Sports Association. (1987). *Commitment to excellence: IRSA club self-rating guide*. Boston: IRSA.

Kays, B.L. (1982). Methodology for on-site soil analysis. In P.J. Craul, (Ed.) *Urban forest soils: A reference workbook*. USDA Forest Service Consortium for Environmental Forestry Studies.

Kraus, R.G., & Curtis, J.E. (1990). *Creative management in recreation, parks, and leisure services*. St. Louis, MO: Times Mirror/Mosby.

Peterson, J.A. (1987). *Risk management for park, recreation and leisure services*. Champaign, IL: Management Learning Laboratories.

Rochman, S. (1997, April/May). Preparing for the worst. *Athletic Management*. 15-18.

Siderelis, C.D. (1979). Winter. Workload cost tracking. *Trends*. National Park Service and the National Recreation and Park Association, 31-36.

State of Pennsylvania. (1979). *Park maintenance management manual*. Harrisburg, PA: Bureau of Recreation and Conservation.

Sternloff, R.E. & Warren, R. (1984). *Park and recreation maintenance and management*. New York: John Wiley & Sons.

United Educators Insurance Risk Retention Group, Inc. (n.d.). *Athletic liability: self-assessment audit*. Chevy Chase, MD: author.

United States Department of the Interior, National Park Service. (1986, January). *Concessions: NPS 48*, Washington, D.C.: Government Printing Office.

CHAPTER 19

Evaluation of Marketing

What Will I Learn in This Chapter?
I'll be able to:

1. Explain how organizations market a service by using the mix of product, price, connection, and distribution.

2. Recommend evaluation approaches and tools for measuring the effectiveness of advertising, public relations, promotions, and brochures.

This chapter applies the process of evaluative research to assessing the effectiveness of a leisure service organization's marketing program. Marketing has become a management tool of vital concern in sport, recreation, park and tourism organizations because it facilitates the use and delivery of services.

To illustrate, in 1996 the National Recreation and Park Association joined forces with a team of partners to initiate a joint safety venture for personal watercraft (Johnson & Blaicher, 1997). Ride Smart From the Start was designed to help personal watercraft owners be more responsible boaters. To gain national visibility for the program, a marketing strategy that relied heavily on producing electronic and print media resource materials for public service announcements was implemented. As a result, Ride Smart From the Start received substantial financial and credibility boosts midway through its first summer with a grant by the U.S. Coast Guard. This in turn translated into an upgrade to full-color resource materials and an even broader distribution process. Requests for the materials poured in from across the nation, and groups like the Army Corps of Engineers, who are responsible for enforcement on many lakes and rivers, expressed strong interest in supporting the program. Thus, this safety program's success benefited from the application of marketing.

As another example, research has been conducted on health clubs. In one study commissioned by the International Health, Racquet and Sports Club Association (Dreyfuss, 1997) it was reported that some adults stay out of health clubs for fear their saggy, out-of-shape bodies will look out of place among the trim young athletes they expect to see in that setting. This same study noted that non-exercisers tend to see clubs as failing to pay attention to their problems—such as embarrassment in not being able to sustain an activity (women, for instance, who have to quit an aerobics routine before it is over, and men who cannot lift the same amount of weight as those around them). The American Sports Data's National 1997 survey of 1,180 adults also confirms this (Dreyfuss, 1997). This study found that 37 percent of those who considered themselves overweight said they would be more receptive to joining a health club if they were less intimidated by the type of people who already belong.

Results such as these have implications for marketing. Your agency might modify advertising campaigns accordingly. For example, instead of featuring trim young athletes (unless this is the specific target audience you want), ad campaigns should feature sensitivity to encouraging a new person to the exercise program.

Marketing encompasses determining what can and does motivate a person to participate in or use a provided service. There are literally dozens of definitions for marketing. Fortunately, most of these definitions are variations on a broad consensus that marketing is consumer oriented (Middleton, 1994). We have chosen a definition first proposed by Kotler (1991, p. 16): The marketing concept holds that the key to achieving organizational goals is in determining the needs and wants of target markets and delivering the desired satisfactions more effectively and efficiently than competitors. It is implicit in Kotler's definition, as well as in that of others, that *marketing* comprises the following elements:

- The attitudes and decisions of leisure service users (target markets) about the utility and value of available goods and services, according to their needs, wants and interests, and ability to pay.
- The attitudes and decisions of leisure service providers (organizations) about the utility and value of their services, according to their organizational environment and long-term objectives.
- The ways in which leisure service providers communicate with users, before, during, and after the service, and distribute or provide access to their services.

(adapted from Middleton, 1994, p. 17)

In other words, the main point in any marketing system is the link between the attitudes and decisions of the two parties—the leisure service providers and the leisure service users. Evaluative research can be used to assess the effectiveness of this link.

This chapter discusses the use of evaluative research to determine the effectiveness of three marketing tools used by leisure service providers to influence the attitudes and decisions of leisure service users. These tools are: advertising, public relations, and promotions. But before this is covered, let us first establish a more solid grounding for these marketing tools by discussing the marketing mix.

The Marketing Mix

There are four principle factors that organizations use to market a sport, recreation, park or tourism service. In order to enhance leisure service users' attitudes and decisions about a service, we manage these four factors within what is called the *marketing mix*. The marketing mix refers to controlling these factors—somewhat like pulling levers or controls—so that the leisure service is delivered to the targeted users accurately and thoroughly. What are these four factors? They are product, price, connection, and distribution (Middleton, 1994). To mix them for marketing means we coordinate them in order to effectively provide the services of our organization.

Product

Product is the program or service offered to prospective users or participants. For example, within the area of tourism, the product could be the hotel, the theme park, the guided tour, or the restaurant. To expand, the product also includes such service characteristics as the interior design of the hotel; the grooming of the staff at the theme park; the quality of the food served during the guided tour; and the cleanliness of the restrooms at the health club. The product, in other words, includes all those things associated with a high-quality experience when using a particular leisure service. Most leisure organizations offer several services. For example, fitness clubs may have dozens of separate products ranging from aerobics to tai chi classes, from outdoor to indoor swimming pools, and from single-use to separate saunas and whirlpools for female and male patrons.

Price

Price refers to the terms required to acquire the product. Sometimes the terms required are financial—the cost of the tour or the meal. Sometimes the terms required are the possession of particular qualities, such as being at least 55 years of age in order to sign up for discount rates to enter a national park, or being at least four feet tall to qualify to ride a rollercoaster at the theme park.

Connection

Perhaps the most obvious of the factors in the marketing mix are those techniques that connect the service providers' product with service users. These techniques include promotions, advertising, brochures, and public relations. The effort is focused on making prospective program participants or service users aware of the service products in order to stimulate demand (Middleton, 1994). It is also the goal of promotions, brochures, advertising, and public relations to provide information to help potential participants decide, and generally provide incentives to use and purchase the leisure service. This marketing mix factor is termed *connection* because it is integrally linked to the other factors of product, price, and distribution; the application of evaluative research to the factor of connection is the purpose of this chapter.

Distribution

For marketing purposes, *distribution* means both the actual destination or place of the leisure service (such as Orlando, Florida for Disney World), and the other points of access for a service (such as the travel agency that booked the trip to Disney World). Distribution also could include the computerized reservation system for picnic shelters in the city park, or the receptionist in the fitness center office who keeps track of the squash court sign-ups.

Advertising

Advertising is an important marketing tool. As one of the techniques in the connection marketing mix factor, advertising functions to communicate about leisure services through the use of the media. More specifically, *advertising* is paid, nonpersonal communication through various mass media....to inform or persuade members of a particular audience (Krugman, Reid, Dunn, & Barban, 1994, p. 12). Most typically, leisure service organizations advertise services in such media forms as daily newspapers, network and cable television, magazines, web sites, and direct mail. Yet there are many possible media sources and leisure service organizations should select those that will best advertise their particular services. See Figure 19.1 for media form ideas.

Figure 19.1: Media forms.

Television (national, regional, network, cable, commercial, public)

Radio (national, local, commercial, public)

Newspapers (national, regional, local)

Magazines (in house, trade, popular, specialty)

Consumer magazines (weeklies, quarterlies)

Magazine supplements

Commercial consumer guides (for hotels, campsites)

Cinema advertising

Billboards

Transportation sites (airports, buses, train stations, taxis, undergrounds)

Directories and yellow pages

Exhibits (display space on stands or bulletin boards)

Direct mail (using purchased address lists)

Door-to-door distribution (an alternative to direct mail)

Web sites

One advantage of advertising is that it reaches a large group of potential service users for a relatively low price per exposure. It can also be adapted to either mass audiences or specific audience segments, and can be successfully used to create instant service awareness (Kurtz & Boone, 1992). For example, for a tourism organization, such advertising messages as the following created instant identification with the organization and its services—some of which we still remember today:

We try harder (Avis).

I love (heart) New York (New York State).

Only one hotel chain guarantees your room will be right (Holiday Inns, Inc.).

There are, however, disadvantages to advertising. One that relates to evaluative research is that advertising does not permit totally accurate measurement of results. This is because advertising works in concert with other marketing tools in an uncontrollable market environment (Krugman et.al., 1994). Let us explore this difficulty more thoroughly, as well as identify ways the effectiveness of advertising can be measured.

In trying to discover whether a particular advertisement has accomplished its objective, evaluative research is needed. Some advertisements are more effective than others, and leisure service organization managers need to determine what is and what is not working. Further, evaluative research can be thought of as a way to help ensure that the money invested in advertising was well spent.

Limitations of Evaluating Advertising

There are, however, some barriers to measuring advertising effectiveness. For one, isolating the effects of advertising from the many other variables that bring people to your organization to use your service is difficult. While we might like for the research to be able to point and say, "This ad produced these program participants," the numerous factors that influence the participants' decisions to participate make this a very difficult task. Instead, we most often must be satisfied to measure more indirect indicators.

Another barrier to evaluating advertising is that consumers are quite complex and unpredictable. This means that evaluative research of advertising must be done relatively quickly, such as within several weeks of the ad's appearance. We cannot wait for months for the evaluation results before making decisions about the next steps in our advertising program.

Given the barriers to the evaluation of advertising, it is no wonder that leisure service organizations sometimes rely on consulting firms. While such assistance is typically quite expensive, some organizations consider it worthwhile because of the firm's demonstrated expertise. For example, for print ads, Gallup & Robinson Inc. uses a sample of 150 adults for its Magazine Impact Research Service (MIRS) and its Rapid Ad Measurement (RAM) (Fletcher

& Bowers, 1991). MIRS posttests ads by assessing the performance of individual ads, overall print campaign effectiveness, and creativity of the advertising strategy. RAM pretests magazine ads for name recognition, idea communication, and buying attitude. Gallup & Robinson Inc. also provide evaluation service for broadcast advertising. The firm provides on-air pretesting of new commercials and posttesting of existing commercials set within prime time programming. The evaluation can measure the commercial's ability to make an impression, the feelings that the commercial evokes, the commercial's ability to persuade, and its overall effectiveness (Fletcher & Bowers, 1991).

Data-Collection Techniques for Evaluating Advertising

Most organizations, however, evaluate advertising effectiveness themselves using simpler techniques. For example, we might judge the personal watercraft safety campaign advertisement (Figure 19.2) sponsored by the National Recreation and Park Association to have

Figure 19.2: Advertisement example.

been effective based on the number of requests that came in for informational materials. Although we don't know exactly the impact the ad had on making people more responsible users of personal watercraft, we do have an indirect indicator of success.

If your organization wishes to conduct its own evaluation of the advertising program, it would be helpful to select an approach according to a classification scheme proposed by Krugman et.al. (1994, pp. 221-223). This scheme classifies the data-collection techniques according to pretesting versus posttesting, and communication versus action effects. Follow along with Figure 19.3 as we explain.

Figure 19.3: Classification of advertising effectiveness measures.

| | Effects Examined | |
	Communication Effects	Action Effects
Timing of Evaluation		
Pretesting	Focus groups	Market tests
	Projective techniques	Inquiry/direct response
Posttesting	Recall tests	Measures of past sales
	Awareness & attitude tests	

(based on Krugman, et al., 1994, p. 223)

1. Pretesting and posttesting. One way of measuring advertising's effectiveness is to categorize evaluation assessments according to whether they are conducted before the ad is printed or broadcast (pretesting) or after exposure (posttesting). *Pretesting* allows you to estimate participant reactions to proposed ads and use the results to finalize the ad copy or release timing. *Posttesting*, on the other hand, occurs once the ad actually has run in the media. A follow-up with posttests is conducted to determine message effectiveness.

2. Communication and action effects. A second method of classifying the measurement of advertising effectiveness is to focus on communication-effect or action-effect. *Com-*

munication-effect research is based on the premise that advertising communicates. This is typically what is evaluated by consulting firms such as Gallup & Robinson Inc. discussed above. That is, the evaluation measures the ad's ability to make an impression or evoke a feeling. *Action-effect* research determines the impact advertising has on inquiries, participation, sales, and other behaviors of people in response to the ad.

As noted in Figure 19.3, these four schemes may be classified into a matrix that includes some of the more common research data-collection approaches used to measure each combination (Krugman, et.al., 1994). First, pretesting communication effects often involves the use of focus groups. In these small group meetings, subjects are asked to discuss how they feel about a specific ad or advertising campaign. Usually the ads are in unfinished form, and based on input from the focus group, are revised and finished afterwards. One of the problems associated with focus groups to pretest communication effect, however, is that individual members may go along with the group and not reveal what they really think.

Another approach to measuring how well an ad communicates prior to its issue is projective techniques. Projective techniques avoid the problem of direct questioning ("Do you like the ad?") and instead are indirect by asking respondents to describe their feelings (Krugman, 1994). A trained interviewer probes individuals about their feelings and motivations about the product or service and the message of the ad. For example, typical questions are: What thoughts come to your mind? and What does this ad tell you about yourself? The point is to discover underlying feelings as a means to inferring what the ad is communicating. Projective techniques are excellent at probing in depth, yet the validity of the results depends on the skill of the interviewer.

Communication effects may also be determined through a posttesting format. For example, recall tests ask respondents what ads they remember. Before they are interviewed, respondents must prove they have read the magazine, newspaper, etc. by recalling details of at least one article within it. Then, the respondents are handed cards showing the names of services or products advertised and asked to make a list of those ads they recall having seen. Finally, respondents are asked a series of questions about each ad on their list, testing their recall of content and persuasive power. Ads are scored according to name recognition, idea communication, and favorable attitude (Krugman, et.al., 1994). Another technique for posttesting communication effects is the awareness or attitude test. Prior to the advertising campaign, a benchmark measure of awareness of the service or product is taken. After the advertising campaign, a second measure is taken to determine if and how much awareness and attitudes have changed as a result of the advertising (Krugman, et.al., 1994).

Shifting attention to measuring action effects from advertising (Figure 19.3), pretest measures include market tests and inquiry/direct response tests. The purpose of market tests is to establish the potential impact of an advertising program before your organization invests lots of money. Market tests can take many forms, but most often the impact of an ad at a small local level is used to gauge what the reaction might be on a regional or national level. For example, a market test would attempt to answer whether the personal water craft owners at a neighborhood lake became more safety conscious as a result of a localized advertising campaign.

Inquiry/direct response measures are used to check the potential behavioral effect of advertisements (Krugman, et al., 1994). This can be very straightforward. For example, a YMCA fitness center could run an ad about an upcoming open house membership campaign, and offer a gift to all persons who show up at the center during the open house. Attendence at the open house could provide an indication of how many people heard or saw the advertising message. Admittedly, however, some who show up at the open house may not represent a sincere interest in joining—wanting only the free gift.

While there are numerous techniques for evaluating advertising effectiveness, a popular approach is the measurement of past sales. Measures of past sales are a way of posttesting action effects, or to measure whether advertising actually affected participation. For example, to evaluate an advertisement for a new museum exhibit, as visitors arrive to view the exhibit they could be asked whether they saw or heard the ad and how much it influenced their coming. While this is a useful way to relate advertising to participation in a service, many nonadvertising variables can also influence participation. For example, a visitor to the museum may have seen the ad in the local newspaper and been encouraged to visit the museum by a friend. Which was the more effective—the ad or the friend?

Public Relations

Public relations is a management function that uses communication to enable relationships between an organization and its publics (McElreath, 1993). Thus, public relations is a very important tool for leisure services organizations. While advertising is always media based by definition and public relations is not, public relations may involve use of appropriate media. Yet public relations also utilizes other strategies. For example, a public relations program for a sports club might include the activities presented in Figure 19.4.

Before discussing options for evaluating an organization's public relations, a distinction must be made between a public relations program and a public relations campaign. A *public relations program* is a sustained effort that often has an ongoing objective, such as sustaining employee cooperation within the organization or maintaining positive community relations (McElreath, 1993). A *public relations campaign,* on the other hand, has a fixed time period to accomplish its objectives, such as a campaign to reduce employee absenteeism, or to overcome an unfavorable stereotype about an organization (McElreath, 1993). Both programs and campaigns use a variety of communication activities, and often the same activities, but the distinction between program and campaign is important in order to measure effectiveness.

Figure 19.4: Examples of public relations activities for a sports club.

Activity	Purpose	Example
Press releases	To draw attention to favorable news events or to combat unfavorable news	Such favorable news as a member winning the city marathon, or such un-favorable news as food poisoning in the club dining room
Receptions	To influence targeted guests with a particular message about the organization	To celebrate the opening of the club, new manage-ment, remodeling, etc.
Personality appearances	To draw attention to an organization's name or service	Autograph signing by an Olympic athlete, or clinic given by a professional athlete
Staged events	To increase participation through exposure to the facility	Sports field day featuring non-competitive sports

Range of Evaluation Methods Available

A wide range of evaluation research approaches can be used to measure the effectiveness of public relations programs and campaigns. One is that through traditional library resources and computerized databases, a public relations manager can analyze media content. Special attention will be given to this approach in the next section on press clippings. In addition to media content analyses, other evaluation methods used in assessing public relations include in-depth interviews, request analyses, participant observations, testimonials, and case studies.

For example, the researcher could conduct in-depth interviews with key opinion leaders within the targeted public. Also, a request analysis could be conducted by systematically recording incoming phone calls and correspondence in order to ascertain requests for information and services. In terms of testimonials, written and verbal comments from satisfied members of the target public can be collected and summarized. Finally, a case study can be used. One way to accomplish this is to summarize and prepare public relations campaign materials for submission to a professional awards competition, such as the gold medal awards program for community recreation departments sponsored by the National Park and Recreation Association. Further, when such an award has been won, it can be used in a public relations program!

Maintaining a record of all communication activities for purposes of conducting a documents analysis is another option for assessing public relations. Likewise, one of the most widely used research techniques in public relations evaluation is the focus group. As well, survey research and public opinion polling are frequently used.

Systematic Use of Press Clippings

Some public relations managers clip out articles about their organization from newspapers and magazines, put the clips into a scrapbook, and then brag about the amount of positive public relations garnered. There is, however, a much more systematic and valid technique for analyzing press clippings. Here are some suggestions (based on McElreath, 1993):

1. Collect and organize the clippings from all media sources (prints and transcripts) according to each specific public relations campaign. Conduct the following steps according to each separate campaign.

2. Using the circulation figures for each publication, calculate the total gross impressions. That is, multiply the circulation count of the media source by the number of different photos and/or articles. For example, a feature article with a photo for the summer day camp appears in a local newspaper with a readership of 15,000 households. Thus, 15,000 X 2 = 30,000.

3. Next, estimate a percentage of the circulation that could be considered part of the public relations campaign's target audience. With these estimates, calculate what is termed the total effective impressions. So, assume the target audience estimate for the summer day camp example above is 5 percent: .05 X 30,000 = 1500.

4. For newspaper clippings specifically, now measure the number of column inches of each of the articles and photographs, and add them to derive the total column inches for the campaign as well as the average column inch per article. So, suppose the summer day camp article and photograph totaled 15 column inches, and because there was only one article in the newspaper, this is likewise the average column inch per article.

5. Using the following scale, assign a value for the position of each print article or photograph: 6 = front page or front cover

     5 = front page of a section

     4 = prominent page position inside a section

     3 = neutral position

     2 = short copy in back of publication

     1 = one paragraph buried in publication

Thus, let's assign the value of "5" to the day camp article since it appeared on the front of the Life Style section of the newspaper.

6. **Assign a value for the content** of each print placement according to the following scale:

> 6 = three key points covered without photo
>
> 5 = two key points covered with photo
>
> 4 = one key point covered, with photo
>
> 3 = one key point covered, without photo
>
> 2 = negative coverage

So, we score a "4" to the summer day camp article because it discussed only how creatively the program is funded, along with a photograph.

7. **Similar scales can be developed and scored** for radio and/or television coverage for the public relations campaign.

8. **These measures can stand alone as separate indicators** of the effectiveness of the public relations campaign, and/or can be assembled into an overall score by multiplying the answers from steps 3, 4, 5, and 6. In terms of the day camp illustration, 1500 X 15 X 5 X 4 = 450,000. This then, can be compared with the analysis of media coverage for another public relations campaign. Suppose the new park master plan coverage resulted in a score of 1,240,000. Did the summer day camp generate more or less effective coverage?

These procedures for evaluation are actually a form of content analysis. They are followed after the public relations campaign is implemented to assess its overall impact.

Promotions

Promotions serve as short-term incentives to encourage participation in a program or use of a service. Promotions are aimed at quickly moving the leisure program or service toward the potential participant or consumer. Promotion essentially deals with activities that support advertising and public relations. For example, coupons, contests, sweepstakes, games, exhibitions, displays, and demonstrations provide a reason for advertising, and can become a component of a public relations campaign.

Coupons can be used as a promotion device by offering potential participants a reduction in the price of the service. Coupons are the most heavily used form of promotion (Krugman et al., 1994). They range from discounts on theme park entrance fees to a reduced price for a first-time trial fitness class. Contests, sweepstakes and games are promotions that focus on generating enthusiasm among potential participants. While the popularity of these techniques grew in the 1980s, they have declined somewhat in the 1990s (Krugman et.al., 1994). A contest involves participants competing for prizes based on their skill, or other characteristic. For example, an on-site one-day landscape painting contest at a state historical landmark might bring people to the site who would not otherwise come. A sweepstakes involves chance by requiring participants to submit their name to a drawing. Sometimes there is a charge to enter the drawing. An example is a "jackpot inning" at a baseball game. Fans entering the game purchase sweepstakes tickets. Then, a fan's name is drawn during the seventh inning; if a home run is hit during that inning, the fan wins the cash jackpot. A promotion using a game is a form of sweepstakes that lasts over a longer period of time. For example, each time participants use the gym they are given a Bingo number. When a participant has acquired a Bingo match, she wins a year's free membership, or pair of racquetball goggles!

By their nature, promotions are task-oriented marketing techniques (Middleton, 1994). This means they are specifically targeted to achieve certain results. Thus, evaluating their effectiveness requires measurement of whether the target task was achieved. That is, did the promotion fill the seats, raise admissions, draw a crowd, etc.? The evaluation should measure the recreation class sign-ups or the hotel bookings achieved during the promotional period. Inevitably it will not be possible to separate the sales promotion effects from effects of other marketing strategies, such as current advertising, but short-run promotional efforts provide the best opportunity marketing managers have to measure the results of marketing expenditure with some precision (Middleton, 1994).

Brochures and Other Printed Materials

Printed materials are also a part of marketing, and include such publications as brochures, leaflets, window posters, and table tents. It is probably obvious from the wide range of items included here that printed materials perform a wide range of functions in marketing leisure services. These include:

- **Creating awareness.** Many prospective participants will gain initial awareness through printed materials first seen in a retail store, library, restaurant, or other location outside the recreation facility itself. The battle for awareness is fierce, and the design of frontcovers is therefore very important. In fact, the role of front covers is like that of the packaging of products in a grocery store—they are designed to attract the attention of people who pass by.
- **Promoting participation.** To serve a promotional role, brochures need to be designed to stimulate prospective participants to participate. In this role printed materials act in the same way as advertising.
- **Providing education.** Healthy ways of spending free time, ecologically sound environmental behaviors, and other such educational messages are a growing role for brochures and other printed materials.

Like other aspects of a marketing program in a leisure services organization, it is important to evaluate the effectiveness of brochures and printed materials. However, as with promotions, it is generally difficult to distinguish with any real precision the singular effectiveness of printed communications from the other elements of the marketing mix as a whole. There are, however, some possible ways to study the impact of print materials (based on Middleton, 1994):

1. **As a way of deciding between different cover designs and content,** conduct a focus group with members of the target audience.

2. **Measure the results of a brochure** by conducting what is called a *split-run*. Two different brochure formats are distributed to matched samples of the targeted audience, and program sign-ups or event registrations that result are compared. Using direct mail to distribute the brochure or flyer and then coding the registration form to be returned according to which brochure was sent is a relatively easy way of doing this.

3. **Measure reaction to print material** through a telephone or mailed questionnaire sent randomly to brochure recipients.

4. **Measure participant recall of brochures** by conducting brief structured interviews when participants arrive at the reception desk.

Main Points

- Marketing the services of sport, recreation, park and tourism organizations requires the mixing of the factors of product, price, connection, and distribution. The connection marketing factor, as it is typically used in leisure service organizations, includes advertising, public relations, promotions, and brochures and printed material.

- Evaluating advertising is often imprecise due to difficulties in isolating the effects of advertising from the many other reasons that bring people to your organization's services. Often indirect indicators must be relied on in determining an ad's effectiveness.

- When evaluating advertising directly, techniques for pretesting and posttesting an advertisement's communication-effect and action-effect include focus groups, projective techniques, recall tests, awareness or attitude tests, market tests, inquiry/direct response measures, and measures of past sales.

- A range of methods is available for evaluating a public relations program and a public relations campaign. A systematic critique of press clippings is recommended.

- Usually evaluating the effectiveness of promotions requires direct measurement of whether the target task was achieved. That is, counting the number of seats filled in the auditorium, etc.

- There are various ways of measuring the ability of brochures to create awareness, promote participation, and provide education. One idea is to conduct a split-run, whereby two different brochure formats are distributed to matched samples of the targeted audience, and subsequent program sign-ups or event registrations are then compared.

Study Questions

1. What are the factors in the "marketing mix"? Why is it labeled a "mix"?

2. Within which marketing mix factor do the often used strategies of advertising, public relations, promotions, and printed materials fall?

3. What is the goal of each of these strategies? How can evaluative research help determine if these goals have been met?

4. What is the difference between directly and indirectly evaluating advertising?

5. What is the difference between a public relations program and a public relations campaign?

6. How do you recommend the effectiveness of promotions be evaluated?

7. In evaluating brochures, what is a split-run?

References

Dreyfuss, I. (1997, Feb. 18). Shyness keeps sedentary out of health clubs. *The Washington Post*, p. 20.

Fletcher, A.D., & Bowers, T.A. (1991). *Fundamentals of advertising*. Belmont, CA: Wadsworth.

Johnson, W.C., & Blaicher, J. (1997, February). Ride smart from the start. *Parks and Recreation, 32*(2), 66-67.

Kotler, P. (1991). *Marketing management: Analysis, planning, implementation and control* (7th Ed.). London: Prentice-Hall International.

Krugman, D.M., Reid, L.N., Dunn, S.W., & Barban, A.M. *Advertising: Its role in modern marketing*. Fort Worth, TX: The Dryden Press.

Kurtz, D.L., & Boone, L.E. (1992). *Contemporary marketing* (7th Ed.). Fort Worth, TX: The Dryden Press.

McElreath, M.P. (1993). *Managing systematic and ethical public relations*. Madison, WI: Brown & Benchmark.

Middleton, V.T.C. (1994). *Marketing in travel and tourism*. Oxford, UK: Butterworth-Heinemann.

PART IV: MISE-EN-SCÈNE

In the original French, *mise-en-scène* means staging an action, and it was first applied to directing staged plays. Today, film directors use the term to signify the director's control over what appears within each film frame, including setting, lighting, costumes, and the actions of the actors. By controlling the mise-en-scene, the film director stages the event for the camera (Bordwell & Thompson, 1997).

To conclude our presentation on evaluative research in leisure services, the mise-en-scène expression and its function serve as a useful analogy. Thus, for the book's finale, let us pull together all the mise-en-scène of evaluative research and consider it again as a complete production. We will do this in two ways. First, evaluative research is reviewed as a process model—that is, what the whole picture of evaluative research looks like. Second, using the model as guide, a checklist of the steps in evaluative research summarizes the book's chapters.

Based on Grosof and Sardy (1985), the evaluative research process is perhaps best modeled as a double-ended funnel positioned on its side (see figure). At the left, or beginning, the funnel is widest to signify that evaluation studies are initially steered by leisure and evaluation literature, the desires of stakeholders, and the evaluator's own background. Then the funnel narrows, signifying that as the evaluation project proceeds, focus is narrowed as choices about sampling, design, data collection procedures, and data analysis are made. As the findings emerge, and lead to conclusions, which in turn are implemented, the funnel widens again to indicate the desired impact of the research on improving services.

If we could use a zoom lens to magnify the funnel model, we would be able to see more of the detail of evaluative research steps. To extend our summary, let us now review these details in a checklist format—all the props and sets we will need for conducting a systematic evaluation.

Stage One: Defining the Focus of the Evaluation
Understand the issue (Chapters 1, 2, 4, 5):
• Hold discussions with research clients and/or organization director.
• Review the literature.

The evaluative research process.

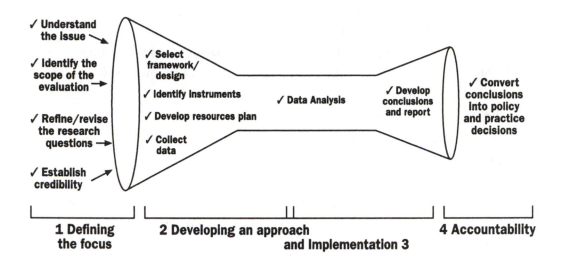

From *A research primer for the social and behavioral sciences* (p. 385) by Grosof, M.S. & Sardy, M., (1985). Orlando, FL: Academic Press. Adapted with permission of the authors.

- Gather information from experts and other interested parties.
- Conduct site visits.
- Consider quantitative and qualitative data perspectives.

Identify the scope of the evaluation (Chapter 6):
- Develop a conceptual framework.
- Draft a problem statement.
- Draft a purpose statement.
- Draft a statement about the significance of the problem.
- Frame research questions, objectives, and/or hypotheses.

Refine/revise the research questions (Chapter 6):
- Negotiate the study's scope with client/organization director.
- Determine any scope limitations.

Establish credibility with client/organization director (Chapter 2):
- Maintain continuous communication.
- When appropriate, negotiate interim reports.

- Form advisory group.
- State study limitations up front.

Stage Two: Developing an Approach

Select a preliminary research design (Chapters 3, 7, 8):

- Define the desired degree of generalizability (population, geography, time).
- Outline the analytic comparisons required to answer the research questions.
- Select a preliminary design.
- Define the study population.
- Decide on probability or non-probability sampling.
- Develop sound estimates for numbers of study participants.

Stage Three: Deciding the Implementation Plan

Make preliminary decisions about procedures and data collection approaches (Chapters 2, 9, 10, 11, 12):

- Identify likely instruments.
- Assess the validity, reliability, and normative data for instruments being considered.
- Determine the appropriate level of measurement needed and then assess existing instruments' level of measurement.
- If required, develop own instruments.
- Pilot and finalize instruments and data collection procedures; is triangulation possible?
- Draft preliminary analysis plan.
- Solicit input from advisory group and client regarding research design and implementation plan.

Develop resource plan (Chapters 2, 3, 10):

- Select data collection sites or access to secondary data.
- Obtain authorization (including human subjects approval) for data collection.
- Develop a plan for personnel resources.
- Develop a plan for financial resources.
- Prepare a task outline for the research activities.
- Check time estimation to make sure time has been allowed for data collection, data analysis, reporting, follow-up, and project management.

Collect data (Chapters 3, 10):

- Check data for relevance, accuracy, reliability, and completeness.
- Refine/revise data collection procedures as necessary.

Analyze quantitative data (Chapters 3, 11):

- Construct frequency distribution tables and graphs.
- Calculate proportions, ratios, or rates.
- Calculate measures of central tendency and variability.
- Calculate measures of relationship or measures of differences according to which are more appropriate.

Analyze qualitative data (Chapters 3, 12):

- Prepare notes.
- Focus on the collected data.
- Prepare data displays.
- Draw conclusions.
- Verify conclusions.

Stage Four: Accountability

Write final report (Chapters 3, 13):

- Organize the content.
- Decide on writing style.
- Draft final report.
- Solicit input from advisory group regarding recommendations.
- Proofread.

Present final report orally (Chapter 13):

- Develop oral report from written report.
- Decide on appropriate visual and/or auditory aids.
- Practice delivery.

Convert conclusions into policy and practice decisions (Chapter 14):

- Make useful recommendations that logically follow findings.
- Disseminate recommendations.
- Choose recommendations for implementation.

Hopefully you are now ready to conduct your own evaluations. Our goal has been to equip you with the staging elements you need, from framing the research question to converting the final report into management decisions. You are ready. Lights, camera, action!

ABOUT THE AUTHORS

Carol Cutler Riddick is a professor of recreation studies at Gallaudet University and also holds an adjuct appointment in the Department of Sociology at the University of Maryland. She also completed both a B.A. in sociology and M.S. in health planning from Florida State University, a Ph.D. from Pennsylvania State University, and a post-doctorate in applied gerontological research (funded by the Department of Health and Human Services' Administration on Aging and the Gerontological Society of America [GSA]). She is a Certified Leisure Professional, an elected Fellow in the GSA, has held various appointed and elected positions in the Society of Park & Recreation Educators, co–chaired the Leisure Research Symposium, and served on the editorial boards of the *Journal of Leisure Research*, *Therapeutic Recreation Journal*, and *Leisure Sciences*.

An active advocate of research and evaluation, Dr. Ruth Russell has dedicated over thirty years to practicing and teaching it. She is professor of recreation and park administration at Indiana University, where she has also served as the director of the Leisure Research Institute and associate dean of the faculties. She received her B.S. from West Virginia University, her M.S. from The Pennsylvania State University, and her Re.D. degree from Indiana University. As a teacher, and as a practitioner and consultant in recreation, park, tourism, and sport agencies, she has published numerous articles and lectured widely on the importance of evaluation to the accountability of leisure services.

INDEX

A

A priori explanation of phenomena, 88–89
Abstracts, 70–71
Accessibility characteristics of a program, 291
Accidental sampling, 158–160
Accreditation model approach, 7, 120
Accuracy of records, 175
Action-effect research, 374–375
Advertising, 370–375
Affective domain, 308
Agency accreditation, 39–40
Alternation ranking, 332
Alternative hypothesis, 112, 113
Appendices, of written report, 263
Applied research, defined, 4–5, 8, 9
Archival documents and records, 174–175
Assessment, 305–316
    focus for, 306
    instrument for, 306
    tools for, 307–316
Attitudes, in data collection, 187
Attributes, in data collection, 187, 238–240
Audience, for written report, 263–264
Authenticity of records, 175

B

Background section of report, 252
Bar graph, 216–217
Basic research, defined, 8, 9
Behavioral objectives approach, 6, 120
Behaviorally-anchored rating scales
    (BARS), 332, 333
Beliefs, in data collection, 187
Beneficence, 45–46
Bias, selection, 122, 123, 125–126
Bibliographies, 71
Brochures, 379–380
Budget, 28, 32–33, 35

C

Case study, 138–139
Causal relationships, 296–297

Cause, construct of, 8–9
Census, 133, 150
Central tendency, measures of, 219–222
Checklists, in performance appraisal, 324, 328
Chronicalist voice, 256–258
Cluster sampling, 155
Clustering of data, 244–245
Coding of qualitative information, 235–236
Cognitive domain, 312–313
Commission for Accreditation of Park and
    Recreation Agencies (CAPRA), 39–40
Communication-effect research, 373–374
Comparative focus approach, 7, 120
Competence, 52
Complete participant, 200
Comprehensive Evaluation in Recreational
    Therapy (CERT), 311–314
Concepts, measurement of, 167–178
Conceptually driven sampling, 155–156
Concessions, 357–359, 360
Conclusions
    drawing, 242–245
    section of report, 254
    verifying, 245–247
Concurrent validity, 172
Confidentiality, right to, 49
Confounding, 120–121
Connection, in marketing mix, 369–370
Consistency, 136
Construct validity, 172
Constructs, 245
Content analysis, 140–142
Content validity, 171
Continuous documents, 174–175
Contracting, 357–359, 360
Control group, 122, 126, 128–129
Convenience sampling, 158–160
Correlative questions, 110, 111
Cost-benefits analysis, 7, 295
Cost-effectiveness analysis, 6–7, 295–296
Critical incidents, 332
Cross-analysis, 244–245
Cross-checking, 136
Cross-sectional survey, 133
Crowd control, 355–356

D

Data collection, 185–202
    for evaluation of advertising, 372–375
Data displays, 237–242
Deception, 50
Deductive logic, 88–89
Descriptive questions, 109, 110
Descriptive statistics, 212–213
Design of a facility, 351–353
Diaries, in performance appraisal, 332
Direct costs, 32–33
Discrepancy theory, 291, 292
Dissemination plan, 35
Distribution, in marketing mix, 370
Document analysis, 140–142
Domain, 238–240
    affective, 308
    cognitive, 312–313
    emotional, 313
    psychological, 313
    psychomotor, 313–314
    social, 314

E

Ecological fallacy, 99
Effect, construct of, 8–9
Effectiveness, absolute vs. relative, 110, 111
Efficiency assessment, 295–296
Effort evaluation, 293–294
Efforts approach to cost measurement, 6
Emotional domain, 313
Employee development plan, 337–339, 340
Employee education, 39–40
End-result program evaluation, 293
Episodic records, 174
Equivalent time series design, 129–131
Essays, in performance appraisal, 332
Ethics, 43–58
    defined, 44
    government regulations concerning, 54
    professional organization codes of, 54, 55–56
    qualities of, 45–52
    standards of, 52–54
Ethnographic study, 136–137
Evaluation. *See also* Evaluative research, Evaluators
    defined, 2, 5
    of marketing, 367–380
    of physical plant, 245–363
    of programs, 286–303
Evaluative research. *See also* Evaluation
    benefits to practitioners, 6–7
    defined, 3–4, 5
    defining the scope of, 97–114
    designs for, 119–143
    differences from other types of research, 7–9
    supervision and maintenance of, 25–38
Evaluators
    internal vs. external, 18
    psychological attributes of, 92
    relationship with program personnel, 20–25
    reporting responsibility, 19–20, 21
    training and experience of, 92, 341
Ex post facto design, 134–135, 161, 162–163
Ex post facto explanation of phenomena, 89
Exclusiveness, 215
Executive summary in written report, 263
Experimental group, 122, 126
Experimental mortality, 122
Experimental research design, 126–127
Experimental setting, 125
Explanations, testing, 246–247
Expressed demand, 308
External audit, 136
External validity, 123–125

F

Face validity, 171
Facilities and equipment, evaluation of, 348–353
Facts, in data collection, 187
Fairness, 52
Feedback, 50
Felt need, 307–308
Focus groups, 193–197, 198
Focused summary, 234–235
Formative evaluation approach, 6
Frequency distributions, 213–217
Fringe benefits, 33, 35
Full-Time-Equivalents (FTE), 293
Functional abilities, assessment tools for, 308, 311–314

G

Gantt chart, 28, 31
General references, 68–71

Generalizability, 90, 123, 161, 281–282
Goal-free evaluation approach, 7
Goals of program, 287–289
Grammar, in written report, 258–261
Grand-tour questions, 113, 114

H

Harm, physical vs. psychological, 45–46
Hawthorne effect, 125
Histogram, 216–217
Historical study, 143
History, effects of, on internal validity, 120
Honesty, 50–51

I

Ideographic interpretation, 90
Impact questions, 110, 111
Inclusiveness, 215
Indexes, 68–69
Individuals, comparison of performance among, 332
Inductive logic, 89
Inductive thinking, 232–233
Informed consent, 56–58
Inputs approach to cost measurement, 6
Inquiry, structured vs. unstructured, 89
Instruments
    choice of, 168–178
    effects of, on internal validity, 121–122
    reactivity of, 172–175
    reliability of, 175–177
    sources for, 177–178
    validity of, 171–172
Integrative diagram, 244
Integrity of results, 50–51
Internal consistency reliability, 176
Internal validity, 120–123
Inter-observer reliability, 175–176
Interval scale of measurement, 210
Interviews
    descriptive information, 192–193, 194
    discovery, 193, 195
    problem-solving, 193, 195
    structured, 188–189
    unstructured, 192–193
Introduction
    of oral report, 266
    to proposal, 26
Inventory tracking of equipment, 356

J

Journals, 72–74
    for dissemination of evaluation results, 278
Judgmental validity, 171

K

Knowing, ways of, 2–3

L

Labeling effect, 46
Leisure attributes, assessment tools for, 307–308, 309–310
Literature analysis, 75–79
Literature review, 26, 63–81, 252
    functions of, 64–66
    synthesis of, 79–81
Literature search, 66–75
Literature sources
    primary, 66–75
    secondary, 66–67
Longitudinal survey, 133

M

Maintenance of facilities, 348–353
Management by objectives (MBO), 324, 325–327
Management-oriented monitoring approach, 6
Marginal participant, 200
Marketing, evaluation of, 292, 367–380
Marketing mix, 369–370
Matching, 129
Matrices, 237–240, 241–242
Maturation, effects of, on internal validity, 121
Measurement
    of concepts, 167–178
    of costs, 6
    instruments for, 168–178
    logic of, 168
    of program outcome, 291–301
    scales of, 208–212
Media, 370–371
Median, 220
Member checks, 136

Memoing, 236–237
Metaphors, in drawing conclusions, 244
Methods, section of report, 252–253
Mid-point review, 38
Mise-en-scène, 383
Mission statements, 286–287
Mode, 220–222
Motive of evaluation, 12

N

Networks, 240–242
Nominal definition, 168
Nominal scale of measurement, 208–209
Non-directional hypothesis, 112, 113
Nonequivalent control group design, 128–129
Nonexperimental designs, 132–135
Nonprobability sampling, 155–160
Non-reactive measures, 173
Normative data, 170–171
Normative questions, 109–110
Notes preparation, 233–234
Null hypothesis, 112

O

Objectives of program, 288, 289–290
    criteria for, 290
    measurability of, 289
    specificity of, 289
One-group pretest-posttest design, 131
One-time posttest design, 131
Open space, evaluation of, 345–348
Operating procedures, of facilities, 353–357
Operational definition, 168
Ordinal scale of measurement, 209–211
Organization citizenship, 322
Organization of reports, 250–256
Organizations, effects of programs on, 293–294

P

Parallel forms reliability, 176
Participant observation, 197–202
Passive participant, 200
Peer review, 73
Performance appraisal, 319–342
    communicating results of, 337–339
    examination of, 339, 341–342
    responsibility for, 335, 336

    timing of, 337
Persistent observation, 135
Person loading, 27–28, 30
Personal documents, 140
Personnel, 27–28, 39. *See also* Staff
    appraisal of, 292, 319–342
Physical plant, evaluation of, 292, 345–363
Physical tracing, 173–174
Pie chart, 215
Pilot study, 131, 178–179
Policy space, 12
Polygon, 217
Population, 149–150
    at-risk, 290
    in-need, 290
    target, 290
Posttesting, 126–127
    and evaluation of advertising, 373
Predictive validity, 171–172
Pre-experimental designs, 131–132
Preferences, in data collection, 187
Press clippings, and public relations evaluation, 377–378
Press releases, and dissemination of evaluation results, 279
Pretesting, 126–127
    and evaluation of advertising, 373
Pretest sensitization, 121, 125, 127
Preventive maintenance, 351
Price, in marketing mix, 369
Primary data, 143
Printed materials, role of, in marketing, 379–380
Privacy, right to, 48–49
Probability sampling, 150–155
Procedures and methods, 26
Product, in marketing mix, 369
Professional conferences, and dissemination of evaluation results, 279
Program
    outcome measures, 291–301
    planning, 287
    satisfaction with, 291
Prolonged engagement, 135
Promotions, 378–379
Proportion, 218
Proposals, 25–35
    organizational review of, 35–36

weaknesses of, 37
Psychological domain, 313
Psychomotor domain, 313–314
Public records, 140
Public relations, evaluation of, 375–378
Purpose of evaluation, section of report, 251–252
Purpose statement, 98–104
    qualitative, 103–104
    quantitative, 99–102
Purposive sampling, 156–157

Q

Qualitative framework
    analysis of information in, 231–247
    compared with quantitative framework, 85–93
    data collection tools for, 187–192
    defined, 86
    purpose statement in, 103–104
    research designs for, 135–143
    research questions in, 114
Quantitative framework
    analysis of information in, 207–226
    compared with qualitative framework, 85–93
    data collection tools for, 192–202
    defined, 85–86
    purpose statement in, 99–102
    research designs for, 120–135
    research questions, objectives, and hypotheses in, 109–114
Quasi-experimental designs, 128–131, 162–163
Questionnaires, 188–189
Quota sampling, 157–158

R

Random selection, 126
Range, 222–223
Rate, 218–219
Rating scales, in performance appraisal, 329–333
Ratio, 218
Ratio scale of measurement, 210
Readability of report, 263–264
Realist voice, 256–257
Recommendations
    acceptance of, 275–276
    based on evaluation results, 271–282

    choosing among, for implementation, 280–281
    dissemination of, 276–280
    negative or controversial, 278
    section of report, 254–256
Records, 174–175
Recreation skills, specific, assessment tools for, 314–316
Redundancy, in written report, 261
Referent validity, 168
Reflective controls, 130
Relative comparisons, 217–219
Reliability
    internal consistency, 176
    inter-observer, 175–176
    of instruments, 175–177
    parallel forms, 176
    test-retest, 176
Replication of findings, 246–247
Reports
    oral, 265–268
    preparation of, 249–268
    written, 256–264
Representativeness
    of data, 245–246
    of records, 175
    of a sample, 160–161
Research designs
    for qualitative framework, 135–143
    for quantitative framework, 120–135
Research hypothesis, 108–114
Research objective, 108–114
Research question, 108–114
Research reviews, 66–67
Respect, 46–50
Respondents, recruiting of, 36–37
Response rate, 133
Results, section of report, 253
Rigor, 135–136
Risk management, 359, 361–363

S

Sample, 149
    expert, 157
    extreme case, 157
    heterogeneous, 156
    homogeneous, 156–157

representativeness of, 160–161
time, 157
Sample size, 89, 161–163
Sampling, 149–164
Sampling error, 160–161
Science
    defined, 4–5
    paradox behind, 4
    uncertainty principle of, 4
Scientific process, 4–5
Search term, 67–68
Secondary data, 143
Selection bias, 122, 123, 125–126
Self-determination, right to, 46, 48
Significance statement, 104–106
Simple random sampling, 152
Site inventory, 346, 347
Situational responsiveness, 9–13
Skills matrix, 27, 29
Snowball sampling, 160
Social artifacts, 98–99
Social domain, 314
Social ecology, 10–13
Solomon randomized four group design, 128
Staff, 18–25. *See also* Personnel
    commitment to evaluation, 12
Stakeholders, 10–12
Standard deviation, 223–224
Standardization, 170
Standards
    comparison of performance to, 324, 328–332
    and open space evaluation, 346, 348
Static-group comparison design, 132
Statistical regression, 122
Stratified random sampling, 152–154
Style, of written report, 256–262
Subsuming, 244
Summative evaluation approach, 7, 120
Survey research, 132–134, 161, 162–163
Systematic sampling, 154–155
Systems analysis approach, 6–7, 120

T

Table of contents for written report, 263
Testing, effects of, on internal or external validity, 121, 125

Test-retest reliability, 176
Theory
    defined, 106
    grounded, 107
    in qualitative studies, 107–108
    in quantitative studies, 106–107
360-degree appraisal, 335–337
Time budget, 27
Time frame of evaluation, 12–13
Time line, projected, 26–27
Time-lag survey, 133
Triangulation, 90, 185–186
Travel costs, 32–33, 34

U

Unit of analysis, 98

V

Validity
    concurrent, 172
    construct, 172
    content, 171
    criterion, 171–172
    external, 123–125
    face, 171
    of instruments, 171–172
    internal, 120–123
    judgmental, 171
    predictive, 171–172
    referent, 168
Variability, measures of, 222–224
Variables, 99–102, 112, 125–126, 168, 296–301
    bridging, 299
    dependent, 100
    independent, 100
    input, 296–301
    intervening, 100, 296–301
    program operation, 299
    relationship between, 101–102
Verb tense, in written report, 258
Visual aids, for oral report, 266
Voice, of written report, 256–258
Volunteer sampling, 158–160

W

Wordiness, in written report, 261